Hoover Institution Publications

Burden of Empire

An Appraisal of Western Colonialism in Africa South of the Sahara

Published for
The Hoover Institution on War, Revolution and Peace
Stanford University, Stanford, California

Burden of Empire

*An Appraisal of Western
Colonialism in Africa
South of the Sahara*

by

L. H. GANN

and

PETER DUIGNAN

FREDERICK A. PRAEGER, *Publishers*
New York · Washington · London

FREDERICK A. PRAEGER, *Publishers*
111 Fourth Avenue, New York, N.Y. 10003, U.S.A.
77-79 Charlotte Street, London W.1, England

Published in the United States of America in 1967
by Frederick A. Praeger, Inc., Publishers

Library of Congress Catalog Card Number: 67–26216
Printed in the United States of America

Preface

The breakdown of Western empire in Africa has produced a tidal wave of printed matter. Over the last fifteen years printing presses have run off more surveys, handbooks, and travelers' reports than during the entire heyday of European rule in Africa. The publication of yet another work therefore requires some justification. We do not aim at a complete chronicle of empire in Africa, a task which would require many tomes and a lifetime of research. There is, however, room for a reexamination of some major assumptions that now govern much of historical and sociological research on modern imperialism in Africa. Some of these have acquired the prestige of a well-established doctrine, which presents the danger of impeding further thought on the subject. The various tenets of the new orthodoxy do not, of course, all follow like a well-constructed syllogism. Many scholars and statesmen may well hold only one or two of the views outlined below and violently disagree with the remainder. Yet there is something like a postcolonial climate of opinion. Certain arguments recur again and again in lecture rooms, seminars, and social gatherings, in learned publications and popular journals. These have a kind of inner unity, and merit a brief summary.

The history of Africa, the argument goes, is obviously the history of Africans, not that of its conquerors, and against the vast time span of Africa's past, the imperial period is but a brief interlude. Western conquest in Africa, starting in the 1870s and 1880s, therefore formed but an episode. The "new imperialism" arose from the inner needs of an overripe capitalist system which called for protected markets and even more for new opportunities for Western investors' growing stock of capital. Relying on their temporary military superiority, the whites conquered Africa and introduced new techniques of government and economic exploitation. Under the imperial aegis Africa nevertheless remained poor. Its economy, where not deliberately distorted to suit the victor's purse, was stagnant. African living standards were stationary or declined.

v

Western man, the argument continues, used the peoples of Africa
and their natural riches for his own selfish purpose. His activities
therefore help to account for Africa's present backwardness. Empires
in Africa greatly contributed to the accumulation of Western capital
resources and present-day Western prosperity. One continent's loss
was another's gain. But Africa, at long last, revolted against the white
conqueror and has achieved its political liberation, with the exception
of a few remaining bastions of Western rule. This victory forms only
one of the many struggles in the emancipation of underprivileged
classes and races all over the world. African political independence,
however, is meaningless without economic independence. Economic,
or even cultural, colonialism continues to threaten emergent Africa,
and the battle must continue until the levers of financial, commercial,
and industrial power pass into black hands and until the last remnants
of Western colonialism are liquidated.

We believe that many of these views are wrong and that others
stand in need of modification. We are critical of what seems an unduly
philanthropic approach to world affairs, of an outlook which springs
from a justifiable attempt at cultural self-criticism—commendable
within limits—but which nevertheless is as much a distortion as the
old-fashioned flag-waving view of history. Social and political scientists, historians, and clergymen have reacted, and rightly so, against
the "gunpowder-and-grapeshot" interpretation of history. They no
longer tolerate the smug moralizing which led so many Victorians to
describe Africans as lesser breeds and their way of life as a foul
catalogue of lying, stealing, gluttony, polygamy, debauchery, witchcraft, and cannibalism. But often the pendulum has swung too far
the other way. Scholars who are bitterly critical of the real or alleged
crimes committed by white men in Africa will often gloss over the
grimmer aspects of both precolonial and postcolonial Africa. Edwardian novelists used to delight in depicting clean-limbed young
Englishmen who carried the Union Jack to the jungle and supposedly
brought civilization to darkest Africa. However, these Edwardian
"prettifiers" have been succeeded by writers of another generation
who romanticize the African past, ignore its cruelties and shortcomings, and heap their disapproval on white colonizers alone. This
transformation of values has affected all social studies; it sometimes
finds expression in a complicated jargon which hides unacknowledged
and often contradictory value judgments behind a pretentious terminology.

We hold that cultures differ objectively in the number of choices
which their members can make and in their ability to develop man's
potentialities. Matabele society, for instance, possessed some admira-

ble features. Warriors belonging to the ruling stratum were trained to display courage, fortitude, and self-respect. But the number of effective alternatives open to a Matabele fighting man (not to speak of those available to his slave or his abducted concubine) was very limited. He might earn renown in battle. He could accumulate wealth in the shape of horned beasts. He could marry many wives and, if successful, gather a large following of kinsmen and captives. But these achievements exhausted the limits of his choice. This is hardly surprising; the resources of Matabele society were small. Drought might destroy the crops, disease might strike down the cattle, and war and pestilence might wipe out a whole community. The margin of survival remained small even at the best of times, and there was relatively little room for innovation or experiment. It is our contention that imperial rule helped to bring about major social, economic, and ideological changes which in turn vastly extended social opportunity. The Matabele warriors' modern descendant can make a living as a teacher, a trader, a bus owner, a civil servant, a farmer, or a tailor. This advance was not only relative, but absolute. It was made possible by a great cultural transfusion in which the West took the leading part and which was not limited to technical factors alone.

In reexamining these issues, we have taken the historical approach and have divided this work into three separate parts. The first, which deals with "concepts and realities of imperialism," outlines various political theories with regard to Western imperialism in Africa and seeks to show how far these were compatible with what actually took place in the African bush. These chapters are primarily concerned with the history of ideas. They may be read in isolation from the rest; they may even be left out altogether by anyone not interested in this particular subject. The second part attempts a more detailed interpretation of developments in sub-Saharan Africa from the 1870s to more recent days. We have tried to illustrate, among other things, that there was not one imperialism but many, that the rulers even of one nationality no more formed a single undifferentiated mass than did their subjects. We have attempted to give characteristic instances of different patterns of imperial enterprise. A short concluding section gives a brief survey of decolonization and sums up our own views.

In our discussion of African history during the colonial era, we have taken the now unfashionable view that the rulers, the decision makers, must necessarily occupy a more important part in a historical treatise than their subjects. We have also excluded from consideration the question of what has been called "psychological exploitation"— the effects of colonialism on the minds and emotions of Africans. The subjective reaction of African people to conquest and alien rule we do not feel capable of measuring. For readers interested in these matters we recommend René Maran's *Batouala*, O. Mannoni's *Prospero and Caliban: The Psychology of Colonization*, and Frantz Fanon's *The Wretched of the Earth*, though we do not happen to agree with these authors. We also believe that African history cannot be artificially separated from the annals of white colonization in Africa. We do not thereby wish to belittle the value of African history proper, any more than a historian of the Roman Conquest in Britain would denigrate the worth of the island's earlier Celtic past by emphasizing the doings of Latin-speaking soldiers, administrators, and colonists within his period. But we cannot see much value in an approach which regards the activities of white men as merely part of European history and arbitrarily tries to take them out of the mainstream of African history.

After 1910 the Union of South Africa has generally been excluded from the discussion on the grounds that South Africa then attained dominion status and ceased to form part of the European imperial system in the political sense. We are aware that this classification lays us open to attack. South Africa, one may argue, may have formally become independent in 1910, but white South Africans continued to rule over the black people. South Africa thus practiced "internal colonization"; its history should therefore properly be regarded as part of imperial history. The South African case is not, however, unique. In 1956 the Sudan Republic became independent. Native-born Muslims nevertheless continued to rule over the Negroes of the south, in much the same way that the Amhara of Abyssinia still lord it over the Somali in the southeastern portion of Ethiopia. No historian has, however, suggested that developments in modern Ethiopia or the Sudan form part of the imperial story; hence no exception can be made for Afrikaners or English-speaking South Africans either.

The problems of North Africa have also, for the most part, been excluded from this book. Geographically the Maghrib forms part of the African land mass, but historically and culturally it is linked to the Mediterranean basin and the Near East. Such divisions can never be absolute. The Mediterranean littoral helped to shape developments in the desert, savannah, and forest belts to the south. References to North and South Africa have therefore been made where these appear necessary, but in the main, we concentrate on the immense region that stretches from the Limpopo River to the Sahara.

We have also had to face the question of how to cope with the current political vocabulary. Since about the early 1950s, the terms imperialism and colonialism have become almost synonymous. Political scientists may well object to this apparent confusion of terms.

We nevertheless have followed current usage in employing these terms to denote the exercise of political power, based on an internationally recognized status of sovereignty, enabling the rulers to make direct governmental and administrative decisions in a territory under their flag. We have eschewed the use of these highly controversial terms to describe purely economic relationships between two countries or the kind of indirect political influence that may be exerted between sovereign nations.

We are aware that we have been selective in our approach and have often concentrated on those areas with which we are most familiar from our own past research. There is also some repetition; similar data and similar interpretations have been used in different contexts. We have not brought to light any new facts and have relied widely on the work of other specialists. This is unavoidable, for historical events hang together and cannot be neatly grouped into pigeonholes with mutually exclusive contents. We have moreover tried to introduce some comparative material and have in a somewhat discursive fashion strayed a good deal into more general fields. We hope nevertheless that this volume may make some contribution not only to what might be called the semipopular history of Africa, but also to the great debate that now goes on about the future relations between what are inaccurately called the developing and the developed parts of the world.

The authors would like to express their gratitude to Professors Peter Bauer of the London School of Economics, Henri Brunschwig of the University of Paris, Gordon A. Craig of Stanford University, J. D. Fage of Birmingham University, Richard Hammond, formerly of Stanford University, and G. Wesley Johnson of Stanford University. These scholars kindly read the manuscript and offered valuable criticism and advice. All opinions expressed, and any errors that may remain, are, however, the responsibility of the authors.

We also wish to express our appreciation to Miss Nancy Clark and Mrs. Evelyn Boyce for editing and for proofreading the manuscript, to Mr. London Green for preparing the Index, and to Miss Liselotte Hofmann and Mrs. Eve Hoffman for typing the several manuscript drafts.

The writers are also much indebted to the Relm Foundation, whose generosity has helped make possible the publication of this work.

L . H. GANN
PETER DUIGNAN

Hoover Institution
May 12, 1966

Contents

PART THREE: DECOLONIZATION

MAPS

PART ONE

Concepts and Realities of Imperialism

1. Fallible Yardsticks

*The more carefully we examine the history of the past, the more reason we shall find to dissent from those who imagine that our age has been fruitful of new social evils. The truth is that the evils are, with scarcely any exception, old. That which is new is the intelligence which discerns and the humanity which remedies them.**

Men's minds are limited, and historians—like everyone else—perforce wear blinkers to see. Theirs is a work of selection, where at every moment objectivity is at stake. Marxist critics have thus claimed that historians are subject to class bias. Psychologists have attempted to show that apparently rational judgments are influenced by subterranean currents of the mind, sometimes forgetting that the relevance of an argument has nothing to do with its psychological mainsprings. However, students of the past are also limited by their raw material. They depend, to a much greater extent than many realize, on a complicated administrative machinery which supplies them with the tools of their trade in the form of files, memoranda, debates, and commission reports. The evidence produced, selected, and preserved by administrators, government statisticians, archivists, filing clerks, and record managers helps to determine the very nature of subsequent research.[1] Even ethnohistorians, who put their trust in the spoken word, depend on an outer framework of government whose existence they sometimes take for granted. Strangers can set up camp only where person and property remain secure; the fact that students of preliterate societies have preferred to work under the Pax Britannica, the Pax Belgica, or a stable indigenous government, rather than

* Thomas Babington Macaulay, *The History of England from the Accession of James II,* I (Chicago, 1888), 380.
[1] Lewis H. Gann, "Archives and the Study of Society," *Rhodes-Livingstone Journal,* No. 20 (1956), pp. 49–67.

3

in a disturbed province torn by intertribal warfare, has in itself influenced the nature of ethnological research.

Historians moreover are not immune to the general currents of thought that flow through their society; they too are subject to intellectual fashions, and their books are a product of their age. In the early nineteenth century, for instance, as cultured Englishmen became more conscious than their ancestors of social evils in the slums of Lancashire and the plantations of Jamaica, a more humane spirit influenced politics and administration alike. This new ethos produced a bulky literature of royal commissions and commissions of inquiry reports which stood out as "one of the glories of the early Victorian age."[2] Commissions of inquiry, however, stressed evils. They were set up when things went badly, rather than when they were going well, and the literature based on such reports naturally caught something of their critical tone. Moreover, contemporaries used this material to produce further literature in current political battles; Tory gentlemen would retort to assaults from industrialists by castigating conditions in Lancashire cotton mills, of which they rarely had personal knowledge. Such attacks on the "millocracy" gained added fervor from the romantic movement, with writers as different in their outlooks as Marx and Engels and Disraeli and Belloc referring to an idyllic rural England which hardly ever existed, but which appeared, rather, through the mist of time and romantic sentiment.

Many subsequent historians caught this mood. In the nineteenth century they frequently misjudged the realities of "Old England," just as a hundred years later they misunderstood the problems of twentieth-century Africa. Scholars—often unacquainted with the practical side of manufacturing even in their own countries—failed to grasp the difficulties that faced the early millowners. They often made little or no allowance for the relative poverty of early Victorian England and for the lack of financial, administrative, and industrial resources that became available only to later generations. They placed unrealistic emphasis on the grim and destructive aspects of early industrialization. As a result, terms such as the "Bleak Age" and the "Hungry Forties" were absorbed into the folklore of British socialism. Many scholars mistakenly accepted as a fact that during this so-called period of dark misery English people had less to eat, lived in filthier hovels, and suffered more sickness than ever in their country's history.

As the reforming mood of this era spilled over into the colonies, colonial administrators too began to produce reports and statistical

---

[2] Thomas S. Ashton, "The Treatment of Capitalism by Historians," in Friedrich August von Hayek (ed.), *Capitalism and the Historians* (Chicago, 1954), pp. 33–63.

abstracts which critics could use as ammunition. In fact, the better administered, and hence the better documented, a colony was, the more glaring its shortcomings appeared. Political parties and newspapers at home used colonial reports to belabor their party opponents in power, and in time this created a new climate of opinion which was sometimes more hostile to the colonial powers than the facts warranted. In 1893, for instance, the pioneer administration of the British South Africa Company[3] in Rhodesia became involved in a war against the Matabele, a warrior people accustomed to raiding their neighbors for women and cattle. The company had a good case for using force to end Matabele sovereignty, but chartered company rule was unpopular with British Radicals and with many missionaries. Humanitarians distrusted Cecil Rhodes as a scheming money maker of boundless political ambitions. Many people disliked the whole theory of allowing so-called backward races to be administered by a commercial enterprise. The chartered company moreover incurred bitter criticism as a rapacious clique of financiers and monopolists determined to do violence to innocent "natives." Radical speakers such as Henry Labouchere contrasted the company's militant methods with the milder means employed by supposedly more impartial imperial officials, overlooking the fact that during the same period imperial administrators were pacifying Nyasaland with methods just as rigorous. A few years later, in 1897, the chartered company thoroughly reformed its administration in Southern Rhodesia. But the reputation acquired in the earlier 1890s clung to the company's name, with the result that a quarter of a century later Sir John Harris, the secretary of the Aborigines Protection Society in London, in pleading for the ending of the British South Africa Company's charter in 1920 could still serve up the same mixture of historical truth and falsehood that had done service in the 1890s.[4]

Europeans also utilized the colonies to criticize one another on national, social, and religious grounds. David Livingstone, the famous Scottish explorer and mission doctor, harshly berated the Portuguese. Livingstone was a patriotic Protestant, a free trader, a keen advocate of permanent white settlement in Central Africa, an ardent believer in Britain's civilizing mission, and in some ways a forerunner of Cecil Rhodes. He detested the Portuguese for their record in the slave trade, for their inefficient or corrupt administration, for their Catholicism, and for their restrictive commercial policies. His books

[3] The company was granted a Royal Charter in 1889. For further material on chartered companies see Chapter 13, pp. 203 ff. and *passim*.

[4] See John H. Harris, *The Chartered Millions: Rhodesia and the Challenge to the British Commonwealth* (London, 1920), *passim*.

helped to publicize long-standing abuses in the Portuguese colonies, but sometimes they gave an even more depressing picture than was justified by the facts.

The British also incurred a good deal of dislike and envy. Some Continental writers, romantic critics of industrial society, helped to elaborate a tenacious stereotype, the picture of the hypocritical Briton who went to the colonies with a Bible in one hand and a mail-order book in the other, a man who spoke of God and meant cotton.

The tradition of European mutual criticism persisted throughout the imperial period. Early colonization led to abuses, especially in territories which long remained underadministered and inadequately supervised. Reports of these evils were seized upon by critics at home —with material published by colonial reformers used as further ammunition—in political attacks on both domestic and foreign policy. The charges, whether exaggerated or not, tended to stick and created a public image which often persisted long after the elimination of the original abuses; the publications of these reformers thus served to reinforce the stereotype.

German and Belgian colonization provides many examples. In the early 1900s the Germans brutally suppressed a series of uprisings in South-West Africa and East Africa. The rebels suffered heavy casualties and were crushed.[5] In 1906 the German Social Democrats and the Catholic Center Party fell upon the colonial question and used this issue for a series of sharp attacks on the government at home. Bülow, the German Chancellor, had in the meantime appointed a new man to the German colonial ministry, Bernhard Dernburg, a banker of high ability. Dernburg started a major reform program, and under him and his successors conditions greatly improved in the German colonies. But the old image proved difficult to eradicate, even in Germany. During World War I the Allies used German material concerning abuses in the Kaiser's colonies for propaganda purposes, and in the battle of mutual recrimination among the European colonial powers, the reputation of imperialism as a whole became tarnished.

Belgian experience was similar. The Congo Free State long suffered from lack of money and effective administration; King Leopold faced the task of pacifying a vast area with a tiny budget more fit for ruling a county than a country. The administration tried to escape from its difficulties by an unwise concessionary policy; there were atrocities

[5] In 1897 the Germans in South-West Africa suppressed a rising on the part of the Swartbooi Hottentots at Franzfontein. In 1903 the Bondelswart Hottentots at Warmbad took to arms. In 1904 a great Herero rebellion started at Okahandja; in the same year Hendrik Witbooi led a major Hottentot rising. The colony was finally pacified in 1907. In 1905 in East Africa the Germans suppressed a major outbreak, known as the Maji-Maji Rising.

against native people; there was forced labor. Humanitarian critics in Britain as well as in Belgium, Germany, and other countries had a good case, but their stories lost nothing in the telling. The Congo was described as a gigantic slave plantation, run for the profit of a rascally king and rapacious shareholders, who reputedly made enormous profits by robbing and starving the Africans. Leopold's rule was pilloried as so bloodthirsty that the African population in the Congo, it was claimed, had diminished by more than half. The facts, of course, were rather different. There were atrocities, but the Free State did good work in suppressing Arab slave traders and indigenous raiders. Policing, however, was expensive, and the state always lacked money. Its trouble was not that it built up a vast, oppressive state machinery, but that it remained weak and could not control the area. The Congo, a country as big as Western Europe, could not be effectively administered with the slender means at Leopold's disposal; far from being exploited, many tribal communities probably never even realized that they lived under the flag of the Congo Free State, or indeed anyone else's flag. Statistical estimates concerning the effects of the Congo Free State's policy on the native population are quite meaningless; there were no censuses, and even to this day no one knows exactly how many people live in the Congo Republic. In 1904 the Belgians appointed an impartial commission of inquiry. This confirmed the existence of many abuses but put the matter into a clearer perspective. In 1908 the Belgian state reluctantly assumed control of the Congo and initiated a series of important reforms; copper mining rather than the collection of ivory and rubber became the economic foundation of the colony. Once more, however, the original impression of widespread exploitation and excessive profits tended to stick, and the story of "red rubber" became part of anti-imperial folklore. Criticism and countercriticism affected even the most rigorously objective scholarship. Henri Rolin, a distinguished Belgian jurist, thus had fault to find with the Belgian Congo's neighbors. His admirable account of early British administration in Rhodesia, the first of its kind, seems to have been influenced to some extent by the way in which the British had previously run down his countrymen in the Congo.[6] Critiques of colonialism, in other words, were transported into the sphere of national competition.

A further factor was the inclination of nineteenth-century writers to criticize things alien to the traditions of middle-class Europe. African tribesmen commonly had a bad press from missionaries and settlers, but these attacks often had effects very different from those originally intended. Many expatriate clergymen and planters in Africa

[6] See Henri Rolin, *Les lois et l'administration de la Rhodésie* (Brussels, 1913).

produced doleful accounts of the way in which black people sup-posedly idled through the day, supplied with the means of sustenance by bountiful nature. Such tales had little relation to reality; they were born of the difficulties experienced in turning tribesmen into wage-workers. However, they had the unintended effect of making condi-tions in Africa seem more attractive than they were in reality, and the white colonizers' record sometimes came to be judged by unrealistic criteria.

Many explorers also drew fanciful accounts of new El Dorados in the interior. These stories continued a long-standing Western tradition of the unlimited fertility which the tropical countries supposedly en-joyed and of the boundless wealth to be won from the trade in luxury goods from the gorgeous East. The commerce in spices, silk, gold, and precious chinaware—though speculative and often dangerous—had in the past yielded great profits to the fortunate. Some of these expecta-tions were later applied to the tropical areas of Africa.[7] In the second half of the nineteenth century, for instance, enthusiastic travelers such as Carl Mauch and Thomas Baines wrote of golden riches beyond the Limpopo River in southern Africa and of the long-lost Ophir from whence Solomon reputedly drew his wealth. Such reports, born of a strange mood of frontier romanticism, later found their way into promoters' prospectuses. Financial speculators—some honest and some crooked—wished to attract funds, and in doing so they vastly exaggerated the riches of, say, Central or East Africa; they also played down the amount of capital that would be needed for develop-ment purposes for creating the administrative infrastructure required for new enterprises.

Expansionist-minded statesmen such as Chamberlain in Britain and Ferry in France used similar arguments. Ferry was determined to extend the French empire to compensate France for the loss of Alsace-Lorraine, but he met with a great deal of domestic opposition. Colonization was expensive, and he had to persuade unwilling parlia-mentarians to vote money for imperial expansion. He bitterly opposed the critics who argued that most Africans only wanted to buy guns and liquor and that colonization and trade of any other kind would not pay. Ferry had to paint Africa's economic possibilities in the most glowing colors, and sometimes he became quite unrealistic in his assessments; but Radical and Socialist critics in turn used these very assumptions to censure the doings of white capitalists and adminis-trators in the colonies. Were these new countries not capable of yield-

---

[7] For a detailed and stimulating discussion of this see Philip D. Curtin, *The Image of Africa: British Ideas and Action, 1780–1850* (Madison, Wis., 1964), pp. 58–87.

ing enormous wealth? Why, then, were the natives so poor? Why did Europe allow them to be exploited? Why would colonial administrators not do more for the aboriginal populations? Many European intellectuals, in fact, shared the economic suppositions that made early investors put their money into shaky Rhodesian gold mines. They overestimated the profits that might be made by capitalists and underrated the vast sums required before an underdeveloped country could be profitably exploited. They failed to allow for the cost of transport and other services or for the lack of social capital, which could be built up only over long periods of development. Colonialists and their critics thus fell victim to the same misconceptions, and these misconceptions have lived on to make the task of evaluating the imperial record even more complicated.

2. Mid-Nineteenth-Century Colonialism

The first of the great social issues in the colonies that exercised the minds of Europe was slavery. The abolitionist movement revealed many features which characterized subsequent imperial reform campaigns. Abolitionism was linked to a growing interest in social welfare at home, to a new spirit of sensitivity to evils long taken for granted, to social conflicts within the metropolitan countries, and to rivalries among the European powers. The campaign began with an attack against the legality of the seaborne slave trade. Denmark made an honorable start by outlawing slave traffic in 1792. After a long struggle the British prohibited slave traffic to their subjects in 1807 and subsequently used their diplomatic and naval influence to prevent foreigners from making profits from the trade.[1]

The humanitarians then turned upon slavery as a domestic institution. The abolitionists now had a good deal of published material to draw on; they started their campaign at a time when conditions in the slave islands were not quite as bad as they had been in the past. Helped by a new climate of opinion, the British abolitionists won all along the line, and in the 1830s slavery was eliminated from all British possessions. The British compensated slaveholders in the West Indies and the Cape; they also made extensive grants to Spain and Portugal in return for engagements to end the traffic from their dominions south of the Equator, shouldered heavy financial responsibilities in founding Sierra Leone as a settlement for freemen, and disbursed vast amounts of money to patrol the coasts of Africa.

British policy backed philanthropy with cash and played a major share in putting an end to slave commerce. France followed suit in

---

[1] In 1807 the United States abolished the slave trade; Holland followed in 1814; Sweden put an end to this commerce in 1815; France stopped the commerce from 1821 onward.

1848, when the newly established republic abolished slavery in all French territories.[2] The final elimination of seaborne slave traffic resolved more and more into diplomatic negotiations concerning the right of search and maritime policing, an issue too technical to arouse the same fervor that abolitionism occasioned in the past.

In the 1830s and 1840s the problems of white-settlement territories moved more into the intellectual foreground. Many Victorian reformers thought of such countries as Canada, Australia, and New Zealand in terms of solving Britain's domestic difficulties. Great Britain was supposedly overpopulated; future generations would not be able to feed all the surplus mouths at home. Britain possessed a more numerous working class without property than any other country. Revolution seemed to lurk round the corner. In 1834 Edward Gibbon Wakefield, a hardheaded middle-class optimist, predicted that "if it were to come to a trial of strength between the two parties [the rich and the poor] in open warfare (which God forbid!), the result must inevitably be favourable to the great majority."[3]

There were, of course, also military factors of a more technical kind which seemed to favor the cause of insurrection at the time. Town-bred insurgents, armed with muskets and entrenched in narrow, winding streets, formed a greater potential threat against organized armies than they did toward the end of the century, when superior staff work and transportation, repeating rifles, and better artillery swept away the European revolutionary's barricades as effectively as the African warrior's wood-and-mud stockade. Wakefield, a Radical reformer, thus thought of settlement colonies as a kind of safety valve for a mother country threatened by potential popular violence. In a long *viva voce* discussion between a remarkably literate colonist and an equally accomplished though skeptical statesman, he set out his whole theory of colonization. Black slaves, white bondsmen, or even free but starving Irish paupers would never make satisfactory laborers in the Antipodes; colonization must rest on a superior kind of workman found in England. The emigration of surplus hands would rid Britain of an awkward social problem, find employment for excess capital to be invested overseas, and prevent the dissolution of the empire. Britain must promote systematic settlement by abolishing free grants of colonial lands in favor of sales at fixed prices. By such means, emigrants would be forced to seek employment for some time

[2] Slavery as a legalized institution survived in the Americas until the second part of the nineteenth century. The United States abolished slavery in 1862 (effective 1863), and Brazil abolished it in 1888.

[3] See Edward Gibbon Wakefield, *England and America: A Comparison of the Social and Political State of Both Nations* (New York, 1834), p. 119.

before being able to buy their own farms, employers would get sufficient manpower, and land sales would provide cash for sending yet more people overseas.[4] Colonization, however, would succeed only under a limited form of self-government. Remote control from London, feebly and incompetently exercised, would never work. Privileged officials appointed from home (the "mother country") might give themselves the airs of demigods; but they could not in fact vie with the better class of settler in qualities of mind, manners, and morals.

These ideas exercised great influence in Britain; they seemed to dovetail with the need for economy and even appealed to the very people whom the "colonial reformers" lampooned as "Little Englanders." The British subsidized overseas settlement. They also moved away from older policies of imperial centralization which their fathers derived from the supposed lesson of the American War of Independence—that concessions to colonists only encourage revolution. In 1837 an abortive rising in Canada discredited traditional policies, and reform became the order of the day.

Responsible government probably saved the empire. But the influence of the reformers should not be exaggerated. Their activities were confined to a few years, their idea of limited local self-government to some extent miscarried, and the remnants of imperial control over such things as crown lands and tariffs crumbled away. Colonies moreover seemed expensive. The British, preoccupied with expanding their industries at home, aimed at low taxation, laissez faire, and limited public expenditure, but this policy could never be fully carried out. The needs of economy conflicted with humanitarian demands and the ambitions of local governors in, say, Hong Kong or the Gold Coast. Slavery was put down, but slave owners required compensation and naval patrols to track down slave traders proved expensive. Subsidized emigration was expected to solve domestic problems, but few operations cost more money than settling farmers on a strange soil. The frontier, whether in New Zealand or South Africa, also produced perennial military problems. The British treasury consistently advocated retrenchment in West and South Africa and the restriction of imperial power to strategically vital areas. Many missionaries and traders, on the other hand, wanted the imperial power to assert its authority in the distant interior; in South Africa, for instance, mission-

---

[4] Edward Gibbon Wakefield (ed. and one of the writers), *A View of the Art of Colonization, with Present Reference to the British Empire: In Letters between a Statesman and a Colonist* (London, 1849). For a detailed discussion of Wakefield's views as anticipatory of subsequent imperialist doctrine in the late nineteenth and early twentieth centuries see Bernard Semmel, "The Philosophic Radicals and Colonialism," *Journal of Economic History,* XXI, No. 4 (December, 1961), 513–525.

aries called for men and money to protect the African tribes inland against Boer settlers and also against the depredations of other African raiders. The British thus careened between these two opposing policies, with the result that imperial taxpayers in the end had to disburse even bigger funds.[5]

By the standards of the time, British colonial expenditures remained high even in the palmiest days of laissez faire. In 1815 the British paid £6 million to Holland in compensation for the Cape Colony. In 1820 the government advanced £50,000 to take 5,000 British settlers to Albany in South Africa. This scheme in turn entailed a considerable military outlay, for "Kaffir Wars" continued to be a drain on the Exchequer for the first three-quarters of the century. The Australian convict settlements absorbed large sums, amounting to as much as £300,000 a year; Parliament made numerous grants in aid of emigration; £20 million was spent in 1833 to compensate the slave owners, but this did not end expenditure on the slavery account. Toward the end of the last century a knowledgeable British consul estimated that Britain's bill to suppress the traffic in human beings ran to something like £5 million, not counting naval casualties.

In 1833, argued an early Victorian economist, the annual cost of empire stood at over £2,300,000. British government revenue during the 1830s and 1840s never exceeded £50 million a year, and every class in society was clamoring against what it regarded as the excessive weight of taxation. Yet, continued the expert, Britain owed none of its prosperity to colonial possessions. The country derived infinitely more advantage from its intercourse with the United States. The American trade had no drawbacks; Britain was not obliged to purchase American commodities which it could obtain more cheaply elsewhere, nor was it forced to keep up armaments for the protection of extensive regions on the other side of the Atlantic.[6]

Britain, confident in its industrial and maritime superiority, thus turned toward free trade. At home manufacturing overcame agricultural interests. The Corn Laws disappeared from the statute book in 1846, the Navigation Acts disappeared in 1849, and free trade became part of rarely challenged orthodoxy. Free trade, however fairly administered, might in practice, of course, benefit British trade. Imperial policy demanded, and free-trade doctrines admitted, that each colony should, insofar as possible, bear the cost of its own administration. Revenue-producing tariffs therefore had to be imposed

[5] See John S. Galbraith, *Reluctant Empire: British Policy on the South African Frontier, 1834–1854* (Berkeley, Calif., 1963).

[6] Cited in Lillian C. A. Knowles, *The Economic Development of the British Overseas Empire* (London, 1924), pp. 93–100.

locally. At Freetown and Lagos, for instance, duties were put on imported liquor, lumber, and tobacco, most of which came from the United States. Textiles were lightly taxed; British merchants accounted for most of the trade in cloth, so that Lancashire had to pay little in the way of colonial revenues.[7] Free trade was a firmly established creed, held with considerable moral fervor, and the British settler colonies began to lose popularity when they departed from this principle.[8]

On the Continent public interest in overseas territories remained even slighter. The French old colonial empire owed too much to the Bourbons' desire for prestige and royal dignity, to past efforts of the Catholic Church, and to an outworn doctrine of mercantilist control to command the loyalty of the nation. Although the French Revolutionary and Napoleonic wars deprived France of the bulk of its transmaritime possessions, these blows injured none but a small group of shipowners, merchants, and planters. The great majority of Frenchmen, preoccupied with political struggles at home and military campaigns abroad, got used to having no colonies. The economic foundations of the colonial empire crumbled. Sugar made from European sugar beets competed ever more successfully with the colonial product made from West Indian cane. In addition, the planters suffered from a serious manpower problem, as the decline of the slave trade deprived the sugar growers of imported labor and slavery finally disappeared.

Abolitionism, however, never became a popular movement in France capable of evoking the same interest in colonial affairs as in Britain. The French antislavery movement was led mainly by secular-minded intellectuals; one of its principal advocates was the Abbé Grégoire, a former *prêtre constitutionnel,* but his name held no appeal for the Catholic masses. Abolitionist enthusiasm was strong among French Protestants, and they produced a number of outstanding missionary statesmen who generally took an Anglophile line, but Protestantism remained numerically weak. Some of the outstanding Protestant pioneers of the Gospel, such as François Coillard, employed their energies in British spheres of influence; Protestantism did not make any great impact on public opinion at home, and the

[7] John D. Hargreaves, *Prelude to the Partition of West Africa* (London, 1963), pp. 106–107.
[8] Carl Adolf Gottlieb Bodelsen, *Studies in Mid-Victorian Imperialism* (reprint of 1924 ed.; London, 1960), pp. 13–22. In 1859 Canada imposed a protectionist tariff. The British neither could nor would interfere with the Canadians' decision, but British faith in the desirability as well as the permanence of the imperial connection received a serious shock.

"nonconformist conscience" hardly affected decision making in the colonies.

Otherwise French governments were subject to many of the same pressures that affected the British. There were the exigencies of a "turbulent frontier" in Senegal; there were demands for expansion from local traders such as Victor Régis, a well-connected Marseilles merchant on the African West Coast. Local governors sometimes managed to impose their views on Paris. French governments in general would try to satisfy Catholic missions and strategically placed trading interests, but France as yet lacked any broad currents of public opinion with an interest in tropical Africa. When high policy demanded that sectional interests should be overridden, this was done without qualms. An important commercial treaty with Britain in 1860 thus abolished duties on most imported raw materials. This ended many long-established commercial privileges affecting commodities such as Senegalese gum, a merchandise important in the local West African setting but of small account for French trade as a whole.[9]

French governments were, however, influenced more than the British by their citizenry's supposed thirst for martial glory. Successors of Napoleon I wrongly imagined that they were still expected to win victories on the battlefield. They failed to realize that the Napoleonic legend was now a weapon for the domestic opposition rather than a desire for warlike successes. Charles X thus meant to gain popularity for his dynasty by seizing Algeria in 1830; he succeeded only in giving employment to the army by embroiling French troops in endless guerrilla wars. In the eyes of British contemporaries, Algeria became a symbol of imperial folly. Louis Philippe sought prestige in protecting French missions in the Far East; Napoleon III sent soldiers to the Crimea, Italy, Mexico, China, and Cochinchina but never gained his fundamental objective of consolidating power at home; in the end he endangered the very basis of his monarchy.[10]

The Germans showed even less interest in colonial affairs than the French, although missionary enthusiasm did strike a chord in the hearts of the pious. German sailing ships became a common sight around the world; in Zanzibar, for instance, the Sultan concluded a trade agreement with the Hanseatic cities of Northern Germany in 1859. Emigrants left the Fatherland for the Americas. However, concern with colonies as such remained negligible. Germany stayed divided. Austria and Prussia, the two great Germanic powers, were concerned only with Continental problems. The duel between Hohen-

[9] Hargreaves, *Prelude to the Partition,* pp. 91–144.
[10] Henri Brunschwig, *Mythes et réalités de l'impérialisme colonial français, 1871–1914* (Paris, 1960), *passim.*

zollern and Hapsburg, the struggle for unification, and constitutional and social conflicts at home absorbed all Germany's energies.[11]

Throughout Western Europe interest in colonial affairs thus remained confined to a limited number of specialists. The most powerful lobbies perhaps were missionary societies, whose middle- and lower-middle-class supporters provided funds for mission stations and avidly read evangelical publications. Some missionaries and humanitarian merchants dreamed of opening Africa to the Gospel and to Christian commercial enterprise, arguing quite correctly that only legitimate traffic in tropical produce like palm oil and cotton would do away with the ravages of the slave trade and give Africans alternative export goods.

Geographers, often associated with missionary enterprises, represented another intellectual pressure group. Organizations such as the African Association, formed in Britain in 1788 with the special object of exploring the interior, the Société de Géographie de France, or the German Centralverein für Handelsgeographie, founded in 1863, all justified their activities by pointing to the practical utility of their work. One of these societies was the International Association for the Exploration and Civilization of Central Africa, founded in 1876 by King Leopold II of Belgium. The society was originally formed for scientific and humanitarian objects, but it soon became an instrument for Leopold's private empire building in the Congo, where Belgian colonization subsequently received international sanction in the guise of the Congo Free State.

Other special-interest groups played their part. The French army had a vested interest in the expansion of Africa's military frontier and was sometimes able to shape policy with scant reference to its political superiors in Paris. A number of British, German, and French mercantile groups, interested in tropical goods like cocoa and palm oil, had a natural concern with colonial questions. However, the great majority of Europeans stood aloof. Except for geographers and specialists in tropical medicine, European scholars displayed relatively little interest in empire matters, while social critics remained primarily concerned with domestic affairs. Even Karl Marx, who knew a great deal about British colonial history, had little to say on the imperial questions of his time. He linked the earlier stages of "primitive capital accumulation" with colonial expansion, which, with all its attendant cruelties, had helped to usher in the rosy dawn of capitalism, and castigated Wakefield's settlement scheme on the grounds that Wakefield wished to manufacture wageworkers. Marx's sympathies went

[11] Henri Brunschwig, *L'expansion allemande outre-mer du XVe siècle à nos jours* (Paris, 1957), pp. 45–87.

to white settlers in the Antipodes, though not to Maori or Australian aborigines, for whom he found no word of sympathy.[12]

In some respects Marx even defended the cause of colonialism in India. The British might be actuated by the vilest of self-interests in initiating a social revolution on the subcontinent, but whatever their crimes, they were a tool of history: "English interference . . . [in India] produced the greatest, and to speak the truth, the only social revolution ever heard of in Asia."[13] They broke up traditional forms of society and smashed Indian domestic industry. They also began to regenerate a backward society by establishing for the first time a political unity, destined to be strengthened and perpetuated by the electric telegraph. The British built a modern "native army"; they introduced a free press and private property in land; they created an educated Indian class, endowed with the requirements for government and imbued with Western science; they provided India with railways; they initiated regular and rapid communications with Europe through steam vessels. Therefore they would be unable to prevent the growth of modern industry; factory work would in turn break down hereditary division of labor, the base of the Indian caste system, and thereby usher in a happier future for the subcontinent.[14]

Marx believed that in such a case the bourgeoisie were unwitting agents of a great dialectical process whereby capitalism conquered the world and destroyed more backward forms of social organization, such as feudalism, before it perished in turn of its own inner contradictions and gave way to socialism. This view in one respect paralleled that of such humanitarian bourgeois reformers as David Livingstone, great medical missionary and explorer, who looked to "commerce and Christianity," to steam transport, missionary propaganda, and permanent white settlement, to spread civilization in Africa and do away with the slave trade and depredations of petty warlords. Marx was, in fact, as convinced of Germany's cultural superiority over the Slavs as British colonial reformers were of their mission to Anglify backward races, white or black.[15] Neither Marx nor Livingstone re-

[12] Karl Marx, *Capital: A Critique of Political Economy:* Vol. I, *The Process of Capitalist Production,* trans. by Samuel Moore and Edward Aveling, ed. by Friedrich Engels, rev. and amplified according to the 4th German ed. by Ernest Untermann (Chicago, 1906), 838–848.

[13] Karl Marx in the *New York Daily Tribune,* June 24, 1853, quoted by Karl A. Wittfogel, "The Marxist View of Russian Society," *World Politics,* XII, No. 4 (July, 1960), 497.

[14] See John Strachey, *The End of Empire* (London, 1961; New York, 1964), pp. 48–51.

[15] Karl Marx, *Revolution und Kontre-Revolution in Deutschland,* trans. into German by Karl Kautsky (6th ed.; Stuttgart, 1920), pp. 97–100. Marx considered the smaller Slavonic nationalities in the Austrian empire religious-

proached Western capitalists for being too warlike, or too interventionist, or expansionist-minded. Livingstone felt ashamed that his country did not do more to put down Arab slave traders in East Africa and called down God's blessing on anyone who would. Marx did not anticipate a new imperialist scramble, and far from scolding the Western bourgeoisie for being colonialists he reproached the British and French capitalists for their timid and pacifist policy concerning tsarist Russia.

In summary, few European thinkers of the day thought that Western colonization was wrong in itself; hardly any were afraid of making what it has become the fashion to call ethnocentric value judgments. None predicted a scramble for colonies or thought that overseas issues would ever dominate future policies. Publications on colonial questions remained limited in number, and colonization remained an affair for specialists, in which Europeans as a whole took little interest.

This state of affairs continued until about the beginning of the 1870s and later gave rise to a strange doctrine of discontinuity. Both Marxist and nationalist historians subsequently discovered a caesura in European development. From the 1870s on, Europe supposedly began to turn outward, embarking on a new career of conquest overseas which contrasted with the more pacific, laissez-faire, free-trading past. There was, in fact, no such chasm. British and French power during the period from 1815 to 1870 simply continued to expand as of old, and the doctrine of discontinuity fitted only Germany and Italy, two recently united nations. British politicians of the mid-Victorian era might fling the epithet "Little Englander" at their rivals, but no responsible British statesman of the period seriously meant to break up the empire. Colonial reformers might proudly maintain their stand for imperial unity, but they usually exaggerated the differences between themselves and their opponents, who basically shared their assumptions.[16]

Early Victorian Englishmen enjoyed an unparalleled naval and industrial superiority over their competitors; access to overseas mar-

---

minded "reactionaries" and backward peasants, who betrayed the revolution of 1848. The Slavs of Germany, Marx argued, had long since lost their political vitality; they must perforce follow in the footsteps of their more powerful neighbors, like the Welsh in Britain, the Basques in Spain, the Bretons in France, and the French and Spanish creoles in North America. The Bohemians and Dalmatians were "dying nations," a phrase used by Marx, a German Communist, with the same gusto as done later by Lord Salisbury, a British Tory. Kautsky's preface tries to explain away these sentiments in the light of conditions in 1896.

[16] John S. Galbraith, "Myths of the 'Little England' Era," *American Historical Review*, LXVII (October, 1961), 34–48.

kets was easier than ever before or since. British governments accordingly saw no reason to enlarge the bounds of formal empire and thereby incur more expense if they could avoid it. Indirect influence and universal free trade remained the ideals, though the Redcoats often had to intervene in practice. "Native" governments might prove hostile to British trade, or they might not be able to protect person and property. British arms constantly had to be used on the turbulent frontiers of empire, either to protect existing commitments or to establish what soldiers regarded as a strategically more favorable boundary line. The search for a defensible frontier itself was likely to provoke trouble. In South Africa, for instance, Boer and British settlers competed for land with seminomadic Bantu, while the colonists' cattle formed an ever-present temptation to warlike border tribes. In 1820 the British tried to cover the Eastern Cape by establishing English settlers as a barrier against the Bantu. The border, however, remained too thinly settled to provide real protection; the area instead became an irresistible attraction to Bantu cattle rustlers with grievances against the newcomers. Settlers and tribesmen could not be kept apart; both moved to and fro across the boundary. Governments then tried to enforce security by more advanced lines of demarcation, but each new boundary further compressed the territory of the indigenous tribes and ultimately led to further conflicts, with the result that the imperial power, regardless of its original intentions, reluctantly kept adding to its commitments.[17]

Although no European state deliberately aimed at massive expansion overseas, the number and extent of European acquisitions kept going up. The territories brought under white sway between 1815 and 1870, the supposedly preimperial era, fill an impressive list. Britain's Indian empire continued to grow; Assam, the Punjab, Lower Burma, Jansi, Nagpur, and Oudh all succumbed to the British raj. Pioneers pushed their way deeper into Canada and Australia, while settlers and Redcoats fought the Maori in New Zealand. The British acquired a chain of bases for their fleet, including Singapore, Aden, and Hong Kong. In Africa the British held on to the Cape in the post-Napoleonic peace settlement. They annexed Natal in 1843, turned the Gold Coast into a crown colony in the same year, and seized Lagos Island in 1861. British soldiers in Africa fought as far afield as the Eastern Cape and Abyssinia.

The French conducted a long and bitter war in Algeria, which ended only with the surrender of Abd-el-Kader in 1847; General Louis Léon César Faidherbe vastly extended French power in Senegal during his governorship from 1854 to 1865. Even the Portuguese

<hr>

[17] Galbraith, *Reluctant Empire*, pp. 41–52.

tightened their grip on some outlying possessions in Africa, and the Spaniards fought a war with Morocco and seized Tetuán in 1860. This expansion did not, however, make a very profound impression on the consciousness of Europe. Systematizers have been unable to find a common historical pattern for a movement composed of so many different facets. Hong Kong was acquired as a trading base with a specifically economic function; Queensland was born of Australian internal settlement; acquisitions such as the Punjab in India or Basutoland in South Africa stood out as evidence that an existing empire would always tend to expand its boundary against more backward communities until it met with some immovable political or geographical obstacle.[18] Social theorists usually had only a limited interest in these matters; they preferred to think about such vital questions nearer home as German or Italian unity, the progress of industrialization in Europe, or the future distribution of power between the social classes. Europe therefore remained inward-looking, and the great change in its intellectual climate had to await the last quarter of the nineteenth century.

[18] D. K. Fieldhouse, " 'Imperialism': An Historiographical Revision," *Economic History Review*, 2d Ser., XIV, No. 2 (1961), 201.

3. Imperialism—The Highest Stage of Nationalism?

Six years after the last army of the Confederate states surrendered at Appomattox Court House the victorious German invaders in Paris proclaimed the King of Prussia to be German Emperor. The United States and the Reich emerged as unified, great nations, and the world balance of power rapidly shifted in their favor. In time Germany as well as the United States abandoned the British-oriented free-trade tradition, rapidly built up new industries, and dreamed of manifest destiny. Germany owed its unification to a military monarchy, not to old-fashioned liberals. The French *levée en masse* could not beat the invaders, and after the failure of the Communards' rising of 1871, revolutionary traditions and militant nationalism began to diverge. To an increasing extent nationalism, or at any rate chauvinism, and the thirst for glory, became the property of the Right in both French and German politics. As the strands of liberalism and nationalism became separated, the social question moved into the foreground of public attention. Nationalism found a new challenger in the form of proletarian internationalism with the founding of the First International in 1864, and the shift in the interstate balance of Europe was accompanied by an equally striking change in its ideological constellation.

European thinkers were living in an age of tremendous expansion. Advances in geology, archaeology, and so-called scientific history widened the frontiers of knowledge, and studies such as astronomy and geography made vast new contributions to man's knowledge of space. Christianity similarly extended its boundaries. In this respect the nineteenth century proved an age of paradox. On the one hand, this era saw a concentrated assault on all religious creeds, more thoroughgoing and better conceived than any in the past. Many secular thinkers triumphantly proclaimed that either mankind as a

whole or a particular section of it—the Nordics, the proletariat, or
some other elite—was fundamentally good and did not need the
creaking crutches of religion. These views seeped through to a wider
public, and the churches lost much of their former hold. On the other
hand, at the very time when so many prophets foresaw the end of
religion, Christianity gained access to new areas of recruitment.

The Church became engaged in a worldwide crusade to make good
its losses at home by conquests overseas. The age that sent white explorers, prospectors, and soldiers of fortune to remote frontiers also
witnessed a tremendous outburst of ecclesiastical pioneering. In men
such as David Livingstone, European Christianity produced martyrs
of a new kind. Livingstone combined scientific knowledge with an
enthusiastic belief in economic development, a profound evangelical
purpose, and a deep conviction of his country's historical mission.
Evangelicalism of this sort went hand in hand with a social purpose.
Many missionaries related the problems of the poor at home to those
of the "heathen" abroad; they tried to apply lessons learned in metropolitan countries to mission fields overseas, combining their faith
with an unquestioning belief in limitless progress. Christianity, contrary to any nineteenth-century analyses, remained a growing religion.

Evangelization was accompanied by an unquestioning mood of cultural self-confidence, which found perhaps its most powerful mode
of expression in the sense of nationality. In the end, neither Christian,
proletarian, bourgeois, nor aristocratic internationalism could successfully challenge the nation-state's prestige. Not only did nationalism strengthen its hold over the imagination of Western and Central
Europe, but European nationalist ideals seeped outward into the
Balkans and the Middle East. The industrial revolution might profoundly change Europe's internal balance of power, but national prestige was still assessed in territorial rather than technological terms.
Europeans continued to dream of their country's greatness by measuring its acreage, just as peasants and landowners measured their
wealth in real estate. To many Western thinkers, progress, nationality,
and territorial expansion seemed almost synonymous.

This mode of thinking remained characteristic of all great European powers, particularly of Germany. The mood of the newly formed
Reich was an odd blend of confidence and apprehension. There was a
naïve trust in a magnificent though ill-defined future, and at the same
time a dread of potential perils, of a danger that in reality already lay
in the past. Although Bismarck took the Social Democrats, with their
revolutionary phraseology, at their own word, the era of internal
uprisings was over. Bismarck suffered from the nightmare of coalitions
and dreaded the kind of situation which Frederick II faced in the

Seven Years War, when Prussia had to fight on three fronts. Yet Germany was in less danger from attack in the 1870s and 1880s than ever in its history.

The Germans deplored the departure of so many people to foreign countries, especially to the Americas. Economists proved that the Fatherland was losing men and money which went to build up competitors; nationalists regretted that so many valuable citizens would give up their German speech and become lost to *Deutschtum*. The stream of emigration soon dried up as displaced German peasants went to seek their fortunes in Germany's own industrial cities. However, some writers then anticipated that with increased urbanization the Reich would increasingly become dependent on foreigners for strategic raw materials, that the Fatherland would no longer be able to supply all its citizens with enough food, or that the growing factories would no longer command sufficient markets. Despite these fears, advances in agricultural science and techniques greatly added to Germany's crops. Germany, like the other European countries, produced more cattle and grain with an almost stationary agricultural population, while industrial products improved in quality and found more customers.

Fear of the uncharted future nevertheless remained widespread, especially among intellectuals, and some Germans began to look overseas for the solution to their country's real or imagined problems. In 1879 Friedrich Fabri, an ex-mission inspector, published a little book which gave expression to this mood and which drew heavily on the arguments of English mid-Victorian imperialists. The German population, Fabri predicted, might amount to 80 million by the end of the century; the Fatherland would not accordingly be able to feed itself, and only emigration would prevent overpopulation. Since the settlers who were now leaving Germany's shores went mainly to foreign countries, especially to the United States, where their skill and capital were lost to the Fatherland, Germany must find settlement colonies of its own, preferably in the temperate portions of Latin America. Colonization would counteract social democracy by providing a safety valve. Germany must learn from Britain, which had set a splendid example by granting self-government to its Canadian, Australian, and South African colonies, with the result that no colony nowadays thought of cutting its ties with the United Kingdom. Germany must be prepared to give large initial subsidies to such colonies and rely on indirect benefits through expanded trade and shipping to pay for the investment. Germany must also learn from Britain how to rule tropical "trade colonies." Nations such as Haiti and Liberia could not govern themselves; the white man must bring effective administration and economic progress to backward tropical populations. Europeans faced a great moral task in these long-neglected lands, and Germany must take its share in Europe's new cultural mission, govern in the natives' own interests, and employ that same "genuine humanity" which the British showed in India. Both settler and trade colonies would repay such efforts by providing markets for a metropolitan economy hit by a lengthy period of economic recession.

Fabri also tried to link protectionism to imperialism. Originally there was no connection between the two. Bismarck introduced a higher tariff regime in 1879, but his reasoning had nothing to do with colonial designs. Britain and France acquired vast possessions in a period of relative free trade. The Austro-Hungarian monarchy, on the other hand, imposed heavy tariffs to shield Bohemian industrialists and Hungarian landowners from foreign competition, but the Hapsburgs took no part in colonial enterprise. Fabri now argued that protectionism would pay only if combined with effective colonial policy designed to enlarge German markets. The Reich, in Fabri's opinion, had expanded its industries too quickly and now had no choice but to seek colonies; the fault lay with the Americans, who had suddenly closed their gates to German products by an ill-considered policy of high tariffs. Overseas expansion, Fabri added in a strange roundabout fashion, would also help the German navy. The German empire did not really need a strong fleet; its fate would in the last instance be decided by Continental armies. Germany should at all costs avoid an arms race with Britain, especially at a time when rapid technological change in naval armaments might soon render the most modern vessels obsolescent, but it did require some ships to show the flag, and in the long run only colonies would make naval power pay.[1]

Fabri's book embodied much of the reasoning that later justified German colonization. His moderation, however, was lost on most other theoreticians of German colonial enterprise. As an ex-missionary, Fabri admired British trusteeship policies in India; he deplored unreasoning navalism. But much of German colonial thought soon ran into more radical channels, and the German Colonial League was more militant. A network of organizations sprang into being, all marked by the same blend of cloudy romanticism and national stridency. Bodies such as the Pan-German League, with their romantic chauvinism, appealed in the first place to academically trained people, teachers, professors, senior civil servants, and men who prized their reserve officer's commissions even more than their doctoral dissertations. Businessmen came only second in the ranks of the Pan-German

---

[1] D. Friedrich Fabri, *Bedarf Deutschland der Colonien? Eine politsch-ökonomische Betractung* (3d ed.; Gotha, 1884), *passim*.

League. Industrial workers and artisans showed much less interest and continued to give their allegiance mainly to the Social Democratic and center parties, rather than to right-wing organizations. The sober-minded German farmers kept aloof; for all the Leaguers' talk about finding new living space for the healthy sons of the soil, the wine-growers and cattle farmers themselves were uninterested, and pan-Germanism remained mainly a city product.[2]

The French too, after their defeat in 1871, became more conscious of colonial matters. Some intellectuals and politicians began to look upon colonies as a consolation prize for losses in Europe. Algeria was making good progress; between 1835 and 1876 the number of white people there went up from some 11,000 to over 300,000. France, with its almost stationary population, could now point at least to one province which experienced rapid demographic expansion. Farmers, ruined by a dreaded vine disease caused by the phyllox-era, found new land on the other side of the Mediterranean; civil servants got promotions more quickly in the colonies, where administrative manpower was scarce; French officers, tired of the dull routine of provincial garrisons, got a chance to show their mettle in action, and sometimes to govern regions as big as European principalities. People of this kind, drawn from various political persuasions, formed a numerous group, so that the French colonialists, unlike the German variety, derived much of their strength from the political center, from men who believed in the Republic and detested the thought of a monarchist revival. Churchmen looked to the colonies as an expanding mission field. Aristocratic families sought to serve their country overseas at a time when they could not or would not work for the hated Republic at home. Above all, the colonial idea appealed to a section of the French intelligentsia—journalists, professors, and senior civil servants, who projected their nationalism overseas and looked to colonial enterprise to regenerate France.[3]

French writers published a considerable number of books on

[2] Mildred S. Wertheimer, *The Pan-German League, 1890–1914* (New York, 1924), p. 65, gives details of the social composition of the Pan-German League. In 1901 the league had a total membership of 19,796. Of these, 9,921 were classed as academic, or as belonging to liberal professions; 5,288 were businessmen, 2,859 were industrial and handworkers, and only 444 were farmers.

[3] Henri Brunschwig, in *Mythes et réalités de l'impérialisme colonial français, 1871–1914* (Paris, 1960), pp. 113–115, shows that between 1889 and 1893 the French "colonial party," a loose parliamentary group, was comprised of 61 persons from the Republican Center, 10 from the Left Center, 12 from the nonmonarchist Right, and 7 Royalists or extreme Right. Of 92 deputies of the *groupe colonial*, there were 52 intellectual and professional people, 13 serving or retired civil servants, 4 officers, 14 merchants and bankers, and 9 landed proprietors.

colonial questions. Outstanding among these was a massive tome by Paul Leroy-Beaulieu, a laissez-faire economist with an encyclopedic knowledge of history and labor questions.[4] Leroy-Beaulieu regarded colonization as the expansive force of a people, its "multiplication across space," a living proof of its vitality in every sphere. Colonization, he argued in characteristic fashion, would prove not merely an economic but also an intellectual boon to the colonizers. The great experience of opening up new territories could not help but broaden the horizons of the motherland. Who could doubt that intellectual achievements would be multiplied among a people that could recruit its liberal professions from the four corners of the world? Writers would find untold encouragement in being able to address their books to global audiences. The new colonial communities would in time build up an intellectual life of their own, just like the United States, which had already made such splendid contributions to literature, philosophy, and history. Colonization would also provide inestimable economic benefits, and here Leroy-Beaulieu, like most of his contemporaries, stressed above all the market aspect of empire. If only the French abstained from imposing ill-considered restrictions on their commerce, they would find countless new customers in the colonies.

Leroy-Beaulieu represented the views of a generation that could see no necessary connection between colonialism and protectionism. France acquired the bulk of its overseas possessions before 1892, when the Méline tariffs passed onto the statute book and surrounded France with a high customs barrier. In the same vein Leroy-Beaulieu combated the view, widely held in his day, that the export of capital would injure the metropolitan economy and should therefore be restricted. The more funds a country imported from France, the more French goods that country would buy. Capital exports, he argued with much force and common sense, would add to the world's wealth, effect a more efficient distribution of resources, promote the specialization of labor, and open up new wealth overseas. French capital investments abroad also formed a kind of financial reinsurance—an argument designed to appeal to a nation that had seen the disasters of 1871. Investments placed overseas would be immune from domestic upheavals and were desirable from the national point of view as an emergency reserve. Leroy-Beaulieu deplored the reluctance of many French investors to risk their money in Algeria or Indochina. He accepted the views of John Stuart Mill, later elaborated for different purposes by such critics of imperialism as Hobson and Lenin, that funds invested in the colonies would yield better returns

[4] See Paul Leroy-Beaulieu, *De la colonisation chez les peuples modernes* (2d ed., rev., corr., and enl.; Paris, 1882). Yves Guyot, *Lettres sur la politique coloniale* (Paris, 1885), furnishes a skeptical reply.

than at home. He did not furnish detailed statistical evidence to uphold Mill's contention, but insisted that French investors, including people with small savings, should show some daring and lend their money in pursuit of *la grandeur nationale* as well as profits.

Leroy-Beaulieu also furnished a detailed colonial program. The core of the French empire was Algeria. The French in the first instance acquired the country for purely political and fortuitous rather than economic reasons. Now the territory's wealth exceeded all expectations. By 1930—a hundred years after the original French occupation—the territory would assuredly contain 3 or 4 million whites; there would be enough Europeans to effect the peaceful and progressive absorption of the Arab population. France would dominate the western and central Sudan, and one-fourth or one-fifth of the immense African continent would receive the imprint of French civilization. Such splendid prospects were worthy of some effort and financial sacrifice. He concluded with one of those future-directed perorations so characteristic of socialists and colonialists alike of the time: the future beckoned the bold; the people who colonized the most would be the first power on earth, and even if this were not true today, it would assuredly be so tomorrow.

This climate of opinion made itself felt in Britain as well, where the confidence of the mid-Victorian period sometimes gave way to a more apprehensive mood. The British had become conscious of the worldwide shift in the balance of power. British fleets still controlled the world's oceans, but what of the future? Sometime around 1870 the British lead over all its competitors in world trade had reached its maximum. From then on, though British figures still kept increasing, those of other nations rose faster, and Britain's share in the whole diminished. In the decade between 1871 and 1881 the United Kingdom for the first time produced less than half the world's supply of steel. The slump, which began in the mid-seventies, was worldwide, but the agricultural depression was Britain's own. In the 1880s the British birthrate began to fall.[5] The old religious certitudes were weakened and were transmitted into more secular gospels, of which Kipling's type of service imperialism was one. Many theoreticians now came to look upon colonies as insurance against an uncertain tomorrow, dominated by huge land powers centered upon Berlin, St. Petersburg, and Washington. British national and imperial feeling became more vigorous at the beginning of the 1870s, after the formation of the German empire.

In 1868, when Gladstone formed his first government, separatism

[5] David C. Somervell, "The Victorian Age," in William N. Medlicott (ed.), *From Metternich to Hitler: Aspects of British and Foreign History, 1814–1939* (London, 1963), pp. 73–99.

was still part of the country's political orthodoxy. Liberals and Conservatives, including Tories like Disraeli, commonly assumed that the
settler colonies must sooner or later cut their links with the motherland. Outlying white dependencies were supposed to be diplomatic,
military, and financial liabilities rather than assets. In 1869 the
Colonial Secretary pointedly refused a request from New Zealand
for the retention of an imperial force on the disturbed North Island.
London similarly turned down in the harshest possible language an
application from New Zealand for a loan. Black colonies enjoyed no
greater esteem; the government quite openly contemplated the cession
of Gambia to France, and many Britons imagined—though wrongly—
that it aimed at progressively liquidating the whole empire.

In the early 1870s attitudes began to change. The nation found a
new pride in its overseas commitments; a new imperialism was born
which from the outset owed nothing to toryism or jingoism, to high
finance or to monopolies, but found its roots in popular radicalism,
humanitarianism, and the strength of national sentiment. A new
movement, largely composed of colonials, especially Australians,
protested against the supposed desire of English statesmen to turn the
colonies adrift. Advocates of the imperial connection tried to prove
that the colonies were in fact of material assistance to Britain. They
emphasized the need for imperial unity, with attention confined entirely to the white-settlement colonies. This stress on the imperial
connection at first had nothing to do with a reaction against free trade;
on the contrary, it made some appeal to followers of the Manchester
school, who hoped that closer union within the empire would counteract protectionist trends in the colonies. Imperialism also retained its
old link with the cause of social reform, and many Radicals continued to advocate state-aided emigration as a remedy for poverty
at home.

These ideas became more popular. The Reform Bill of 1867 had
given the vote to the urban workers, many of whom had brothers and
cousins in New Zealand, Australia, or Canada. They regarded these
territories as their own, as places worth keeping, unlike India which,
for all its imperial romance, only provided posts for the upper classes.
Imperial feeling also derived strength from an undercurrent of fear.
Gladstone had disestablished the Irish Church and had made economic concessions to Irish tenant farmers, and many British owners,
who resented interference with property rights, believed that this
and subsequent land legislation on Gladstone's part might be applied
in England itself. Numerous well-to-do British people thus rallied
to the imperial cause. Gladstone's subsequent fight for Irish autonomy
and the way in which he supposedly knuckled under to Irish violence

helped to split the Liberal Party in 1886. From then on the liberal unionists provided reinforcements for the imperial camp.

Developments abroad seemed to underscore the importance of imperial consolidation. Only big powers would survive, and the best way to hold onto national greatness was to strengthen imperial ties. Poets such as Tennyson caught this mood. Disraeli, with his inimitable skill for picking up ideas in his party's cause, veered around. In a great speech at the Crystal Palace in 1872, he established the new connection between conservatism and empire, a policy which stood for the assertion of British prestige rather than for territorial expansion. By the end of the 1870s the term imperialism, which had once signified no more than Napoleon III's military dictatorship, had passed into popular speech, and in the process it acquired a variety of meanings. Many linked it with jingoism of the drumbeating, anti-Russian variety, a popular sentiment among many British workers. Others came to associate it with the reaction against liberal pacifism. Such romantic writers as James Anthony Froude idealized empire for noneconomic reasons. Froude praised the white-settlement colonies because he hoped to reproduce in these distant countries a simpler state of society and a nobler form of life than he found in England. Like some German and pan-Slav romantics, he wished to save his country from the perils of industrialization; a colonial population of healthy, clean-cut, sunburned farmers would compensate England for the supposed biological deterioration of its city dwellers.

This romantic, antirational element did not play as big a part in British as in German imperialism. A far more representative writer was Sir John Seeley, a distinguished Cambridge historian. Seeley cared little for race, but a great deal for the state. He envisaged the expansion of the British overseas as the true key to British history, the European and the colonial policy of England forming two sides of the same coin. He disapproved of both the bombastic self-congratulatory and the pessimistic imperial schools and considered the British colonies merely extensions of the British nation. The white-settlement colonies would be able to hold together under one banner and thereby rival Russia and the United States, the superpowers of the future. The Indian empire, Seeley admitted, did not really fit into the pattern of British settlement colonies. The British acquired the subcontinent under rather special circumstances; most of the fighting was done by Indian troops, who possessed no feeling of nationality. Having once taken over, the British could no longer pull out. Their dominion would last as long as they could rely on the tacit consent of a vast but heterogeneous population. To Seeley, the sentiment of imperial unity appeared as a kind of "pan-Anglism," but Seeley's pan-Anglism, for all its lack of realism, remained a good deal more attached to common sense than pan-Germanism. The British, Seeley believed, enjoyed no special biological superiority over brown-skinned people. They would never be able to resist the force of nationalism. If ever the people of India acquired a sense of national cohesion, Britain must change course, Seeley predicted. Once Britain's relations to India should ever come to resemble, however remotely, those of Austria to its Italian subjects, the British would have to haul down the flag.

These views were not in themselves outstandingly original. The assertion that colonists remained Englishmen beyond the seas (a view that ignored the force of colonial nationalism) was not new. The argument elaborated by Seeley, that science would facilitate imperial union by diminishing distance, was a commonplace of the time. The fear that England without its colonies would be dwarfed had frequently been advanced before. Other British writers had foreseen the possibility—distant but by no means unthinkable—that British rule might have to yield to a westernized Indian nationalism. Britain's cession of the Ionian Islands to Greece in 1864 had, in fact, taken place precisely in response to such a national sentiment. But Seeley gave a well-written and logical statement of the imperial case; his arguments were both moderate and convincing. His historical interpretation, which made overseas expansion the pivot of English history for the last two centuries, was impressive.[6] Seeley's views corresponded to a changed climate of opinion. This new opinion was more responsive to imperial greatness, more tolerant of state expenditure, more willing to maintain the empire for reasons that transcended financial profit and loss calculations.

Seeley, Fabri, and Leroy-Beaulieu were nationalists above all; each considered colonial greatness an outward expression of the national destiny of his country, a mood which dominated much of European thinking until the present century.

[6] See Sir John Robert Seeley, *The Expansion of England: Two Courses of Lectures* (London, 1891). For a detailed discussion of Seeley's work see Carl Adolf Gottlieb Bodelsen, *Studies in Mid-Victorian Imperialism* (reprint of 1924 ed.; London, 1960), pp. 149–176.

4. The Imperial High-Water Mark and the Turn of the Tide

Despite the influence of men like Seeley, Fabri, and Leroy-Beaulieu in their respective countries, empire building in Africa never became a really popular cause until the partition was over. In Britain the daily papers of the 1880s and 1890s catered to middle-class tastes. The board school alumni, taught to decipher print but not much else, confined their reading to the Sunday newspapers, which had, since the middle of the nineteenth century, learned how to serve up a popular diet of crime, sports, and sex. Even the new dailies developed in the 1890s continued under the spell of *The Times;* it was perhaps not until 1903 that the flavor of such journals as *Tit-Bits* seeped into the daily papers. The London press, like that of almost any other country, used the news from Africa as ammunition for domestic political struggles. The copy sent in by correspondents—long, detailed, and often unreadable—became the raw material of controversies which made only a very limited appeal to the new literates, whom the Education Act of 1870 had equipped with a bare knowledge of the "three R's."[1]

Imperialism in Africa at first therefore lacked a popular mass basis. The builders of the new African empire, men like Goldie and Johnston, received little encouragement from home, and did not ask for it. Imperialist books do not seem to have made much of an impact on the majority of those ordinary people who actually carried white rule to Africa. Scholars who search through the letters and diaries of early Rhodesian farmers, transport riders, civil servants, and soldiers will find no references to Darwin or Gumplowicz, Benjamin Kidd or Kipling, whose writings are supposed to have created a major change in the late nineteenth-century climate of opinion. The ideas of these

[1] James A. Edwards, "Southern Rhodesia and the London Daily Press, 1890–1893," *Occasional Papers of the National Archives of Rhodesia and Nyasaland,* No. 1 (June, 1963), pp. 58–70. Even the *Daily Mail,* which first appeared in 1896 and which many assume to have been the first popular daily, originally saw itself as a conscious imitation of *The Times.*

31

writers may have gained some popularity after the partition of Africa was over, but they never became the subject of discussion around the campfires in the Rhodesian bush. In Germany colonial romanticism made a somewhat greater impact, but even there writers like Hermann Löns only produced their mournful lyrics about safaris and askaris and a beautiful soldier's death when the partition of Africa was already an accomplished fact.[2]

The personal motives of the empire builders, great or small, almost beggar description in their variety. Generally there was some economic motive—the wish to make money or build a career. None, however, sought solely for profits. Some, like Sir Alfred Sharpe, an early Nyasaland commissioner, first went to Africa as big-game hunters. Cecil Rhodes and others suffered from a weakness of the lungs and sailed for the Cape in search of a better climate and a longer life. An unhappy love affair drove Frederick Lugard to seek oblivion in the African bush. Doctors went abroad to study new medical problems or, like Godfrey Huggins, later a Rhodesian prime minister, to better his income and support aging parents. There were bankrupt swindlers. There were refugees from tsarist oppression or from Continental conscription laws. English gentlemen's sons who could not get through Sandhurst or failed to pass the difficult Indian civil-service examination might turn to Africa for an administrative career.

At first sight the only safe generalization that seems possible is that the empire builders rarely resembled the stereotype of the clean-shaven, beef-eating, pipe-smoking Englishman of colonial fiction. Henry (Harry) Hamilton Johnston, an outstanding administrator, self-taught soldier, and indefatigable writer, was a small-statured, squeaky-voiced art student. George Grey, a magnificent Rhodesian mining pioneer and a born leader of men, stammered so badly that his subordinates avoided looking him in the face when asking a question, so as not to aggravate his impediment. Hermann von Wissmann, a brilliant German administrator, was a drug addict. Rhodes was a dreamer who loved books and despised soldiers. The missionaries presented an equally varied picture. They comprised some of the intellectual elite of the British working class—Livingstone, a textile worker turned doctor, and Robert Moffat, an ex-gardener who became a great linguist, scholar, and evangelical statesman. They also included people of much higher social position, such as Bishop Colenso, a Cambridge wrangler and a former fellow of St. John's, whom Zulu skepticism turned to a critical examination of the Pentateuch.

[2] For a contrary interpretation see William L. Langer, *The Diplomacy of Imperialism, 1890–1902* (2d ed.; New York, 1960), pp. 67–96.

Yet despite this extraordinary diversity of motivation and background, the majority of empire builders shared certain ideas about what they believed to be their mission. They felt convinced that Europe represented the highest kind of civilization, that progress was inevitable, and that history was on their side. Africa was a continent of darkness, to be redeemed by hard work, the profit motive, the Gospel, or a combination of all three. The empire builder was a patriot; he believed himself to be serving both his cause and his country. Administrators and missionaries, even some farmers and traders, normally stood for a doctrine of trusteeship. They were convinced that money making, however laudable, could not serve as the sole excuse for empire. The conqueror, in their view, had a mission. To rule was also to serve. The humanitarian would feel ashamed of individual outrages which white men might commit against black, but as far as colonization as a whole was concerned, his conscience was clear. Empire represented progress, and progress was sacred. The ideological initiative lay with the white man, and throughout the earlier history of African imperialism, the intangible factor of morale favored the colonial as against the indigenous ruler.

The details of the "scramble for Africa" will be discussed in a chapter later on. At this point suffice it to say that the partition of the continent subsequently assumed in the eyes of Europe a dramatic quality which it did not always possess at the time. In the late 1870s European map makers still showed the great African land mass as a continent of outposts. Algeria was French; South Africa was British. British and French colonizers had established a number of enclaves along the West Coast, but only in Senegal was there any penetration in depth. The Portuguese maintained an ill-defined and shaky rule over the coasts and some inland stations in Angola and Mozambique. The Turks still claimed suzerainty over the North African seashore from Egypt to Tunis, though real power had long since slipped from their grasp. The sultanate of Zanzibar, another Muslim kingdom, had established an extensive sphere of influence in East Africa, but the Sultan wielded little power away from the seashore. Elsewhere the map was blank. Cartographers had no colors to indicate the territories controlled by indigenous rulers, and Westerners regarded these regions as an enormous no man's land.

Thirty years later geographers presented a very different picture of Africa. Only Ethiopia, Morocco, and Liberia remained independent.[3] The remainder of Africa was painted over in imperial blues, reds, and greens, indicating the formal ownership by metropolitan powers. Within just a generation a few European states seemed to

[3] Most Europeans assumed that in time even these "anomalies" would disappear. Tripolitania was still Turkish, only to be lost to Italy in 1921.

have effected the quickest and most extensive land occupation in history.

The late nineteenth century saw a series of sharp diplomatic struggles in Europe of which the scramble was to some extent a by-product. The public at home became increasingly concerned over these disputes. Negotiations among the metropolitan powers, especially at the international conference over the Congo, 1884–1885, and over the Anglo-German treaty of 1890, produced a great deal of literature on colonial questions. Many of these works purported to show that the nation to which the writer belonged had failed to obtain an adequate share of the vacant territories suddenly thrown on the diplomatic real-estate market. There was also a boom in soldiers' reminiscences. Retired captains and colonels told adventurous stories of how, say, the British overthrew Lobengula, the Matabele paramount chief in Southern Rhodesia, or of how the Germans conquered the East Coast Arabs in what was later Tanganyika. European opinion became accustomed to viewing the partition as a rapid, well-planned, and dramatic process, full of colorful deeds, sudden disasters, and splendid victories.

The realities of the scramble did not quite conform to this spectacular image. Inland expansion was at first a slow process, starting in many cases from bases long in existence. In the last third of the nineteenth century European penetration picked up increasing momentum, though the imperialists continued to meet many domestic obstacles, with each new annexation involving conflicts against advocates of economy or of caution within the metropolitan countries. The "new imperialism" finally reached its high-water mark in the 1890s. In 1895 Joseph Chamberlain took charge of the British Colonial Office, determined on a policy of massive imperial consolidation and development. France was wedded to an annexationist policy. Germany thought in terms of a *Weltpolitik*.

The year 1896 in many ways formed a turning point in the story. In that year Abyssinian warriors, well supplied with modern rifles, inflicted a decisive defeat on a strong Italian expeditionary force at Aduwa. The Italian army lost fully one-half its effective power. Italian expansionism—a policy pursued largely to divert social discontent and anti-Austrian irredentism at home—suffered a decisive check. Aduwa, not the outstanding Japanese successes over Russia between 1904 and 1905, marked the first great modern victory of a colored people over a European power. Aduwa made a deep impression among American Negroes;[4] it also produced an echo in the minds of a few educated

---

[4] Many American Negro writers during this period looked to Ethiopia as the black man's defender, and numerous Negro churches in the United States and Africa used the word "Ethiopian" in their names.

black men in South Africa. But otherwise the Ethiopian victory, unlike the Japanese campaigns of the subsequent decade, found slight response. The majority of Africans in other parts of the continent neither knew nor cared about what happened in distant Abyssinia. Humanitarians in the metropolitan parliaments could not regard the cause of unknown Amharic feudal lords as their own; the Ethiopian military feat caused no stir in the Socialist ranks of Western Europe. On the contrary, empire in Africa for a short time began to arouse popular enthusiasm. African colonization became more widely associated with a sense of social and cultural mission. Military might now seemed justifiable as a means of bettering the condition of the subject races. British writers such as Kipling defended imperial expansion in moral terms; the concept of trusteeship for tropical Africa merged with the ideas of Anglo-Saxon kinship and the imperial bonds of brotherhood to produce a powerful creed which for a few years intoxicated the British masses.[5]

The Ethiopian victory, in fact, gave a short-lived impetus to imperial expansion. The British bitterly regretted the Abyssinian success, not because they felt humiliated at a black triumph, but because the Italian defeat apparently left the way open to a two-pronged French advance from east and west into the Sudan, Egypt's hinterland. For this and other reasons the British decided to invade the Sudan and secure their hegemony over Egypt. The French could make no headway against British opposition, and in 1898 they pulled out at Fashoda. But in Europe itself the French gained a handsome diplomatic dividend from the Italian disaster. Crispi, the pro-German Premier, fell from office; Franco-Italian relations improved, and later on in 1902 Paris concluded a secret agreement with Rome, recognizing Italian claims to Turkish-owned Tripolitania. The French subsequently moved into Morocco and the Italians invaded Tripolitania. This Italian victory in turn helped to set off a nationalist war of liberation of the Balkan peoples against the Ottoman Empire. Between 1912 and 1913, Serbian, Montenegrin, Greek, and Bulgarian arms inflicted a series of crushing defeats on the Turks, eliminating all but a few remnants of the last Asian empire in Europe.[6]

On the northern shore of Africa, European imperialism, in competition with decadent Muslim states, continued to advance until just before the beginning of World War I. However, the real decline of the imperial cause in Africa began on the southern tip of the continent,

[5] See Richard Koebner and Helmut Dan Schmidt, *Imperialism: The Story and Significance of a Political Word, 1840–1960* (Cambridge, Eng., 1964), pp. 196–220.

[6] In defeating the Turks the Balkan peoples effected a revolution in the balance of power which helped to set off World War I.

where a great metropolitan power clashed with a white African people. In 1896—three months before Aduwa—the Afrikaners of the Transvaal inflicted a humiliating defeat on an unofficial filibustering force led by Leander Starr Jameson and financed by Rhodes's British South Africa Company. On January 2, 1896, the "raiders" laid down their arms at Doornkop. From the purely military point of view the battle was a petty affair. Only some 600 men were involved on the British side, compared to the 8,300 Italians killed or captured in the Ethiopian campaign, but politically the results of this fight were just as far-reaching. The raid indeed formed a historic landmark. Rhodes's venture contained all the elements of indirect aggression, which totalitarian strategists elaborated in the twentieth century in a different context. The chartered company's plans involved the organization of an armed uprising within the borders of a nominally friendly state, the dispatch of "volunteers," the employment of mass propaganda, and the connivance of supposedly neutral statesmen at home. But the venture was bungled in comic-opera fashion. The raid deepened existing cleavages between Boer and Briton in South Africa; it helped to isolate Britain, and world sympathy went out to the Boers in a way which it had not to the Amhara. "Stock-exchange imperialism" stood discredited; anticolonialism of a relatively new kind developed in response to the real or alleged iniquities committed by an overblown empire against a small nation. The raid also gravely weakened the British position north of the Limpopo. In preparing for the invasion of the Transvaal the chartered company denuded Southern Rhodesia of its military police. The Matabele and many Mashona peoples seized the opportunity to rise against the white man, and the chartered company became engaged in a war of survival. The native uprising was seized upon by the Radical enemies of the charter at home and occasioned bitter criticism of its administration.

South of the Limpopo the failure of the Jameson Raid damned indirect methods of imperial infiltration. The British imperial power now turned to direct pressure on the Transvaal to wring political concessions from the Boers. The Transvaalers replied by seizing the military initiative, and in 1899 war broke out to decide whether Briton or Boer should rule over South Africa. The British would not give way, because they saw the Cape and its vast hinterland as an indispensable link in a great imperial chain.

Compared with these great political issues, the economic questions were of only secondary importance. The British did not fight to make their mining concerns on the Witwatersrand safe against the exactions of unenlightened pastoralism. The Transvaal government, though inefficient, did not threaten British gold investments on the Witwatersrand; nor did the mining companies have sufficient cause to stir up hostilities because of the financial burdens laid upon them by Boer corruption and red tape. The Transvaal administration could usually be "squared"; its financial demands were not nearly so heavy as the charges laid upon mining concerns by the British South Africa Company's government in neighboring Rhodesia.[7] And the majority of Boers had no wish to set the economic clock back. Both Radical and Socialist well-wishers of the Afrikaners and British war propagandists mistakenly described the Boers as bewildered Biblical herdsmen, at war with a capitalist system which they did not understand. The Afrikaners in fact had no intention of destroying the gold industry. The great mining ventures provided them with a steady revenue and a growing market for their farm produce. The Boers therefore had no wish to drive out the *uitlanders*. What they desired was political supremacy (a supremacy they did not attain until half a century later). Both sides were also influenced in their political planning by the absence of reliable demographic statistics. Milner and Kruger, the chief contenders on the opposing sides, each believed that British immigrants would ultimately outnumber the Afrikaners in the Transvaal. Britons and Boers thus based their policies on future-directed assumptions that had no basis in fact. These preconceptions, however, added a special element of bitterness to the struggle which, from the British point of view, got completely out of control.

The conflict began as a small colonial venture of the limited-liability variety, financed on a shoestring and fought against an enemy thought hardly superior to warlike Indian mountaineers. Initially the war was waged in the traditional manner, with fixed rules designed to protect civilians and confine hostilities to white fighting men. But the struggle soon became increasingly bitter and turned into a South African civil war, with 53,000 locally recruited and mainly English-speaking soldiers taking up arms against their Afrikaans-speaking neighbors, who mobilized a total of some 87,000 men. In addition, the British Empire as a whole made the greatest military effort in its history. The dispatch of almost 400,000 men to fight on the other side of the world was an unprecedented feat. The struggle, so confidently begun, ended as a halfway house to total war in which farms were burned, civilians rounded up, and the Boers driven to the borders of despair.

The British won a barren victory in the field; the imperial idea sustained a blow from which it never recovered. From the military point of view the conduct of the war brought scant prestige to the British ruling class. In Britain imperialists such as Milner found themselves isolated. The war had never been popular; public opinion was only roused by the initial Boer ultimatum and the disasters of the

[7] Lewis H. Gann, *A History of Southern Rhodesia: Early Days to 1953* (London, 1965), p. 158.

"black week." Wartime chauvinism soon evaporated, and war in the end deprived imperialism of its hold on most of the educated.[8] Milner lost the support of the "academic unionist" Liberals and of radical imperialist publicists such as Dilke and Stead. Militant imperialism thus began to lose its appeal.

After the Boer War the British became increasingly preoccupied with social questions at home. There were strikes; there was syndicalist and suffragette agitation; there were the intractable Irish issue and Ulster militancy. In the economic sphere the British middle classes had to cope with the problems occasioned by a slower rate of industrial expansion. Brains and capital to some extent drifted from industry into landownership, politics, and the professions. Observers remarked upon the loss of drive among second- or third-generation entrepreneurs. There was an even more diffused feeling of biological decline, occasioned to some extent by the reduction in the size of families, a process which began in business and professional circles and gradually spread down the social hierarchy. Many British thinkers became more self-questioning; their changing attitudes reflected a general shift in values which affected the Western world as a whole.[9]

Healers and philosophers, affected by this mood, tried to get beyond the apparently superficial realities of the reasoning mind and to chart the dark currents of the subconscious. Critics of contemporary life attempted to understand the hidden realities of society. The obvious explanations for commotions such as the Boer War, cast in the language of blue books and white books, no longer sufficed. The secret motives of the conflict had to be uncovered, its sordid reasons unmasked. Some writers thus began to interpret the whole conflict as a dubious promoter's scheme, hatched in secrecy. Their reasoning owed a debt to conventional imperialist critiques of other peoples' imperialism and to the pronouncements of imperialist statesmen such as Chamberlain and Ferry, who had promised golden rewards to the investors of their respective countries, if only they would give financial support to the policy of colonial expansion. Now these arguments were turned against those who had initiated them, to become part of a new anti-imperial ideology. Colonialism and finance capital came under bitter attack, both from traditionally pacific Radicals and from Catholic republicans such as Hilaire Belloc. These sentiments sometimes blended with anti-Jewish outbursts against "hook-nosed financiers" from Johannesburg, who had supposedly pushed Britain into an inglorious war.

[8] See Eric Stokes, "Milnerism," *Historical Journal*, V, No. 1 (1962), 47–60.
[9] George L. Mosse, *The Culture of Western Europe: The Nineteenth and Twentieth Centuries; An Introduction* (London, 1963), p. 230.

This "financial-conspiracy" school of thought was a relatively new phenomenon. The contemporaries of Louis XIV or of Frederick the Great and the Earl of Chatham had been well aware of the economic motives of their rulers, but it had never occurred to them to regard kings and ministers as the puppets of faceless financiers. The beginning of the nineteenth century, however, saw an important change. The disdainful, aristocratic poetry of Lord Byron's "Don Juan" presaged the economic determinism of subsequent Marxist and social-liberal writers.

> Who hold the balance of the world? Who reign
>   O'er congress, whether royalist or liberal?
> Who rouse the shirtless patriots of Spain?
>   (That make old Europe's journals squeak and gibber all).
> Who keep the world, both old and new, in pain
>   Or pleasure? Who make politics run glibber all?
> The shade of Buonaparte's noble daring?—
> Jew Rothschild and his fellow-Christian, Baring.
>
> Those, and the truly liberal Lafitte,
>   Are the true lords of Europe. Every loan
> Is not a merely speculative hit,
>   But seats a nation, or upsets a throne.
> Republics also get involved a bit;
>   Columbia's stock hath holders not unknown
> On 'Change, and even thy silver soil, Peru,
> Must get itself discounted by a Jew.[10]

Karl Marx and later socialist writers provided what they regarded as the scientific foundation for this romantic view of modern history, but Marx did not link the colonial expansion of his day to the machinations of finance capitalists. The first formulation of this theory fell to bourgeois critics of Western society, and perhaps the foremost of these was John Hobson, an English writer and economist.

Just before the outbreak of the Boer War, Hobson visited South Africa as a newspaper correspondent. He sharply criticized British policy on the subcontinent, and his hatred of Milner's methods soon broadened into a root-and-branch condemnation of imperialism. Hobson's views in some ways anticipated those of Keynes. He argued that the underpaid workers of Britain did not receive sufficient wages to buy their own products. The capitalists accumulated huge profits, but, unable to find adequate returns at home, they had to put their money into overseas territories in order to earn bigger dividends. Hobson thus linked empire building abroad with underconsumption at home. He

[10] "Don Juan," canto XII, stanzas V and VI, *The Poetical Works of Lord Byron* (London, 1928), p. 784.

showed by means of statistics how enormously the British Empire had expanded over the last twenty years or so. He also demonstrated the vast increase in Britain's foreign investments. He then linked these two phenomena by a causal chain, arguing that territorial growth was the effect of investments abroad:

> Over-production in the sense of an excessive manufacturing plant, and surplus capital which cannot find sound investments within the country, force Great Britain, Germany, Holland, France to place larger and larger portions of their economic resources outside the area of their present political domain, and then stimulate a policy of political expansion so as to take in the new areas.[11]

The competition of rival empires formed the principal characteristics of modern imperialism.

Hobson's interpretation of empire building was not solely confined to financial and economic motives. He stressed the "moral and sentimental factors" that helped to produce modern imperialism; he denounced the politicians who became the financiers' willing accomplices, having been led astray either by direct financial interests in their business schemes or by the desire to divert domestic discontent into adventures abroad. He similarly condemned the ecclesiastical, academic, military, and administrative hangers-on of imperialism and the cheap jingoism of the masses, the popular chauvinism born of "the lust of the spectator, unpurged by any personal effort, risk or sacrifice, gloating in the perils, pains and slaughter of fellow-men." But the greatest fault lay with a small number of monied men engaged in banking, broking, bill discounting, loan floating, and company promoting. These were the true villains. Hobson continued, with bitter passion:

> United by the strongest bonds of organisation, always in closest and quickest touch with one another, situated in the very heart of the business capital of every State, controlled, so far as Europe is concerned, chiefly by men of a single and peculiar race, who have behind them many centuries of financial experience, they are in a unique position to control the policy of nations. No great quick direction of capital is possible save by their consent and through their agency. Does anyone seriously suppose that a great war could be undertaken by any European State, or a great State loan subscribed, if the house of Rothschild and its connexions set their face against it?[12]

[11] John Atkinson Hobson, *Imperialism: A Study* (London, 1902), p. 85.
[12] Hobson, *Imperialism*, p. 64.

Hobson expressed Byron's sentiments in prose, and as prose they made even better reading. Still, Hobson was not content to let matters rest with invective or analysis. He was an optimist at heart and believed that matters could be put right peacefully. Modern imperialism was not inevitable; it benefited only a small, parasitic section within the bourgeoisie, whose power might be destroyed by reforms. Let the peoples of the West rid their countries of tariffs and monopolies. Let them invest their savings at home rather than abroad and thereby give more employment to their own workers. Let them increase the purchasing power of the poor and thereby put an end to underconsumption and the perpetual cycle of slumps. Let them clear their minds of "kilometrisis" or "milomania"—the prehistoric passion for land, dating back from the childhood of the race, when a wide range of territory was necessary for the community's food supply. Let them stamp out the glowing embers of militarism—and then, Hobson said, all would be well.

Hobson's ideas were not entirely original; however, his hatred of monied men and monopolies, his loathing of secret compacts and public bluster, fused all existing indictments of imperialism into one coherent system. He induced British, and later world, opinion to accept his own definition of the term. His ideas influenced German nationalist opponents of the British Empire as well as French Anglophobes and Marxists; they colored the thoughts of American liberals and isolationist critics of colonialism. In days to come they were to contribute to American distrust of Western Europe and of the British Empire. Hobson helped make the British averse to the exercise of colonial rule; he provided indigenous nationalists in Asia and Africa with the ammunition to resist rule from Europe. As a modern historian has put it, there is now "an international *communis opinio* for which economic imperialism has become an accepted fact."[13]

Hobson seemed to put forth a brilliantly convincing argument, but in correlating the expanding acreage of British territorial acquisition with the figures of British capital exports he performed some interesting intellectual jugglery. Closer analysis, even in the days preceding World War I, showed that the bulk of British capital exports avoided tropical areas and went to regions of white settlement both within and outside the empire. More than half of Britain's colonial and foreign investments were placed in the Americas. Britain's greatest borrower

---

[13] See Richard Koebner, "The Concept of Economic Imperialism," *Economic History Review,* 2d Ser., II, No. 1 (1949), 1–29; see also D. K. Fieldhouse, " 'Imperialism': An Historiographical Revision," *Economic History Review,* 2d Ser., XIV, No. 2 (1961), 187–209.

was the United States, a country which Britain controlled neither politically nor financially and which until about 1897 frequently pursued an anti-British course. The Union Jack, in other words, did not generally follow upon British investments.[14]

The financial interpretation hardly squared with the political facts even in southern Africa, the area foremost in Hobson's mind. Because of his Radical background, Hobson could see nothing wrong with colonial activity which consisted in the migration of settlers to vacant or sparsely populated foreign lands, where the newcomers established local self-government in close conformity with the mother country's institutions. Empire building of this type was "a genuine expansion of nationality." Democratically minded colonists were virtuous. This preconception prevented Hobson from seeing how much imperial expansion owed to settlers on the periphery of the empire, not only in South Africa but also in Australia and New Zealand.

Hobson also misinterpreted the Boer War. The British did not attack the Transvaal to acquire new gold mines, and victory did not change the property relations on the Witwatersrand. The "Rand lords" made good money under Kruger's government and remained politically divided in their allegiance. Even Rhodesia, a chartered company-

[14] George Paish, "Great Britain's Capital Investment in Individual Colonial and Foreign Countries," *Journal of the Royal Statistical Society,* LXXIV, Part 2 (January, 1911), 186, shows that by 1910 British investments (in thousand pounds sterling) were distributed about as follows:

Grand total, all countries	3,191,836
Total foreign countries	1,637,684
Total British colonies and India	1,554,152

The principal borrowing countries were:

United States	688,078
Australian Commonwealth and New Zealand	380,050
Canada and Newfoundland	372,541
South Africa	351,368
Argentina	269,808

The tropical areas in British possession absorbed only the following amounts:

West Africa	29,498
Straits Settlements	22,037
British North Borneo	5,131
Hong Kong	3,104

For a more recent breakdown of British foreign investments during the high tide of imperialism, see Harvey H. Segal and Matthew Simon, "British Foreign Capital Issues, 1865–1894," *Journal of Economic History,* XXI, No. 4 (December, 1961), 566–581. Segal and Simon calculate that only 25 percent of the capital called up during the period went to the tropics, as against 65 percent to regions of new settlement, although the tropics participated more substantially in the upswing of the late 1880s.

ruled territory, supposedly the monopolist's paradise, did not fit the Hobsonian pattern. Rhodes did not annex the country beyond the Limpopo River because he failed to place his surplus capital elsewhere. Indeed, a financier with purely economic motivations such as Barney Barnato, another great diamond magnate, put up strong resistance to Rhodes's design of using revenue from diamond mining to finance territorial expansion into the "far interior." Rhodes had to squeeze Barnato out of his financial empire to acquire freedom of action.

Having conquered Rhodesia, the chartered company maintained only a limited measure of economic control. The company acquired the territory's mineral rights and imposed a bitterly unpopular charge on all mining companies wishing to operate in the country. However, anyone could invest if he paid the required royalty. The only real monopoly concerned diamonds, which were reserved to Rhodes's financial associates at Kimberley. Prospectors could not find these gems, and this particular privilege remained an academic one, while the company's income from royalties and land sales continued for a long time insufficient to cover its outlay. Trade as such was free; there were no all-powerful boards to monopolize exports in special commodities, and economic development suffered less from official interference than in, say, French or Portuguese territories under the direct administration of the state. Although chartered company investors were supposed to make enormous amounts of money, profits were hard to gain in a new and underdeveloped country where all administrative services had to be started from scratch, and from 1890 to 1923 the company did not pay a penny in dividends.

Even the South African gold industry was not as lucrative as legend had it. The new rich from Johannesburg, who amassed millions on the Rand and then put up mansions in Park Lane, acquired in their time a sort of archetypal quality; they stood out as the bloated, exploiting, cigar-smoking, "kaffir-baiting," warmongering money makers par excellence. But investors could also lose a great deal of money on the Rand; large gains in some mines were balanced by low profits or losses in others. The mean yield of capital invested in the Rand mines for the first forty-five years after their effective exploitation amounted to no more than 4.1 percent.[15] Most British investors preferred smaller risks and smaller gains. The gold speculator, willing to put up risk capital, took second place to the rentier, anxious to secure a safe income. In 1911 Paish calculated that over 60 percent of Britain's foreign investments had been employed in the construction of railways,

[15] S. Herbert Frankel, *Capital Investment in Africa: Its Course and Effects* (London, 1938), pp. 91–92.

either directly by British companies or indirectly by government loans.[16] Railway lines, of course, yielded lower profits or none, especially in new countries, where the provision of transport preceded development, and the lines long remained underused.[17]

Hobson's analysis bore no more relation to the realities of Continental empires. German colonization in the Bismarckian era took place at a time when the Reich disposed of relatively little surplus capital. German savings at first went mainly into industrialization at home. The cartelization of German industry and the decisive role of German banking in industry dated only from the beginning of the present century. Lenders willing to risk their money outside the borders of the Fatherland preferred the Americas or adjacent countries in Central and Eastern Europe, where British competition was weak. While British funds played an important part in the development, such as it was, of the German colonies in southwestern and East Africa, the authorities at Berlin found considerable difficulty in getting their own capitalists to put up money for these territories. Bankers in Berlin or Frankfurt who were willing to divert funds to Africa often preferred British possessions such as the Transvaal to Germany's own.

Applied to Italian, Portuguese, or French imperialism, Hobson's interpretation made even less sense. Italy remained chronically short of investment capital even for domestic purposes—hence many of its social troubles—and conditions were no better in Portugal. The majority of French capitalists were not interested in their empire. French financiers experienced constant political pressure to make their investments serve the purpose of their governments. Great sums of money flowed to Russia, where they cemented the Dual Alliance, but the French colonial empire remained the Cinderella of the Paris bourse.[18]

[16] Paish, "Great Britain's Capital Investment," p. 185.

[17] For more detailed criticism of the theory of economic imperialism see the following outstanding articles: Richard J. Hammond, "Economic Imperialism: Sidelights on a Stereotype," *Journal of Economic History,* XXI, No. 4 (December, 1961), 582–598, and David S. Landes, "Some Thoughts on the Nature of Economic Imperialism," *ibid.,* pp. 496–512.

[18] Herbert Feis, *Europe, the World's Banker, 1870–1914: An Account of European Foreign Investment and the Connection of World Finance with Diplomacy before the War* (New Haven, Conn., 1930), gives a detailed account. According to Feis's figures on p. 51, France had invested a total of 45 billion francs by 1914. This was distributed as follows (in billion francs):

Russia	11.3
Remainder of Europe	16.2
Latin America	6.0
French colonies	4.0
Egypt, Suez, South Africa	3.3
Asia	2.2
United States, Canada, Australia	2.0

Hobson himself recognized that Russian imperialism fell completely outside his categories. The tsarist monarchy was obviously not plagued by an excess of domestic capital seeking new opportunities for investment. He got out of this difficulty by arguing that Russia was a special case. Russian expansion was "primarily Asiatic in its achievement"; the Russians proceeded by the direct extension of their boundaries on land and aimed primarily at settlement for agricultural and industrial purposes (a description which by no means fitted Russian expansion either in the Baltic or in Central Asia). In his view Russian empire building was therefore "of a more normal and natural order" than that of Western states,[19] the implication being that territorial acquisitions in backward regions were somehow exonerated if conquests were made by land. However, Hobson (and his ideological descendants in the Afro-Asian world of the 1950s and 1960s) never explained why overland expansion should be more "natural" and less reprehensible than the seaborne variety. Modern followers of Hobson or African nationalists do not explain—to put the question in modern European terms—why Hitler's only truly imperialist venture should have been the naval invasion of Norway.

Hobson, like Lenin after him, also laid himself open to attacks on other grounds. He did not consider the poverty of precolonial Africa. Instead he wrote of European firms in foreign parts almost as if they were so many pirate gangs looting the indigenous people of their riches. But the mines sunk in the Transvaal during his own days were not booty which Rhodes and company stole from Boer or Bantu; they formed a new kind of wealth, which would not have come into existence except for the *uitlanders'* enterprise and their willingness to risk their own or their clients' money on the Rand. Hobson also underestimated the difficulties in the investor's path. Most profitable investment in underdeveloped countries required extensive economic and social overheads—schools and harbors, power plants and roads, railways and telegraph offices. In most of Africa these infrastructures did not exist, and many investors who miscalculated failed to make money. Hobson simply took the existence of such facilities for granted and failed to see that only simple industries, such as slave catching and ivory hunting, can do without this essential social capital. Nor did he take any account of the constabulary aspect of imperialism. Like so many other liberal intellectuals brought up in the pacific climate of an Anglo-Saxon country, he also assumed the existence of such institutions as a police force, law and order, and an incorruptible administration. Few underdeveloped regions, however, possessed such services. Hence the rich in poor countries often preferred to hoard their funds

[19] Hobson, *Imperialism*, p. 22.

in Paris or London rather than use them at home, where, according to Hobson, they should have been able to make more money. Hobson moreover had nothing to say on the question of risk; he ignored the dangers from war, disorders, and default faced by any lender who placed his funds in foreign fields.

In spite of these omissions and inconsistencies, anticolonialism of the Hobsonian variety slowly began to make converts in the decade preceding World War I. Its concepts at first appealed to Radical and pacifist critics of society more than to British Fabian Socialists; many Fabians remained wedded to a hard-minded, almost Milnerite doctrine of imperial rule justified by efficiency. Bourgeois humanitarians took a harsher line. Edward Morel provided English-speaking readers with scathing condemnations of French and Belgian practices in the Congo; Henry Nevinson castigated conditions in Portuguese Angola and São Thomé. These and other writers piled up numerous instances of colonial iniquity—many real enough, some exaggerated, and not a few invented. In doing so, they helped to build up a widespread conviction that these examples characterized imperial rule as a whole, that Western empires in the tropics were built on consistent, and withal highly profitable, systems of exploitation. Colonization supposedly yielded enormous gains to the undeserving rich and provided jobs for their even less deserving sons. The condition of the exploited Africans supposedly continued to deteriorate. Financiers and their hangers-on were thought to be poisoning the international air. Their secret cabals would ultimately lead to war, and only the sunset of empire would bring peace to a troubled world.[20]

[20] See, for instance, the following works by Edmund D. Morel, *The British Case in French Congo: The Story of a Great Injustice, Its Causes and Its Lessons* (London, 1903), *King Leopold's Rule in Africa* (London, 1904), *Great Britain and the Congo: The Pillage of the Congo Basin,* with an introd. by Sir A. Conan Doyle (London, 1909), and *Morocco in Diplomacy* (London, 1912), as well as Henry W. Nevinson, *A Modern Slavery* (London, 1906), and Henry N. Brailsford, *The War of Steel and Gold: A Study of the Armed Peace* (London, 1914).

5. Pre-Leninist Critiques of Colonialism on the Continent

Hobson's critique of empire was based on Radical and humanitarian as much as economic assumptions. It fitted in with British religious traditions and made a considerable appeal to the nonconformist conscience. This humanitarian outlook was also found in writers on the Continent. Jean Jaurès, the great French Socialist reformist leader, condemned French intervention in Morocco not only for its expenditure in money and men, but also on the grounds that the venture was morally unjust.[1] Continental critiques usually owed more, however, to Marxist or nationalist condemnations of other peoples' empires. The latter line of reasoning gained much ground, especially in Germany, where opposition to British imperialism became popular among most writers favoring territorial expansion and a more active *Weltpolitik*. Foreign powers, headed by perfidious Albion, had supposedly tried to prevent German unity.[2] By the time Germany had found its unity, the argument continued, alien powers had preempted the best parts of the world. Germany should therefore redress the balance. Germans were more vigorous, younger, and better qualified to rule. England, the new Carthage, was slipping into wealthy decadence. Let the Reich assert its power, and the German Eagle would prevail.[3]

The concept of a decadent Carthaginian oligarchy which levied

[1] Jean Jaurès, *Contre la guerre au Maroc* (Classiques français du socialisme; Paris, 1936), *passim*.

[2] For a scholarly refutation of this view see Günther Gillessen, *Lord Palmerston und die Einigung Deutschlands: Die englische Politik von der Paulskirche bis zu den Dresdener Konferenzen (1848–1851)* (Lübeck, 1961), *passim*. This legend, as incorrect as it was influential, later reappeared in new guises throughout many newly unified countries of the Afro-Asian world.

[3] See Gerhart von Schulze-Gaevernitz, *Britischer Imperialismus und englischer Freihandel zu Beginn des zwanzigsten Jahrhunderts* (Leipzig, 1906). Schulze-Gaevernitz himself was relatively moderate and asked his compatriots not to speak of British "decadence." Others, like Werner Sombart during World War I, took a much more extreme position. See, for instance, Werner Sombart, *Händler und Helden: Patriotische Besinnungen* (Munich, 1915).

tribute on the whole world naturally pleased many of Britain's economic competitors. Ideas of this nature appealed even more to the anticapitalist ethos of many intellectuals, soldiers, and bureaucrats in Germany and elsewhere. Detestation of the "rich, overfed Western imperialists" became an article of faith among numerous right and left wingers in Central and Eastern Europe.[4] Defeat in World War I only strengthened this image in the minds of many German intellectuals; the Western peoples continued to be regarded as the wicked "haves," engaged in an unholy conspiracy against the virtuous "have-not" countries. The class struggle was thereby lifted from the national to the international plane, and militant nationalism acquired pseudo-Marxist overtones. German writers tried to strengthen their thesis by contrasting the supposedly shallow, materialistic, rationalist, machine-ridden nature of the West with the deeper, truer, soul forces of the German folk. Notions of this kind also appealed to subsequent generations of intellectuals in colonial and ex-colonial countries. The world's proletariat came to be identified with the Afro-Asians, and world capitalism with the West as a whole. This interpretation also colored liberal thought in Western Europe and North America, where good will toward emergent nations sometimes blunted the critical faculties of scholars and journalists.

Theoreticians within the Marxist camp shared many of the basic assumptions about Western imperialism held both by Western bourgeois pacifists and by Anglophobe nationalists. Marxists, however, used these concepts as weapons in the class struggle and formulated their theories according to the political strategy they wished to adopt. But they encountered many difficulties, for Marx's writings could be used to justify the most diverse courses of action. Marx had died in 1883, firmly convinced that capitalism would not survive him for long. Economic crises were bound to become more numerous and more severe. The workers of the West would become more miserable and militant; the proletariat at the same time would receive constant reinforcements from a dispossessed peasantry and the dying class of impoverished shopkeepers and craftsmen. Revolution was just around the corner, but the revolution would be a domestic European struggle and would be decided within the West. Marx had dismissed colonial expansion as an essentially precapitalist phenomenon. He stressed not so much the expansive nature of Western capitalist society, but its alleged inability to find a proper balance between the output of capital equipment and consumer goods. Colonialism was to him a matter of

---

[4] Within a generation or so, similar views found a comparable response among intellectuals and party officials in many parts of Asia and Africa, where the West often came to be viewed in terms similar to those popular in Wilhelminian Germany about Great Britain.

secondary importance, though he did draw attention to the gold discoveries in Australia and California as a temporary stabilizing factor within the capitalist world economy.

These essentially mid-Victorian ideas seemed to bear no obvious resemblance to the problems of the early twentieth century. Capitalism, far from contracting, was extending its sphere of operations over the whole world. Production had steadily increased; living standards had continued to rise for the bourgeoisie and the workers alike. Worse still, nationalism could not be eradicated from proletarian minds. State-run social-welfare schemes had given the workers a greater stake in the existing order. In racially mixed countries, such as the Austro-Hungarian monarchy, nationalism had become even more virulent.

The first original contributions toward an explanation of these discrepancies came from the Marxists of the right, those who believed in evolutionary socialism and justified their stand by the argument that capitalism still had some life left. The most important center of the new Socialist thought was Vienna, the capital of a multinational empire, a state torn by social and racial hatreds within and wedded to a highly protectionist customs policy and a strong foreign policy abroad. Socialists like Otto Bauer, the offspring of a wealthy manufacturing family, thus spent a great deal of time investigating the relationships of nationalism, capitalism, protectionism, and finance capitalism. Bauer's theories emphasized the impact of a steadily expanding population on the stability of capitalism. The Slavonic peoples of the empire maintained a high birthrate—hence the growing number of Hapsburg subjects continued to provide factory owners in Vienna and Brno with more customers. Bauer concluded that steady demographic expansion might shore up the capitalist system by ensuring some kind of equilibrium between production and consumption.[5]

Rudolf Hilferding, another "Austro-Marxist," and later a German cabinet minister, came to similar conclusions via a somewhat different argument. Hilferding produced a brilliant pioneer study on finance capital, which analyzed the cartelization of industry and the dominant role of the banks, a marked feature of the German (though not so much of the British) economy of his day. He agreed with Hobson that modern imperialism was the product of capital exports, but he believed, like Bauer, that the rich had a choice in the matter, that imperialism was not an absolute necessity for the continued existence of capitalism.[6]

[5] The best general discussion in English of these problems is found in Earle M. Winslow, *The Pattern of Imperialism: A Study in the Theories of Power* (New York, 1948), pp. 148–214.

[6] Rudolf Hilferding, *Das Finanzkapital: Eine Studie über die jüngste Entwicklung des Kapitalismus* (Marx-Studien, Blätter zur Theorie und Politik des wissenschaftlichen Sozialismus, Vol. III; Vienna, 1910), *passim*.

The doctrine of free choice also appealed to more moderate German Socialists like Karl Kautsky, a leading theoretician of his party. Kautsky tried to convince his fellow countrymen, both of the right and of the left, that the Reich did not necessarily have to acquire either colonies overseas or adjacent dependencies in Europe to keep its economy afloat. When World War I broke out, Kautsky met with bitter opposition from a great army of German annexationists who looked forward to a German-dominated bloc comprising the non-Russian borderlands of the tsarist monarchy, Belgium, northern France, and the Balkan Peninsula in addition to the Hohenzollern and Hapsburg monarchies.[7] Kautsky also found to his distress that some of his own Social Democratic comrades were only too ready to find excuses for German designs at territorial expansion, and in 1915 he produced a short study entitled *National State, Imperialist State and Association of States,* which is now little known, but deserves to be remembered as a classic on the subject of imperialism.[8] Kautsky's monograph first analyzed precapitalist modes of imperial expansion and showed that most modern forms of imperialism were still influenced by archaic motives. The ancient forms of empire rested on military power, on exploitation through tribute, or on forced labor. Absolute monarchies like Russia (or, as he might have added, Prussia) acquired new territories to increase the number of taxpayers and to provide more jobs for officers and bureaucrats to strengthen the state machinery. Russia remained bound to this policy, but at a heavy cost to its national wealth. The Russians, according to Kautsky, would have done better to build up their economic potential by domestic reforms in education, agriculture, and industry. Instead they pursued the line of least resistance and wasted their substance in empire building. The fact that even Russian industries were becoming more efficient had nothing to do with territorial expansion. The Russians owed these successes to the influx of foreign capital and, indirectly, to the rise of the Russian labor movement.

Another early form of expansion, Kautsky noted, rested on mercantile monopolies and the search for luxury goods such as furs, ivory, and spices. British, French, and Russian frontiersmen rapidly occupied vast areas in North America and Siberia; the rush for ivory and rubber helped to open Africa. But colonization based on such simple "robber" economies could not last; the treasures of nature were quickly looted, and modern technology and advanced methods of

[7] See Fritz Fischer, *Griff nach der Weltmacht: Die Kriegszielpolitik des kaiserlichen Deutschlands, 1914/18* (Düsseldorf, 1961).

[8] Karl Kautsky, *Nationalstaat, imperialistischer Staat und Staatenbund* (Nürnberg, 1915).

agriculture alone provided adequate substitutes. The old-style mercantilist economies based on trade monopolies, Kautsky believed, necessarily displayed a warlike character. Industrial economies, however, tended toward pacific expansion. Factory owners gained no advantage from wars, which would only disrupt world trade and kill their customers. Industrial capitalists desired free competition, both for their workers on the labor market and for the merchants on the commodity market. The greater the number of traders who competed for manufactured goods, and the greater the number of merchants who engaged in the sale of raw materials, the more the factory owner would benefit. Military and naval power was almost irrelevant in such calculations. The merchant fleet of Norway considerably exceeded in size that of much bigger powers like France and Italy, and Belgium had developed a great industrial complex and formed the center of a vast shipping trade, yet neither Norway nor Belgium needed navies. Kautsky also opposed those Germans who saw empire as the answer to overpopulation. In more recent periods of history, emigrants came from backward rural areas such as Poland or the most neglected portions of Germany and went to highly populated industrial regions whose factories afforded employment. The "living-space" argument was therefore archaic.

Kautsky at the same time denied that the export of capital must inevitably tend toward imperial expansion. The British example seemed to prove the opposite. The most important British imperial territories from the standpoint of investment and trade were the white-settlement colonies. Indeed, the relative importance of Canada and Australia as borrowers of British capital had been increasing in recent years, while the value of India and other colonies had diminished.[9] These white-settlement territories were not, however, acquired as the result of modern finance capitalism. Nor were they colonies in the true sense of the word. The white dominions were now self-governing democracies of an advanced kind, tied to the motherland through a loose association. Leagues of states (run on what we would now call Commonwealth lines) corresponded in Kautsky's views to the highest state of capitalism: "An association of states, not a nationally mixed state

---

[9] The figures quoted by Kautsky for the value of capital exports in *Nationalstaat*, p. 38, were as follows (in million pounds):

	1908–1910	1911–1913	*Increase or decrease*
Canada	91.5	132.3	+40.8
Australia	28.9	35.4	+ 7.5
South Africa	20.9	14.5	− 6.4
India	46.4	12.7	−33.7
Other colonies	38.0	18.8	−19.2

[like the Austro-Hungarian], and not even a colonial state, represents the form of empire required by capitalism to attain its last and highest form, before the proletariat takes over."[10]

India stood in a different category. The British, Kautsky mistakenly believed, levied a heavy tribute from the subcontinent through taxation. They also developed commerce on a vast scale. So great was the importance of the Indian empire that the bulk of British possessions in Africa, and elsewhere in Asia, were acquired primarily to safeguard the route to India, with British strategy hinging on the Cape and on Egypt and the Suez Canal.[11] The Indians, Kautsky continued, paid a heavy price for the Pax Britannica, but they also derived many benefits from British rule. Capitalism, Kautsky argued in line with Marx's reasoning, brought to India modern postal and railway communications, a free press, and other innovations. The British maintained peace through a small, inexpensive standing army. A single glance toward Europe would show the Indians that independence would bring them much heavier military burdens. The new Indian middle class of merchants, intellectuals, bankers, shopkeepers, landowners, and such wished ultimately to shake off the British yoke, but they realized that they were not yet sufficiently strong to take over. If British rule ended right away, India would break up into a number of despotic states engaged in constant feuds; hence the Indian National Congress was willing to wait and would not give trouble to the British while the war lasted.

Kautsky's analysis of imperialism in Africa was equally interesting. Socialist theoreticians claimed that modern imperialism was characterized by the export of capital and the fusion of industrial and agrarian protectionism, but Great Britain, the most highly developed capitalist state at the time of the scramble, did not in fact take the initiative in the race for African colonies. The joint interests of British working-class consumers and shipowners, both more powerful in the island kingdom than anywhere else, prevented the country from adopting protective tariffs and forced its industrial capitalists to find new markets with free-trade methods. It was France, not Britain, which had set off the scramble. The root cause of French imperialism, however, was not financial. French colonialism was originally archaic in character, resembling more the Russian variety. The French empire, by

---

[10] Kautsky, *Nationalstaat,* p. 75. Freely translated.

[11] Kautsky's interpretation thus agreed in many ways with the thesis put forward by John Gallagher and Ronald Robinson, two modern British scholars who arrived at similar conclusions on the basis of documentary material not available to Kautsky. See Ronald E. Robinson and John Gallagher, *Africa and the Victorians: The Climax of Imperialism in the Dark Continent,* with Alice Denny (New York, 1961).

increasing the number of salaried posts, served the interests of the army and the bureaucracy, and of those classes from which the military and civil service drew its recruits—that is to say, the intellectuals, the petty bourgeoisie, and the farmers. It was only subsequently that French imperialism had become a tool of industrial and finance capitalism. Germany, after a period of initial reluctance, had also acquired several possessions in Africa, but German hopes for vast wealth from the Dark Continent, Kautsky realized, were doomed to disappointment. In relation to the total trade of the imperialist powers, this African commerce was small.[12] The relative insignificance of the African trade explained why, despite recurrent crises like the Fashoda and Morocco conflicts, African problems had never led to war between the great powers: the risks of war did not correspond to the stakes involved. The only territories which at that time were really valuable for the purposes of European capitalism were South Africa, Egypt, and Algeria. South Africa, however, had already attained political independence. Egypt was approaching that status, and Algeria would in time follow suit. Once these countries had become masters in their own house, they would maintain home rule against all comers. German wartime schemes for a new profitable African empire, Kautsky implied, were therefore unrealistic.

The real cause of World War I was to be found neither in the contradictions of imperialism nor in the economic competition among the great Western manufacturing states. German nationalists might claim that envious British capitalists wished to smash their Teutonic competitors, but such a policy made no economic sense, for the German trade alone was worth practically as much to the British as their commerce with the entire Indian subcontinent.[13] Imperial disputes among the Western states had, in fact, all been settled before the war broke out. The real storm centers of Europe were the Ottoman and Austro-Hungarian monarchies, which were all threatened by nationalist movements. Kautsky, a native of Prague, and much more familiar with the realities of Eastern Europe than a writer like Hobson, maintained that

[12] Kautsky showed, for instance, that in 1912 France exported goods to the value of 6,234 million francs. Of these, 108 million francs' worth went to French Africa. The export to Belgium alone was ten times as large, amounting to 1,024 million francs in 1911. Germany's total exports in 1913 amounted to 10,770.3 million marks; of these goods, only 54.1 million marks' worth went to its colonies. Kautsky, *Nationalstaat*, pp. 53, 70.

[13] In 1912 Britain imported goods to the value of £70 million from Germany and £52 million from India. At the same time Britain exported £59.6 million to Germany and £59.7 million to India. For the Reich the importance of the German colonial trade compared with the British trade was quite insignificant. Kautsky, *Nationalstaat*, pp. 70–71.

capitalism played but little part in these battles. Serbia, for instance, was still a backward peasant state struggling for nationhood. Austria was importing capital, not exporting it. Such expansionist policies as were pursued in Vienna and St. Petersburg were preimperialist or precapitalist in origin. This applied even to the economic struggles involved; the economic clash of interest between Serbia and Austro-Hungary derived from agrarian motives.[14]

The arms race—which became a cause of the very conflicts it was designed to prevent—imposed its own logic on policy, with the date of mobilization becoming a vital military factor. In earlier days conflicting states formulated certain demands against their neighbors; then they mobilized; then they went to war. Now the order was altered in a disastrous fashion. The great powers mobilized, but mobilization pushed them into war to avoid losing the strategic initiative. Having embarked on a limitless struggle, the belligerents proceeded to formulate limitless war aims. Instead of fighting for a simple, well-defined objective such as the acquisition of a province, statesmen chased the mirage of total national security and fashioned their war aims accordingly. Only a policy of compromise and disarmament, Kautsky believed, would end this threat of total war and total conquest. Kautsky thus asked himself whether existing imperialism might not be supplanted by a new superimperialist policy, based on agreement among the capitalist powers. In such a case capitalism might survive for a time; the system might then expand its productive capacity to its fullest extent, until such time as the proletariat would take over.

[14] The great Hungarian landed magnates opposed the import of Serbian agricultural products into the monarchy and thereby dealt a severe blow to the interests of the Serbian peasantry. These local clashes, however, acquired a new importance as a result of the international competition in armaments.

6. Lenin's View of Imperialism

European empire building in the late nineteenth century was no more than a short chapter in the much longer story of Western expansion around the globe. Imperialist and socialist writers in the twentieth century, however, endowed the colonial policies of British, French, and German colonizers with an importance infinitely greater than statesmen such as Lord Salisbury and Bismarck had themselves been able to see in their handiwork. Yet if Seeley and Rhodes and Hobson and Lenin had little in common, they did agree on one thing—that imperial expansion represented the focal point of European history in their day. From the first decade of the 1900s controversy about the true character of Western imperialism thus assumed a decisive role in the doctrinal struggles that shook the socialist movements of the world.

The combatants in this great debate, Kautsky on the one hand and Rosa Luxemburg and Lenin on the other, were not particularly interested in the history of Western colonization as such. Their interpretation of imperialism was not based on the desire to find the facts; they wished to forge swords for their ideological armory. They all looked to theory as a means of changing the world, and they designed their weapons for the kind of battle they meant to fight. Moderates like Kautsky wished to establish socialism peacefully and therefore maintained that neither world empires nor world wars were inevitable. The bourgeoisie could be forced into reform by parliamentary procedures. Hence the socialist parties should be organized on a democratic basis and utilize existing constitutional machinery to the full.

Revolutionary socialists like Lenin found this point of view abhorrent. Lenin was convinced that the bourgeoisie had outlived its progressive role; capitalism was past reform, and the time was ripe for a violent overthrow of the existing order. However, left to themselves, the proletariat of all countries would only develop a trade-union consciousness, combine into labor organizations, strike for higher wages, and compel the government to pass reformist legislation. The revolution must therefore be organized by a tightly disciplined party—a cross between a crusading order and a conspiratorial movement—which

55

would determine both the strategy and the tactics of the revolution and would guide the masses into the path of historical inevitability. Lenin thus regarded Kautsky's brand of reformist, "opportunist" socialism with deadly antipathy, and the dispute over imperialism became a great battleground. He particularly seized on Kautsky's doctrine of free choice for the bourgeoisie. Lenin, in his way, was a predestinarian. The bourgeoisie, he believed, could not *choose* between an imperialist and a nonimperialist way. The advanced Western countries had to turn to empire building, no matter where their leading statesmen's personal preferences might lie. Imperialism had to lead to world war; there was no alternative. Revolutions were not won by compromise with the class enemy, by pacifist effusions, or by silly sentimentalism. Kautsky's supreme fault lay in fundamentally misrepresenting the course of history, and his arguments—Lenin concluded in the polemical style customary among comrades engaged in controversy—were repulsive in a person who had not yet been officially certified as feeble-minded.

Lenin thought much better of Hobson, a bourgeois and a social liberal who had never made any pretense of being a socialist. Lenin showed how middle-class writers such as Hobson and Heymann demonstrated that production within capitalist economies was being concentrated in an ever-decreasing number of enterprises. This recent type of capitalism was distinguished by monopoly and also by an entirely new feature, the dependence of the industrialist on the banks. In this transition stage capitalism became "overripe." Capitalism, Lenin argued, developed at an uneven pace in the different parts of the world. Monied men could not find sufficient profitable investments at home because of the backward systems of agriculture and the impoverished state of the masses in the Western countries. The capitalists therefore had to invest their funds in backward regions, where land, labor, and raw materials cost less and profits were higher. The export of capital went hand in hand with the economic partition of the world among a small number of cartels, trusts, and syndicates; this division of the world among a few capitalist combines was the driving force behind the political division of the world. Finance capitalists naturally extracted the greatest profits where they could exercise direct political rule over a subject country. Monopolists could, of course, also make money in subject states enjoying formal independence, but foreign financiers in general strove for empire. Or to put the matter into different words, modern imperialism formed but a special stage of capitalism.[1]

[1] V. I. Lenin, "Imperialism: The Highest Stage of Capitalism," *Imperialism and Imperialist War (1914–1917)* (Vol. V of *Selected Works;* New York, 1935), pp. 3–119; see especially p. 81.

Lenin picked out three major regions of highly developed capitalism with elaborate means of transport, trade, and industry: the Central European, the British, and the American areas. Imperialist rivalries among these giants had sharpened because Germany had only a restricted territory and a few colonies; the creation of a [German-dominated] Central Europe was still a matter for the future, though it was being born in the midst of World War I. German capitalism represented a younger form which was at war with the older British robbers, but socialists must impartially destroy them all. The world war being fought at the time was the necessary result of imperialism in its monopoly stage. The world imperialists now battled to annex not only agricultural regions, but even highly industrialized countries. This expansive tendency was inherent in contemporary capitalism because the world had already been partitioned. Imperialism also entailed strategic conquests for the purpose of weakening the adversary. There was nothing the capitalists could do about this state of affairs. The characteristic feature of world capitalism was the uneven nature of its development. The big industrial countries developed at varying speeds; the distribution of the world's riches among the big powers constantly lagged behind their varying economic and military potentials. The world's embattled monopolists could solve the internal contradictions of their system only by war. Kautsky, Lenin wrote, misled the masses when he talked about the possibility of peaceful compromise between capitalists, but even traitors like Kautsky were themselves but the product of a given social situation. The capitalists in the advanced countries, by exploiting the backward parts of the world, managed for a time to rake in superprofits, and their loot enabled them to corrupt certain sections of the Western working class, as well as many of their leaders. Only revolution could smash imperialism; only the class war could bring peace to a strife-torn world.

Lenin's pamphlet was a clear call to battle. The period of waiting was over; the worldwide assault on the bourgeoisie must begin. Marx and Engels had assumed that the workers would first seize power in the advanced industrial countries of the West and had attached little importance to events in the colonies. The workers' victory in Western Europe and America would be the crucial event of future history and would tremendously accelerate the course of revolution all over the world. Marx, of course, had never indicated that every country would necessarily have to go through the preordained stages of feudalism, capitalism, and revolutionary socialism, like a three-stage rocket. He did, however, put the main historical emphasis on the advanced countries in the West, and he was convinced that most nations would have to make two revolutions, first a bourgeois-capitalist and then a socialist one. Marx was an optimist who believed that his doctrines would help to inspire workers the world over, but even he would have been surprised that one day Congolese levies would march to war brandishing spears and poisoned arrows, ostensibly under the banner of revolutionary socialism.

Lenin gave a new twist to Marx's doctrines. He shifted the main initial battleground to Europe's agricultural periphery and maintained that revolutions in the more backward countries would set off social struggles in the advanced West, thereby revising Marxist classical doctrine. Lenin also gave a new emphasis to contemporary socialist thought on the role of the bourgeoisie. Marx, with his nineteenth-century optimism, had believed that Western capitalists were still performing a progressive function in the backward parts of the world. He had held that a social system became ripe for overthrow only when it became an impediment to continued economic development and had therefore looked with hearty approval upon the work of, say, British railway builders in India. Lenin now denied that capitalists could do any good, even though their activities still kept adding to the means of production available to the world. Bourgeois professors, he angrily expostulated, depicted railway building in the colonies as a civilizing and democratic enterprise, but such ventures, with private property the means of production, "have converted this work of construction into an instrument for oppressing a *thousand million* people [in the colonies and semicolonies]."[2] He thereby cut Marx's doctrine of progress from its economic moorings; the achievement of railway companies in providing employment, facilitating trade, and hence increasing production had become irrelevant.

Lenin at the same time maintained that the entire system of bourgeois-capitalist states formed a single, coherent whole, ready for overthrow. For this reason, a decisive Communist success could set off world revolution by a chain reaction. There was no need for revolutionaries in backward countries to wait their turn until the advanced proletariat in Britain, France, and Germany had mounted the barricades. What mattered was the existence of a revolutionary situation and the ability of a disciplined, tightly organized party to mobilize the masses. In a multinational state like Russia, the oppressed minorities would join the revolutionary forces. The downtrodden people in the Western colonies would supply another reserve army for the proletariat. Lenin's doctrine of imperialism thus not only justified the seizure of power and the establishment of a minority dictatorship in a backward country like Russia but also led to a substantial modification of the classical concept of world revolution, with the underdevel-

2 Lenin, "Imperialism," p. 8.

oped countries being assigned a major role.[3] Leninism in effect called on the downtrodden of the new world to redress the balance of the old.

Lenin's doctrine also explained why the Western workers had proved Marx wrong, why they had refused to revolt earlier, and why they had fought for their own countries in the world war. Imperialism with its superprofits had enabled the capitalists to bribe some of their wage slaves and thereby split the workers' ranks. The Leninist view of imperialism did away finally with all reformist hairsplitting about the extent of increasing poverty through the appropriation of surplus value. The workers' lot, Marx had predicted, would steadily get worse under capitalism. In fact, this had not happened; Western, and to some extent even non-Western, standards of living had gone up since the industrial revolution. Reformists therefore argued that Marx had meant a "relative," not an "absolute," increase of the Western workers' misery. In Lenin's view, such debates were academic. Advanced capitalism led to imperialism; imperialism caused war; war, with its ghastly slaughter in the trenches, meant an increase of misery which not even Marx had been able to foresee. Now the cup was running over. The revolution was at hand; mankind would emerge from the valley of dry bones and march forth to a new and better life.

Lenin's work on imperialism at first had only limited impact. It was published in Petrograd in April, 1917, when the outcome of the revolutionary struggle still seemed uncertain. A few months later Lenin and his associates overthrew the Kerensky government and established themselves in supreme power. Lenin then consolidated Communist rule against its enemies from within and without, and had other things to think about than elaborating general theories of imperialism. Three years later, however, his booklet was published in French and German and soon gained an unchallenged place both in Communist and in non-Communist circles. The new editions displayed greater anti-Western bias than before. Lenin now feared the victorious British, French, and American capitalists more than the defeated Germans. He still thought of Germany as a potentially revolutionary country and as a possible ally against the West. In the past he had received support from the Kaiser's government in his agitation for an end-the-war policy in Russia. The son of a Russian civil servant ennobled for long and faithful service to the Tsar, Lenin was a man of letters and was contemptuous of businessmen; he did not therefore regard German officers with quite the same loathing as Western capitalists. Thus his preface to the new French and German editions described the Versailles Treaty, dictated by the United States, France, and Britain, as "much more brutal

[3] Boris Meissner, "Soviet Russia's Foreign Policy: Ideology and Power Politics," *Modern Age*, VIII (Winter, 1963–1964), 7–24.

and despicable" than the Brest-Litovsk Treaty, which Imperial Germany had forced on Russia in 1917.[4] In retrospect this seems a strange judgment, yet these comments were in keeping with his ambivalent outlook toward wartime Germany, whose empire building he disliked but whose dedication to the military virtues and efficiency he could not help respecting.

Lenin's theories raise numerous questions of a fundamental kind. Like Marx, he believed that the realities of man's existence lay in the economic basis of society and in the relations of production developed thereby. Politics and ideology formed nothing but the superstructure raised on these foundations. This interpretation, however, fails to account fully for the forces of religion, nationality, and military power, all of which played a vital role in the makings of modern imperialism. Just as the major religions have continued to exist through many different economic systems and have proved compatible in turn with feudalism, capitalism, and socialism, so nationalism fails to conform to the rigid mold of Marxism-Leninism. The politics of nationalism were profoundly influenced by economic factors. German businessmen, to mention just one example, clearly preferred a united Reich to a mosaic of small principalities, each with their own customs and currencies. But however vague and ill-defined, the sense of German nationality is infinitely older than German capitalism; its creation has nothing to do with middle-class or even feudal interests. The birth of an Israeli nationality, composed of disparate Jewish groups brought together from the four corners of the earth and united in the twentieth century by a revived Biblical tongue, cannot be explained in terms of Jewish middle-class interests. Marxist theoreticians could not and did not predict such a development.

Nor does the economic interpretation fully account for the military realities of history. Since the beginnings of mankind, the means of production have determined the means of destruction. Tribal economies produced lances and bows; simple manufacturing economies produced flintlocks and bayonets. The tribal economy which gave rise to the massed spear crescents of the Zulu could not, of course, in the long run defeat armies supplied by modern industry. The regiments of Frederick the Great, however brilliantly led, would not have been a match for those of the smallest Balkan state at the beginning of the twentieth century. Muskets could never beat machine guns. Economic realities, in other words, provided the irreducible minimum required by military leadership. But within this framework there is always a wide field open to voluntarist factors—such noneconomic factors as discipline, morale, and leadership. Prussia in the Seven Years War

[4] Lenin, "Imperialism," p. 9.

was economically much weaker than the coalition of Russia, Austria, and France arrayed against Frederick the Great, but the Prussians won because they were better led and because they could march and fire faster. In the nineteenth century German history taught the same lesson; the Franco-German war of 1870–1871 ended in a German victory despite the fact that from the industrial and demographic point of view France was then Germany's equal. The French might have made better use of strategic railways; they might have made better use of their manpower resources; they might have deployed their mitrailleuses more effectively on the battlefield; they might have built better guns. But they did not, and Germany became the greatest power on the Continent.

The argument can, in fact, be carried further. The broader the economic basis, the more indeterminate its superstructure. Or to put the matter more simply, the more a country can produce or purchase, the wider its choice of possible policies. The industrial economy of the nineteenth century permitted an infinitely greater number of military alternatives than the pastoral and raiding economy of the Zulu. What was true in the military sphere applied equally to all others. The more varied a society's economic potential, the greater its freedom to strive for varied ends. Military power and empire form a possible objective, but only one of many. The very shape which armed might or foreign dominion can assume may greatly vary within the framework of comparable economies and cannot be explained solely by a materialistic interpretation of history.

Lenin's more detailed analysis owed a great deal to German scholarship and to the German example. Cartels, dominated by banking capital, did indeed play a major role in the economic structure of the Reich. Even in Germany, however, the growth of monopolies and the amalgamation of the banks occurred only after the turn of the nineteenth century—some two decades after Bismarck made his bid for colonies. Manfred Nussbaum, a modern historian in the German Democratic Republic, thus points out that the original acquisitions of German colonies *preceded* the consolidation of monopoly capitalism. Many German business interests, he concedes, were apathetic toward overseas expansion; colonialist pressure groups owed much more to the leadership exercised by civil servants, officers, and adventurers. Bismarck's colonial policy, as will be shown, owed much more to diplomatic than to economic motives. Germany in the 1880s had scarcely any capital for export to Africa; German industry was not yet trustified. Nussbaum therefore argues that Bismarckian policy sprang not from the search for investment opportunities, but more from the desire to secure new markets and raw materials. German capitalism underwent a basic change at the turn of the century, and only then did German monopolists begin to use Germany's overseas possessions in the fashion described by Lenin. Nussbaum thus successfully negates application of the Leninist thesis to the German colonial empire, but he does not explain how even in the 1880s a relatively small section of German capitalists should have been able to impose their wills on a man like Bismarck, whom Nussbaum himself describes as a *Junker*. Nor does he account for the infinitesimal part that tropical Africa played in German trade at the time.[5] Later on German industrialists formed cartels of great size, and German banks assumed a dominant position in the economy. But even then, German bankers placed only very small amounts of capital in the overseas dependencies of the Reich. The reforms instituted by the banker Dernburg in the Kaiser's colonial empire did not greatly improve the position. Pan-German writers sorrowfully continued to chide their countrymen for their lack of interest in Africa, and the bulk of Germany's investors would not put their money into what they still regarded as the Dark Continent.

Lenin's thesis that modern imperialism formed nothing but the superstructure of finance capital in search of investment opportunities makes even less sense for countries like Japan and Italy. Both these powers strove to extend their overseas possessions at the end of the nineteenth and beginning of the twentieth century; both at the same time were so deficient in capital that they had to import great sums of money from abroad. Poverty-stricken Portugal was even worse off; Portuguese politicians assuredly did not try to hold onto their country's overseas possessions because Lisbon lenders held too much cash.

Lenin's interpretation is no more helpful when applied to British policy. During the heyday of British imperialism, industry in the United Kingdom was neither cartelized nor trustified. The British colonies were open to the free trade of all nations. Banks did not have the hold on the economy in Britain that they had in Wilhelminian Germany. Many British economic writers, in fact, complained with some justice of inadequate coordination between British banks and British industry. The great houses handling foreign loans remained independent of the rest of the London money market. The money market stayed divorced from manufacturing industry, which, until after the end of World War I, financed itself from sources in the provinces.[6]

[5] See Manfred Nussbaum, *Vom "Kolonialenthusiasmus" zur Kolonialpolitik der Monopole: Zur deutschen Kolonialpolitik unter Bismarck, Caprivi, Hohenlohe* (Studien zur Kolonialgeschichte und Geschichte der nationalen und kolonialen Befreiungsbewegung, No. 8; Berlin, 1962), *passim*.

[6] W. H. B. Court, "The Communist Doctrines of Empire," in William Keith Hancock (ed.), *Survey of British Commonwealth Affairs:* Vol. II, *Problems of Economic Policy, 1918–1939,* Part 1 (London, 1940), 293–305.

The example of American capitalism lends no more support to the Leninist thesis than does the British example. In the United States imperialism did indeed see a short hour of triumph in 1898, during the Spanish-American War, but the fight for Cuba owed little to big industrial trusts or financial corporations, and American desire for territorial acquisitions overseas soon became sated. Americans never thought of building an empire in Africa, even though until the 1860s they were one of the leading trading nations in West and East Africa. They never even considered staking out claims to the German colonial heritage on the Dark Continent as a *quid pro quo* for helping the Allies in World War I. From the purely economic point of view, the big American industrial concerns acquired greater financial resources than the big banks themselves, so that Lenin's view lacks any contact with reality when applied to the structure of capitalism in the United States.

Lenin's analysis, moreover, paid no attention to the vast amounts of British capital sent overseas before the 1870s and 1880s, before the new imperialism began. To give just one example, the founding of the Standard Bank of South Africa in 1862 was an important event in both British and South African economic history. The bank opened its doors at a time when capital was plentiful on the London market and when a great many similar institutions were being formed overseas with the help of British funds. The bank was also one of the first to be set up on the basis of recent British joint-stock banking legislation. Yet at this period there was no desire in England to pursue an active imperial policy—despite the pressure of capital available for loans overseas.

The omission of earlier British capital exports from their analysis enabled Communist theoreticians to assume a "qualitative change" in the character of British capitalism. On this basis they built up a false doctrine of discontinuity in British colonial policy. Lenin's omission also had the advantage of absolving him from a closer analysis of the relations between a creditor and a debtor country. Guided by the experience of weak countries like Egypt and Tunis, he assumed that foreign bankers would always be able to manipulate the policies of a debtor state in their own interest. The history of Europe itself, or of North America, does not bear this out. In the early nineteenth century British investors already had begun to look overseas for investment opportunities. Capital, however, rarely followed the flag, and the bulk of British loans went to European countries. Prussia and France, for instance, borrowed vast sums in London to finance their industrialization. British financiers, British entrepreneurs, and British engineers thus played a valuable part in developing the economic potential of various Continental countries. Neither France nor Prussia, however, was reduced by these loans to political dependency on the United Kingdom. The same applies with even greater force to the United States. British financiers placed huge sums in the United States; British immigrants continued to pour into the United States throughout the nineteenth century, and many of these Anglo-Americans subsequently attained high positions in the land of their adoption. But American isolationist folklore notwithstanding, the British could no more run affairs behind the scenes in Washington than they could in Berlin.

French experiences with Russia were no more encouraging. The French, after concluding a military convention with the Tsar in 1892, and a full-scale alliance two years later, poured vast sums into the Russian empire for the purpose of strengthening their ally against Germany. Paris, however, could never impose its will on St. Petersburg; the Russians, on the contrary, held the stronger hand.

Lenin's thesis of monopoly capitalism naturally links imperialism to protective tariffs. National monopolies cannot, after all, be set up if foreign importers may compete freely with native-born capitalists. In a like vein, Jules Ferry, the great advocate of French colonialism, argued that the closure of markets in protectionist states forced other countries to seek protected outlets by colonization. Empire building, in the view of both, was a good way of getting a country over trade crises.

The theory which links protectionism to empire is attractive, but it does not work out in practice. Britain, Belgium, and Holland were all major colonial powers, but their merchant and consumer interests successfully stood in the way of high tariffs. The United States, on the other hand, lacked an overseas empire. After the Civil War, however, American duties quickly went up, reaching a level higher than any in Europe. The Americans stuck to high tariffs despite their aloofness from world affairs, and long before they embarked on an expansionist policy during the Spanish-American War of 1898. In Germany, Bismarck placed imposts on industrial and agricultural imports in 1879, when he broke with the National Liberals and turned toward the more conservative Center. No one at the time linked his tariff increases to colonial designs. Much later, German dependencies such as East Africa still had to rely heavily on British manufactured goods and British capital for their development.[7] Bismarck's tariff of 1879 should, in Ferry's interpretation, have restricted Franco-German trade, but in fact, commerce between the two countries grew steadily. French colonization, Ferry's propaganda notwithstanding, was hardly affected by trade cycles. The conquest of Madagascar and French intervention

[7] See William O. Henderson, *Studies in German Colonial History* (London, 1962), pp. 58–86.

in Morocco took place at a time when French trade was booming. The seizure of Tonkin, on the other hand, was accompanied by a slump.[8] Colonies in fact could not provide France with a profitable monopoly because France could not supply all the required goods. Imperial markets remained limited in size, so that colonial trade formed a relatively small proportion of French commerce as a whole.[9]

Ironically, the French Colonial Party turned against protection from 1900 on. The explanation for this is simple. The Méline tariff of 1892 taxed most colonial produce entering France, to safeguard French farmers. The French thereby hurt many agricultural producers in the colonies, including their own settlers. The tariff also placed heavy imposts on foreign manufactured products and thus injured French-Algerian colonists in their capacity as consumers.

In other words, French capitalists, like those of any other nation, could never work in unison; they represented many different interests, and could never enforce a genuinely monopolistic policy. As far as France was concerned, Lenin's description of national monopolies harked back not so much to the highly developed capitalism of the new imperialism, but to the "military capitalism" promoted by Napoleon to beat the British.

Lenin, of course, would have given little consideration to such criticism. He was a systematizer who thought in terms of rigid categories. Businessmen and their allies, in his view, formed a cohesive class, conscious of a common economic interest. By the end of the nineteenth century, "dominion over palm and pine" was for these people not a poet's fancy, but a banker's necessity. If they wished to present their shareholders with attractive balance sheets, they had to extract additional wealth from underdeveloped countries, either by direct exploitation or by squeezing more surplus value out of native workmen. According to Lenin, it was precisely this ability to use guns for gain which made imperialism a more efficient means of money making than the Manchester system.[10]

In fact, the bourgeoisie were never capable of making such a sim-

---

[8] For further details see Henri Brunschwig, *Mythes et réalités de l'impérialisme colonial français, 1871–1914* (Paris, 1960), pp. 82–101.

[9] Between 1882–1886 and 1909–1913, during the height of French imperialism, the proportion of French trade with the colonies rose from 5.71 percent to 10.20 percent only. The bulk of this trade was with Morocco, Algeria, and Tunis, not with sub-Saharan Africa. In the case of Germany the trade which the Reich carried on with its colonies between 1894 and 1913 was less than 0.4 percent of its total trade.

[10] See David S. Landes, "Some Thoughts on the Nature of Economic Imperialism," *Journal of Economic History*, XXI, No. 4 (December, 1961), 496–512.

ple decision, because they never formed a united front and could never agree even on specific issues. Throughout the nineteenth century European middle-class groups fought bitter struggles against other middle-class groups over subjects as diverse as franchise and foreign policy, tariffs and taxes, factory laws and food prices. Then, as now, millowners in the same line of business competed against each other. Producers within the same industry clashed with consumers. Traders held out for one course of action, manufacturers for another, farmers for a third, mining companies for yet a fourth. To mention just one example, in the interwar years the world's great copper producers in Chile and the Belgian Congo, the United States and Northern Rhodesia, could never maintain a common production policy for any length of time; the low-cost producers usually pressed for increased output quotas and the high-cost producers generally preferred restrictions, so that international price fixing soon broke down.[11]

Even within the same territory, mammoth companies in the same line of business sometimes followed divergent courses. In Northern Rhodesia, for instance, the two largest concerns, the American-dominated Rhodesian Selection Trust and the South African–based Anglo-American Corporation, frequently failed to agree with each other on specific political or economic issues. Both wielded influence, but during the very heyday of colonial rule neither of them ever managed to dominate the country's politics. Even in a backward and relatively undifferentiated economy like that of Northern Rhodesia, the state machinery throughout the colonial period responded to pressures infinitely more complex than the real or imagined machinations of copper magnates. A British governor had to consider the interests of farmers and traders, of civil servants and railway men. He received instructions from London based on political and economic considerations at home that far transcended local interests; he also tried to satisfy demands from missionaries and humanitarians; last but not least, he was animated by a spirit of public service which aimed at making the state an impartial arbiter between competing interests and an instrument for public welfare as a whole. Northern Rhodesia presented a comparatively simple picture. The political processes in Britain itself were far more complex. Here the interests of the British workers and employees played an infinitely greater part than Lenin's interpretation allowed, and no economic pressure group was ever sufficiently well organized to control the state.

Lenin was on equally shaky ground when he argued that working-class reformism was but the bastard child of imperialism. He assumed

[11] Lewis H. Gann, *A History of Northern Rhodesia: Early Days to 1953* (London, 1964), pp. 251, 256–257.

that colonialism enabled the metropolitan bourgeoisie to bribe local working-class leaders and some of their followers into betraying the revolution. It is true that reformist socialists like Bernstein and even radicals like Bebel found some advantages in imperialism. But the industrial advancement and the rise in real wages of Western Europe did not, in fact, mirror the growth of empire. Between 1860 and 1914 the workers' purchasing power went up in Britain, France, and Germany alike. But the rise in real wages began well before the start of the new imperialism and had its origins in superior industrial and agricultural techniques. Working-class militancy, moreover, never mirrored the size of empire. Britain, with its extensive dependencies, had a powerful reformist working-class movement. Norway, Sweden, Switzerland, Denmark, and the United States, on the other hand, all lacked colonies, yet the workers of these countries were no more inclined to mount the barricades than their British comrades. Portugal and France, for their part, had appropriated a big slice of the imperial cake. The French and Portuguese colonies were indeed considerably larger in relation to the size of the motherland than Germany's, yet French proletarians developed a much greater tradition of militancy than those of Northern Europe.

The matter of "bribing" the Western European working class raises the question of the extent to which imperialism paid in cash. Lenin believed that investors were bound to make more money in the colonies than at home, because land, labor, and raw materials would cost them less overseas. The bankers knew better. A large amount of risk capital was lost. European statesmen like Bismarck and Leopold II, and even financial imperialists like Rhodes, had to think up the most ingenious ways to secure monetary support for colonial ventures. A great deal of cash was, of course, invested; some of it yielded excellent dividends. However, the characteristic lender in Germany or in Britain was not the merchant adventurer out for superprofits, but a rentier who sought slow but steady returns in the form of fixed-interest securities, pegged at a modest level.[12]

Even more fundamental to Lenin's view of history is the concept of exploitation, which formed the very core of his theory and exercised a profound influence on all critiques of imperialism, no matter from what quarter. What is exploitation? Marxists give a confident answer which is linked to their theory of surplus value. This concept is so essential to much of contemporary thought as to merit additional discussion. Marx assumed that commodities derive their value from the labor which is necessary to produce them under given technologi-

12 Richard J. Hammond, "Economic Imperialism: Sidelights on a Stereotype," *Journal of Economic History*, XXI, No. 4 (December, 1961), 594.

cal conditions. Capitalists are able to exploit their workers and to accumulate more cash because they have a monopoly on the means of employment and can thus buy labor at cutthroat rates—rates which are just enough to keep workers alive and able to perpetuate their kind. In exchange for wages, the employer buys the worker's labor, a commodity that produces more than it costs. The mill hand or miner may, for example, earn enough for his maintenance in six hours, but because he has sold his labor, he may be made to work for eight hours, and the two-hour difference represents unpaid labor appropriated by the capitalist. Machinery, in Marx's view, creates no surplus value. It is labor, and labor alone, which provides the capitalist's ill-gained profits. Applied to a modern African situation, the argument implies that if, say, a Zambian mine pays its shareholders high dividends, the money disbursed to investors has been wrung from Zambian mine workers. Whether Zambian labor conditions are good, bad, or indifferent, the black man suffers from exploitation by the very nature of the economic arrangement under which he works.

This postulate, however, begets numerous difficulties. The capitalist, thirsting for surplus value, introduces more and more machinery in order to cut down the time required for the workers' maintenance and to increase the number of hours available for the production of surplus value. Marx then explains that machinery itself represents the product of sweated labor. Mechanization in underdeveloped countries should therefore logically be linked with the increased exploitation of highly skilled labor in the more advanced countries. Lenin and his followers did not, however, make this point explicit. Instead they considered imperialist enterprise as a form of superexploitation which gave the metropolitan working class a small share of the colonial spoils.

Marx's law of surplus value also has other weaknesses. Marx, in the first instance, attempted to explain prices. But the value of a commodity cannot be explained simply in terms of past costs. Value also looks to the future and to use in the future. Marx and his pupils gave scant attention to the question of how far competing capitalists had to outbid one another for labor. It makes no sense to speak of monopoly when the alleged monopolists have to bargain against one another. For Marx, as for many of his modern successors in the postcolonial era, the individual worker and the individual employer had no real existence, except insofar as they represented the class to which they belong. There is little suggestion that work and management alike are human functions. Marx was interested only in the relations between class and class and paid little attention to the individual abilities or talents which permitted any one member of the bourgeoisie to survive within his class because of his superior endowments as an organizer, planner, or manager. Marx had no theory of cost accounting, yet his abstruse calculations purported to show not what the value of a commodity ought to be from a moral point of view, but what it actually is within the framework of a capitalist economy. Thus Marxist theory fails to meet the test of practice. For example, in a situation where the Soviet Union successfully competes on the world market, Soviet economists, like their capitalist counterparts, must take into account both the value of their capital investment and the laws of supply and demand. No Soviet trading company which has to buy British machinery in London or sell Russian timber in Hamburg calculates prices on the basis of relative labor investments in the goods involved. Soviet traders in the world market must adjust their prices according to how much others are willing to pay—and they do. Hence interpretations of exploitation based on the theory of surplus value have little relevance to colonial Africa.

Charges of exploitation are, however, also made in a more general form. We can do no better at this point than to summarize a discussion by David Landes, a modern economic historian who has devoted much attention to the subject.[13] For most people the term "exploitation" stands for low wages, low in relation to profits, low in relation to wages in other countries or other occupations. The charge is rarely precise, but the moral stigma is all the more inescapable. However, for serious work as opposed to political pamphleteering, this imprecision will not do. Landes therefore adopts a definition linked to the exercise of political dominion, formal or informal: "Imperialist exploitation consists in the employment of labor at wages lower than would obtain in a free bargaining situation; or in the appropriation of goods at prices lower than would obtain in a free market. Imperialist exploitation, in other words, implies nonmarket constraint." So defined, exploitation is by no means the necessary consequence of imperialism, direct or indirect. "It makes no sense, for example," writes Landes, "to talk of exploitation by oil companies in Venezuela or sugar refineries in [pre-Communist] Cuba when these not only pay a freely negotiated wage, but a wage distinctly higher than that prevailing in the sector of indigenous enterprise."

Even in this strict sense, exploitation has, of course, gone hand in hand with imperial conquests. In the early 1890s, for instance, settlers in Rhodesia often used forced labor from neighboring villages. These extortions accompanied a primitive kind of farming, where white pioneers raised a little maize and small herds of "scrub cattle,"

[13] See Landes, "Some Thoughts on the Nature of Economic Imperialism," especially pp. 499–501.

with few opportunities to sell their surplus. The concept of forced labor met with bitter opposition from London, and the "imperial factor" soon put an end to the practice. But perhaps even more important was the fact that forced labor proved incompatible with a more highly developed form of capitalist farming, not to speak of more complicated mining and manufacturing ventures. A more indirect form of pressure was the obligation laid on Africans to pay taxes in cash, which could be earned only by selling crops or by signing on for a month or two with a white employer. Here again, however, the importance of monetary imposts as a labor incentive soon diminished. The Rhodesian economy, for example, expanded; Africans earned more, and they got used to buying pots and pans, blankets, bicycles, and other commodities from the village store. A capitalist market economy replaced pressure by economic inducements.

The second form of direct appropriation mentioned by Landes concerns the enforced sale of commodities. The most notorious example of this was the "culture system" of the Dutch East Indies, under which the peasants of Java were required to devote part of their lands to certain cash crops and to deliver these to the government at fixed prices. Such arrangements, however, left much to be desired even from the metropolitan country's point of view. Satisfactory performance could not easily be enforced from free native cultivators. The system therefore did not generate as much wealth for the nationals of the imperialist powers as the proponents of forced cultivation had anticipated. Direct exploitation in the sense defined by Landes played only a minor part in the operations of Western imperialism in Africa during its later stages. There was, however, a good deal of direct exploitation in the early phase of imperial occupation, though it was never comparable in intensity to the exploitation practiced in precapitalist societies like those of Carthage and ancient Rome.

From the political point of view, however, such flaws in Lenin's thesis did not matter. Lenin proceeded on the basic Marxist assumption that employers made their money by appropriating the surplus value of labor. His theory excluded the "service" element in a capitalist economy. Bankers and factory owners, in his view, made no significant contribution to their country's prosperity, either as planners or organizers or as distribution agents. Real wealth was created by the laboring classes alone. Exploitation was therefore inevitable—even in a free-market economy that eschewed slavery, forced labor, or the direct appropriation of other people's goods. Any profits made by a capitalist firm formed, *ipso facto,* evidence of exploitation.

This doctrine, based on a normative judgment of social deserts, could not be proved. But Marxism-Leninism provided its followers with a creed both logical and Messianic in character, and Lenin's philosophy had a tremendous appeal. By linking exploitation with foreign tyranny, and foreign tyranny with war guilt, Lenin forged new ideological weapons of great strength. In wielding these weapons, Leninists were not afraid to throw in *ad hominem* arguments for good measure. Scholars who defended the constructive sides of imperialism, who wrote of the schools, hospitals, and colleges put up by colonialists, were, in Lenin's view, simply lackeys of the bourgeoisie who were singing for their suppers. They had a vested interest in whitewashing the black record of empire; hence their arguments must be worthless. This conclusion, of course, does not necessarily follow, but bourgeois controversialists were usually too riddled with guilt feelings to turn the charge against its makers. For many intellectuals, Lenin's doctrine became hallowed by political success and acquired profound influence far beyond the ranks of orthodox Marxists. Leninist arguments came to dominate the great debate on colonialism and continue to shape the climate of opinion to this day.

7. The Colonial Debate Between the Two World Wars

In 1919 the German plenipotentiaries placed signature to the peace treaty with the Allies and associated powers. The German, Austro-Hungarian, Ottoman, and Russian monarchies had all crumbled. The first great bid for a German-dominated Europe had come to nought, and the Western powers stood supreme. The Kaiser's possessions in Africa went to the victors. Moroccan and Senegalese fighting men participated in the occupation of the Rhineland; the sight of black soldiers in horizon-blue uniforms gave some support to the French notions of "a hundred million Frenchmen" to restore the demographic balance of power on the Continent in favor of France. The British had won all that their most ambitious strategists could have desired at the end of the nineteenth century. With British troops in occupation of Palestine and Iraq, the Suez Canal was held more firmly than ever before. South Africa was linked to the empire by a successful wartime partnership that secured South-West Africa to the Union. No foreign power could threaten any of Britain's African territories.

Britain and France stood at the zenith of their imperial might, but at the very moment of success, real power was slipping from their grasp. Both were exhausted. American strength now far exceeded that of any individual European state; only American military might had been able to turn stalemate into victory. With the American armies arrived Wilson's program for reconstructing the world on anti-imperialist lines. Self-determination was to change the historical pattern of Europe. Old-fashioned colonial annexations fell into disrepute, and empire now seemed justified only on the assumption that it would benefit the ruled and not the rulers.

The concept of colonial trusteeship was, of course, familiar enough even to Victorian imperialists like Kipling, but now this ideology became part of an internationally accepted doctrine against which Germans and Turks were supposed to have offended. Trusteeship principles were built into the postwar settlement which disposed of ex-enemy colonies as mandates rather than as objects of legitimate conquest. Imperial ideologies found themselves on the defensive in the West. Russia and America, the two potential superpowers, began to compete for the minds of men in Europe and in many parts of the Westerners' periphery. Wilson meant to end the old balance-of-power system and thought in terms of democratic self-determination, based on the Fourteen Points, which would remold the world on the principles of the American founding fathers. Lenin continued to count on world revolution which would unite Europe's proletariat with the colored races in a common struggle and remake the universe in the Communist image. The bulk of German, Austrian, Hungarian, and Turkish opinion remained unreconciled to the various peace settlements, and the conquerors themselves became skeptical of their gains.

In France communism gained numerous converts, among both the intelligentsia and the industrial working class. The extreme Left backed all colonial rebellions, and the long war against Abd-el-Krim saw the beginning of a new chapter. Abd-el-Krim, a great Moroccan chieftain, resisted the armies of France and Spain until 1926. The Moroccan campaign of the 1920s already foreshadowed certain essential features of the Algerian war in the 1950s and 1960s. There was the same solidarity between the French extreme Left and the colonial insurgents; there was the same breach between the European Algerians, even those at the most modest social level, and the metropolitan Left; there was the same sympathy for the Left among intellectuals as little suspect of being Communists as Georges Duhamel and Henri Torrès, who put their names alongside those of Louis Aragon and André Breton on a manifesto deploring "the spilling of blood in Morocco."[1]

In Britain the bulk of the intelligentsia experienced a similar revulsion against imperial ideals, though in the Anglo-Saxon countries this reaction owed more to the strength of Wilsonian and Hobsonian concepts than Leninist ones. Ireland, Britain's oldest overseas colony, fought a successful guerrilla war (1919–1921) against the British ascendancy and provided an example to future colonial revolutionaries of how to attain independence by partisan tactics. British as well as American and French intellectuals made Ireland's cause their own; the Irish question also became part of the wider imperial issue, the questioning of colonialism. The British intelligentsia in this respect were ahead of the masses. Disillusionment with empire was re-

[1] Paul-Marie de la Gorce, *The French Army: A Military-Political History*, trans. by Kenneth Douglas (New York, 1963), pp. 212–215.

flected to some extent in falling recruitment figures for some overseas services. Even the Indian civil service, once a coveted plum for university graduates, found difficulty in filling all its vacancies. Many educated men were stricken with a deep feeling of guilt, both about the Versailles Treaty and about the real or supposed injuries inflicted upon the defeated Germans. The issue of war guilt became linked with colonial controversies and the question of how far empire could be justified in moral terms. Even Kipling's imperialism had possessed a profoundly religious strain; "dominion over palm and pine" was defensible only if it agreed with God's purpose, while an unrepentant imperial people would see its far-flung navies melt away and become one with Nineveh and Tyre. These religious arguments continued to operate in a secular form. Rivalry for colonial territories, ran the argument, was wrong in itself; empire served no moral purpose, and the struggle for overseas dependencies had precipitated, if not directly caused, the world war, and thereby brought a terrible judgment on the West.

Colonial empire and small wars in exotic places had moreover lost most of the popular glamour they once possessed. In the 1890s minor last stands, such as the destruction of the Shangani Patrol in the Matabele War of 1893 in Southern Rhodesia, became renowned as heroic tragedies. Writers seldom tired of depicting white frontiersmen or professional soldiers in the colonies as bold adventurers, willing to face dangers which the petty clerk from Peckham would only read about in his Sunday paper. But once the petty clerk from Peckham—or from Paris—had gone through the slaughter of the Somme, he ceased to be impressed by minor sideshows like the Matabele War or the campaigns against Abd-el-Kader, and colonial ideals lost much of their former prestige. On a more sophisticated level, war also produced a more general reaction against all the beliefs of preceding middle-class generations—the businessman's standard of value, the glorification of economic individualism, and the Victorian ideals of sexual morality. Victorian middle-class people in some way tended to identify African tribesmen with the "lower orders" of society at home. Now African tribesmen gained from the comparison. To some intellectuals, all that was not bourgeois became praiseworthy, and the colonial races were likened to the European proletariat in its real or supposed virtues.

The great slump in the early 1930s further affected the climate of thought. Britain, France, Belgium, and the Netherlands, with their great dependencies overseas, suffered as much or more from unemployment as smaller states without empires. The Soviet Union during the same period went through a social crisis of far greater proportions; there were mass liquidations and famines, and human life was destroyed to an extent unknown to the West in peacetime. However, to many intellectuals Russia was sufficiently remote to be romantic; Soviet excesses were widely denied or explained away, and Soviet ideals had a profound appeal for many young academic people in the West.

The full force of social criticism instead turned against Western empire. What was the point of having colonies? Perhaps Lenin was right in linking empire with the internal decay of capitalism, and capitalism with increasing misery for the masses both at home and abroad. In a more limited sense, the worldwide glut in raw materials worked against both the economic and the political interests of all white producers in the colonies—be they tobacco farmers in Rhodesia, winegrowers in Algeria, or mining magnates on the Northern Rhodesian Copper Belt. African peasants, working the land with simple methods, seemed more crisis resistant; they also had as yet made fewer political demands than white settlers, so that European colonists in Africa began to meet with a particularly heavy barrage of criticism from home. In a period of falling demand, customers seemed more important than raw-material producers; native Africans were far more numerous than the small group of emigrant farmers and miners from Europe. Some economists therefore began to stress the future potentialities of indigenous mass markets as against the traditional role of colonies as sources of primary products.

Among Europeans and Americans the debate on colonialism produced, broadly speaking, two main schools of thought. The first contended that colonialism in its existing form did not really pay. This group was comprised of moderate socialists, bourgeois reformers, and pacifists in the Hobsonian tradition, the majority of whom wished for peaceful change, put their trust into some kind of international planning, and generally looked to the League of Nations to reform the world. They might be described as the "tender-minded." The second school of thought, the "tough-minded," thought that Western colonialism paid all too well, but they arrived at varied and diametrically opposed conclusions from this premise. The Communists and their allies demanded revolutionary action and hoped that colonial toilers would join the ranks of a worldwide proletarian army, while the right wing of the anti-Western school, comprised of numerous nationalists in Germany and Italy, the defeated or disappointed nations, considered that the spoils of empire should be taken from the "have" and given to the "have-not" nations, that the soft should give way to the fighters, the fierce, and the fertile.

Within the Western countries, the humanitarian and reformist school enjoyed more influence than any other. The most convinced imperialists themselves became more apologetic in tone; scholarly administrators such as Lord Lugard now justified British rule in terms of the "dual mandate," whereby the metropolitan powers had a duty both to their African subjects and to the world at large.[2] Lugard, however, never became a popular writer. Among the educated the Hobsonian tradition carried more weight, and perhaps the ablest writer within this school was Leonard Woolf. Woolf was a Cambridge man who had acquired practical administrative experience overseas in Ceylon and later turned to publishing and journalism. In the old tradition of the colonial reformers, he approved of white-settlement colonies like Australia and New Zealand but looked with distaste at African colonization. No part of the Dark Continent, in his view, was suited to become a "white man's country," not even Algeria or South Africa, where European settlers remained a minority. The African dependencies in no way added to the military strength of the motherland. Trade with the tropical areas remained small, and Woolf argued that on examination the import and export figures of these dependencies would show that "the ideas of imperialists with regard to the importance of African colonial possessions as sources of wealth are delusions."[3]

The story of African empire, in Woolf's view, was a sad tale of consistent exploitation and neglect. With striking lack of consistency, he derided imperialists both for robbing the colonies and for making them yield so little trade. At the same time he stressed what he regarded as the peculiar abuses brought about through colonization by white settlers. Postwar progressive thought in this respect introduced a new note. Lenin, and Hobson in his earlier vein, had regarded imperialists more or less as an undifferentiated mass of exploiters, and their censure stressed the vices of big monopolistic concerns such as the chartered company; yet both had sympathized with the Boers against the Britons. The postwar period saw a major change in this attitude. Anti-imperialists became more hostile to white colonists in Africa; the attack started with an intellectual assault on the British emigrants occupying the northern and southern ends of the arc of British settlement in Africa—in Kenya and South Africa. White Kenyans became associated with the British landed aristocracy and a widely discredited military caste in Britain. The humanitarian conscience rebelled at forced labor and came to look at the Kenyan estate economy in much the same light as abolitionists once viewed the West Indian slave plantations.

[2] Lord Lugard, *The Dual Mandate in British Tropical Africa* (Edinburgh, 1922).
[3] Leonard S. Woolf, *Economic Imperialism* (London, 1920), p. 55.

South Africa came under serious fire when an Afrikaner nationalist-labor coalition came into power in 1924. The new rulers at Pretoria put a large English-speaking community into the unaccustomed position of being a political minority. Only the Southern Rhodesian settlers did not as yet incur the same amount of odium. Rhodesia, went the argument, still possessed vast untilled acres from which white men could not legitimately be excluded. The progressives' real bugbear was the British South Africa Company, which governed Southern Rhodesia until 1923 and incurred bitter criticism from white Rhodesians and British humanitarians alike. The Rhodesian leaders who negotiated in London for responsible government thus met with a friendly reception from missionaries, left-wingers, Radicals, and humanitarians.

A few years later, however, this temporary alliance between Rhodesian settlers and progressives broke down, while the image of the Algerian *colon* or the white Kenyan became similarly tarnished in France. British reformist opinion especially began to change the priority of disesteem given to different types of colonizers. Trading and mining concerns, from being the most detested regiment in the army of imperialism, rose slightly in progressive estimation. Mining concerns were, after all, only too willing to promote lower-paid African workers into jobs previously held by more highly remunerated white men, and commercial companies seemed indispensable for the task of distributing native-grown crops. The settlers, on the other hand, came to be viewed as exploiters in a more consistent fashion than in the prewar days, when they appeared to the "enlightened" public to be victims as much as accomplices of colonialism. The settlers were accused of always stealing the best lands from their African neighbors; they enforced social and economic color bars. In the 1920s and 1930s, moreover, the settlers themselves lost much of their social dynamism. Rhodesia, Algeria, and Kenya attracted only a trickle of white emigrants. The local whites themselves dreaded the competition of newcomers on an apparently overstocked labor market, and their fierce nationalism militated against the large-scale absorption of white foreigners.

Such being the prevalent climate of opinion, Woolf and his bourgeois fellow reformers, as well as most British colonial officials, regarded Britain's West African possessions as the brightest spot in an otherwise depressing African scene. In Nigeria and on the Gold Coast white men could not acquire land; Africans produced tropical crops as free men on their own soil. Of course, Woolf ignored the way in which African tribesmen in white-settled Mashonaland were also expanding their maize crops and adding to their pastoral wealth during this period. He took no account of the way in which the Rhodesian and South African economies did, in fact, give employment to black artisans. Nor did he consider the administrative color bar involved in not appointing local Africans to senior positions in the imperial civil service, a kind of discrimination that owed nothing to settler initiative.

Woolf also displayed serious deficiencies as a historian. In trying to give chapter and verse for his theory of economic imperialism, he made numerous factual errors and could never resist taking a swipe at empire builders who risked their lives in policing disturbed regions. In the late 1880s Lugard, later a great British administrator, offered his services to the African Lakes Company, a Scottish trading concern engaged in hostilities against Arab slave traders. According to Woolf's interpretation, Lugard satisfied himself that shooting the native slave raiders of Nyasaland was as good a cause as mowing down the Abyssinians of Abyssinia, the Burmese of Burma, and the Afghans of Afghanistan.[4] He did not mention that the slave traders in question were Arabs, not Nyasa—an omission characteristic of many Western humanitarians of the period, who could see neither merit nor justification in the constabulary function of imperialism. Woolf's views had a wide appeal, not only among Socialist writers, but also among many conservative theoreticians of colonial trusteeship, and even among British administrators themselves.

Most American writing on imperialism followed essentially similar lines. American, like British, academicians generally felt disillusioned with the outcome of the war. Many blamed the munition makers, the "merchants of death"; others censured the Wall Street bankers, who supposedly pushed the United States into battle against Germany in order to secure the loans made to France and Great Britain. American historians also were generally shocked by the secret treaties concluded by the Western Allies during the war. Much of subsequent Western research on the origins of World War I and the war-guilt question rested on *Die grosse Politik der europäischen Kabinette,* the German collection of diplomatic documents on the outbreak of the war. The Germans, having gotten their version out long before anyone else, generally got their story accepted, and for many years most Anglo-Saxon professors and their students tended to look at recent history through the spectacles provided by German editors.[5] They

---

[4] Richard J. Hammond, "Economic Imperialism: Sidelights on a Stereotype," *Journal of Economic History,* XXI, No. 4 (December, 1961), 582–598. See also Leonard S. Woolf, *Empire and Commerce in Africa: A Study in Economic Imperialism* (London, 1919).

[5] See, for instance, Sidney B. Fay, *The Origins of the World War* (New York, 1928).

generally rejected the Establishment's former assumption of German war guilt, and accepted the economic causation of war as a commonplace. The international struggle for markets, raw materials, and investment opportunities, in their view, caused colonialism, and colonialism led to war. Most American and British historians thus took little account of the deliberate attempts at empire building in Europe made by the Kaiser's Germany during World War I. Instead they remained preoccupied with European colonization in Asia and Africa; here the Germans had played only a minor part, and the German record seemed no worse than that of the Allies.

Liberal scholarship in the West continued to regard overseas imperialism as the main culprit. Not only was empire wicked, but it was also unprofitable. Neither the colonizers nor the colonized drew much profit from these ungodly enterprises. Imperialism, in the liberal scholar's view, was merely one of the many illusions that clouded men's minds.[6] Among the most intelligent economic analysts belonging to this school of thought was Grover Clark, an American scholar. His statistical material is too detailed to be summarized and also contains a number of gaps which would require extensive further research to be filled. Nevertheless, a few instances may be given to illustrate his argument.[7] "No French government finance figures [covering expenditure on the empire] are to be had for the years 1918 to 1921, inclusive. Direct colonial expenses for the rest of the time from 1894 to 1934 were 8,814 million francs. This was 4.6 per cent of the colonial trade for the same period, which was 193,461 million francs or 14.7 per cent of the total trade. Dividing the total defense expenditures in this same proportion we get 32,134 million francs as the proportion indirectly chargeable to the colonies. With the direct colonial expenses, this makes 40,948 million francs, or 21.1 per cent of the colonial trade in this period." Italy was a much worse example. "All of Italy's trade, imports and exports together, with all of her colonies, from 1894 to 1932, was worth 5,561 million lire. This was less than one per cent of her total external trade in the same period. In the twenty years 1913 to 1932—the records do not go further back—Italy spent on her colonies 6,856 million lire." "Britain's record on its face points to the conclusion that the amount of trade is in inverse rather than direct ratio to the amount of political control, since the figures for the United Kingdom's trade back to 1894 show that of the trade with the overseas British coun-

[6] See, for instance, Parker T. Moon, *Imperialism and World Politics* (New York, 1927).

[7] Grover Clark, *The Balance Sheets of Imperialism: Facts and Figures on Colonies* (New York, 1936), pp. 10b, 11a, 12a, 14a, 14b.

tries a steadily increasing share has been with the Dominions which are self-governing, and a steadily decreasing share with those regions which are controlled from London." In 1894 only 49.0 percent of the value of Britain's gross trade with all the British countries was with the self-governing parts of the empire. In 1934 it was 59.9 percent. But this was not all. "The British countries as a whole now do with Britain a considerably smaller share of their total trade than they did in the middle of the nineteenth century, or in 1894: 36.1 per cent for 1929–1933, compared with 48.7 per cent for 1854–1863, and 47.3 per cent for 1894–1903." Even as a population outlet, the British Empire was of only limited importance. "Of the 28 million of all nationalities who sailed to other continents from British ports from 1886 to 1933, precisely 5.0 per cent went to the British territories other than the Dominion areas. . . . The Dominions got 38.8 per cent, and the United States 51.6 per cent."

The remedy was simple. Countries capable of standing on their own feet should be granted the right of self-determination, like the states of Eastern Europe. Backward areas not yet in a position to form nation-states of the approved parliamentary pattern must be placed under the tutelage of the League. The mandate system should be extended to include all Western colonies. These projects, of course, ignored the unfortunate experiences with international action over the Congo; nor did they take into account the very inadequate benefits brought about by multinational intervention in Macedonia before 1914. But designs for the internationalization of empire gained luster from the idealistic hopes placed in the League or some other form of global organization; they continued to haunt British and American thought before, during, and after World War II, and ultimately hardened into a new political orthodoxy.

From Western liberal criticisms of imperialism, we go on to Continental variants of the same theme. Liberal Continental scholars also stressed what they regarded as the irrational aspects of empire building, but they often followed a different line of reasoning. In 1919 Joseph Alois Schumpeter, an Austrian scholar, published a brilliant little work which described imperialism as a form of social atavism. Schumpeter agreed to some extent with Marx. He showed how the living conditions or the relations of production prevalent in any given society would produce a certain political or ideological superstructure. In his view, however, the roof did not necessarily cave in when the foundations decayed. Certain attitudes, certain psychological habits, might survive long after the original conditions justifying their existence had passed away. The Assyrians regarded war and chase as a kind of sport. Warlike habits continued not merely as a means, but also as an end, giving rise to one of the most merciless and bloodthirsty imperialisms ever known to history. Schumpeter applied a comparable analysis to Arab imperialism (he might have spoken in similar terms of the wars waged by Masai and Matabele warrior communities in Africa).

Capitalism, Schumpeter's argument claimed, was essentially pacific in nature; imperialism was occasioned by precapitalist survivals in the body politic. Schumpeter applied similar reasoning to explain the growth of modern trusts and cartels. Organizations of this nature could pursue a monopolistic policy only behind protective tariffs. Protective tariffs, however, did not automatically stem from competitive systems. They were the results of political action, and only benefited minorities within the bourgeoisie. They did not derive from capitalism as such, but rather from the financial interests of the absolutist monarch, of the older type of state power. Capitalists unfortunately were not sufficiently conscious of their own interests; even the most powerful monied men often took over the preconceptions of an older, war-oriented, landowning nobility—an observation, one might add, which was true to some extent of imperial Germany, but hardly for nineteenth-century France, Belgium, or Britain. Imperialism, Schumpeter continued, was only the heritage of the autocratic state, the outcome of precapitalist forces which the older monarchies had reorganized. Imperialism, in other words, stemmed from the living conditions not of the present, but of the past. Put in terms of the economic interpretation of history, imperialism sprang from the relations of production that had prevailed in days gone by; empire was a social atavism.[8]

Schumpeter made a contribution to the postwar debate on imperialism by emphasizing not only its economic, but also its noneconomic elements. He ably stressed the time lag that so often allows outworn ideas to survive and to captivate men's minds long after the objective conditions behind such concepts have passed away. He claimed men acted emotionally in acquiring empires. He nevertheless laid himself open to serious attack. Many of his economic theories did not hold water. Protectionism flourished both in the United States, which never knew monarchical power in the nineteenth century, and in Germany, where kings and princes had ruled for centuries past. The movement toward autarchy in the 1930s could not possibly be interpreted as a revival of eighteenth-century absolutism, but only as a response to the strains and weaknesses of contemporary capitalism.

Furthermore, imperialism even in its early manifestations was not necessarily irrational. Roman expansionism strengthened the great landowners' control of the state apparatus and helped to head off in-

[8] Joseph Alois Schumpeter, *Imperialism and Social Classes,* trans. by Heinz Norden, ed. and with an introd. by Paul M. Sweezy (New York, 1951).

ternal land reform. Foreign conquests provided Rome with a golden stream of tax money and cheap grain which the Roman ruling class employed in a thoroughly "Leninist" fashion to buy off their internal proletariat with bread and circuses. Nineteenth-century Britain, to take another instance, was not run by a professional warrior class; yet the British vastly added to their possessions in the last century, and many British capitalists did profit from empire.[9]

With his Germanic background, Schumpeter stressed only outworn feudal concepts of personal honor and national prestige as motives for expansion. Otherwise, his is a theory of chaos. Imperialist statesmen do not seem to act for any very good reason—yet men like Rosebery and Salisbury argued quite rationally for or against the acquisition of any particular territory. In oversimplifying, like the Marxists, he completely misses the complexity of the motives involved. Rhodes's financial backers believed that money might be made in British South Africa Company shares, and many of them held quite sincerely that they were putting up cash for a laudable cause. Schumpeter ignores the philanthropic and missionary element in imperialism—the campaign against the slave trade, the steady lobbying on the part of humanitarian pressure groups anxious to make the British government annex unprofitable regions at great expense to the taxpayer for the benefit of tribesmen. He has nothing to say of the very real idealism of missionaries like François Coillard, who devoted his life to the evangelization of fever-ridden Barotseland toward the end of the last century. Coillard went through incredible dangers and hardships; he saw his wife and scores of his companions die from tropical disease, and he himself perished by the Zambezi. Although he was French, he played an active role in bringing Barotseland under British protection, in the conviction that British rule was an engine for progress, that only the Queen's government could modernize the country, put an end to the chronic civil wars within and the raiding outside its borders, and protect the Barotse against the activities of white gold seekers.

A similar spirit of self-sacrifice animated early medical officers, agricultural advisers, and administrative officials in the field.[10]

[9] For a good Marxist critique of Schumpeter's views see Murray Greene, "Schumpeter's Imperialism—A Critical Note," in Harrison M. Wright (ed.), *The "New Imperialism": Analysis of Late Nineteenth-Century Expansionism* (Boston, 1961), pp. 62–67.

[10] For the medical side of imperialism see, for instance, Michael Gelfand's trilogy, *Tropical Victory: An Account of the Influence of Medicine on the History of Southern Rhodesia, 1890–1923* (Cape Town, 1953), *Northern Rhodesia in the Days of the Charter: A Medical and Social Study, 1878–1924* (Oxford, 1961), and *Lakeside Pioneers: A Socio-medical Study of Nyasaland (1875–1920)* (Oxford, 1964).

Schumpeter does not discuss these constructive sides of imperialism, nor does he make any serious attempt to differentiate between one form of expansionism and another, or to go into the question of whether there were not, in fact, many different types of modern imperialism.

World War I and its aftermath also produced extensive anti-Western literature in industrialized Germany. German nationalist writers looked for a scapegoat who would account for Germany's defeat and subsequent financial breakdown. Some blamed the Jews; others blamed the British; many blamed both. The British, in this view, had deliberately encircled an overmighty competitor to despoil the Fatherland of its trade and colonies. Cunning, purposeful, and energetic, the island people were also hypocritical and decadent. The bloated, Jew-ridden Western plutodemocracies lived on the world's colonial loot. But Germany, the proletarian nation, must have its place in the sun. German nationalists regarded the return of the colonies as a matter both of national prestige and of profit. Their ideas found expression in an enormous and now, for the most part, unreadable literature, cast in the peculiarly humorless mold of German chauvinist invective. In 1933 Franz von Papen, a leading nationalist, sadly mused[11] how the sight of a gigantic brick elephant at Bremen recalled to him all the great natural wealth still locked in the heart of Africa. Germany, according to Papen, needed colonies to feed its people, house its surplus population, meet its foreign credit engagements, and spread its civilization.[12] Such arguments became commonplace in Germany, Italy, and Japan.[13]

During the interwar years Marxists more than any others insisted on what they called "unity of theory and practice." The philosopher's job, in Marx's view, was not to interpret the world, but to change it. Ideology was nothing but the handmaiden of political strategy. Marxist thought thus mainly hinged on elaborating methods for the struggle against capitalism and cannot be separated from practical politics. Africa during this period played only a very minor share in Communist thinking. The main battle against Western imperialism centered on Asia. In 1920 the Second Congress of the Comintern saw a strenuous debate between Manebandra Nath Roy of India and Lenin concerning the tactics which Communists should adopt toward the colored races. A compromise solution laid down that the International should for the time being collaborate with the revolutionary

[11] In an article in the *Saturday Evening Post*, September 30, 1933.
[12] Article cited in Louis L. Snyder (ed.), *The Imperialism Reader: Documents and Readings on Modern Expansionism* (Princeton, N.J., 1962), p. 453.
[13] Wolfe W. Schmokel, *Dream of Empire: German Colonialism, 1919–1945* (New Haven, Conn., 1964).

movement in the colonies and backward countries, without, however, merging with it. Three years later this thesis was applied more specifically to the Negro problem; "Resolution on the Negro Question," the thesis of the Fourth Comintern Congress, asserted the necessity of supporting every Negro movement which undermined or weakened capitalism. The Communists believed, quite wrongly, as the facts showed later, that the American Negroes were peculiarly qualified to play a leading part in the liberation struggle of the entire African race. The Communists had made no real progress in Africa itself. Advanced socialist thought of the revolutionary variety remained confined to a small minority of Arabs and of European settlers in North Africa and to a tiny body of English, Jewish, and Bantu intellectuals and trade unionists in South Africa.[14] The growth of a Negro working class in the Americas and the development of an African consciousness among American and West Indian Negro leaders seemed to show more promising chances for agitation; hence much of Communist strategy concerning black people centered on the New World.

Communist thought on the Negro problem was strongly influenced by Stalin's views on the national minority problems in Eastern Europe. In 1928 the Comintern committed itself to a policy of supporting territorially separate black republics in the United States. This decision unwittingly mirrored similar segregationist ideas current among British humanitarians and missionaries, who then generally supported separate native reserves and separate development for the native tribal communities.[15] However, from the tactical standpoint this move turned out to be a disaster. The Communist parties in South Africa and the United States continued weak and could make little headway. Communist thought remained largely confined to a small section of the Negro diaspora in the metropolitan countries, the West Indies, and the United States. The Soviets in the main had to rely on Communist parties in Western Europe to infiltrate the colonial territories.

Stalin, like his predecessor, envisaged the world in almost Mani-

[14] See Colin Legum, "Pan-Africanism and Communism," in Sven Hamrell and Carl G. Widstrand (eds.), The Soviet Bloc, China and Africa (Uppsala, 1964), pp. 9–29, and George Padmore, Pan-Africanism or Communism? The Coming Struggle for Africa (London, 1956), especially pp. 289–379.

[15] The Southern Rhodesian Missionary Conference warmly supported the policy of segregation inherent in the Southern Rhodesian Land Apportionment Act, 1930. For a theoretical justification of apartheid written by a Christian socialist missionary in Southern Rhodesia at the time, see Arthur S. Cripps, An Africa for Africans: A Plea on Behalf of Territorial Segregation Areas and of Their Freedom in a South African Colony (London, 1927). Today these segregationist views survive among the Afrikaner nationalists of South Africa and the Black Muslims in North America.

chaean terms as divided into the armies of light and darkness, with the socialist camp on one side arrayed against the capitalists on the other. He elaborated Lenin's theories of how Communists must make full use of all the divisions among the enemy's ranks—that is to say, the class struggles within the Western countries, the rivalries among the imperialist powers, and the contradictions between the colonizers and the colonized. At home Stalin bloodily suppressed all effective national minority movements and liquidated theoreticians like Sultan Galiev, who wished to adapt socialism to the particular needs of the Muslim communities. Abroad, on the other hand, he tried to merge the ambitions of all oppressed ethnic groups, European, Asian, or African, into the greater struggle for world revolution. In so doing, of course, he always gave priority to the needs of the Soviet Union and strictly subordinated agitation in other parts of the world to the internal and external policies of the "fatherland of the world's working classes." The need to find allies against Hitler among the Western capitalist democracies for a time induced Stalin to soft-pedal the anticolonial movements in the later 1930s, and the struggle against imperialism was revived with full vigor only after World War II.

On the theoretical plane Communist thinkers confined their analysis of imperialism to an industrious exegesis of the Leninist-Stalinist scriptures. Outside Russia variants of the Marxist thesis stressed the works of Rosa Luxemburg, who had placed special emphasis on the importance of the noncapitalist sector, both within and outside the main bourgeois states. Luxemburg believed that neither the workers nor the capitalists could consume all they produced; hence capitalism had to expand constantly, both into the backward areas on the periphery and into the little islands of precapitalist enterprise, handicraft, and agricultural industries within the capitalist states. This process could not, however, go on indefinitely and was bound to collapse. Fritz Sternberg, a German Marxist, enlarged on this theme; he argued that the smaller the noncapitalist sector within a capitalist country, the greater was its need to expand into the underdeveloped spaces overseas. Britain, according to this argument, ruined its traditional peasantry. The British farming population became proportionately smaller than that of any other country, hence the island kingdom had to build up a big colonial empire in Africa and elsewhere. These dependencies gave the country an opportunity to get rid of both surplus capital and surplus goods. The more capital was absorbed in the colonies, however, the smaller became the investors' profit, and the system therefore could not last.[16]

[16] See Rosa Luxemburg, *Die Akkumulation des Kapitals: Ein Beitrag zur ökonomischen Erklärung des Imperialismus* (Leipzig, 1921), and Fritz Sternberg, *Der Imperialismus* (Berlin, 1926).

This argument, presented with a wealth of statistics, did not explain how the incorporation of backward Matabele warriors or of starving Bemba tribal farmers into the sphere of British capitalism would supply the purchasing power that was lacking at home. The continued survival of American capitalism, according to this reasoning, would similarly depend on the existence of backward rural enclaves in the Appalachians and the Deep South. The thesis led to the even more preposterous conclusion that a colony like Rhodesia would yield big profits only as long as foreign companies invested small amounts of capital within its borders. Conversely, returns would fall as more mine shafts, mine hospitals, and railways were built with the shareholders' money—an assumption that would have moved any London mining board to merriment.

Explanations of imperialism thus varied widely, but most of these theories had something in common. European thinkers, whether Marxist or fascist, reformist or revolutionary, still looked upon tribal Africans in much the same way as the old-fashioned white missionary had; they saw a great, undifferentiated mass of faceless blacks. For the nineteenth-century evangelists, black people were damned souls to be saved; for the socialists of the 1920s and 1930s they were wage slaves to be freed. Black people produced profit, the argument went, so all the capitalist had to do was to turn on the tap, and out would squirt a golden jet of surplus value.

There were, of course, differences in outlook and degrees of sophistication. The late 1920s and the 1930s saw major changes in the views of colonial administrators themselves. British theorists of indirect rule and, in a somewhat different form, French advocates of association wished to eschew violent upheaval; they hoped to utilize indigenous institutions for the cause of social betterment, and thus build up the colonies by slow degrees. Reforming British officials, as well as the settler-run administration of Southern Rhodesia, encouraged ethnographic and statistical research. Retired administrators such as Lord Lugard and Sir Harry Johnston promoted academic investigation at home. The gospel of "development," as well as colonial crises, strikes, parliamentary pressures, and immediate administrative needs, produced great series of official reports on social, financial, and economic problems in the colonies. Many missionaries also became more sophisticated in their approach. The International Mission Council set up a department of social and industrial research. Both clerical and secular scholars tried to apply in Africa the lessons learned in the study of so-called underprivileged social or ethnic minorities in Western Europe and America. The combined efforts of these investigators, most of them employed or subsidized by the colonial powers, in time helped to provide the critics of colonialism with factual ammunition. Colonial governments themselves published extensive material on wages, wage differential, housing, and educational conditions of the kind not available for areas of Russian settlement in Soviet Asia or for more backward independent countries like Liberia. There was, however, a time lag in the compilation of such facts and their evaluation in the more theoretical studies of empire. Moreover, the gulf between different academic disciplines took much time to be bridged. Scholars generally took insufficient account of the extreme material backwardness of Africa, of the intricacies of divergent kinship systems, social habitat, and customs. Many failed to allow for the great diversity of Africa's geographical, ecological, and climatic conditions. Most remained unfamiliar with the findings of anthropologists, who were then only beginning to work in Africa. The black man continued to be widely looked upon as no more than an exploitable or exploited commodity. Further investigation into the realities of imperialism had to await the development of more Africa-centered studies.

8. Pan-Africanism, Imperialism, and Négritude

The word Africa does not figure in any early Bantu vocabulary; it is perhaps the most important article of export which Europe ever sent south of the Sahara. The Negro people originally lacked any geographical conspectus of their land mass as a whole; they had no sense of ethnic unity. In Britain, America, and the West Indies, however, the black diaspora for the first time became aware of similar racial origins; they absorbed the culture of the West, and by the end of the eighteenth century dissident Negro religious sects had begun to adopt the term African into their nomenclature. Negro missionaries subsequently carried their own forms of nonconformity to various parts of Africa, where their teaching made a considerable impact. In addition, free Negro settlers from the New World carried this "black-consciousness" back to Sierra Leone and Liberia. These black-settlement colonies produced a small middle class of their own. Many English-speaking West Coast Africans made a name for themselves in trade and administration; men such as Dr. Samuel Johnson and Bishop Samuel Adjei Crowther attained some distinction in the realm of letters. So did Surgeon Major James Africanus Beale Horton, the first Negro to attain a regular commission in the British army. In many respects Horton typified the "new African." The son of a liberated slave, he looked beyond tribalism toward a high sense of African unity; in 1859 he predicted in a doctoral thesis that the Ibo, Yoruba, Krumen, and others would by intermarriage produce the finest race of Africa. In subsequent works Horton bitterly attacked current ideas of the African's inborn inferiority. He refused to be bound by the simple dichotomy of nation and tribe which dominated European thinking and argued with firm conviction that black people were perfectly capable of attaining "a real political government and national independence." Horton therefore would have nothing to do with "the false theories of modern anthropologists," who placed the Negro

88

people near the bottom of the human ladder, and stressed instead the beneficent part which education would play in the regeneration of the Negro race.[1]

The late nineteenth century also produced a handful of intellectuals who stood for what might be regarded as an early form of *négritude*. Outstanding among these was Edward Wilmot Blyden, a West Indian scholar who made his name as a teacher and diplomatist in Liberia. In the cultural sphere Blyden's doctrines bear a curious resemblance to notions expressed earlier by German romantics such as Johann Gottfried von Herder; in the political field Blyden had something in common with the Russian *narodniki,* who extolled what they regarded as the Russian peasant's primitive socialism against the supposedly materialistic, money-making creeds of the West. Blyden spoke, perhaps for the first time, of the "African personality." The African had his own contribution to make to the happiness of mankind; he had a deeper and more spiritual faith than the European. Religion, in Blyden's view, had originated in Ethiopia, and thence spread to Asia via Egypt. The African's close communion with nature resulted in a system of cooperative socialism, family solidarity, communal landownership, and government which brought democratic justice to all. According to Blyden, the deterioration of African life was the result of the slave trade and of the baneful influence of Western Christianity, which came to Africa as the handmaiden of oppression. Africans must work out their own destiny; Liberia should become a beacon shining into Africa's splendid future.

The bulk of the African intelligentsia, however, backed the cause of empire. Men like Johnson, Crowther, and Horton, born of servile ancestry, regarded colonial rule as a social revolution which overthrew domestic slavery, gave a new chance to the disinherited, killed ancient superstitions, and deprived corrupt indigenous aristocracies of ill-gained power. They thus shared the optimism of their white Victorian contemporaries about imperialism. Had they read Marx, they would have agreed with his views on the "progressive" nature of capitalism in the backward parts of the world. Even Blyden, for all his belief in the African personality and his interest in African studies, thought that European classical languages would form the most effective disciplinary study in African university education. He also extolled the philanthropy of no less a personage than Leopold II and in 1891 eulogized the British administration at Lagos in terms that might have made Cecil Rhodes blush.[2]

[1] George Shepperson, "An Early African Graduate," *University of Edinburgh Gazette,* No. 32 (January, 1962), pp. 23–26.

[2] See Robert W. July, "Nineteenth-Century Negritude: Edward W. Blyden," *Journal of African History,* V, No. 1 (1964), 73–86.

The alliance between the new African intelligentsia and imperialism, however, proved short-lived. The full story of the educated African's progressive disenchantment with white colonial rule remains to be written and will form a key chapter in the annals of the African continent. As a rough generalization, disillusionment with the imperial factor first struck the Negroes of North America, the West Indies, and Europe. Their critical spirit, fed from Western anticolonial springs, seeped into West Africa and then into other parts of the continent. The last areas to be affected were territories like Rhodesia, where European settlers developed their own form of "protonationalism," in opposition to black nationalism.

The ending of slavery in the Western hemisphere did not result in immediate equality for black men. Lincoln, the liberator, himself bitterly opposed full integration; most American writers believed that the different races of mankind were unequally endowed and different in natural capacity. The existence of independent black states such as Haiti and Liberia did nothing to improve the African's image. On the contrary, textbooks were wont to cite the chronic poverty, turbulence, and corruption of these countries as proof that black people could not govern themselves in a civilized fashion. Booker T. Washington, a distinguished American Negro educator, tacitly accepted the charge of Negro backwardness; he determined to lead his people out of the darkness through education and changes in their social environment. Others put their trust in territorial separation and worked for the repatriation of freed Negroes to their ancestral shores in Africa. Toward the end of the last century a new group of Negro intellectuals appeared on the American scene. They took a more uncompromising stand in the struggle for civil rights and demanded more militance in defending the independence of Haiti, Liberia, and Ethiopia. They fought for equality, both on the individual plane, as between Negroes and whites, and on the international stage, as between Western and existing or future African nations. They also took much interest in Negro history and argued that the Negro—far from being mankind's eternal Peter Pan—had made a major contribution to the progress of humanity.[3]

The movement struck an answering chord among black expatriates in London, where black people from Africa, the West Indies, and North America found themselves in a position to meet with those of like mind from other parts of the world. There were no restraints on organization or debate. There were newspapers and libraries.

[3] See Immanuel Wallerstein, "Pan-Africanism as Protest," in Morton A. Kaplan (ed.), *The Revolution in World Politics* (New York, 1962), pp. 138–139.

There were many intellectual stimuli, and London thus became the meeting ground of the world's earliest pan-African conference. The participants, called together in 1900 by Henry Sylvester-Williams, a West Indian barrister, were mainly black delegates from England, the United States, and the West Indies, with a sprinkling of visitors from Africa. The meeting put the term "pan-African" into circulation and stressed the need for equality between the races. This concept found expression in the famous statement by William Edward Burghardt Du Bois, a radical American Negro scholar, that "the problem of the twentieth century is the problem of the color line." But otherwise the conference achieved little. In the United States interest centered on the internal situation; the pan-African idea lay dormant until Du Bois made a dramatic new move at the end of World War I. In 1919 he succeeded, through the support of Blaise Diagne, a black deputy from Senegal in the French Chamber of Deputies, in convening the Second Pan-African Congress at Paris.[4] This gathering contained French African parliamentarians and American Negro officers, businessmen, and intellectuals, who among them wielded a good deal more influence than their predecessors in London. Drawing their inspiration from the liberal and reformist thought of the time, they advocated trusteeship in terms not very different from those of liberal colonial administrators. The congress insisted that the governing powers in Africa should safeguard natives against loss of land, forced labor, exploitation from foreign capital, and other abuses. The colonial powers ought to promote education and give the indigenous people of Africa more share in local and tribal government, with a chance of ultimately rising to the higher offices of state. Du Bois would also have liked to internationalize colonialism by placing former German, and perhaps also Portuguese and Belgian, dependencies under international trusteeship. He added, more significantly, that the Negroes in the two Americas and the West Indies, the black governments of Liberia, Haiti, and Ethiopia, as well as educated natives in white-ruled Africa, should have some say in the disposal of the Kaiser's former transmaritime possessions.[5]

Subsequent pan-African congresses in the 1920s continued to speak in a moderate tone but wielded little influence. The movement was mainly confined to intellectuals, its arguments cast in a rigidly rationalist mold. The genuine mass movements which arose among American Negro poor and among backward African villagers more commonly displayed an intensely emotional or religious bent. In

4 Wallerstein, "Pan-Africanism as Protest," pp. 139–140.

5 George Padmore (ed.), *Colonial and Coloured Unity: A Programme of Action; History of the Pan-African Congress* (Manchester, Eng. [1947?]).

America, Marcus Garvey for a short time attracted an immense following with a fantastic scheme for leading the black citizens of the United States out of the "house of bondage" back to the "promised land" of Africa. Garvey had no appeal for black intellectuals and members of the middle class, who generally supported organizations such as the National Association for the Advancement of Colored People and the pan-African congresses. He opposed socialist solutions and looked to the day when Negroes would boast of their own millionaires. He bestowed fanciful titles and bombastic honors upon his followers and flattered their egos by an inverted racism which exalted the black at the expense of the white. Garvey for a time exercised a considerable influence on a subsequent generation of African nationalists, including Kwame Nkrumah, Ghana's first president.

In the meantime sub-Saharan Africa had also begun to stir. The second half of the nineteenth century had already seen some early manifestations of what later became known as nationalism. Economic development on the Gold Coast provided the material conditions for the development of new ideas, new loyalties, and new forms of association. The progress of education and the absence of an effective system of colonial censorship allowed new views to be expressed through the printed word. The superimposition of a foreign bureaucracy, centralized and efficient, helped to give the country a new sense of unity. The creation of representative institutions of the British colonial type introduced a new element into politics and helped to precipitate opposition from the governed. Many of Ghana's nationalist campaigning devices are of late nineteenth-century origin. The earliest recorded boycott of European goods took place in 1874; African politicians demanded popular representation in the legislative council in 1882; a strike broke out in 1896, and a year later politically conscious Africans formed the Aborigines' Rights Protection Society to voice their aspirations.[6]

Gold Coast nationalism at first remained confined to a tiny middle class and flowed in constitutional channels. Sub-Saharan Africa later produced similar but also more militant movements. In Nyasaland during World War I, John Chilembwe, an American-educated African, unsuccessfully tried to shake off British rule and set up a revolutionary black theocracy in the lakeside protectorate.[7] In the Congo, in Northern Rhodesia, and elsewhere, black prophets sprang up and

[6] See David Kimble, *A Political History of Ghana: The Rise of Gold Coast Nationalism, 1850–1928* (Oxford, 1963).

[7] See George Shepperson and Thomas Price, *Independent African: John Chilembwe and the Origins, Setting, and Significance of the Nyasaland Native Rising of 1915* (Edinburgh, 1958).

foresaw—in one form or another—a "second coming," a day of judgment, when the white man's evil trinity of government, Church, and big business would crumble into dust, and the black elect would inherit the kingdom. Whereas Garvey looked to Africa, some of these African preachers looked to America. In Northern Rhodesia in the 1920s, for instance, stories went around the bush that the British were too stupid to manufacture things like airplanes and that the aircraft in the country were all made by Americans; the Americans would come to liberate the country from the English and would bring untold wealth to the black people. The movement of the prophet Kimbangu in the Belgian Congo and the Dini ya Misambawa along the Kenya-Uganda border bore some similar features. This reaction, of course, was by no means uniform. Where Europeans fully dominated tribal society, or where the sense of tribal identity no longer retained its old force, as among the scattered Mashona of Southern Rhodesia, this type of response did not occur to the same extent. In regions such as the Belgian Congo and Kenya there were, however, just enough whites to disturb tribal life seriously, but not enough to dominate it completely. Anti-European sentiments found expression in a more overt manner. Sects such as the Watu wa Munga (the People of God sect) among the Kikuyu in the 1920s condemned almost everything of European provenance; they also bore a Messianic character which, to some extent, later affected many African nationalist movements of a more secular kind. But prophesying of the religious variety on the whole made a limited impact on the new Africans. The emergent class of Western-trained black people—medical assistants, schoolmasters, and agricultural demonstrators—generally realized that they could not yet take over the state. They were too dependent on state employment to take a more militant stand and in the interwar years usually confined their efforts to minor demands of a local nature.

Although it may have been weak in Africa itself, the pan-African movement received a major access of strength after World War I through support from British Labour Party experts, the Fabian Society, and such leading intellectuals as H. G. Wells. At the same time, some African students came to Britain and socialism made a tremendous appeal to these expatriate youngsters. The average African student absorbed his learning from pacifists and humanitarians, from reformist writers such as Woolf, and above all from such distinguished Socialist academics as Harold Laski. Pan-African pioneers such as George Padmore thus elaborated a creed which differed little from Hobson's. The conquest of Africa arose from economic causes; colonial annexations resulted from the exigencies of developed capitalism in the West, which created a new demand for tropical raw materials, overseas markets, and later for additional investment opportunities. The colonies, in Padmore's view, became dumping grounds for the sons of the bourgeoisie, who went abroad as officials, technologists, and settlers—an echo from British nineteenth-century descriptions of the empire as "a vast system of outdoor relief for the upper classes." Imperialism, in Padmore's interpretation, was politico-economic parasitism by a few highly industrialized and well-armed powers living at the expense of humanity. Worse still, imperialism went hand in hand with the arms race and led to recurrent wars.[8]

According to Padmore and his political companions, the colonial powers' burden of guilt was all the greater, since they had obtained their original accumulation of capital from the ill-gotten profits of the slave trade and other forms of robbery. His argument did not take account of the agricultural, scientific, technological, commercial, and administrative revolutions that provided the indispensable framework for industrialization in the West, nor did it explain why the vast wealth which the Iberian Peninsula had once obtained from the silver mines of Peru and the spices of the Indies was not similarly transmuted into industrial capital. Overseas exploitation had in the end ruined rather than enriched the might of Spain and Portugal. The thesis resembled Hobson's or Lenin's in that it gave no credit to entrepreneurial ability or technical expertise, but it did provide both a historical explanation and a framework of moral values; it allocated a central place to the colonial issue in human history, and therefore proved attractive to all colonial students, from whichever country they might hail.

The emergent pan-African ideology mirrored most of the views contained in British Left Book Club publications of the time or in British progressive journals. Africa—like the world at large—appeared as "through a glass, darkly," as a land where poverty ruled amid plenty and where progress was held back by the machinations of "guilty men." This type of reasoning, however, was not revolutionary in character. Pan-Africanism of the Anglo-Saxon variety put its trust in legal means and thereby reflected its intellectual environment. In the 1930s, moreover, the fascist and Nazi threats began to loom on the horizon. Mussolini conquered Ethiopia, the last independent black kingdom on the continent, and progressives looked to the Western powers to stop him. The Nazis elaborated their racial theories, which proclaimed Jews to be devils incarnate and Negroes to be half-brothers to the ape. Africans, like British progressives, therefore

[8] George Padmore, *How Britain Rules Africa* (London, 1936).

adopted a somewhat ambivalent outlook toward countries like Britain, especially when the Communists backed "popular-front" tactics and the Left seemed united. Britain might be capitalist and imperialist, but it obviously did not practice the excesses of European totalitarianism. Laski could lecture with impunity in London; in the colonies British courts and British district commissioners on the whole retained popular respect.

Many pan-Africanists or socialists thus sought the explanation for the Western capitalists' relative moderation in the existence of colonial empire. German capitalists, according to this view, lacked the colonial resources of the West. They were at the end of their tether and therefore kept Hitler in power to hold the German workers down, while the Western bourgeoisie, with their worldwide empire, had no need for such bloody methods. Although there was no explanation of why the faceless men who supposedly ran Nazi Germany from under cover could not remove their alleged servants or make them do their bidding when Germany was obviously about to crash into the abyss, the "progressive" interpretation again gave a central place to the colonial empire in world politics. It also provided intellectual consistency for Hobsonian beliefs, which became part of a new orthodoxy and have continued to affect anticolonial thought to the present day.

World War II gave a great impetus to anticolonial beliefs both in the metropolitan countries and in their African dependencies. France, Belgium, and Holland, three old established colonial powers, all collapsed under the blows of German arms. The Belgian Congo and the French African colonies were progressively removed from their respective mother countries' direct political control and functioned as semiautonomous units under the control of local administrators. In some ways Hitler involuntarily played a role in the French-speaking African colonies similar to Napoleon's in the Iberian Peninsula, where Napoleon's invasion cut the cord which linked these countries to Latin America and thereby set off the liberation of the South American continent. The sudden military breakdown of Western empire in southeastern Asia gave another profound shock to the colonial system. Even some of the most convinced white imperialists in the distant Rhodesian backwoods, loyal army officers rich in medals and memories, began to question their own handiwork, which, they argued, had neither protected the "natives" against Japanese aggression nor generated a spirit of genuine loyalty to the ruling power.

Anticolonial thought also owed a great deal to American inspiration. The United States was born of an anticolonial revolution and looked with distrust upon the imperialist struggles of the Old World which—it was said—had caused two world wars. In the nineteenth century the Americans had stood for the "open-door" policy in China; in the twentieth century they advocated similar solutions for Africa. The older colonial powers moreover lost prestige. Britain, France, and Holland could not effectively resist Japan in the Far East. Americans therefore questioned the wisdom of fighting for the reconquest of other peoples' colonies. Surely the GI's sacrifice abroad should not be transmuted into profits for British mercantile interests. American soldiers overseas were also often impressed by the poverty of the people; many attributed this misery to the alleged iniquities of colonial rule. In addition, there were a number of more organized pressure groups. Many economic lobbies disliked foreign tariffs. Protestant mission societies looked askance at countries like Belgium and Portugal, which put obstacles in the way of American evangelization. Most Protestant churchmen hoped to apply Wilsonian solutions to Africa, and in 1942 a great Church Conference on African Affairs pronounced in favor of guardianship, to be followed by independence for the black colonies. Nationalist China, America's favored ally in East Asia, was as resentful of colonialism as was Russia. Roosevelt was responsive to all these currents, and despite the existence of strategic reasons and other lobbies more favorable to the cause of European empire, American policy thus generally favored the anti-colonial cause.[9]

Within Africa action by local white authorities helped to promote a new and questioning spirit. In Northern Rhodesia the administration tried to influence African public opinion by means of a propaganda campaign involving leaflets, talks by district commissioners, broadcasts, and motion pictures in the villages. These activities were designed to explain the war, account for shortages and other economic strains, and get black people to join the armed forces; they had the unintended effect of spreading political consciousness, as did the policy of recruiting African soldiers, who went abroad in large numbers and sometimes picked up new ideas overseas. In many parts of sub-Saharan Africa revolutionary concepts became secularized. Men began to hope for basic political changes initiated by their fellow citizens, rather than for a supernatural transformation of society brought about by God. Greater economic affluence and the development of a more vigorous press also played their part in this ferment, as did improved education and the provision by the colonial powers of bursaries to African students for courses of higher studies in London or Paris.

[9] Maurice Levallois, "Les tendances anti-colonialistes des Etats-Unis, de l'U.R.S.S. et de la Chine," *Renaissances,* No. 15 (October, 1945), pp. 22–38.

Most important of all, the general intellectual climate of opinion in the West was favorably inclined to such aspirations. Western statesmen subscribed to the principles of the "four freedoms," the Atlantic Charter, and the United Nations. They denounced Germany's racism and military conquests. Now the hour of judgment seemed to have come for their own empires. Genuine believers in the old system, including groups as diverse as the Rhodesian and Algerian settlers and professional French army officers, increasingly found themselves in intellectual isolation. The bulk of Western opinion makers had lost faith in their imperial mission and no longer possessed a living creed which would justify colonialism.

A new generation of African nationalists in the meantime began to clarify the issues. They rejected assimilation, demanded independence outright, and tried to organize mass movements to secure these ends. The Fifth Pan-African Congress, held at Manchester, England, toward the end of 1945, stood out as a landmark on the road to decolonization. The congress assembled a few months after the British Labour Party had gained power, and it displayed a mood of striking optimism. The most significant thing about this gathering was the plebeian character of its membership. In addition to learned leaders from the Western Hemisphere, there were representatives from political, trade-union, and farmers' organizations in Africa; there were many nationalist-minded men, including future African leaders such as Nkrumah and Jomo Kenyatta. The congress marked the beginning of a new era in pan-Africanism, its transformation from a protest movement of Western European and American Negroes against inequality to an African-led movement for the ending of colonial rule.[10] The congress adopted a philosophy of quasi-Marxist socialism and vigorously denounced Western rule. Its resolutions now denied the progressive character of colonialism; the congress members—unlike men such as Horton or Johnson in the past—asserted that the advent of British, French, and Belgian dominion had brought social regression instead of progress. Colonialism rested on systematic exploitation; devices like indirect rule, partnership, guardianship, and the mandate system could not serve the political wishes of the people. Alien domination, in the delegates' view, had inhibited the industrialization of West Africa, with the result that living standards had fallen below subsistence level. Africans were being robbed of their land; the administrations had prevented the formation of independent trade-union and cooperative movements, operating without official interference. Foreign monopolies had seized Africa's mining wealth; West Africa's foreign trade was virtually controlled by a clique of white merchants; the preva-

10 Wallerstein, "Pan-Africanism as Protest," pp. 142–143.

lence of monocultures in colonial Africa proved the colonial powers' incapacity for government. Alien rule had failed to improve the health, education, or nutrition of the people; organized Christianity in West Africa was identified with this political and economic exploitation. There was only one solution—complete and absolute independence.

The interesting feature about these arguments is that they became more uncompromising in tone precisely at a time when the Western powers had become more intent on reform. In Northern Rhodesia, for instance, the British Labour government itself promoted trade unionism for Africans who had not hitherto formed labor organizations of their own. White settlers clamored for the creation of secondary industries; white union leaders agitated for boons such as the eight-hour day, from which African workmen also benefited. After World War II the provision of medical, agricultural, educational, and other social services for the colonies steadily improved. The colonizers' efforts, however, could not meet the "revolution of rising expectations"; they may to some extent even have added to the ferment they were trying to prevent. Pan-Africanist polemics, which mirrored these discontents, superficially bore a Leninist tinge, but orthodox Communist influence in fact remained small. If bibliographies may be said to provide an intellectual pedigree, the selected reading lists furnished by the Pan-African Congress is conclusive. Recommended reading included American Negro scholars such as Du Bois, West African politicians such as Obafemi Awolowo, liberal British colonial administrators and scholars such as Lugard, and, above all, British reformists—Rita Hinden, Lord Olivier, Leonard Woolf, and Norman Leys—whose somewhat pragmatic cast of mind influenced politically conscious Africans in the English-speaking areas more than any other political philosophy.

In French Africa political thinking at first took shape in relative isolation from that of English-speaking Africa. Educated people from Bamako were much better informed about events in Bordeaux than in Bulawayo. Cultured Africans in Lagos knew more about what was happening in London than in Lomé. The main port of entry for outside ideas was Senegal on the West Coast, where for many years several African communes had enjoyed the full privileges of French citizenship. In the late 1920s a Senegal Social Party came into being. In the 1930s Senegalese socialists took part in the French popular front; the popular-front regime gave an impetus to political and labor-union organization in other territories besides Senegal. A number of socialists and even a few Communists obtained official positions in French West Africa, especially as teachers. The new

French-speaking African elite thus learned to adapt the theoretical framework derived from Jaurès and Lenin to their own local problems. African politicians played some part in French metropolitan politics, in a way that would have been unthinkable in the highly decentralized British African empire.[11]

The war years and their aftermath saw a number of Communist successes. In 1943 General de Gaulle's Free French government took over power from the Vichy administration in West and North Africa. For tactical reasons, De Gaulle cooperated with the Communists, who formed various groups for Communist study in African cities such as Dakar, Bamako, and Conakry. Between 1945 and 1947, French Communist participation in a tripartite government at Paris provided further opportunities for infiltration, but the Communists at the same time found themselves in a serious quandary. As participants in a "bourgeois" government, they had to give temporary support to attempts at maintaining the French hold over Algeria and Indochina. (The Communists could come out in open support of the Viet Minh only after they had been expelled from the French coalition government in 1947.) Many African nationalists thus came to look upon European Communists as just one more group of white politicians who manipulated Africans for their own purposes.[12] Communists, for their part, stuck to Stalin's intransigent view that African nationalists merely represented a petty bourgeoisie incapable of genuinely revolutionary action, and hence they failed to make full use of their opportunities.

French-speaking Africa also acquired a different literary and philosophical tradition from that of British Africa. The British, on the whole, did not aim at cultural assimilation. Their empire remained decentralized; the African reaction to their rule generally took political rather than literary forms. The French had a dual political tradition which oscillated between assimilation on the one hand and association on the other. The assimilationists were centralizers, heirs to revolutionary and Jacobin ways of thought; they looked to an empire of "a hundred million Frenchmen" who would enjoy the blessings of the French Revolution and also form an effective counterweight to Germany. The advocates of association, many of them traditionalists or royalists, held fast to the Girondin tradition of decentralization; they believed in provincial and local loyalties and, like the centralizers, carried their creed to the colonies. French methods

---

[11] Thomas L. Hodgkin, *African Political Parties: An Introductory Guide* (Harmondsworth, Middlesex, Eng., 1961), especially pp. 39–40.

[12] See, for instance, George Padmore, *Pan-Africanism or Communism? The Coming Struggle for Africa* (London, 1956).

of government were influenced by these competing concepts of government and shaped further by local needs or the impact of domineering personalities on the spot. In practice, French methods of rule usually differed less from the British ways than Paris politicians asserted. France also practiced various forms of indirect rule, and association generally took pride of place over integration; in the end much of the assimilationist tradition remained confined to the French Left.[13] Nevertheless, there were real differences; the French did produce a relatively numerous group of Gallicized West Africans who, together with French-speaking West Indian Negroes, played an important part in the literary and political life of Paris. In 1939 Aimé Césaire, a Negro writer from Martinique, wrote his poem "Cahiers d'un retour au pays natal," in which he first used the term *négritude*.[14]

Négritude, the cult of "blackness," struck an answering chord among West African intellectuals. There was a new nationalism, ill-defined, but tinged with romantic European notions extolling the deep spiritual qualities of the poor, the downtrodden, and the primitive; this fused with the French revolutionary tradition which gave a profoundly ethical significance to the real or supposed characteristic of peasants and proletarians. This romantic creed appealed precisely to those intellectuals most strongly exposed to French cultural assimilation; it gave a special coloring to the French West African campaign against imperialism and extended the struggle into the literary and philosophical sphere in a way which more pragmatic English-speaking pan-Africanists had never envisaged.

The outstanding apostle of the new faith was Léopold Sédar Senghor, a Senegalese poet-politician. Senghor was educated at French lycées at Dakar and Paris; he became a teacher and subsequently took a distinguished part in French politics. Later he rose to be the undisputed leader of his own country. Senghor could read German as well as French and was deeply influenced by German romantic thought. He also owed much to the philosophy of Maurice Barrès, a French nationalist and conservative man of letters who proclaimed the values of inherited folkways, of French provincial life as against the soulless centralizing capital, and who wrote of the unbreakable bonds between the living and the dead.[15] Senghor saw

[13] The main exception in this respect were French right-wing advocates of *Algérie française*.

[14] Wallerstein, "Pan-Africanism as Protest," p. 144.

[15] For this and other aspects of Franco-African cultural relations, see Jacques Louis Hymans, "L'élaboration de la pensée de Léopold Sédar Senghor: Esquisse d'un itinéraire intellectuel" (doctoral dissertation, University of Paris, 1964).

the doctrine of *négritude* as the direct outcome of French assimilationist policies. Africans might learn mathematics in the French tongue, but they should never lose their black spirituality. They must continue on their fervent quest for the Holy Grail, their "collective soul." "Its whereabouts was pointed out to us by that handful of freelance thinkers—writers, artists, ethnologists, and prehistorians—who bring about cultural revolutions in France. It was, to be quite precise, our teachers of Ethnology who introduced us to the considerable body of work already achieved in the understanding of Africa, by the University of Oxford."[16]

From these writers, artists, and teachers, Senghor continued, Africans learned how the slave trade and the early years of colonization ravaged Africa like a bush fire, wiping out images and values in one vast carnage. The world's loss was all the greater, since Negro civilization had flourished in the upper paleolithic age, and Africans had helped to make the neolithic revolution which so profoundly affected the technology of early man. The roots of African civilization had, however, retained their vigor and would once again produce new grass and green branches. The key to the understanding of Africa lay in *négritude,* the whole complex of civilized values—cultural, economic, social, and political—which characterized the African Negro world. These values were formed essentially by intuitive reason. This sentient reason expressed itself emotionally through that self-surrender, that coalescence of subject and object, the archetypal images of the collective soul—above all through primordial rhythms, synchronized with those of the cosmos. The sense of communion, the gift of mythmaking and of rhythm, were the essential elements of *négritude* which observers would find indelibly stamped on all the works and activities of the black man.

From the political standpoint, *négritude* broadened the attack on imperialism. Padmore had censured the colonial powers for bolstering up outworn chieftainships and decadent social institutions and for not westernizing Africa with sufficient speed. Senghor now blamed the white man for doing precisely the opposite—for brutally destroying indigenous cultures and robbing the people of their soul. In theory the two charges seemed contradictory; in practice they fused into an all-out condemnation of imperialism. In 1956 the editors of *Présence Africaine,* a Negro literary journal, thus convened a World Congress of Black Writers and Artists at Paris, the first major pan-African meeting since 1945. The congress had a cultural purpose, but the poets backed the politicians in arguing that political independence

[16] Léopold Sédar Senghor, "What Is 'Négritude'?" *West Africa,* November 4, 1961, p. 1211.

was the first requisite for a cultural renaissance. *Négritude* concepts thus blended with the more traditional critiques of empire, the humanitarian and reformist views and those of the Leninist and romantic nationalists. The new anti-imperialism adopted selected arguments from past European Continental attacks on Anglo-Saxon supremacy and the alleged softness of "Anglo-Americans." Disillusionment with aesthetically or socially repulsive aspects of urban industrial civilization was fused with attacks on capitalism. Imperialism now became a slogan, a word of reproach endowed with so many different and sometimes contradictory meanings that exact definition was impossible. Fundamentally, however, this protest was clear enough. African nationalists wanted to stand on their own feet; they demanded international respect. "Economic penetration, cultural assimilation, ideological domination, psychological infiltration, and subversive activities" all seemed dangers against which the continent must stand on guard.[17] Home rule was not enough; Africans must also achieve cultural independence and at last face the white powers on terms of ideological equality.

[17] Kwame Nkrumah, *I Speak of Freedom: A Statement of African Ideology* (New York, 1961), p. 128.

9. Communism, Colonialism, and Neocolonialism

The development of pan-Africanism presents some striking parallels with the rise of Balkan nationalisms in the late eighteenth and nineteenth centuries. During their stay abroad Balkan exiles, like expatriate Africans of a later generation, learned how to ask new questions and helped to transmit new ideas to their homeland. In Eastern Europe foreign or foreign-educated scholars played an important part in recording the traditions of the past which then helped to cement a national view of history. In twentieth-century Africa, European anthropologists, ethnohistorians, and archaeologists performed a similar function. Balkan and African nationalists alike commonly placed great stress on the glories of days gone by. Serbians mused over the splendors of Stefan Dušan's tsardom; Gold Coast students drew new inspiration from the long-lost magnificence of Mali and Ghana. Thinkers of both groups often displayed the same curiously ambivalent outlook toward Europe. Some unreservedly wanted to emulate the institutions of Britain, France, and Germany; others concurred in the sentiments of Laza Kostić, a nineteenth-century Serb writer who admonished his countrymen not to seek "salvation in the West, where the shopkeeper and the broker rule."[1]

Both types of nationalism commonly displayed a profound belief in redemption through suffering. African theorists of *négritude* envisaged the history of their continent as one vast martyrdom, where weeping blacks bore the burden of the world. The new nations might lack the well-filled treasuries or the far-flung navies of older countries, but surely they possessed something infinitely more precious—a greater humanity and a deeper spirituality than their neighbors. Most

[1] L. S. Stavrianos, "The Influence of the West on the Balkans," in Charles Jelavich and Barbara Jelavich (eds.), *The Balkans in Transition* (Berkeley, Calif., 1963), p. 210.

emergent nation states, moreover, produced a *terra irredenta*. The southern Irish dreamed of annexing Ulster (where the majority did not wish for Dublin rule). The Serbs looked to the southern Slav territories of the Hapsburg monarchy. Modern pan-Africanists turned their eyes toward Angola, Mozambique, and South Africa, which they saw as a part of Africa's bleeding soil, groaning for liberation.

Here the European parallels end. The Balkan Peninsula, heir to the Byzantine tradition, played a leading part in the development of European civilization up to the Renaissance and the Turkish conquest; it was only after about the fifteenth century that the cultural disparity between Western and Southeastern Europe began to widen. The culture gap between sub-Saharan Africa and Europe, however, was not only much greater, but also of much more ancient origin. Whereas Eastern European nationalism had had since the eighteenth century strong religious foundations—a man's creed determined his nationality—in sub-Saharan Africa neither the religion of the European missionaries nor the ancient spirit creeds could serve as a cement for nation building. Tribal systems of various kinds have persisted to the present day, whereas in most parts of precolonial Africa economic contact between Europe and the interior remained of a slender kind. The Balkans, on the other hand, from the eighteenth and nineteenth century on developed new middle classes of their own, which showed a strong preference for Western ideas in the political sphere. In Africa indigenous urban and entrepreneurial traditions remained weak. In East and Central Africa the bulk of new enterprise owed its origins to white planters, to industrialists and mineowners, and to Indian shopkeepers. Even in West Africa, European merchant houses and Lebanese village traders played a major role in economic development. These differences, of course, should not be exaggerated. West Africa, for instance, also had trading cities of long standing. Many eighteenth-century West Africans made money in the slave traffic; later on Nigerian traders—usually ex-slaves—developed the commerce in palm oil.[2] The Gold Coast subsequently bred a vigorous and relatively prosperous peasantry who planted cocoa and often educated their sons on the proceeds of trade, agriculture, and moneylending.

The bulk of modern African nationalist politicians, on the other hand, started as schoolteachers or as minor government officials and clerks; they owed their education to foreign missionaries or to colonial government bursaries. They possessed little experience in

[2] See Kenneth Onwuka Dike, *Trade and Politics in the Niger Delta, 1830–1885: An Introduction to the Economic and Political History of Nigeria* (Oxford, 1956).

independent economic enterprise and were naturally inclined toward *étatiste* solutions which accorded with their previous experience and expectations in life. Over most of twentieth-century Africa westernization came from above, from the colonial powers, from white settlers or other foreign agents. The African nationalist's view of Europe inevitably became more ambivalent than that of the Balkan revolutionary. The *comitadji* despised his Turkish overlord as backward, but no African nationalist could ever regard the British, the Belgians, or the French with the same kind of contempt. The Balkan peoples, moreover, had a much richer cultural equipment. Throughout the harshest days of Ottoman domination they retained an ancient linguistic and historical tradition. Whereas the Greek Orthodox Church continued to transmit a sacred liturgy and a tradition of literacy which only Ethiopia and some islamized portions of the Sudan could faintly match in black Africa, the memory in Africa of medieval empires like Zimbabwe had more of an archaeological than a popular luster. Moreover, it was European scholars who dug up these ancient ruins. It was European policy makers who created the territorial units which subsequently sought independence as sovereign states. Northern Rhodesia and the Gold Coast owed their very existence to colonial administrators. They lacked a common language or a common precolonial history. African nationalists subsequently tried to "naturalize" these European creations by tagging nativistic name plates such as Mali or Ghana onto the colonialists' handiwork; black party secretaries nonetheless had to start where white district commissioners left off.

The new nationalities, devoid of linguistic, religious, or ethnic homogeneity, for the most part lacked the images, with all their emotional content, that a Serbian or Greek motherland could provide to its Balkan citizens. The purely colonial origins of these artificial states had to be ignored, and Africans found themselves committed to the massive task of reshaping the past in order to forge the future. The very nature of politics itself put a premium on a visionary approach that sought for rapid, "voluntarist" solutions. Pan-Africanists of the twentieth century all longed for unity, for power, for prestige— assets which Gambia or Zambia could not provide on their own. The only ideological tools at their disposal were a common emphasis on skin color and the common memory of imperial rule. The real or assumed excellences of *négritude,* the varieties of African socialism, and the iniquities of colonialism formed the main bonds which might link up congeries of new states, geographically dispersed, economically underdeveloped, and plagued with divergent political interests. Most important of all, pan-Africanism developed at a time when liberalism had already declined in the West and socialism in different guises had become the major ideological force in Europe. In the 1920s and 1930s European socialists were readier than conservatives to mingle with expatriate Africans on terms of personal intimacy; they would listen to claims for national independence with much more sympathy than the Establishment. Socialism appealed to the poor; Africans regarded themselves as the underprivileged of the universe. In all the Afro-Asian states of the twentieth century socialism thus enjoyed the same intellectual reputation which liberalism had commanded in the emergent states of Southeastern Europe and Latin America a hundred years earlier.[3] Most pan-African and African nationalist thought became tinged with collectivist strains; henceforth most African politicians could say with identical conviction, "We are all socialists now!"

In the struggle for the minds of Africa, Soviet communism thus enjoyed a number of natural advantages which Western creeds could not easily match. The Soviet system was totalitarian and Messianic in character; Russian statesmen wielded infinitely greater power within their country than their Western counterparts; moreover, they gained renown both as decision makers and as party ideologues. These achievements were greatly prized by African leaders like Nkrumah, who similarly played a threefold role in running a party, governing a country, and elaborating a political philosophy to explain and justify his activities. There was the same emphasis on the "struggle," the "battle," and the "combat." As Alexander Dallin, a modern expert on Soviet affairs, puts it, "Particularly to the young intelligentsia, trade unionists, and 'activists' of the new Africa—themselves in part susceptible to an elitist, authoritarian, and manipulative outlook and impatient for rapid and dramatic change—the Soviet experience must loom as an admirable accomplishment."[4]

Communists spoke in the same clear, resonant tones that once rang through Western Christian missionary propaganda in Africa; there was none of the apologetic note that now characterized the bulk of Western scholarship and diplomatic statements about Europe's imperialist past. There was none of the Western cultural guilt feeling. There was a simple and, on the face of it, uncomplicated faith that promised ultimate victory. The Russians, moreover, were unburdened by a colonial past in Africa; their own territorial expansion in Europe

[3] For a romantic statement of this view see Frantz Fanon, *Les damnés de la terre,* preface by Jean-Paul Sartre (Cahiers libres, Nos. 27–28; Paris, 1961).

[4] Alexander Dallin, "The Soviet Union: Political Activity," in Zbigniew Brzezinski (ed.), *Africa and the Communist World* (Stanford, Calif., 1963), p. 44.

and Asia—like that of nineteenth-century America—was land-bound; Russian annexations did not suffer from pollution by salt water. African nationalists, like Hobson before them, were thus willing to make excuses for Soviet expansion which were not applied to Western conquests based on seapower. Between 1945 and 1956 the Russians succeeded fairly effectively in switching all accusations of imperialism against the Western powers. The Soviet conquest of countries such as Latvia and Lithuania was forgotten. The NATO states themselves, for all practical purposes, seemed to agree that the Communist occupation of Europe beyond the Elbe was irreversible.

The military stalemate in Europe, and the Westerners' unwillingness or inability to carry the "cold war" into Russian-occupied Europe, now appeared to imply that the world's uncommitted nations would determine the world's future balance of power. The charge of colonialism was thus largely confined to the remnants of Western overseas empire. In the postwar period the Eastern-bloc states, following the precedent set by Turkey's expulsion of the Greek minority after World War I, effected mass transfers of population, unparalleled in scale though not in cruelty; some 20 million people were shifted from regions as far afield as Eastern Poland and East Prussia, Sakhalin, and Silesia, Karelia, and the Crimea. These expulsions, carried out on a race rather than a class basis, succeeded in establishing clear ethnic boundaries. Nevertheless, world opinion in the main remained content to confine diatribes against apartheid or segregation to the limited disabilities imposed on dark-skinned people in southern Africa and the United States. Neither Western propaganda nor the Western intelligentsia as a whole proved able or willing to oppose this massive misrepresentation of facts. For the great majority of African intellectuals the Communist regimes of Eastern Europe possessed the legitimacy derived from a universal suffrage, however objectionable some Communist practices might appear in other respects. The electorate might be able to vote for only one party, but each citizen had the right to cast his ballot, which supposedly assured him of rights equal to those of his neighbors.

African politicians thereby projected their Western-inherited traditions onto a very different screen. In British colonial territories elections for the local legislature genuinely influenced political decision making. The polling booth was a real center of power, not part of a political façade to disguise the power monopoly obtaining in a single-party dictatorship. Under the Union Jack, however, the franchise had generally been restricted by property, educational, or other qualifications. The British limited the franchise precisely because the franchise possessed real importance. The struggle against the colonial power therefore revolved to a considerable extent about the right to cast the ballot. The principle of "one man—one vote," adopted by all African leaders, stood out to some extent as a symbol of emancipation from traditional ties. The slogan emphasized individual rights as against tribal obligations. Manhood suffrage, linked to militantly populist slogans, assumed an almost sacramental quality in the eyes of emergent Africans. Communist power in the Eastern European states was anointed with the triple oil of universal suffrage, social purpose, and a revolutionary phraseology. Its legitimacy was not challenged. Many African as well as Western intellectuals adopted the curious double standard whereby the peoples of Angola were entitled to self-determination, but not those of Eastern Germany—for East Germans, after all, were entitled to the vote.

Soviet policy, however, lacked sufficient flexibility to make full use of these natural advantages. Stalin on the whole regarded the colonial struggle as a sideshow. He apparently felt convinced that communism would win Africa as a result of political victory in Europe and used the colonial issue to embarrass the West in the United Nations. He tried to divide the NATO allies by claiming that American millionaires were endeavoring to push out the older capitalists from the colonies in order to replace the rule of francs and pounds sterling by the tyranny of the dollar. He insisted that only the working class could lead the struggle for independence and that only the Communist Party could direct the proletarian liberation campaign. Since Africa contained even fewer Communists than industrial workers, this policy was doomed to failure. Russians for a time nevertheless persisted in their mistakes. Their theorists at first refused to recognize the realities of decolonization in countries where Western powers had relinquished their rule. Moscow believed that new nations such as India, and later Ghana, had acquired no more than a fictitious independence, since Western financiers could still pull the strings from behind the scenes. The revived "two-camps" philosophy of the world could not envisage effective neutrality; whoever did not support the "forces of peace" must necessarily be their enemy. The Soviet rulers moreover suffered from a habit of mind which made them debate in public the strategy and tactics of revolution. Open discussion continued on the problem of achieving a proletarian revolution through shifting class alliances, in which the confederates of today would be destroyed the morning after, until the vanguard of the proletariat wielded undivided power. Nationalists such as Nkrumah found themselves labeled lackeys of imperialism, and even the most progressive leaders of African nationalism were judged unfit to defeat the capitalist enemy. Soviet strategists also found difficulties in appreciating the essential characteristics of African society. These societies continued to differ sharply, not only from those of Western and Eastern Europe, but also from those of Asia, with the result that many of the revolutionary analogies employed proved fallacious.

The second phase of Communist activity in Africa grew out of the Bandung Conference of 1955, held two years after Stalin's death. Russia did not participate in the meeting; China did, and Moscow realized that, if it was to have any influence in Asia and Africa, it would have to come to terms with the new anticolonial movements, led mostly by non-Communists. The African states were in the main moving toward independence by nonrevolutionary methods; hence the Soviets had to change their view toward the national bourgeoisie of the new countries. In 1956 the Communist Party Congress admitted that independence could be achieved under nationalist middle-class leadership. Africa now assumed a much higher priority in Soviet planning. Non-Communist leaders were praised; the Soviets cooperated with bourgeois governments; the local pro-Soviet Marxist-Leninist parties pleaded for "united fronts of independence" to build a "national democracy" that would ultimately serve as a steppingstone to workers' and peasants' governments on the Soviet model; at the same time the West was continually attacked and accused, in the accepted Leninist fashion, of gross exploitation.

In the ideological sphere the Soviets strengthened their hand by improving their academic standing in African studies. In the late 1940s Soviet Africanists had begun a more forceful polemic against colonial rule on the one hand and against "bourgeois" Africanists on the other. The latter's factual material was used; but Western authors were accused of deliberately falsifying the African's past, of belittling the black man's cultural achievements and innate capacities.[5] Even left-leaning Western anthropologists found themselves labeled—much to their surprise—as agents of imperialism. This ideological campaign, cast in academic dress, suffered, however, from numerous weaknesses. Cadres were inadequate. Soviet African studies largely remained, and to some extent still remain, based on secondary material. Soviet scholars confined most of their efforts to forcing Western research into the framework of Marxism-Leninism, without making new factual discoveries of their own. In addition, there was dispersion of effort. Communist spokesmen later agreed that until the Twentieth Congress of the Communist Party their academic workers had held "rigid and dogmatic views," that they had neglected serious work in their areas or, at any rate, had lacked the necessary sophistication. After 1957, however, academic work was adequately coordinated and

[5] See David Morison, *The U.S.S.R. and Africa* (London, 1964), pp. 59–72.

subsidized. In 1959 the Africa Institute opened its doors in Moscow, and Soviet propaganda made further advances in the academic sphere.

Throughout this campaign Moscow's overriding object remained ultimate "nonexistence" for the capitalist West; but the long-term liquidation of the enemy would be effected by "salami-slicing" tactics rather than by open assault. The Soviets now believed that the balance of economic and military power was inevitably shifting against NATO. The capitalists, in their view, could no longer deal with Russia from a position of superior strength, and the nuclear stalemate was bound to assist the Russian cause. The collapse of the colonial system was genuinely improving the strength of the Eastern bloc. As Soviet strategists gave increasing emphasis to nonmilitary methods of waging the class struggle, they became more willing to admit the "historically progressive nature" of the colonial independence movements. African socialism, pan-Africanism, and African nationalism, of course, continued to be regarded as bourgeois or petty-bourgeois ideologies, characteristic of countries which as yet lacked a class-conscious and cohesive proletariat. Such movements could, however, play a temporarily progressive role. Had Engels not welcomed the Italian bourgeois revolution in the nineteenth century? Italy did not then possess, in the Marxist interpretation of the day, a numerous militant working class; the Italian bourgeoisie was not yet frightened into political timidity, and heroes like Garibaldi could accordingly still achieve miracles.[6] The African independence movements, the product of an even more backward economy, might therefore play an analogous role. In 1961 an authoritative Moscow commentator explained that even though the newly liberated countries for the most part continued to remain in the world capitalist economy, they no longer formed the rear and reserve of imperialism.[7] This contention was difficult to uphold on purely Leninist principles, but it showed greater political common sense than Soviet theoreticians had displayed earlier.

Imperialism nevertheless continued, in the Soviet view, to remain a formidable foe. True enough, the capitalist powers had lost a number of important instruments for exploiting the people of Africa. Since the breakdown of colonial rule, the Western bourgeoisie could no longer expropriate land, forcibly seize mineral wealth or mining rents, impose taxation in favor of a foreign administration, or practice similar extortions. As L. Goncharov, a modern Soviet academician, put it, the imperialists still wielded powerful weapons. The new form of imperialism, called "neocolonialism," followed seven guiding princi-

---

[6] Friedrich Engels, *Über die Gewaltstheorie: Gewalt und Ökonomie bei der Herstellung des neuen deutschen Reiches* (Berlin, 1946), pp. 22–23.

[7] Dallin, "The Soviet Union," p. 12.

ples. The colonialists wanted to maintain the domination of foreign capital in the new states and prevent the breakup of the colonial structure of their economies. They wished to preserve their political bonds with their ex-colonial wards by the formation of communities or alliances, by imposing cooperation agreements with the young states to undermine their sovereignty, by maintaining garrisons and military bases, by using the administrative machinery inherited from the colonial regime as an instrument of policy, by wielding ideological influence, or by using outdated legislation which hindered the development of political democracy. The imperialists aimed at continued profits from colonial countries. They therefore wished to keep the ex-colonial countries backward and to limit their economic activities to the production of raw materials.[8] Soviet writers supported this thesis by an elaborate vilification campaign cast in academic dress. The Mau Mau uprising was represented as an invention of British imperialists who wanted an excuse to suppress a nationalist movement. The British were said to have provoked the shooting that occurred during the labor disturbances at Enugu, Nigeria, in 1948. Western negotiators engaged in independence talks were inspired only by the worst of motives; Western imperialism was devoid of any constructive elements whatever. Soviet writers at the same time drew a sharp distinction between tsarist imperialism in the nineteenth century and Western colonial systems in the twentieth. The former was regarded as a partial good in the sense of leading the peoples of Asia beyond the stages of tribalism and feudalism. The latter was an unmitigated evil. The majority of Soviet writers almost wholly ignored Western achievements in radically transforming African life, though such changes were clearly taken into account in the balance sheet of Russian imperialism in Asia.[9] Writers such as Goncharov made no reference to the economic revolution, to industries set up by Western entrepreneurs in Africa, to factory laws, or to other evidence of social progress. They continued to see Western imperialism as a satanic enterprise without any redeeming features whatever, a point of view difficult to reconcile with their own dialectic.

The Chinese Communists essentially agreed with this diagnosis. Nationalist as well as Communist China had always been opposed to white empire builders; Chinese of all shades of opinion had always

[8] L. Goncharov, "New Forms of Colonialism in Africa," *Journal of Modern African Studies,* I (December, 1963), 467–474.

[9] Mary Holdsworth, "The Application of Soviet Nationality Theory to Africa in Soviet Writing," in Kenneth Robinson and Frederick Madden (eds.), *Essays in Imperial Government; Presented to Margery Perham* (Oxford, 1963), pp. 209–226.

resented the "unequal treaties" forced by foreign barbarians upon the proud Chinese Empire. Chinese and Russian Communists alike, despite their internal differences, applied the same analytical tools to the problems of Western colonialism. Both agreed that "peaceful coexistence" meant the intensification of the class struggle. Both considered the emergent countries as a major theater of operations against imperialism. Both asserted that the United States had replaced Western Europe as the mainstay of colonialism. Both argued that the class struggle justified "wars of national liberation," even in such formally independent countries as Laos or Cameroun. Both were willing to make temporary alliances with bourgeois or even feudalist countries; China established friendly relations with Pakistan and Russia courted Afghanistan. Both powers ultimately aimed at a worldwide dictatorship of parties, centrally coordinated and all equally committed to Marxism-Leninism. China and the Soviet Union disagreed not so much over the strategy of the class struggle, but over tactics and over the vital question of who was to control the world Communist movement. Neither country would allow the other to gain a monopoly of influence within the revolutionary movements of the "third world."[10] Hence the two powers were forced to outbid one another in a new kind of socialist competition on a global scale. In the resulting battle of words, China used a more militant terminology, sometimes infused with a latent antiwhite racism, but Russian and Chinese writers allocated the same central place to neocolonialism in their analysis of the contemporary world. The Chinese professed to fight the same enemy, but, lacking the ability to provide much economic assistance to the new countries, they stressed the importance of military uprising. Their doctrine equated the underdeveloped countries of Asia and Africa with the world's countryside and the industrialized states with a city— a curious analysis of a situation in which a "rural" country like their own had to buy wheat surpluses produced by a "city" country like Canada. The Chinese nevertheless insisted that successful revolution in the world's rural periphery would isolate the urban lands and ultimately play a vital part in the liquidation of capitalism in its Western bastions. At the same time Chinese theoreticians argued that the new countries could learn more from the forced industrialization of China, a poverty-stricken, underdeveloped nation like those of Africa, than

[10] Brian Crozier, "The Struggle for the Third World," *International Affairs,* XL (July, 1964), 440–452. There were, of course, also disputes between the two countries. The Chinese resented what they regarded as inadequate military and economic assistance from the Soviet Union; they censured the Soviets' failure to support Chinese policy over Formosa; they disliked Soviet help given to India. There were also differences of opinion over boundary claims and other matters.

from the experiences of Russia. The dual nature of the assault from both Peking and Moscow on neocolonialism gave the Communists the unintended advantage of conducting a dual strategy; enforced bipolarity enabled the two great conflicting parties to effect some degree of "specialization of labor" in their assault on the Western position in Africa, but to some extent it also weakened their appeal.[11]

The concept of neocolonialism, for very different reasons, also gained almost universal acceptance among the African elites in the emergent countries, sensitive as they were about their newly won independence, suspicious of their former masters, and defensive about their countries' often unimpressive record in social and economic matters. Neocolonialism implied that the former rulers had not really left; they were still pulling the strings from behind the scenes. The slogan, like post-Versailles German charges against the *Zinsknecht-schaft,* the foreign servitude of debts imposed upon the Fatherland, could always rally nationalist opinion against an assumed enemy abroad. Neocolonialism likewise occupied an important place in the thinking of many non-Communist socialists and liberals in the West. The charges proved on some occasions a useful tactical device against domestic opponents and on others a valuable blanket term to give expression to a national guilt feeling.

Communist ideological warfare, however, was not wholly successful in switching the accusation of neocolonialism toward Western capitalists alone. Both Russian and Chinese Communists had also made enemies, sometimes by unwise forms of intervention or by raising economic hopes which they could not meet. The Chinese seizure of Tibet, for instance, somewhat tarnished Peking's image. Interbloc controversy, though inadequately exploited by the West, similarly did some harm to the Communist position. Communist theoreticians of both schools, moreover, weakened their standing by criticizing all forms of pan-Africanism not based on a socialist solution. Soviet writers had some hard things to say about *négritude* as a reactionary, petty-bourgeois ideology. They denied the pan-Africanists' contention that indigenous African society was classless in character and insisted that there was a latent conflict between the national bourgeoisie and proletariat even in Africa. More important still, even left-wing African governments like that of Guinea found unexpected political and economic difficulties in dealing with Communist countries. Some of the

[11] Franz H. Michael, "China in Afrika," in Friedrich-Ebert-Stiftung, *Studien zur Aktivität des Ostblocks in den Entwicklungsländern* (Schriftenreihe der Forschungsstelle; Hanover, 1963), pp. 65–78, and Robert A. Scalapino, "Sino-Soviet Competition in Africa," *Foreign Affairs* (New York), XLII, No. 4 (July, 1964), 640–654.

ablest African theorists thus began to speak of a post-Marxist revolution which must avoid the errors of both capitalist and Communist exploitation and which should range the proletarian nations against *all* the more highly industrialized states, whatever their ideology. Russian economic practices in Eastern Europe themselves came under attack. The Soviet Union, some Africans argued, was creating a new kind of economic imperialism. "By substituting barter exchanges, with profits going in but one direction, for the monetary relations of the capitalist market, the dominant Soviet economy, like any other dominant economy, reinforces its dependence on the economies it controls, and creates, finally, an untenable situation leading to ruptures, silent or explosive."[12] The realities of foreign trade, the argument continued, showed that Soviet theories merely formed a screen for exploitation on a collectivist basis—in other words, Soviet communism might well be the highest stage of imperialism.

These charges, of course, did not vindicate the Western varieties of imperialism, which occidental scholarship and diplomacy usually no longer felt inclined to defend. Westerners were more concerned to rebut accusations against neocolonialism, to deny charges that Paris, London, and Washington were aiming at another form of indirect rule, more sophisticated and therefore more insidious than the kind once practiced by Lugard. Western scholars at the same time began to discount the importance of old-style imperialism; they lengthened the time scales of African history, thereby reducing the chronological import of the imperialist period. They also tried to avoid all ethnocentric interpretations of the African past, and, laboring under a profound sense of cultural guilt, many Western scholars berated their own society for its alleged cultural ethnocentricity. In so doing, they ignored the fact that a sympathetic interest in and a systematic study of alien cultures is a typical feature of modern Western civilization, rarely, if at all, paralleled in any other. It was, in fact, this very search for objective truth that drove Western scholars into the systematic study of African history.

Africans were put into the center of the stage, with the result that the imperial period now appeared to be but a short, and by no means the most important, chapter in a long and checkered story of African evolution. Decolonization now appeared but a reversion to older and well-tried models. Mid-Victorian Britain, went the argument, had aimed at trade, not dominion, security, not conquest. Territorial expansion into Africa appeared as a temporary phenomenon, set into motion by a concatenation of strategic and economic circumstances,

---

[12] See Mamadou Dia, *The African Nations and World Solidarity,* trans. from the French by Mercer Cook (London, 1962), p. 51.

by calculations derived from "a hardening of arteries and a hardening of hearts." The mid-Victorians' "imperialism of free trade," in this view, marked the golden age of British expansion. Late Victorian imperialism was the symptom of defeatism and decline.[13] Britain had always preferred to deal with independent nation states; the statesmen of the 1950s had thus merely continued the traditions of their predecessors a hundred years ago. Imperialism, in this view, seemed but a relic of a past, more irrelevant than shameful. As Sir Denis Brogan, a modern British writer, puts it, "There is no reason to believe that the case for imperialism (there was a case, there is a case) can be argued today."[14] Empire was both dead and damned, and its practitioners had taken their place amid the pomp of yesterday.

[13] Ronald E. Robinson and John Gallagher, *Africa and the Victorians: The Climax of Imperialism in the Dark Continent,* with Alice Denny (New York, 1961), pp. 462–472.

[14] Denis W. Brogan, "The Word That Lost Its Savour," *The Observer,* May 31, 1964.

PART TWO

Colonial Rule

10. Problems of African Historiography

The Negro, more than any other human type, has been marked out by his mental and physical characteristics as the servant of other races. There are, of course, exceptions. . . . But the Negro in a primitive state is a born slave. He is possessed of great physical strength, docility, cheerfulness of disposition, a short memory for sorrows and cruelties, and an easily aroused gratitude for kindness and just dealing. . . . Above all, he can toil hard under the hot sun and in the unhealthy climates of the torrid zone. He has little or no race-fellowships—that is to say, he has no sympathy for other Negroes . . . and, as he is usually a strong man and a good fighter, he has come into request not only as a labourer but as a soldier.*

Sir Harry Johnston, a great British empire builder, was a man of considerable culture and many accomplishments. His views were not those of a low-born Negro baiter; they reflected the prejudices of an age. Tribal Africans, in his view, were barbarous people who had never advanced beyond the first steps of civilization. For Johnston, the chief interest of African history therefore centered on the accomplishments of alien invaders of the Dark Continent. Opinions of this kind find a curious mirror image in the writings of influential Communist scholars today. Endre Sík, a Hungarian Marxist, thus believes that the precolonial peoples of Africa led a primitive life, that some were sunk in the lowest stage of barbarism, and that "scientific" history in Africa primarily revolves around the expansion, the inner contradictions, and the ultimate breakdown of alien, exploitative social systems like Western capitalism transplanted onto the soil of Africa.[1]

* Sir Harry Hamilton Johnston, *A History of the Colonization of Africa by Alien Races* (Cambridge, Eng., 1899), pp. 151–152.

[1] See, for instance, Endre Sík, *Histoire de l'Afrique noire*, I (Budapest, 1961), 17–20.

Such concepts still bedevil our understanding of Africa and its past. No account of the imperial impact on Africa can therefore be complete without listing some of the difficulties facing African historiography and examining the myths and misconceptions that distort the realities of Africa's past. During the last two generations, archaeologists, historians, linguists, and anthropologists have made much progress in reconstructing the earlier African past, but a great deal remains unknown. Many African societies were technologically backward and did not construct permanent settlements. Slash-and-burn cultivators or nomadic herdsmen did not require permanent buildings. The student of African history does not have at his disposal as many architectural monuments—ruins of ancient cities or castles, remnants of stone tablets or figurines—as are available to the majority of his colleagues specializing in early European history. There are exceptions; magnificent reminders of ancient African civilizations survive at Zimbabwe, Meroë, and elsewhere, but these ruins are confined to a limited number of regions, and archaeologists are more often reduced to reconstructing the past through the contents of prehistoric trash heaps. This is a difficult undertaking, for whereas artifacts survive, ideas and social systems do not. It is therefore all too easy to come to mistaken conclusions on the basis of inadequate evidence, especially since the more advanced African societies sometimes suffered sudden breaks in their tradition owing to the irruption of more barbarous neighbors.

Historians have tried to supplement this evidence with documents, but writings of precolonial African provenance, except in Arabic, are few and far between. Most early African societies lacked both the art of committing words to paper and a sufficient degree of labor specialization to maintain a literate intelligentsia. African literary languages were mainly confined to the Sudan and to the maritime cities of the African East Coast. Early Arab, Fulani, Hausa, and Swahili texts still survive to give some idea of earlier days. Future collectors will probably find additional manuscripts when they search for undiscovered documents in faraway countries such as Persia and Arabia; in addition, European archives will certainly yield further information on early Africa. Unfortunately the ravages of time have caused great gaps in these holdings. Old papers are preserved only with great difficulty in tropical countries where white ants and atmospheric humidity pose serious problems even to modern archivists. Early record keepers were far less equal to their task, and much material has been lost or destroyed.

Some historians therefore try to supplement these sources with indigenous folktales, heroic lays, genealogical tables, and personal reminiscences. Brilliant work is now being done at some institutions in correlating such information with knowledge drawn from old documents or from archaeological remains.[2] Such supporting material is, however, often scanty. There are of course exceptions. Many West African societies, for instance, have professional historical remembrancers who pass on their knowledge to their heirs by rote and who do manage to preserve some of their national traditions. But even the best memories falter; old men die; oral recollections are subject to distortion. Oral tradition of recent provenance has a good claim to be heard, and excursions into the more remote past may be significant in elucidating an image which profoundly affected later political relations, but as evidence of what actually happened, the tales are worthless without proper corroboration.

The use of anthropological material occasions similar difficulties. The study of primitive society was originally the preserve of armchair scholars. A writer, sitting in some European capital, laboriously pieced together accounts from sea captains, missionaries, and travelers who told of the strange customs practiced by outlandish tribes. These reports were analyzed, with the various social systems grouped according to some preconceived scheme of social evolution. Gradually the scissors-and-paste students gave way to those who were prepared to study preliterate societies at first hand. Under the impact of men like Malinowski and Radcliffe-Brown, for example, anthropologists from the 1920s on spent long periods with the people they wished to study, and indeed sometimes became almost naturalized citizens of "their villages." The new approach resulted in a major contribution to scholarship and greatly extended knowledge of primitive races and of social problems in general. Few historians nowadays venture into the field of African history without some background of anthropological knowledge. But anthropologists can have their biases, just like anyone else, and no two anthropologists give identical accounts of the same society. Many anthropologists in the past were not, moreover, particularly interested in history. Some were also too much inclined to study "their people" as a separate, self-sufficient entity. Anthropologists study the "customary modes of activity, clusters of ideas and institutionalised patterns of social relations, in communities or social aggregates sufficiently small in scale and simple in organisation to be comprehended as, and analysed as total working systems."[3]

2 For an excellent introduction see J. Vansina, R. Mauny, and L. V. Thomas (eds.), *The Historian in Africa: Studies Presented and Discussed* (4th International African Seminar, Dakar, Senegal, 1961; London, 1964).

3 Daryll Forde, "Social Anthropology in African Studies," *African Affairs*, special issue (Spring, 1965), p. 15.

Such is a distinguished British anthropologist's definition of his craft. But what exactly is a "total working system"? Even the most backward, and apparently most isolated, village communities may for centuries have been profoundly influenced by outside contacts, so that they can no longer be understood as self-sufficient communities. The more civilization advances, the greater is the importance of communications and migrations. Yet many anthropologists have been too much inclined, for instance, when studying an African village, to ignore the labor migrants who had left their homesteads for the cities, but who nevertheless still formed part of the community under investigation. Anthropological evidence, moreover, is not the same as historical evidence. Africans change just as other groups do; the tribal groups studied, say, during the 1920s, were as much the product of age-old social transformation as was our own industrial society. The rate of change may have been slower, but the members of a backward Bantu group living in some remote region of a modern African country simply cannot be identified with their remote ancestors of many hundred years ago.

From anthropology we go on to the more orthodox methods of historiography. Most chronicles of Africa appear in written records created during the colonial period, especially in government files, manuscripts of private provenance, or published works. Unfortunately, this evidence also has many gaps or is liable to distortion. Official records are particularly valuable, but the early period of colonial enterprise is usually understated. There were not many civil servants, and the people on the spot were usually more concerned with immediate tasks than with writing reports. White ants, rats, and careless or inefficient clerks have destroyed a good deal of material; much has been misfiled, lost, or burned. The more recent days, by contrast, are often overdocumented. The administrative revolution brought about by the expansion of the state machinery and the introduction of typewriters, cyclostyling machines, and other devices has filled the files with a mass of ephemeral material, the quality of which is in inverse ratio to its quantity.[4] Decolonization, moreover, may disrupt archival services; the new successor governments sometimes lack the interest, the men, or the money to maintain their old records. Historical investigators must conform to government-imposed rules of access, so that government files cannot usually be used to elucidate the more recent periods of colonial history. Historians also have to cope with the problems of coverage and bias. Sailors, traders, and civil servants were for the most part not interested in the structure of African so-

[4] See Lewis H. Gann, "Archives and the Study of Society," *Rhodes-Livingstone Journal,* No. 20 (1956), pp. 49–67.

ciety per se, but in accumulating information useful for their jobs. Early officials and soldiers were concerned with questions of supply and armaments. The bulk of the early Portuguese records relating to Mozambique, stemming from the beginning of the sixteenth century, are thus very prosaic; there are bills of lading, receipts, and returns of weapons and stores which read like odds and ends from a quartermaster's office. Traders were mainly interested in prices and profits or in other data of an immediately useful kind; it is not easy to use such material for the reconstruction of earlier African societies. The same applies to official files. Most of the early administrators were concerned with a very limited range of problems, such as the maintenance of law and order or the raising of revenue. Early records reflect the nature of this work and thus make the social historian's task extremely difficult. Indeed, the lack of available material will forever prevent the historian of precolonial or early colonial Africa from describing the societies of the time with the same wealth of detail and documentation which, say, a scholar like Elie Halévy could bring to bear on nineteenth-century England. It is only in comparatively recent periods, with the state tackling an ever-growing variety of tasks and with hosts of new record-producing bodies, that files have begun to yield large quantities of reliable data on historical questions.

Finally, we come to the problem of bias. Just how much credence should we give to the white man's and the brown man's writing about the black man? A great deal of the traditional information about Africa must be taken with a grain of salt. The early Arabs and Portuguese both were inclined to draw oversharp contrasts between the heathen and the converted. Pagans often appeared as the unredeemed villains of a morality play, whereas proselytes, by contrast, got an extra-good press. In the seventeenth century, for instance, Monomotapa, the head of the Karanga empire in what is now Rhodesia, concluded an alliance with the Portuguese and became temporarily converted to Christianity, with the result that contemporary best sellers endowed the Karanga monarch with fantastic splendor of the fairy-tale variety. Usually, however, distortion went the other way.

For many centuries Europeans, Americans, and, to a lesser extent, Muslims purchased Africans as slaves; the institution of slavery created an elaborate mythology which rationalized servitude by reference to the Africans' supposed racial inferiority. Stereotypes drawn from the experience of slavery were reinforced by the myth of Africa's infinite wealth. Frontier situations in every age seem to produce such exaggerated tales of boundless riches beyond the hills. Elizabethan and Jacobean Englishmen were shocked by the customs of tribal Irishmen. Ireland, many reflected, was a fair country, with excellent pastures magnificent woodlands, and splendid rivers and harbors; it could be made to prosper, but only if the savage Celtic clansmen were taught a stern lesson and their country was licked into shape. Victorian empire builders, endowed with a similar cultural and economic self-confidence, looked upon Africa the same way. Here was a tropical treasure-house, full of green, lush jungles of supposedly boundless fertility, and riches in gold and diamonds whose exploitation would put the profits of the Eastern spice trade into the shade. The "idle natives" neither would nor could exploit this wealth, but preferred to live a useless existence on the unlimited favors of nature and the labors of their wives. The realities of Africa, of course, bore little relationship to these stereotypes. Even the most luxuriant rain forests might suffer from leached soils and irregular rainfall. Mineral deposits underground would usually require unsuspectedly vast resources of skill and capital for their successful exploitation. But the image of the gorgeous tropics, where wealth might be had for the asking, persisted and has continued in various forms to affect cultural attitudes to this day.[5]

The accelerating pace of industrial development in the West further widened the gap between European and preindustrial societies. A West Coast African war canoe, for instance, could in some ways stand comparison with a small Mediterranean galley of the type familiar to the Portuguese at the end of the fifteenth century. The same war canoe looked infinitely less impressive when compared to an eighteenth-century "East Indiaman" and utterly puny when laid alongside a steam-driven armored vessel. The Europeans developed a host of explanations to account for their superiority, and all these ideologies played some part in besmirching the image of the Negro in the minds of white men.

Geographical materialism, a very ancient creed, envisaged mankind as the helpless product of climate and topography. Hard, cold countries were supposed to breed tough, enterprising, and warlike men. Hot countries were thought to make lazy or soft men. (This theory has, of course, no basis in fact. Indians are industrious; the Kenyan Masai living near the equator comprise some of the most intrepid warriors the world has ever seen.) Economic materialists, by contrast, saw moral and intellectual qualities as the superstructure of the economic system adopted by any given society, a point of view which profoundly affected both Marxist and non-Marxist philosophies of history. Economic materialists did not generally regard Negroes as racially inferior, but they placed the Africans at a very low rung of

[5] See Philip D. Curtin, *The Image of Africa: British Ideas and Action, 1780–1850* (Madison, Wis., 1964), *passim*.

the human ladder by reason of their technological backwardness. Biological materialists, on the other hand, envisaged the achievements of men's minds as the superstructure of certain physiological features. This creed produced whole libraries of biased history which asserted the racial inferiority of Jews, Slavs, Negroes, or any other group whom the writer happened to dislike. Victorian doctrines of progress and evolution similarly created prejudices of their own.

These various streams of thought, sometimes strangely intermingled, received additional tributaries from the occupational experiences of the people directly concerned with the opening up of Africa. The missionaries were one of the most influential groups, and their writings played a major part in shaping Europe's image of Africa. Nineteenth-century missionaries, many of whom sprang from the intellectual elite of the European petty bourgeoisie, tended to regard the precepts of Victorian middle-class morality as absolute. They widely identified themselves with the views of contemporary businessmen, who supplied the bulk of their funds. They believed that men should save and improve themselves. African tribesmen did neither and consequently appeared to their critics as a nation of unemployed. African tribal systems, devoid of economic individualism and in the grip of kingly socialism or of primitive aristocracies, seemed morally wrong to those of peasant stock like François Coillard, the evangelical pioneer of Barotseland. The missionaries also stood for the Western ideal of monogamous marriage and premarital chastity. Africans had very different ideas on the subject, and to most missionaries African family systems, based upon polygamy, seemed vicious. But above all, the missionaries came to preach the Gospel among the heathen. The preachers from abroad faced terrible perils from disease to convert the pagans; yet as often as not African tribesmen either proved unresponsive to the missionary's message or completely changed the significance of what they were taught. Only men of stern, unyielding disposition stayed on under such conditions. Many of these reacted with much bitterness to native conditions and transmitted highly colored accounts of the tribesmen's supposed depravity.

The old-time missionary's grim picture of Africa was strengthened by the impressions of other Europeans in Africa. The Victorian period was the great era of explorers in Africa, who produced bulky, well-illustrated travelogues of little-known countries. The tribal African usually emerged from these massive tomes in an equally unfavorable light. The task of the early explorers in Africa was desperately difficult. Isolated in the wilderness, shaken by fevers, the traveler usually had to depend on African carriers for the transport of his supplies. These hired men did not necessarily share their employer's love of adventure. They might go on strike or desert, and when they did, the result was sometimes catastrophic. In any case, the pioneers of geography had to make their way through strange countries and had to deal with strange peoples whose languages they rarely understood. The reception accorded white strangers was sometimes hostile and, what was worse, always unpredictable. The traveler unfamiliar with the complicated network of tribal family relationships or politics, which he unwittingly became involved in, often could see neither rhyme nor reason in the Africans' doings. Sometimes the natives were friendly and sold food; sometimes they were hostile and showered poisoned arrows on their visitors. Obviously they were not guided by reason; they were "savages" and could not be trusted.

As Africa was gradually colonized, the impressions of the missionaries and explorers were reinforced by those of still other Europeans. Late nineteenth-century soldiers and colonial administrators joined in criticizing primitive Africa. These Victorian servants of empire were, after all, faced with the tremendously difficult task of policing huge areas with tiny military forces. They had to run territories as large as the whole of England on budgets fit only for English parishes. They had to cope with slave traders, warlords, and tough adventurers in search of easy money. They saw that peace was essential to Africa's future progress, and they knew that at the time there was no real alternative to their authority. To them, primitive society was an ever-present reality, not the subject of an academic investigation undertaken sixty or seventy years after the effective pacification of Africa. It is little wonder that they tended to be harsh in their judgments.

If the administrators were inclined to criticize indigenous methods of government or their absence, the European settlers complained of African economic methods. The farmer who half a century ago began to grow tobacco in some lonely spot on the Rhodesian veld had little use for the old-style native villager. The white pioneer could not improve his farm or build better roads so long as his native neighbors continued to practice their age-old shifting cultivation of the slash-and-burn variety; the colonist could not breed superior cattle so long as the tribesman's small and diseased beasts were allowed to graze next to his sleek dairy herds. Above all, the white man needed black labor, and the supply of this commodity seemed most inadequate, especially when the harvest had to be gathered and a whole year's grueling work might be ruined because no "boys" would turn up.[6]

Victorian and Edwardian literature often presented a very biased picture to the metropolitan public, but after World War I the pendu-

[6] See Lewis H. Gann and Peter Duignan, *White Settlers in Tropical Africa* (Harmondsworth, Middlesex, Eng., 1962), pp. 10–11.

lum began to swing the other way. New schools of psychology subjected Victorian moral codes to a scathing analysis. Some scholars, in their criticism of Western man supposedly burdened by new inhibitions and frustrations, began to idealize primitive societies whose members were imagined to be living "in a world which we have long since forgotten, a world in which the whole of nature was filled with the divine breath of life."[7] In America there was a craze for Harlem and for jazz, for the so-called happy, uninhibited Negro of the slums, or for the virtuous peasantry of the world's backwoods, for a world of happy, unspoiled people. This formed part of a wider trend toward a sophisticated escapism, and sometimes toward an almost neurotic permissiveness, which led many intellectuals to denounce Western mechanical civilization and to flee into a world of their own making, where simplicity and irrationality, or even violence and nihilism, were extolled at the expense of the harder bourgeois virtues.

The reaction against Victorian values also affected Western attitudes toward the peoples of Africa. Many Victorians had identified the Africans in some ways with their "lower orders" of the metropolitan countries; so did their descendants, but now the Africans gained from this assumed likeness. The new social consciousness spilled over into the colonies; for some intellectuals everything that was not bourgeois became praiseworthy, and Africans now benefited from their supposed status as "the world's proletariat." Many Western academic people became disillusioned with big cities, "admass," money making, and patriotism of the traditional kind. Some therefore began to look for an idealized past in precolonial Africa and elsewhere. Some writers began to popularize a rosy picture of Africa's antiquity and painted a historical portrait with all the warts left out.[8] A whole new school of writers used ancient Africa as a foil to set off the real or assumed evils of their own society, much as Tacitus had written up the ancient Teutons for his Roman countrymen or as Madame de Staël performed a similar service regarding early nineteenth-century Germany for the benefit of the French.[9] The results of the new African historiography often left much to be desired. They sometimes bore about as much resemblance to the realities of early

---

[7] Carl Gustav Jung, *Essays on Contemporary Events* (London, 1947), p. 65.

[8] See, for instance, some of the books of Basil Davidson.

[9] See, for instance, Heine's comments. "The good lady only saw in our country what she wanted to see; a misty land of spirits where disembodied people, all virtue, wander through snowy fields, and only talk of morality and metaphysics. . . . Everywhere she sees German spirituality; she praises our honesty, our virtue, our educated minds—she does not see our jails, our brothels, our barracks . . . and all that to needle the Emperor [Napoleon] whose enemies we were at the time." Heinrich Heine, "Geständnisse," *Deutschland. II.* (Vol. VIII of *Sämtliche Werke;* Leipzig, 1898), pp. 11–12.

Africa as did the musings of Madame de Staël to Napoleonic Germany or the Irish nationalist image depicting ancient Erin as the land of kings, bards, heroes, and saints to the true condition of the decaying Celtic tribal societies that succumbed to the English during the Elizabethan age.

Anticolonialism of the intellectual variety gained further strength from political decolonization, from a generous enthusiasm for the new emergent nations of Africa, and sometimes also from a collectivized guilt feeling about the real or assumed past crimes committed by Westerners against their darker-skinned fellow men. There was also a general trend toward cultural relativism, which often introduced concealed value judgments through the back door. Views of this kind spilled over into the field of scholarship and to some extent began to affect African historiography. We can do no better than to summarize an otherwise excellent pamphlet written by Philip Curtin, an outstanding American historian in the African field.[10] Curtin places much emphasis on the Europeans' "cultural arrogance," which he associates, among other things, with the rise of Western technological supremacy. There is much value in these strictures, but he gives insufficient attention to the way in which many other peoples who live in preindustrial societies, including Africans, can also hold racist views or be wedded to extreme cultural ethnocentrism. The contempt of the aristocratic black Watutsi for their Bahutu serfs, or of the Matabele for their Mashona "dogs," was an even more extreme feeling of superiority than that felt by backveld South African farmers regarding their Bantu laborers. Orthodox Jews, Muslims, Catholics, Lutherans, and so forth often suffer from "cultural arrogance" toward the adherents of other creeds. Theories of biological superiority have been propounded by Chinese against Westerners and by Japanese against the indigenous Ainu. Curtin emphasizes Western racism, but many prejudices which, on the surface, spring from racial motives can be traced to social rather than psychological tensions. There was almost no difference between the attitude of a late nineteenth-century white settler in Matabeleland toward his black neighbors and that of an English Elizabethan colonist in Ireland who denounced the white Celtic tribesmen for "their promiscuous generation of children; their neglect of lawful matrimony; their uncleanliness in apparel, diet and lodging . . . ; and their contempt and scorn of all things necessary for the civil life of man."[11]

Nineteenth-century Europe, to be sure, developed racist views

[10] See Philip D. Curtin, *African History* (New York, 1964).

[11] Alfred Leslie Rowse, *The Expansion of Elizabethan England* (London, 1955), p. 106, quoting a comment of Attorney General Sir John Davies in James I's reign.

of many kinds. But it was also nineteenth-century Europe, with its interest in scientific history and its literary romanticism, which developed such a widespread and profound interest in other civilizations. Curtin, like others of similar persuasion, is therefore inclined to exaggerate the extent of racial prejudice as opposed to purely political and cultural factors. For instance, he accuses the settler government of Southern Rhodesia of encouraging pseudoscientific racism as an argument for white domination; he fails to mention the valuable and objective work done on African art, history, and archaeology by such government-run or government-supported Rhodesian bodies as the Rhodes National Gallery at Salisbury, the National Museum at Bulawayo, and the Rhodesian Commission for the Preservation of Natural and Historical Monuments and Relics. It was, in fact, white colonial officials, settlers, and missionaries who started all the earlier scientific journals that appeared in Africa. It was under the auspices of colonial governments that the bulk of the more recent investigation into the African past was initiated. It was colonial governments which created the first African archives, thereby providing scholars with an invaluable tool to carry out documentary research into African history.

Curtin, by implication, blames historical writers of the colonial period for confining their researches to the doings of their own countrymen in Africa—ostensibly because racial prejudice caused the colonizers to assume that Africans had no history worthy of investigation, but again he overstates his case. To give one specific instance, the back numbers of the Southern Rhodesian *Native Affairs Department Annual* are full of interesting information about the local African past. The colonial authorities might certainly have done more, but lack of money, manpower, archival, and other resources played an infinitely greater part in restricting research than racial prejudice.

Besides, the fundamental assumption that the history of the Europeans in Africa is not truly a part of African history is extremely dubious, and similar generalizations would not be accepted for any other part of the world. No serious Rumanian scholar, for example, would refuse to regard the record of Phanariot Greeks in Moldavia as part of Rumanian history, even though Phanariot influence on the Moldavian principality was infinitely less than that of the white colonial impact on Africa. The demand made by some scholars (though not by Curtin) for a purely African history, a history free of such regrettable intrusions as white railway enterprise or the evolution of colonial administrative methods, springs from a romanticism that has no place in scholarship.

Curtin's cultural relativism, a creed which he shares with many

Africanists, is liable to internal contradictions. For example, he condemns European writers for calling Africans primitive but sees nothing wrong in referring to Northern Europeans at the beginning of the Christian era as "barbarian."[12] Yet the use of the word "barbarian" implies as rigid a cultural value judgment as the word "primitive." Cultural relativism raises philosophical difficulties of a more fundamental kind. Curtin agrees that on some matters, such as "the needless killing of human beings," people of different cultures can arrive at a common standard, but his emphasis is on "needless,"[13] a word which itself begs the question. He also misses the point of much of our own cultural and religious tradition. The Hebrew prophets condemned human sacrifices to Moloch; their reason was not that it was "needless," but that it was immoral and inhuman. A Canaanite familiar with modern theories of social anthropology would have had difficulty convincing the Hebrews that human sacrifices in Tyre, or for that matter in Benin, performed a vital role in maintaining group cohesion and thereby preserved the cultural pattern of Moloch's votaries. A consistent relativist would, moreover, be obligated to censure the Hebrews' cultural arrogance on the same basis that he now condemns the Victorian empire builders' "ethnocentrism." If value judgments about a culture are themselves illegitimate, why are a relativistic scholar's standards to be preferred to those of a Hebrew prophet or a British district commissioner? Relativism, in other words, is liable to defeat itself, for the relativist may fail by his own standards. He must accept whatever is; he cannot condemn Hitler's Germany, Verwoerd's South Africa, or the practices of cannibalism and ritual murder. Obviously, Africans who believe in their moral system cannot be held morally accountable to another system; no charge of "sin" or immorality can be levied against an African woman who kills her twins. But once conditions change and a higher form of morality—one which allows man to develop his human nature more fully—is introduced and complied with, then a charge of immorality can be made. There is knowledge, there is consent of the will, and the act is forbidden by the new moral system. Curtin is right in criticizing Europeans for making moral judgments about Africans whose tribal practices seemed sinful only to Christians, but there is no reason that a Christian should not examine the value system itself, as distinct from its individual practitioners who acted in good faith.

This somewhat summary discussion is by no means merely aca-

---

[12] Curtin, *African History*, p. 28.
[13] Curtin, *African History*, pp. 23–24.

demic, for relativistic historiography may now be going too far in devaluing the very uncomplimentary, or even blood-curdling, accounts handed to us by eighteenth- and nineteenth-century eyewitnesses of African society. Many of these observers were prejudiced, but their subjective prejudices do not necessarily make their objective observations inaccurate. François Coillard, for instance, may well have been overharsh in his scathing denunciations of late nineteenth-century Barotse society, with its armed affrays, its political murders, its massive liquidations, and its servitude. But this does not render his observations worthless, for his facts were in all probability quite correct. The temptation to paint a prettified portrait of precolonial Africa is as great a pitfall as the old-fashioned interpretation which regarded Africa as the Dark Continent, inhabited by hordes of foul and filthy savages. Both views lead to distortions and misrepresent not only the past of Africa, but the past of mankind as a whole.

Although Curtin criticizes older European views of African history, he has almost nothing to say about the new African history. However, replacing one set of biases with another is no improvement. Some of the current African historical writing is romantic nonsense.[14] The basic theses of the new history include the following: An African past not only existed, but also was glorious and was related to and inspired by Egyptian civilization, and hence predated the glory of Greece and Rome.[15] The advances in black Africa are traced through Egyptian Negro bearers of culture—the Yoruba came from the Nile, and Wolof culture was Egyptian-based. There was no regression among later African cultures; Africans produced no writing because there was no paper, and they did not need writing because they had such well-developed oral traditions. Apparent African regressions were either exaggerated by white racist historians or were due to the effects of the slave trade. The commerce in human beings, conquest, and colonialization stopped the natural cultural evolution in Africa, and seemingly supported the rationalizations of colonialists.[16]

The basic motivation of such thinking is, of course, a nationalistic desire to bolster the Africans' ego and to attempt to find glory in

[14] We exclude from this category the work of African historians such as Dike, Ajayi, Ly, KiZerbo, etc.

[15] Cheikh A. Diop, *L'Afrique noire pré-coloniale: Etude comparée des systèmes politiques et sociaux de l'Europe et de l'Afrique noire, de l'antiquité à la formation des états modernes* (Paris, 1960) and *Nations nègres et culture* (Paris, 1955). A similar view was also held by some American Negro scholars such as Du Bois and Woodson.

[16] The claims of high civilization reached by African Negroes and the qualities supposedly possessed by Africans are used in most cases to offset European stereotypes of Negroes as not being inventive, etc.

past African societies. Praise for precolonial African society may serve the Africans' emotional needs at this time, but understanding for and sympathy with the insecurity of Africans and their concern to find a sense of history should not blind scholars to the dangers and problems of this kind of historical writing. The main problems are that the new history is guided by *a priori* notions (every African nation must have a glorious past, and African historians have the duty to demonstrate this), value judgments are emphasized (the guilt of Europeans in dealings with Africans), and Africans must be shown to be morally superior to Europeans. The notion of European guilt is heavily stressed by writers such as Basil Davidson in *Black Mother*. The double standards and value judgments which make Europeans less moral than Africans are seen in the following charges: the African internal slave trade was excusable, the white slave trade was bad; wars in Africa were caused by Europeans who induced the slave trade; Europeans could have stopped the wars, but the Africans could not; Africans have suffered mainly at the hands of the Europeans, but not at the hands of Arab or indigenous African conquerors. As Austin Shelton concludes in his excellent article (which forms the basis for the above analysis), this stress on value judgments and historical assertion furthers black chauvinism, placing African history in danger of becoming the tool of politicians and special pleaders.[17]

[17] See Austin J. Shelton, "Historiography and 'New' African 'History': A Short Exposition," *Genève-Afrique*, III, No. 1 (1964), 81–89.
Included is a list of works of African and European writers who offend against scientific history. Not that African historians are the first to offend in this fashion; first-generation nationalist historians of any country usually commit such excesses.

11. Africa Before the Partition

Africa's early age is shrouded in darkness. The continent may well have been the cradle of the human race; from time immemorial it has certainly been a vast racial melting pot. Hence there are many different kinds of Africans. From prehistoric times the inhabitants of Africa comprised people as diverse as the Bushmen and Pygmies, small-statured men who eked out a scanty living by hunting game and collecting edible plants. There were Hottentots, pastoralists of slightly taller build than the Bushmen. More important were the Negroes, including the Bantu, black-skinned people speaking a related group of languages. Sometime between 500 and 300 B.C. the Bantu may have begun to move southward from the savannah region east and west of Lake Chad, after they had acquired the arts of agriculture and of metalworking. The Bantu took over land only sparsely occupied by nomadic hunters. To some extent they mingled with the aboriginal peoples, so that the modern Bantu differ as much in physical appearance as Europeans. Today related Bantu languages are spoken from Uganda to South Africa and from the Cameroun to Mozambique. The Bantu are closely related to the Negroes of West Africa, and there is no hard-and-fast racial division between the two.

Africa also contains many different peoples of Semitic speech, whose ancestors came from Arabia and who intermarried to some extent with the inhabitants of Ethiopia and the Sudan. Another distinct group are the peoples speaking Hamito-Semitic languages. The so-called Hamites again do not form a pure race, any more than do the Negroes; they are comprised of people such as the Berber and the Galla, who speak related tongues. The Hamito-Semitic speaking peoples have a variegated cultural heritage. The Hausa, one of the largest numerically in this group, are primarily cultivators, traders, and craftsmen. Others were cattle breeders who usually managed to

133

establish a military superiority over their darker-skinned neighbors practicing a more sedentary kind of agriculture.[1] These multitudinous migrations, the divisions and the blending of different peoples, some of whom subsequently subsisted in relative isolation, turned Africa into a complex ethnic mosaic. It is therefore impossible to speak, as Sir Harry Johnston did, of the "typical" Negro.

The peoples of Africa are divided by ethnic descent and by language. There are hoe agriculturists such as the Ganda, the Tiv, and the Yoruba. The Hausa, Ruanda, Swazi, and many others practice mixed farming. The Jie, the northern pastoral Somali, the Masai, and so forth make their living by herding stock. Scattered groups such as the Mbutu Pygmies eke out a bare existence by hunting and foraging. African forms of political and social organization similarly display a bewildering variety. All the peoples of Africa had some ways of ordering public affairs, of limiting private violence within a community, and of arriving at some kind of public decision.[2] There were wars aplenty in precolonial Africa, but no people in Africa, or indeed anywhere else in the world, ever lived in a state of universal conflict where everyone's hand was raised against his neighbor. What did differ was the scale and nature of organization. African societies ranged from small hordes of Bushmen to groups of middling size such as the Fulani or the Tiv and, finally, to highly organized kingdoms such as those of the Ganda, the Hausa, the Lozi, and the Yoruba. There were also vast differences in the power of African state organizations. The weakest kind of monarchical constitution was found among the Shilluk, whose kingship was symbolical and ritual in nature, lacking administrative power but representing the unity of the nation. Next came the small chiefdoms of South Africa, which were subject to constant segmentation. The Zulu and the Bemba had more highly organized states, where chiefs and princes administered territorial counties on the king's behalf but were able to mobilize their own armies of followers in support of attempts at securing power. The Lozi kingdom was much more highly integrated; here power struggles centered on "the politics of the capital." The king's council consisted not of landed magnates, but of title holders appointed to their positions by the king in council. However, these were not specialized

---

[1] For an attempt to classify the African peoples from a linguistic standpoint see Joseph H. Greenberg, *Studies in African Linguistic Classifications* (New Haven, Conn., 1955). For an earlier classification of Africans on racial lines see Charles G. Seligman, *Races of Africa* (3d ed.; London, 1957), and for a critique of Seligman's views, Philip D. Curtin, *African History* (New York, 1964).

[2] See Lucy P. Mair, *Primitive Government* (Baltimore, 1962), for an excellent study.

bureaucrats, for the kingdom was still too backward in technological and economic development to support a high degree of administrative specialization of labor. The king moved people from office to office, to which estates and followers were attached; social mobility of the brave and the able was still possible. The next type was to be found in "caste" states of cattle-keeping conquerors who had established their dominion over subject peasant peoples. In states of this kind, in Ruanda and Matabeleland, there were radical restrictions on the ability of the conquered to rise to positions of great power. West African states like Dahomey, Nupe, and Zazzau had a more differentiated economy, with slave labor and foreign trade on a large scale. There were great landed magnates, with town and country houses, and factions of aristocrats which vied for the support of city mobs. Mercenaries and mercenary generals entered the arena of politics. Dynastic struggles still went on, but in addition to such faction fights, one account at any rate reports a large-scale peasant revolt.[3] Africa also knew far-reaching differences in kinship systems; some societies traced descent through their fathers, others through their mothers, and there were communities with systems of double descent.[4]

Africa was divided as well into major culture areas. A historian might divide the land mass of Africa into five main regions. Men and ideas have moved across Africa from time immemorial, and the history of this great land mass can no more be shut off into tight compartments than that of any other continent. These divisions do, however, serve some purpose in focusing attention on a number of features in which certain adjacent territories approximate each other more than they resemble distant areas.

The name Africa was first applied to a portion of the continental northern shore, but this area in fact formed part of the Mediterranean world and had little in common with the remainder of black Africa. Its people came from Hamitic, Semitic, or related stock; its vegetation, over vast streches, resembled that of Italy, Greece, or Lebanon; its ports mainly looked northward. The country formed part of the Graeco-Roman, the early Semitic, and later the Arab world; its fate was intertwined just as much with that of the European shores beyond the horizon as with developments in the hinterland, stretching to the equator and beyond. The valley of the Nile, comparable in some ways to a huge, ribbonlike oasis winding from south to north, was the

[3] Max Gluckman, "Civil War and Theories of Power in Barotseland: African and Medieval Analogies," *Yale Law Journal,* LXXII, No. 8 (July, 1963), 1545–1546.

[4] For an excellent introduction giving an anthropological appraisal of selected African peoples see James L. Gibbs, Jr. (ed.), *Peoples of Africa* (New York, 1965).

home of Africa's most famous civilizations. Egyptian statesmen throughout the ages attempted to assert their country's power over the southern stretches of the river. But Egypt, the greatest granary of antiquity, was also more intimately linked to the Mediterranean than to the distant Sudan and, under a long succession of Hellenistic, Latin, and Muslim rulers, shared in the vicissitudes of its neighbors on the littoral.

The lands of the Nile and the Mediterranean shore also maintained contacts with the south, and there was always some cultural cross-fertilization. About five hundred years B.C., Meroë on the Upper Nile became the seat of an important kingdom and developed into one of the great iron-smelting and manufacturing centers. From Meroë, and perhaps also from other areas, the art of working iron spread west and south. By the time Portuguese, French, and Dutch sailors first anchored off the shores of Africa, the indigenous Negro and Bantu peoples all knew how to fashion tools and weapons out of metal.

Africans also learned how to mine gold, and from the early Middle Ages until the discovery of America the western Sudan was the Occident's chief supplier of this yellow metal. The peoples inhabiting the vast savannah belt of the interior, lying between the forests adjoining the coastal areas and the Sahara to the north, made good use of their strategic position as middlemen and built up an important commerce. The savannah, unlike the fever-ridden forests of the south, proved suitable for horses and camels. Mounted warriors, using weapons fashioned of iron, acquired an irresistible superiority over sedentary agriculturists. The Sudan contained a good deal of fairly fertile farm-land permitting a variety of crops, while the country's topography allowed relatively easy communications. From the early Middle Ages on, the savannah was the site of a number of extensive states which rose and fell in succession and which, from an economic point of view, formed part of the Islamic world's extreme southern frontier.

These Muslim or semi-Muslim communities supplied the Mediterranean world with raw materials of high value and rather small bulk, merchandise that could be sent across the Sahara to the Mediterranean and still yield profit. The Sudanic kingdoms did business in metal, salt, precious stones, slaves, and especially gold.[5] These savannah states were ruled by horsemen from the desert or by Negro peoples who had acquired new techniques of warfare, trade, and government. Large areas were unified for varying periods. The empire of Ghana (situated in the western Sudan, not present-day

[5] The Saharan trade is described in E. W. Bovill, *Caravans of the Old Sahara: An Introduction to the History of the Western Sudan* (London, 1933) and a shorter version, *The Golden Trade of the Moors* (London, 1958).

Ghana) reached the peak of its power some time at the beginning of the eleventh century. Later Mali developed a splendid civilization; this reached its highest point in the fourteenth century, when Mansa Musa, the reigning sovereign, dazzled Egypt and Arabia with a magnificent pilgrimage to Mecca. Equally imposing was the empire of Songhai, which reached the apogee of its might in the sixteenth century. The western Sudan as a whole developed a sophisticated way of life, based on trade and handicraft. Skilled craftsmen produced cloth, leather work, weapons, jewelry, and many other commodities; Sudanese merchants traded as far afield as the Gulf of Guinea and the Mediterranean; cities like Timbuktu became renowned for their wealth, learning, and luxury.

At the end of the eighteenth century the Fulani took a leading part in the history of what are now Northern Nigeria and the Republic of Niger. The Fulani were immigrant pastoralists of old standing; many of them became townsmen, adopted the Muslim way of life, and developed an intelligentsia of their own—Fulani militant divines who condemned the lax practices of the existing Hausa ruling class. In Gobir, Usuman dan Fodio, a famed Fulani preacher, finally proclaimed a holy war and enlisted the support of Fulani city dwellers and herdsmen alike. Dan Fodio gained many brilliant successes and established his capital at Sokoto, from which he governed the conquered Hausa states through Fulani lieutenants. Sokoto could not in the end effectively hold onto all its conquests, but Dan Fodio's *jihad* set off other campaigns of a similar type; these created new empires based on the subjugation of many different peoples by well-armed conquerors on horseback or camelback, who turned conquest into a profitable investment by levying tribute on their subjects.

The Sudanic states of the interior traded with the communities dwelling in the forests to the south, but their political power made little headway beyond the "green curtain." Horsemen saw their mounts perish of sleeping sickness in the woodlands; fodder was hard to get; plumed lancers fell easy prey to well-laid ambushes. Trade and technology, however, penetrated southward, and settlers made their way into the northern fringes of the forest area. The introduction by the Portuguese, Indonesians, and Arabs of new crops from Southeast Asia and tropical America provided food for a larger population.[6] The forest people borrowed new ideas and built up a number of kingdoms of varying size and power, on lines strikingly similar to those of the Sudan, with towns of dried-brick or rammed-earth construction and surrounded by earthworks, with developed systems of

[6] For a good general introduction see John D. Fage, *An Introduction to the History of West Africa* (3d ed.; Cambridge, Eng., 1962).

trade and administration, and with flourishing crafts such as weaving
and metalworking. In the second half of the fifteenth century, moreover, Portuguese vessels sailed to West Africa, subsequently penetrat-
ing into the Indian Ocean. Portuguese traders, followed later by
Dutch, French, and English competitors, began to purchase gold,
slaves, and ivory directly from the West Coast, selling guns, gunpowder, cloth, beads, knives, hatchets, rum, and tobacco in exchange.
Sailing ships, of course, could carry goods more cheaply than could
camels; the European intruders opened a new trader's frontier, with
the result that the commercial, and to some extent even the military,
balance of power began to shift southward. Warriors wielding muskets
enjoyed a natural advantage over fighting men armed with only bows
or lances; the gun trade thus helped to initiate a major political revolution, which in time made itself felt in lands as distant as Ashanti
and the Congo.

The impact of these new military and economic techniques produced a great variety of responses and resulted in an enormous diversity of state organizations. During long periods of their history the
Yoruba were divided into independent towns, often at war with one
another. Each city-state was subject to a local king, chosen from an
ancient family associated with the founding of the city. The kings
surrounded themselves with an elaborate ritual, but their power was
limited. There were numerous dignitaries, whose office was often
hereditary. The major decisions were made by a local state council,
which represented the most powerful extended family groups and
sometimes also craft organizations. In many cases royal power was
further limited by secret societies whose officials might also serve in
high administrative capacities in the state and who could try offenses
involving their own members.

The Ashanti state in what is now the middle portion of Ghana represented a more centralized kind of dominion. Ashanti developed
into a confederacy of towns under the leadership of the Asantehene,
the lord of Kumasi. Each town was governed by a council, with representatives from all the great lineages within its confines. Conciliar
rule was subject in turn to checks and balances. In each state the
commoners had a defined constitutional position and established
rights in relation to the chiefs and elders. They could demand the
deposition of unpopular town chiefs and also exercised some influence
on the chiefs' decisions. Kumasi developed a political and ritual
primacy over the various cities, but even so, the Ashanti confederacy
remained united primarily for warfare against outsiders. Kumasi received subsidies from other states, but could neither enforce direct
taxation nor appoint the various officials serving the town govern-

ments. In Dahomey, on the other hand, central power had congealed into a more absolute kind of rule. The king appointed the more important officials throughout his kingdom and enforced his authority through a network of spies, a well-drilled standing army, and hosts of executioners. There was an elaborate court, maintained by taxation, by fines and confiscations, and by the spoils of war and trading profits, which accrued to the king by virtue of his characteristic role as chief merchant. The monarchs of Dahomey became feared as bloodthirsty potentates, though they still had to consult their officials and dared not act against the combined opposition of all their dignitaries.

The African East Coast developed another kind of civilization, maritime in character, a blend of Arab and Bantu elements, looking out toward the Indian Ocean. Many centuries before the arrival of the Portuguese in the Indian Ocean, cities such as Mombasa, Kilwa, and Sofala obtained slaves, gold, and ivory from the tribes of the interior in exchange for cloth, beads, and other commodities. The coastal communities formed part of a "triangle of trade" connecting East Africa with the Red Sea and the Persian Gulf on the one side and Gujarat, Malabar, and Coromandel on the other. These Muslim states were skilled in navigation, stone building, and other arts; they maintained links of ancient standing with the regions inland.[7] Coastal trade in turn gave an impetus to the creation of Iron Age empires such as that of Monomotapa, which during the latter Middle Ages loosely unified most of the lands between the Limpopo and Zambezi rivers.

Muslim merchants and Portuguese missionaries made some attempts to spread their faiths inland, but until the late nineteenth century neither Christianity nor Islam achieved any major conquests in the East African interior. There was, however, one great exception. The lands adjoining the Red Sea had always traded with one another and with the Mediterranean region. Settlers from southern Arabia regularly made their way across the waters; Christian missionaries came in from the north. Some time at the end of the fourth century, Christianity secured a firm foothold in the kingdom of Axum, which carried on a flourishing trade across the Red Sea and for a time even extended its power to the Yemen. Axum could not maintain its greatness, but Christianity did not disappear. The focus of this Afro-Christian civilization shifted to the Amharic peoples of Abyssinia, who, in their mountain stronghold, stubbornly maintained their power against both the Muslims from the north and east and the pagans from the south. The Abyssinians, however, remained in ideological as well

[7] For a discussion of East Africa in precolonial days see Roland A. Oliver and Gervase Mathew (eds.), *History of East Africa,* Vol. I (Oxford, 1963).

as physical isolation from the West. They professed Christianity in its Coptic (Egyptian) form. The doctrines of Rome could make no headway in Abyssinia, which remained a cultural island. Fifteenth-century reports in the West nevertheless greatly exaggerated the power of this state; rumors gave rise to romantic tales about Prester John, a mighty Christian monarch who supposedly ruled an enormous kingdom inland and who might be expected to help the Western Christians against the forces of Islam.[8]

These African kingdoms, emirates, and city-states represented a tightly fashioned political rule of some kind or another. Historians of the Marxist-Leninist school have linked their evolution to incipient class differentiation. In the Marxist view, the emergence of privileged groups of warriors and slave owners led to disputes between the rich and the poor. The wealthy tried to safeguard their position through the creation of rudimentary state machineries; the new states then became more oppressive as internal differences of property and status increased. Such generalizations, however, cannot be accepted without qualification. In the eighteenth century the Bisa of what is now northeastern Zambia played an important part in trade. Some Bisa became richer than their neighbors, but the Bisa nevertheless failed to build up a tightly knit state. The Bemba, another people from northeastern Zambia, developed in a very different fashion. They lived in a harsh, infertile country and gained a scant livelihood from a particularly arduous form of slash-and-burn agriculture. They supplemented their income by raiding and in time terrorized all the tribes on the boundary of their kingdom. Differences in living standards between Bemba noblemen and commoners were not great, yet the Bemba developed an exceptionally rigidly organized state and a very violent form of rule.

> In nearly every village are to be seen men and women whose eyes have been gouged out; the removal of one eye and one hand is hardly worthy of remark. Men and women are seen whose ears, nose and lips have been sliced off and both hands amputated. The cutting off of breasts of women has been extensively practised as a punishment for adultery but . . . some of the victims . . . are mere children. . . . Indeed these mutilations were inflicted with the utmost callousness; every chief for instance has a retinue of good singers and drummers who invariably have their eyes gouged out to prevent them running away.[9]

[8] For a good general history of Ethiopia see Arnold H. M. Jones and Elizabeth Monroe, *A History of Ethiopia* (Oxford, 1955).

[9] Robert Codrington, "Report of the Administrator of North-eastern Rhodesia for Two Years Ending March 31st 1900," in *British South Africa Company: Reports on the Administration of Rhodesia, 1898–1900* (n.p., n.d.), p. 68.

The Bemba state was not exceptional in this respect. The more centralized forms of African kingships commonly had a grim and bloody side to their makeup which is sometimes ignored by modern African historiography. In 1897 the British occupied Benin in Nigeria. They found a gruesome charnel house, a kind of small-scale African Belsen:

> Altars covered with streams of dried human blood, the stench of which was awful . . . huge pits, forty to fifty feet deep, were found filled with human bodies, dead and dying, and a few wretched captives were rescued alive . . . everywhere sacrificial trees on which were the corpses of the latest victims—everywhere, on each path, were newly sacrificed corpses. On the principal sacrificial tree, facing the main gate of the King's Compound, there were two crucified bodies, at the foot of the tree seventeen newly decapitated bodies and forty-three more in various stages of decomposition. On another tree a wretched woman was found crucified, whilst at its foot were four more decapitated bodies. To the westward of the King's house was a large open space, about three hundred yards in length, simply covered with the remains of some hundreds of human sacrifices in all stages of decomposition. The same sights were met with all over the city.[10]

In many West African kingdoms the ruling classes were probably demoralized by the slave trade. The commerce in human beings, however, does not form the sole explanation for the widespread use of terror in precolonial politics. Matabeleland, in what is now Rhodesia, was never implicated in the slave trade, yet precolonial Matabeleland witnessed civil strife of a ferocious nature, with refined forms of torture and ruthless liquidations. Several elements probably entered into this kind of political violence. Most African rulers, like the Roman principate, never effectively solved the problem of peaceful succession. In Barotseland and most other kingdoms of this kind the death of a king was likely to usher in a period of temporary anarchy, with competing factions struggling for the spoils of office. The growth of larger states allowed the pacification of extensive areas, but the evolution of state power, however primitive, also gave greater temptations to the ambitious. Kingships capable of collecting tribute from a large number of subjects and controlling interterritorial trade constituted great economic as well as political prizes; the very successes of African kingship may well have put a special premium on political success and thereby given an extra edge to internal struggles for power.

[10] Report by Captain A. Boisragon quoted in Sir Alan Burns, *History of Nigeria* (6th ed.; New York, 1963), p. 179. See also George Murdock, *Africa: Its People and Their Culture History* (New York, 1959), for discussion of cannibalism and ritual murder.

States like Benin or Ghana and Mali or lesser kingdoms like Barotseland and the Bemba state were, however, comparatively rare. For generations untold the majority of Africans have lived in political communities where men did not hold allegiance to distant superiors. The framework of most African history has not been the centralized state, but a looser polity based on neighborhood and kinship links.[11] In many regions, such as Tanzania and Malawi, centralized governments did not exist over large areas. A political map of precolonial Africa south of the Sahara should really show a splatter of multi-colored blotches, each indicating larger states, all characterized by some economic, administrative, and military division of labor and marked by internal inequalities of political and economic status. These states would expand or contract their territorial influence with the shifting fortunes of trade or war. They would be surrounded by a great ring of smaller communities, organized into what anthropologists call "stateless societies." Map makers would not be able to separate these communities by precise borderlines; they could best indicate them by a scatter of dots. Each of these dots would stand for overlapping neighborhoods, whose members maintained local peace after a fashion but recognized no chiefs and knew only limited differences of wealth and status. The members of such societies nevertheless recognized the rule of law among themselves; peaceful relations between members of the same community were regarded as normal, and there were also certain devices whereby men were able to transcend the ties of local neighborhoods.[12]

Set out on paper, these categories assume a neatly defined quality which they did not in fact possess. Nor do they exhaust the infinite variety in forms of social organization which Africans evolved to suit varying needs. Africa was in constant flux; nothing would be more mistaken than to look upon precolonial African society as static. More powerful kingdoms would expand at the expense of their weaker neighbors or would in turn contract with the decay of central authority. In some areas, as in the southern Sudan during the nineteenth century, successful prophets built up large followings that went beyond local loyalties; in others successful slave traders or warlords, furnished with imported guns, carved out new lordships for themselves which sometimes expanded into larger states until European colonizers put an end to local warfare.

[11] For an interpretation contrary to this see Curtin, *African History,* p. 39.
[12] For an excellent study see Lucy P. Mair, *Primitive Government.* The authors are also much indebted to an unpublished paper by Elizabeth Colson, "Baselines of Change in Africa," Training Brief No. 2, prepared at Boston University for the Agency for International Development (December, 1962).

Many anthropologists nowadays thus refuse to use the terms tribe or tribalism at all. They argue that such designations merely serve to conceal complexity or that they place a mistaken emphasis on the primitive and backward nature of precolonial Africa. Opinions on the use of the word differ; the anthropologists' aversion to the word tribe is not shared by modern African nationalist leaders like Kwame Nkrumah, who talk of tribalism in terms as disparaging as those used by any Victorian missionary.[13] However, anthropologists who reject the word tribe do have a case. The term often conveys the idea of a people united by a common language and culture, with a common feeling of identity stretching back into the misty past. Yet some tribes, in their present form, are modern creations. The Tonga of Northern Rhodesia, for instance, are today known as a tribe. Seventy years ago they lived in small neighborhood communities, speaking related dialects. They then had no common name for themselves, nor did they look upon themselves as members of a single group. It was the needs of British administrators that laid down new tribal boundaries and popularized a new name. Today the Tonga think of themselves as a tribe, but the new tribe owes its existence as much to the Pax Britannica as to the boundaries of Zambia. The Barotse (Lozi) are also described as a tribe. Barotseland, in what is now western Zambia, however, was never an ethnically homogeneous people. The Barotse were simply a dominant group ruling over great congeries of other communities, with different tongues and customs. Yet Barotseland separatism in modern Zambia is called a "tribal" movement. Tribal constitutions, moreover, implied neither social equality nor collectivist methods of production.

Many precolonial African communities knew social or ethnic differentiations as rigid as those of the most caste- or color-bar-ridden societies in other parts of the world. The Matabele were split into sharply divided groups. The states of Sine and Saloum in Senegal were traditionally divided into several classes, with warriors at the top, free peasants in the middle, and artisan and slave castes at the bottom. Members of the lowest caste were not permitted to marry outside their group. There was similar differentiation between the ruling Watutsi and the conquered Bahutu in what later became the Belgian trust territory of Ruanda-Urundi. Among the Bantu of southern Africa, land belonged to the community as a whole in the sense that each tribesman had a traditional right to be allocated a garden

---

[13] The term "tribe," of course, need not necessarily entail a concealed form of cultural criticism. Modern Jews feel no sense of shame when they talk of their ancestors as the "Twelve Tribes." Nor do twentieth-century Germans feel embarrassed in referring to the Bavarian, Saxon, or Swabian components of their nation as *Stämme,* or tribes.

for his use. But each family worked its own land and kept the crops. Kinship groups had cattle of their own; there was no community property. Hoes and axes, fishing nets, spears and bows—means of production in their own right—belonged to individuals. Even stateless societies knew internal differences. Some men had more wives to labor in their fields than others; some owned more cattle or commanded more followers than their neighbors.

On a higher economic level, tribal institutions might be combined with trade. The so-called houses, which made up many Niger delta states, successfully combined tribal with capitalist modes of social organization. Among the Nembe of Nigeria, for instance, a house formed a semiautonomous community, composed of a chief and his relatives, followers, and slaves. The members of each house might reside in a particular quarter of the city; petty chiefs might own parts of a smaller town, farms, or fishing villages. The house acted as a trading corporation; its members might also fish and farm. Houses also operated as military units, each being required to equip at least one war canoe for the navy of its respective city. Houses also acted as associations for the maintenance of law and order; they played a ritual role, and each provided some form of social security for its members and acted as a burial society.[14] "Primitive communism," in other words, is but a myth. So is the concept of history which regards different forms of social organization as mutually incompatible, which ignores mixed forms of social association and arranges tribalist, feudalist, and capitalist in the same mechanical order used by a child in reciting "rich man, poor man, beggarman, thief."

The term tribe must therefore be used with caution. It is diffuse in its meaning and may apply to communities of many different kinds. It cannot be used to describe complicated polities such as the East African city-states. And yet most African societies had certain features in common. With the exception of the great Sudanic empires and the Swahili cities on the Indian Ocean, most African states had to function without a literary intelligentsia; even the greatest Bantu states could rarely maintain professional scribes. Men could store information only in their memories, not on paper or papyrus. This deficiency perhaps helped to give undue prestige to traditional knowledge, and it may have helped to give more power to the old men in the community. Traditional societies were mostly small scale in nature. Bantu law in the main was customary law; the decisions of past chiefs and councils served as legal precedents. Bantu councilors were

[14] For a detailed description see Ebiegberi Joe Alagoa, *The Small Brave City State: A History of Nembe-Brass in the Niger Delta* (Madison, Wis., 1964), especially pp. 11–33.

not so much concerned with abstract rights as with achieving immediate unity and reconciliation by upholding the standards of the "reasonable man."[15] Bantu lawgivers would, however, enforce their decisions with extreme rigor; in many societies criminals were beaten to death, impaled, or mutilated. Tribal communities, of course, had no prisons; the people themselves approved of harsh punishments to keep evildoers in check. The application of the law might vary a good deal according to local circumstances. Among the Matabele, for instance, there was no concept of equality before the law; punishments for crimes were meted out according to the castes of the criminal and the injured party.[16]

In their laws and customs traditional African societies emphasized communal responsibilities, and traditional African education stressed these values to an extraordinary extent. By the age of three or four an African village child would have learned to tell his kinsfolk from others—a difficult task in a society where kinsfolk would run to many dozens. By the age of six he was likely to know the precise terms in which to address each one and how to behave toward them. He would have to know a multitude of food taboos and the penalties of infringement, as well as numerous dance rhythms and games. Small boys and girls would build toy villages, where they performed, by an appropriate division of labor, the chores of pounding manioc, hewing wood, and drawing water, the thatching of roofs, and the making of pots, baskets, and dugout canoes. African youngsters, like peasant children in Europe, were expected to take care of the goats; older boys would look after the cattle and learn all about their diseases. In cattleless country boys would be put to work repairing tools, helping their elders in lopping the branches off tall trees, making nets, and going fishing. Girls were apprenticed from an early age to the difficult art of carrying jars on their heads; soon they accompanied their mothers to the fields to search for wild vegetables, herbs, and spices that would garnish the evening dish. The sternest training came during the years of puberty, when youngsters were formally initiated into the tribal traditions and often had to pass a series of grim tests before being admitted to the privileges of manhood. Many tribes also had initiations for girls, where young women were sometimes subjected to ordeals which seem cruel and coarse by modern standards. In the Loma country of Liberia, for instance, all initiates underwent clitoridectomy with a crude iron razor and with only cold water for

[15] See Max Gluckman, *The Judicial Process among the Barotse of Northern Rhodesia* (Manchester, Eng., 1955).

[16] See, for instance, Thomas Morgan Thomas, *Eleven Years in Central South Africa* (London, 1873), p. 251.

an anesthetic; the operation was so painful that some girls were known to die of shock induced by fear and pain. Rites of this nature nevertheless achieved their aim. They instilled a profound respect for custom and authority; they extolled the virtues of obedience, patience, humility, and resourcefulness. They trained young people for a society which emphasized communal responsibility and stressed a man's duties to his extended family and the ancestral spirits; they stood for a way of life which valued the normal, the "reasonable man," and stamped out all deviates.[17]

This kind of society normally rested on a slender economic basis. Most African societies were at a subsistence level. The Africans generally enjoyed a superfluity of land but usually suffered from extreme poverty in all other kinds of capital. There were, of course, exceptions. In many West African countries land was not nearly as plentiful as in the less thickly populated regions of southern and Central Africa. Some West African societies therefore evolved complicated systems of encumbering the soil with community and individual rights. Various forms of tenancy came into existence to cope with situations where the ground available for cultivation was becoming scarcer. The great majority of Africans, however, never had to worry about the problem of land shortage. Whenever the villagers had exhausted the fertility of their fields, they were able to move farther on. The bush, which stretched out before the village like an endless, rolling sea, was open to all. This fact dominated every other aspect of life. In contrast, the feudal states of medieval Europe knew no such easy advantage for their members; there were landless laborers, professional mercenaries, merchants, or wandering scholars who would never own a field in their lives. Africans had their gardens, and except for a tiny minority, their existence centered on a small village or a scattered group of homesteads. There were exceptions, such as the large towns of Nigeria or the East Coast, but even the largest African states suffered from severe economic limitations. The Monomotapas, the medieval rulers of what became Southern Rhodesia, were mighty monarchs in their heyday, but unlike Joseph in Egypt, they could not stockpile huge quantities of corn to tide their subjects over bad seasons. Joseph could float grain along the Nile to his repositories and the Romans could use ships to tap the grain resources of Sicily and Egypt, but the Monomotapas lacked such a transportation system. Even had they solved the problem of constructing and administering a network of warehouses, they could not have conveyed large quantities of maize or cassava from one part of their vast king-

[17] This reconstruction is taken from George H. T. Kimble, *Tropical Africa:* Vol. II, *Society and Polity* (New York, 1960), 14–18.

dom to another. Salt could be traded fairly easily, but cattle walking on their own feet comprised the only "mobile" source of food which could be shifted about in great bulk.

The economic surplus at the disposal of any African society always remained narrow; a drought, a swarm of locusts, or a barbarian invasion was likely to cause disaster. Tropical Africa suffered from a perennial manpower shortage; in a society that lacked technological resources there simply were not enough people to complete all the jobs that needed doing. The vast majority of African communities had to rely on the power of a man's arms, legs, or back to perform all their labors. There were exceptions: the warriors of the savannah rode horses and camels and the Basuto of South Africa learned the art of mounting ponies. But almost no African community south of the Sahara managed to harness draft animals to pull plows and wagons until European newcomers introduced these new methods of traction in the nineteenth and twentieth centuries. The East Coast city-states utilized wind power to propel sailing ships, but this achievement found few parallels on the West Coast. To hoe the soil or propel canoes, the bulk of prepartition Africa depended solely on human muscle power. African technology, unlike that of Europe in the later Middle Ages, could neither convert the force of wind into rotary motion for the purpose of milling grain nor utilize water to run a mill. African society was also limited in its use of mineral resources. Some communities acquired some skill in mining, but, lacking pumps, they could not dig for ores at any great depth. Many of the ancient workings of Rhodesia were thus abandoned long before their gold resources were fully exhausted.

These technological weaknesses did not, of course, preclude change or progress. In the all-important field of agriculture Africans achieved some major advances; they developed techniques for coping with a wide range of soils and climates, techniques which were relatively efficient for the purpose they served, yet required little physical capital. They domesticated various wild plants and also successfully naturalized Portuguese-imported food crops such as cassava, maize, and sweet potatoes. Later on African farmers on the West Coast made commercial use of cocoa and groundnuts (peanuts). In Abyssinia, in the eastern highlands of Rhodesia, and in Kenya some communities astonished posterity by complicated terracing which conserved the soil on steep hillsides. Tanganyikan and Kenyan cultivators worked out irrigation systems. Africans in a few favored areas such as the Upper Zambezi developed more intensive forms of riverine farming. But throughout most parts of the continent farmers stuck to simple kinds of slash-and-burn cultivation. Cultivators would burn the bush, plant their crops, and move on when the land was exhausted. These systems worked well enough as long as the population remained small and the land plentiful, but they stood in the way of a more intensive type of agriculture. In most parts of Africa the art of replenishing soil fertility by green crops or by the application of animal manure was adapted from European examples only in the late nineteenth and twentieth centuries. There was little idea of deliberately improving the quality of stock. Even such sophisticated African cultures as the Monomotapas' medieval kingdom in Rhodesia thus rested on a very limited technology.[18]

Traditional methods of handicraft, however, rarely seem to have been able to satisfy Africa's internal demand for merchandise. From Christiansborg to Kilwa there was a widespread hunger for goods such as cloth, beads, knives, and axes, which African artisans generally could not turn out as cheaply or efficiently as suppliers overseas, and for merchandise such as muskets and mirrors. Africa produced only a limited number of goods that could be sent abroad in payment for import and were of sufficient value to stand the high cost of transportation. These included slaves, ivory, gold, and gems.[19] Such assets, however, were irreplaceable. Once a mine was exhausted, once elephants were "shot out," an African kingdom might encounter a serious diminution of available supplies and face disastrous social consequences.

These economic weaknesses made themselves felt in both the administrative and the military spheres. Even the most advanced kingdoms, for instance, continually faced a communication problem. The Sudanic states possessed cavalry, and their horsemen could subdue large areas, but communications remained slow and defective. An able and active ruler might retain the reins of government in his own hands and keep his dominions in order by continually moving about with his army, whereas a lazy or foolish successor might let matters slide, and disorder would follow in the wake of weakness. Alternatively, power in the outlying provinces would be delegated to viceroys; sometimes the chiefs of conquered peoples stayed in power, and sometimes the generals of a conquering army were rewarded with

[18] There is a considerable literature on the subject. Especially valuable are Max Gluckman, *The Economy of the Central Barotse Plain* (Rhodes-Livingstone Institute Paper, No. 7; Livingstone, Northern Rhodesia, 1941), for a case study of one particular area, and S. Herbert Frankel, *The Economic Impact on Under-developed Societies: Essays on International Investments and Social Change* (Oxford, 1953), for wider aspects of indigenous economies faced with the challenge of new economic institutions.

[19] Elephants in theory form a replaceable form of wealth, but African kingdoms failed to protect and rationally exploit this form of capital.

a governorship. In neither case, however, could the satrap's loyalty be easily kept. The longer an empire lasted, the more corrupt its administration was likely to become at the center, so that provincial governors and subject peoples had more incentive and opportunity to rebel or cooperate with new invaders.[20]

A kingdom like that of the Monomotapas faced similar problems. In the fifteenth century the Monomotapas managed to build up a great tribal confederacy; hoe cultivation, small-scale industries such as weaving, gold mining, the production of ironware and pottery, and trade in luxury goods enhanced the country's wealth. As time went on, powerful men could afford richer clothes, finer ornaments, and better weapons than their followers. The king used great nobles in his household who formed the nucleus of a rudimentary state organization, comparable perhaps in some ways to that which ran the Anglo-Saxon kingdoms of the heptarchy. But the village community remained the economic basis of society. A tribal aristocracy, headed by the Monomotapas, dominated the state; property differentiation and continual warfare probably widened the gap between the lordly class and the ordinary clan members of the community; this process in turn strengthened the power of the military commander, who turned into an absolute ruler. The state nevertheless suffered much from internal disorders, and by the time the Portuguese settled at the coast, the gold trade from the interior was already declining. The periphery of the Karanga empire was controlled by sons and other relatives of the king, who conquered outlying areas but would not willingly submit to the monarch's orders. The Monomotapas' empire, like other African states, suffered from poor communications; it also faced the problem that its various provinces remained economically undifferentiated and therefore lacked economic ties to hold them together.

Many state builders also failed to solve the perennial problem of keeping militarily abreast of the barbarian fringe on the periphery of their empire. Monomotapas' armies consisted of infantry, armed with battle-axes, bows, and lances that were not one whit superior to those of their enemies. Once the state lost its political cohesion, its military supremacy was gone. In the early nineteenth century the Monomotapas' successor state was easily overthrown by invaders from the south, conquerors of Zulu stock who had perfected the art of fighting in disciplined formations with jabbing spears and oxhide shields. The Sudanic kingdoms, though militarily superior to that of the Monomotapas, suffered from comparable weaknesses. Even the more

[20] John D. Fage, *An Introduction to the History of West Africa* (3d ed.; Cambridge, Eng., 1962), pp. 16–17.

highly organized kingdoms, in other words, failed to secure a military lead against the barbarians at the gate, comparable with that which enabled medieval England or medieval Germany, respectively, to hold back and finally to conquer the Celtic and Slavonic tribal frontiers.

To a considerable extent this lack of social resources was caused by geographical and ecological factors. Aside from the Cape and the Mediterranean coasts, most of the continent is in many respects particularly ill-favored by nature. By moving southward into Central and southern Africa, the Bantu paid a heavy price; they peopled half a continent, but the move cut them off from the Sudanic and forest civilizations of the north. The loss of contact was not merely a question of distance. Most African rivers are unsuitable for navigation; only a few great water sources, such as the Niger, afford access to large boats. Another difficulty concerned coastal shipping. On the West Coast, for example, Africans had large canoes which they used for coastal voyages; but the Sahara coast of modern Mauritania was virtually impassable. Winds and currents prevented Africans from reaching the countries north of the Sahara, and for many centuries Europeans were afraid to sail south for fear of being unable to get back and of being swallowed up in the dark horrors of some mysterious ocean. Fantastic as these tales of boiling seas and leaden waters might be, European vessels in fact could not return until the development during the fifteenth century of vessels capable of sailing into the wind. The southern part of Africa faced even greater difficulties, owing to the frequently stormy seas around the southern tip of the continent. As a result, until the end of the fifteenth century the whole western coast of Africa had no regular maritime contacts with the outside world, and African civilization had to develop in conditions of comparative isolation.

Conditions on the East Coast were much more favorable. The monsoon winds in the Indian Ocean enabled ships to sail south as far as Madagascar with assurance that the wind would change at half-yearly intervals and blow them safely north again. Sailors from India, southern Arabia, and even China could therefore trade with the East African coast. But merchants still faced great difficulties in the interior. Many parts of tropical Africa were, and still are, infested by the tsetse fly, which carries parasites fatal to draft animals. Wheeled carts were therefore useless, and commerce depended on human porterage. African societies had as well to cope with a host of human diseases peculiar to the tropics, sicknesses which were likely to debilitate large numbers of people. Sickness also placed further barriers in the way of foreign contacts. Africa was the home of yellow fever; in addition, most of tropical Africa is a region of hyperendemic malaria. Before the improvement of medical knowledge toward the end of the nineteenth century, a very large percentage of Europeans could expect to die within a year of their arrival. If they survived the first attacks they were somewhat safer, but the initial mortality rate was high enough to discourage extensive penetration.[21] Huge areas thus remained landlocked.

African societies also faced a host of major ecological difficulties. Vast areas suffer from irregular rainfall and drought. Even the verdant forest belts, whose vegetation seems so lush, must cope with soil leaching and sometimes with irregular precipitation, which make farming a gamble. African ethics therefore emphasized the virtues of cooperation rather than individual advancement. There were some societies, like those of the Ganda, where there was a considerable degree of social mobility, but by and large, honor went to the good neighbor and power went to the generous lord. To the Bantu, as to the Anglo-Saxon of old, the king was a *hláford,* a "loaf ward" or bread giver who made gifts to his followers and fed the hungry when the crops failed. In a society with few means of storing food over long periods, generosity was indeed the best policy. The road to power lay through a man's ability to secure the loyalty of his relatives and the allegiance of strangers by judicious gifts. There was also an element of economic compulsion. In many African societies chiefs could enforce short periods of compulsory labor which enabled them to build up a small surplus of food. A powerful ruler moreover collected tribute, but much of this was redistributed in the form of gifts. Niggardliness, on the other hand, was the mark of the bad citizen; the man who took all and gave nothing, whose crops flourished when everyone else's failed, was likely to be killed on charges of practicing witchcraft.[22]

The Bantu believed that the manifold dangers of the material world were duplicated by threats of a supernatural order. They envisaged these perils in terms which accorded with their day-to-day experience. Tribesmen knew no privacy. Everyone knew everyone else. The Bantu therefore interpreted in personal terms many problems which Western man explains by the working of providence, by the statistical laws of chance, or by scientific causation. Africans, on the other hand, accounted for misfortunes inexplicable in rational ways through the operation of witchcraft. This did not mean that they lacked either the

---

[21] This section has been taken from the excellent summary in Curtin, *African History,* pp. 32–33.

[22] See, for instance, Lucy P. Mair, *Studies in Applied Anthropology* (London, 1957), pp. 23–62.

gift of logic or the ability to learn from experience. If an unskilled hunter was trampled to death by an enraged beast, his friends would account for their companion's death by his lack of technical skill, but if a veteran with many tuskers to his credit unaccountably lost his life on a hunt, his death would probably be attributed to sorcery. Someone must have caused his death by magical means. The malefactor thus had to be found and punished, the work of detection normally being entrusted to a skilled diviner.

Tribal life was also thought to be influenced by a whole pantheon of spirits who spoke through human mouths. Most African peoples believed in a supreme being, but God was not concerned with the problems of individuals; he was too remote to be prayed to directly.[23] The tribe, in their view, was guided by tribal spirits who look after matters affecting the community as a whole, such as the provision of rain. Below tribal spirits (the ancestors) like Chaminuka of the Shona of Southern Rhodesia came lesser spirits, who were concerned with districts. Shona beliefs are of course not unique. To this day Lutheran children are still warned in their Shorter Catechism against the perils of practicing witchcraft. The Catholic Church also has its hierarchy of saints. Medieval Europeans venerated specific saints for looking after the affairs of a town, a parish, or a guild; individuals looked up to their own guardian saints, whose names they bore. The Christian religion hinges on the worship of the Trinity, of a God both immanent and transcendent, a diety all-good, all-wise, and all-powerful who cares for each individual soul. These tenets have no equivalent in Bantu thought, which conceived the world to be a spirit-centered universe whose supreme deity normally remained outside humanity's reach. The spirits in turn talked through mediums. Special gifts in abilities such as dancing, hunting, or healing were also attributed to in-dwelling spirits.[24] This type of religion met the needs of its adherents; it did not, however, encourage change. The ancestral spirits liked things done in the accustomed fashion. Moreover, they did not travel well; they remained attached to their ancestral acres, and even foreign invaders would often go to much trouble to humor the ancestral spirits of the vanquished. The Bantu, unlike the Christian or the Jew, had no "portable motherland," a rigidly defined system of faith which he might carry to the ends of the earth. Nor could he

[23] Again, there were exceptions. There is, for instance, some evidence that when Matabele society was faced with a crisis after its defeat by the British in 1893, the direct worship of Mlimo, the Ancient of Days, attained for a time an intensity and also a revolutionary significance unknown in earlier days.

[24] Michael Gelfand, *Shona Ritual, with Special Reference to the Chaminuka Cult* (Cape Town, 1959).

conceive of individual rights, apart from and independent of the community.

This does not mean that Africans could not change inherited ways. Some anthropologists are limited by the notion that primitive communities could not conceive of "engineered social change," but this interpretation is open to doubt. The Book of Samuel tells the story of a deliberate switchover from the mild governance of judges adjudicating disputes between seminomadic kinship groups to the despotic rule of anointed kings controlling a centralized territorial monarchy.[25] African history records comparable examples. The Zulu, under their great chief Chaka, deliberately militarized their society in the early nineteenth century and thereby effected revolutionary changes in their whole way of life. But emphasis in general lay on the group, and individualism was discouraged.

In summary, Africans had developed a multitude of different cultures; they had managed to settle vast areas; they evolved a host of new economic, military, and administrative techniques. There was little in common between a sophisticated townsman from Timbuktu and a slash-and-burn cultivator in distant Malawi. Civilizations such as that of Timbuktu were not, however, typical of precolonial Africa; the great majority of Africans were organized in much simpler communities, which for the sake of convenience are called tribes. Tribal cultures had many achievements to their credit, but they also had many defects which no amount of romanticizing or appeal to philosophies of cultural relativism can explain away. The tribal community restricted the over-all development of the community and of individuals. Its outlook and public philosophy were narrow. Essentially the tribe aimed, successfully or not, at preserving the status quo. Fear of witchcraft restricted innovation. The kinship system, for all its admirable qualities, also made people less venturesome and restricted economic development. Other unattractive aspects in many tribal communities included domestic slavery, the frequent practice of infanticide, the execution of suspected witches, ritual murders, and the widespread custom of killing people to accompany the dead king into the nether world. The mutilation or torture of criminals and the slaughter of prisoners were common. In general, primitive societies showed little concern for humaneness. Few tribal political systems had sufficient resources to pacify large areas over any length of time. Furthermore, Africans lacked the technological resources to exploit fully their land and mineral resources. Tribal society, even at its most advanced level, implied poverty. The ordinary tribesman accordingly had few choices open to him. The sons of a junior wife in Thonga

[25] I Samuel 8.

society in Portuguese East Africa, to take just one example, were not free to prosper and gain status or wealth until the mines and farms of the Rand and Rhodesia gave them an opportunity to work and acquire goods. Previously, by custom all but the children of senior wives had been committed to an inferior status. African leisure was usually enforced leisure; when there was a drought or when stronger enemies attacked the village and murdered or abducted the able-bodied, stole the cattle, or burned the crops, the survivors had little choice but to sit and starve. It was thus the modern money economy that for the first time gave Africans the choice of numerous economic alternatives —and the foundation for liberty.

Sub-Saharan Africa was never able to solve fully its economic problems; its exports were limited and its natural wealth remained small. There was, however, one commodity which for many centuries found an ever-increasing market. This was muscle power, the working capacity of Africa's own sons and daughters. The disastrous combination of an unsatisfied demand for foreign trade goods with an insatiable demand for slaves in the Americas and in the Muslim world resulted in the development of a traffic in slaves that in time came to dominate much of Africa's economic life. In its earliest form this commerce did not originate in the West. Slave dealing in the Sudan dates back to remotest antiquity; the slave trade was Africa's first form of labor migration. From time immemorial, Egypt, North Africa, and the Middle East purchased black people from the south who did duty as servants and farmhands, as soldiers and palace guards, as eunuchs and concubines. But caravans going by land could carry only a comparatively small haul of captives; the demand for slaves in the Mediterranean basin always remained restricted. The Mediterranean produced a limited number of plantation economies. Mediterranean plantations, mines, and workshops—especially those of Carthage and Rome—mainly relied on white prisoners from the more immediate peripheries of their dominions. In West Africa the social effects of this early small-scale commerce probably were limited.

In the seventeenth century, however, commerce in human beings received a tremendous impetus through the sudden and insatiable demand for agricultural labor in the plantations of the West Indies and the Americas. West Africa already possessed an established class of indigenous traders, willing and able to handle "black ivory." Right from the start, the existence of domestic slavery among some of the coastal people provided a readily available stock for export. European sailing ships were able to handle a much larger volume of traffic than camels and dromedaries on the trans-Saharan routes. The traffic reached its greatest extent in the eighteenth century and was finally brought to an end in the late nineteenth century. Statisticians have given conflicting estimates of the number of people involved in this enormous forced migration: some believe that 15 million persons were shipped overseas between the sixteenth and the nineteenth centuries; others put the total loss at as much as 40 million. These figures represent an unimaginable amount of suffering, exceeded possibly only during such human catastrophes as the Thirty Years War in Europe in the seventeenth century or the mass liquidations carried out by totalitarian regimes in the twentieth century. Its social effects are, however, more difficult to calculate. Some historians now largely ascribe Africa's technological and material backwardness to the effects of the slave trade and to the loss of population which the traffic entailed. They also blame this commerce for such perversions as cannibalism, which made its appearance in Nigeria and the Congo and played a major part in shaping the Victorian image of Africa. The evidence is not, however, clear-cut. Barotseland remained relatively sheltered from the incursions of slave traders into the interior of southern Africa. The Lozi ruling class had little interest in exporting much-needed manpower; on the contrary, they preferred to raid their neighbors on their own account. The kingdom was also protected by sheer distance from the main centers of slave dealing in Angola and the East Coast. Nevertheless, Barotseland never attained a higher level of material civilization than the West African states which did participate in slave traffic. Lozi politics also had a dark side, with tortures, liquidations, and other refinements of cruelty that owed nothing to foreign pressure or inspiration.[26] Cannibalism—a custom adopted by some African communities either for ritual purposes or for the sake of obtaining a more varied diet—flourished among people like the Ibo of Nigeria, who were involved in the slave trade; cannibalism, however, was also popular with the Zimba, a conquering horde who terrorized various parts of East Africa during the sixteenth century but did not sell their captives to the Christians.[27]

The effects of manpower losses brought about by the slave trade are equally difficult to assess. Daniel Neumark, a modern economic historian who has gone over the slave-trade figures, estimates that if the total population of West Africa during the slave-trade period stood at no more than 20 million, the average loss would have

[26] See, for instance, François Coillard, *On the Threshold of Central Africa: A Record of Twenty Years' Pioneering among the Barotsi of the Upper Zambezi* (2d ed.; London, 1902), for a very grim interpretation of Barotse life in precolonial days.

[27] For cannibalism among the Ibo see, for instance, Burns, *History of Nigeria*, p. 59. For Zimba cannibalism see Roger Summers, *Inyanga: Prehistoric Settlements in Southern Rhodesia* (Cambridge, Eng., 1958), p. 225.

amounted to a maximum of 0.5 percent a year.[28] Slave depredations, however, were very unevenly spread. The strong and highly central-ized black states of the coastal regions, which managed to monopolize the traffic with the hinterland, prospered amazingly; kingdoms such as Oyo, Dahomey, and Ashanti owed their greatness and prosperity to slave dealing. Thus some areas derived considerable economic benefit from the trade. Oddly enough, it is precisely those parts of West Africa which might be assumed to have suffered most from the slave trade—the Gold Coast and what is now southern Nigeria—that comprise today some of the most advanced and densely populated districts of the country. Even when the slave trade was at its highest, these regions were remarkable for the density of their population and for their elaborate political organization. In some instances the ex-pansion of trade acted as a stimulus to the growth of population by the introduction of American plants and fruit.[29] It also contributed to the development of more centralized forms of political rule. The ex-port of slaves enabled Africans to purchase consumer goods which they could not have afforded otherwise. All in all, slave traffic proba-bly gave even more employment to African than to European dealers. No wonder, therefore, that the British abolition of the slave trade in 1807 led to bitter African discontent on the Gold Coast.

The damage inflicted on parts of Africa was nevertheless disastrous. Outlying regions on the periphery of the slave-trading states suffered with special severity; so did the less densely populated regions, which could not easily stand any additional loss of manpower. Slave trading represented not merely an inhuman system, but also a serious diver-sion of economic resources. Imported guns made warfare more de-structive in its effects; the trade in firearms certainly gave an added advantage to freebooting chiefs, able to acquire the discarded weap-ons of the West for use against less well equipped neighbors and rivals. Slave-trading kingdoms themselves became demoralized. Hu-man sacrifice flourished in Benin; Dahomey at the end of the century presented a picture not of youthful vigor, but of bloodstained de-cadence.

The effect of the slave trade on the metropolitan economies varied a good deal. Slave traffic formed an essential component in a "tri-angle of trade" involving Europe and America, the West Coast of Africa, and the West Indies. Liverpool merchants sent manufactured goods to, say, the Gold Coast, where British factors bartered "black

[28] S. Daniel Neumark, *Foreign Trade and Economic Development in Africa: A Historical Perspective* (Stanford, Calif., 1964), pp. 50–54, especially p. 51.
[29] J. Vansina, "Long-Distance Trade-Routes in Central Africa," *Journal of African History,* III, No. 3 (1962), 387.

ivory" in exchange for knives, cloth, trinkets, guns, and other goods. The slaves were shipped to the New World, and British vessels then returned home laden with bales of tobacco and similar commodities. Slaves provided indispensable manpower for the plantations of the American South, Jamaica, and adjacent islands, thereby lowering the price of sugar, rum, cotton, and tobacco for overseas consumers. The commerce provided employment for a whole army of traders and their factors, shipwrights and sailors, rum distillers and iron manufacturers. In the United States, too, the financial ramifications of the trade affected many elements of society. The West Indian slave plantations provided New England fishermen with markets for dried fish. Landowners benefited from the sale of timber to barrel makers or shipbuilders. Rhode Island in particular made a great deal of money from slave traffic, which played a major part in transforming its economy from an agricultural to a mercantile one. Slave trade was also accompanied by legitimate commerce; African merchants bought ordinary trade goods as well as men and sold manufactured articles in exchange.[30]

Fortunately, however, the traffic in slaves did not always prove an unmixed blessing to its overseas perpetrators. Parsimonious New England slave traders might invest their profits in new enterprises, but a good deal of money was used for conspicuous display, and countries such as Portugal and Zanzibar failed to use their mercantile gains for manufacturing. Slave trading, moreover, was apt to prove expensive. European merchants, obliged to fit out ships and buy valuable cargo such as cloth, East Indian textiles, metal goods, muskets, rum, and so forth, had to risk an outlay very much greater than that of their African commercial partners, who merely supplied the slaves. In the seventeenth century, a slave-trading venture such as that of the Royal African Company had to pay for the upkeep of forts and garrisons; there were constant hazards at sea from storms, pirates, and pestilence; in addition, there were the usual business risks.[31] Small countries like Brandenburg or Courland which tried their hands at the slave trade could not compete, for they lacked transatlantic plantation colonies of their own and could only sell their slaves to planters of other nations. The smaller powers accordingly failed to make their enterprise pay, but even well-established English or Dutch traders might suffer heavy loss.

In the latter part of the eighteenth century, moreover, the slave

[30] Peter Duignan and Clarence Clendenen, *The United States and the African Slave Trade, 1619–1862* (Stanford, Calif., 1963), pp. 5–11.

[31] For a detailed study of such a chartered company see Kenneth Gordon Davies, *The Royal African Company* (London, 1957).

trade became offensive to the British Christian and humanitarian conscience; all the outstanding Western thinkers now considered the traffic incompatible with ideals of Christian liberty and also with a capitalist economy based on free exchange of goods and labor. The final solution of this iniquitous commerce forms no part of this story. Suffice it to say that toward the end of the eighteenth and at the beginning of the nineteenth century the British slaving and West Indian interests, and the whole complex network of lobbies associated with these groups, sustained a series of crushing ideological, political, and economic blows. Britain put an end to its slave trade in 1807; and from then on the island kingdom began to press for abolition of slave traffic by all other powers, both for humanitarian reasons and in order to do away with what was now regarded as unfair competition on the part of foreigners. In 1833 plantation slavery was ended in the British Empire; the United States·followed suit in the Civil War; in Brazil slavery ceased in 1888.

The American plantation economies, based on monoculture and forced labor, underwent a profound transformation. The British especially, and to a lesser extent the Americans, threw their naval, diplomatic, and financial power into the scales against the slave trade. There was a long-drawn-out struggle, extending over several generations, one of the great humanitarian campaigns of history, and at long last the enforced migration of Africans to the New World became a thing of the past. On the West Coast of Africa the traffic in human beings gradually gave way to "legitimate" business in forest produce. This economic revolution profoundly affected the local balance of power in West Africa. It also made an important contribution to economic development in Western Europe. In the nineteenth century Western living standards went up enormously. There was an increased demand for better illumination at night, as well as a greater vogue for personal cleanliness. West Africa produced palm oil and palm kernels needed by British candle and soap producers. Machines required more lubricants, and thus the demand for imported oil went up. Western manufacturers looking overseas for markets began to turn to Africa for expanded sales, so that West Africa was slowly drawn into a worldwide system of legitimate commerce.

But as the Christian slave trade declined on the West Coast of Africa, the Muslim traffic picked up momentum in East Africa. In the nineteenth century slaves were increasingly shipped to the clove plantations of Zanzibar and Pemba, as well as to southern Arabia, Turkey, and Persia. Carriers, many of them slaves themselves, were the only means of transportation under conditions where the dreaded tsetse fly and topographical obstacles made the employment of animal-drawn vehicles either too costly or altogether impracticable. The trade in slaves and ivory commonly went hand in hand. Africa developed into the world's most important supplier of elephant tusks, and outside southern Africa ivory dealers normally did business in slaves as well. African ivory was fashioned into billiard balls and piano keys, into cutlery handles and the knickknacks that used to cram Victorian parlors. At the same time India purchased great quantities of the rings left over from the turning of billiard balls to sell in bazaars as women's bangles. Craftsmen also bought ivory as a raw material for ornaments, statuettes, and other luxury goods. From the south, white hunters made their way across the Limpopo and later across the Zambezi. From the east, Swahili traders penetrated farther and farther inland to find new hunting grounds.

These Arab and half-caste frontiersmen, in most cases, came not as permanent settlers, but to amass a fortune sufficient to retire to the harems and plantations of the coast. Where conditions seemed favorable, they established lordships of their own. Among many of the weaker tribes inhabiting the regions bordering Lake Tanganyika or Lake Nyasa this was an easy matter, for the Arabs possessed breechloaders and knew how to fortify themselves in well-designed stockades. The intruders from the coast also involved indigenous communities in the trade. Prominent among Bantu slave traders were the Yao, who drifted into Nyasaland from the east in small groups, subjugating the native Nyanja. The slave trade was the invaders' chief means of acquiring muskets, rifles, and cloth, but in their case commerce was closely linked to conquest of land for settlement. The somewhat more powerful chiefs had an additional political incentive, for slave trade would provide them with gunpowder and thereby enhance control over turbulent headmen. Another group of raiders consisted of Portuguese half-castes from the Zambezi valley, locally known as Achikunda. In addition, slave caravans made their way inland from Angola. These Portuguese, or Portuguese-speaking Bantu, traders worked through native chiefs, who received guns and powder in exchange for slaves. The chiefs then armed their warriors and engaged in further raids, with the result that the commerce spread rapidly inland. By the end of the 1870s Biheno merchants had penetrated to the Kafue River, and the two invading groups met in the heart of Africa.[32] In addition, Muslim adventurers were also pushing into the interior from the north, down the Nile Valley, raiding and trading with the Nilotic and Nilo-Hamitic races whom they encountered on their way.

The slave trade proper did not by any means draw the whole of

[32] Lewis H. Gann, *The Birth of a Plural Society: The Development of Northern Rhodesia under the British South Africa Company, 1894–1914* (Manchester, Eng., 1958), pp. 9–14.

Africa into its vortex. The tribes of southern Africa did not participate in the traffic to any significant extent; some communities, like the Lozi of what is now Zambia, abstained from selling people on any large scale. Yet even they appropriated foreign muscle power by raiding along the periphery of their kingdom. More serious were the inroads of the South African Zulu and their descendants. In the beginning of the nineteenth century the Zulu of Natal effected one of the great military revolutions of the continent. Zulu warriors learned how to fight in closely disciplined formations, wielding deadly stabbing spears and protecting themselves with huge oxhide shields. The Zulu possessed cattle herds; this four-legged "commissariat" made them to some extent independent of what they could cultivate or capture on the way, giving them a great range of action. The Zulu, and Zulu offshoots such as the Matabele and the Angorni, were thus in a position to live a semiparasitic existence on surrounding peoples. They raided their neighbors for cattle, for women, and for children, whom they incorporated into the tribe, thereby increasing its manpower, with the result that these warrior communities quickly snowballed and spread their power over vast areas of southern Africa, the northernmost offshoots marching as far as Tanganyika.

The trade in slaves and ivory, the steady movement of the "gun frontier" inland, and raiding by indigenous hosts trained in new methods of warfare profoundly affected African life. Long before European settlers or officials arrived on the scene, the Western world had indirectly begun to influence African society. The importation of guns in exchange for ivory and slaves exalted the power of chiefs and gang leaders in possession of improved weapons or of local monopolies. Just as the introduction of the horse and the gun among the Plains Indians of North America added to the ferocity of internecine strife, the advent of guns and powder made African wars worse. It did not matter where the raiders came from, east or west, or whether they captured prisoners for sale or for domestic use; there was always the same story of burned villages, slaughter, and the devastation of crops. Many survivors who escaped starved to death; many others died on the road to captivity. Recovery from such affrays was often difficult for the weaker tribes; primitive economies could not draw on accumulated capital, and the margin of survival was narrow at the best of times. The results could be terrifying, and on this point all contemporary observers agreed. Livingstone, for example, was told by the British consul at Zanzibar that in the early 1860s some 19,000 slaves were sent from Nyasaland to Zanzibar alone. This figure, of course, was exclusive of the numbers sent through Portuguese slave ports, but "those taken out of the country are but a very small section of the sufferers. We never realized the atrocious nature of the traffic until we saw it at the fountainhead. There truly 'Satan has his seat.' Besides those actually captured, thousands are killed and die of their wounds and famine, driven from their villages by the slave raid proper. Thousands perish in internecine wars waged for slaves with their own clansmen and neighbours." Vast parts of Nyasaland were reduced to misery:

> No words can convey an adequate idea of the scene of wide-spread desolation which the once pleasant Shire Valley now presented. Instead of smiling villages and crowds of people coming with things for sale, scarcely a soul was to be seen; and when by chance one lighted on a native his frame bore the impress of hunger, and his countenance the look of a cringing broken-spiritedness. A drought had visited the land after the slave-hunting panic swept over it. Had it been possible to conceive the thorough depopulation which had ensued, we should have avoided coming up the river. Large masses of the people had fled down to the Shire, only anxious to get the river between them and their enemies. Most of the food had been left behind; and famine and starvation had cut off so many, that the remainder were too few to bury the dead. The corpses we saw floating down the river were only a remnant of those that had perished, whom their friends, from weakness, could not bury, nor overgorged crocodiles devour. It is true that famine caused a great portion of this waste of human life; but the slave trade must be deemed the chief agent in the ruin, because, as we were informed, in former droughts all the people flocked from the hills down to the marshes, which are capable of yielding crops of maize in less than three months at any time of the year, and now they were afraid to do so.[33]

Comparisons between the destructive effects of primitive and modern warfare in relation to the recuperative capacity of the societies involved are obviously difficult. Potentates like Msidi, a late nineteenth-century freebooting chief in the Katanga, or Umzilikazi, a dreaded Matabele monarch, employed praise singers, not statisticians. But their wars nevertheless might prove extremely costly. In World War II, Germany, after more than five years of bloody and desperate fighting, lost just under 4 percent of its population on the battlefield. With the assistance of foreign aid West Germany quickly recovered from the devastation of war, and West German national production soon vastly exceeded prewar rates. Traditional African warfare probably called for a proportionately smaller blood toll and in general may have involved less economic dislocation. But the military revolutions

[33] David Livingstone and Charles Livingstone, *Narrative of an Expedition to the Zambesi and Its Tributaries and of the Discovery of the Lakes Shirwa and Nyassa, 1858–1864* (New York, 1866), pp. 412–413, 481.

brought about by Zulu militarization, and by the importation of fire-arms during the nineteenth century, brought a disastrous change for the worse. No one knows what percentage of the tribes attacked by the Matabele, for instance, perished in local wars, but we know that some of these communities, like the Tonga peoples of what is now Zambia, suffered with extreme severity. Recovery from such raids proved more difficult for a weak tribe, depending largely on sub-sistence agriculture, than for a modern industrial community, which can produce far more goods and can spread its risks with greater ease. On a comparative basis strife was therefore likely to be even more destructive among the people of Central Africa during the second half of the nineteenth century than for Western Europe in the first half of the twentieth century. The Bantu could be saved from these wasting struggles and from their general economic and technological back-wardness only by the imposition of stable government. No indigenous power possessed either the technological or the administrative re-sources required for such a task, and the solution at long last came from the West.

12. Europe in Africa
by the Early 1870s

From the Western point of view, Africa of some hundred and forty years ago was still "a continent of outposts," with its interior largely unknown. There was only one great exception. The northern shore, from Egypt to Algiers, was under Turkish suzerainty. On the map the Ottoman Empire appeared to be the greatest colonial power in Africa; but the Caliph's dominions were in decline, Turkish men-of-war had long since ceased to dominate the southern and eastern littoral, and Turkey was now more an object than an independent agent in European policy. The French Revolutionary Wars led to the first great modern irruption of the West into the Levant. Napoleon, having abandoned his plans for a direct invasion of England, determined to strike at the island kingdom's Indian empire by way of Egypt, but the French could not hold their conquests against British sea power. In 1802 the Peace of Amiens restored Egypt to the Sultan; yet the Ottomans could not maintain effective control, and Egypt in effect became a semi-independent state in which Albanians, Greeks, and other Levantine immigrants held most of the key positions. In 1805 Mohammed Ali, a former tobacco merchant from Kavalla who had come to the country in command of an Albanian military contingent, secured the governorship and began to westernize the country with French aid. Mohammed Ali might be likened in some ways to Peter the Great; he liquidated the mutinous Mameluk army and its leaders, introduced the cultivation of cotton and hemp, and built up modern fighting services. Between 1820 and 1822 he conquered Nubia, Sennar, and Kordofan in the Sudan to gain more effective control of the southern trade in slaves and gold.

The French would have liked to cooperate with Egypt. The restored Bourbon monarchy looked for success abroad to offset its waning prestige at home; the conquest of Algiers also would extirpate a nest of Muslim pirates and bring honor to a Christian France. The French at the same time asked Mohammed Ali to cooperate with them, hoping to combine conquests in the Western Mediterranean with designs for expanding their influence in the Levant through the Viceroy's instrumentality. Mohammed, however, pitched his price too high; he also dreaded British intervention, and in the end the French decided to act on their own.[1] In 1830, a time when Britain was too much preoccupied with other issues, the French struck and captured Algiers, but effective conquest took more than half a century. The French met with frequent reverses in the interior, and the fortunes of war began to change only in 1837, when Thomas Robert Bugeaud, a one-time grenadier in Napoleon's army, secured command. Bugeaud, a brilliant military innovator, relied on swift offensive thrusts by self-contained formations which carried their supplies on horses, mules, and camels instead of wagons. He effectively kept the enemy on the move, menaced their food supply, built a network of roads, and encouraged European settlement. His operation benefited greatly from the study of Roman practice. The French, with unshaken cultural self-confidence, regarded their work as a revival of Rome's ancient civilizing mission. The Muslims, for their part, suffered from severe internal dissensions; the Berber mountain tribes would not cooperate with the Arabs, and in 1847 Abd-el-Kader, the greatest of Algerian leaders, finally surrendered. Sporadic resistance continued in certain parts of Algeria until the early 1880s. From then on Muslim opposition to French rule lay dormant until after World War I.[2]

The French began a vigorous policy of colonization; numerous European immigrants entered the country and carved out farms for themselves, most of them in the coastal regions, where communications were better and rain more plentiful than inland. By 1846 the number of Europeans in Algeria already amounted to 100,000, and more kept coming in. In many areas the newcomers displaced the original population; in others they brought unused land under the plow by draining swamps or irrigating drought-stricken areas. Wheat and grape cultivation expanded, communications were improved, and Algeria became a French-speaking settlement frontier, where Christian colonists pressed upon established and relatively numerous Muslim communities. European colonization brought a social revolution

[1] C. W. Crawley, "The Mediterranean," in *The New Cambridge Modern History:* Vol. X, *The Zenith of European Power, 1830–70* (Cambridge, Eng., 1960), 416–441.

[2] For a general introduction see Nevill Barbour (ed.), *A Survey of North West Africa (The Maghrib)* (2d ed.; London, 1962), pp. 1–47 and 201–255. For a detailed history see Charles-André Julien, *Histoire de l'Algérie contemporaine: La conquête et les débuts de la colonisation (1827–1871)* (Paris, 1964).

and met with bitter opposition from within the country. Many Algerians lost their land rights; many detested the foreigners' taxes; some even looked back to the easygoing days of old, when the Turkish rulers were at least fellow Muslims instead of Christian Franks and when government rested on only slender military and administrative foundations.

The white newcomers, for their part, met with great economic difficulties; the majority of French settlers became an urban people, who lacked contacts with the indigenous population. The settlers also encountered harsh criticism from Paris. Napoleon III, like Disraeli, had little interest in overseas extension; whereas the Tory minister once described the colonies as millstones around British necks, the Emperor referred to Algeria as a stone attached to the feet of France. He pronounced Algeria to be "an Arab kingdom," and unsuccessfully tried to promote penetration by great financial companies instead of colonization by farmers and merchants, although the Third Republic reverted to a more active policy of colonization. France also continued to exert considerable economic and cultural influence in Egypt, and by the early 1870s the Tricolor flew over what was then the greatest African colonial empire north of the equator.

In West Africa, French power originally rested in Senegal, where a small factory was first set up in 1645. In the middle of the last century the colony consisted of little more than a small coastal strip with the port of Saint-Louis, which did some trading up the Senegal River. Senegal, like West Africa as a whole, proved unsuitable for European farmers; the country formed part of a soldier's and merchant's frontier, where European firms and French-speaking enfranchised mulattoes dominated the economic scene. The colony suffered from serious fiscal problems. Governors found great difficulty in protecting traders upriver against the exactions of Moorish peoples such as the Brakna and the Trarza. Muslim potentates established alliances with Negro peoples in the vicinity of Saint-Louis itself, so that the French began to fear encirclement. In addition, the French wished to safeguard their expanding inland commerce, which had come to rest more and more on the export of African-grown peanuts. Peanuts were first introduced to the country by Portuguese slave traders and grown for African consumption. In the mid-nineteenth century, however, an odd quirk of fashion suddenly turned peanuts into a profitable export crop. French consumers refused to buy the yellow soap manufactured from palm oil; Marseilles soapmakers thus turned to making a blue marble soap, manufactured by mixing peanut oil with olive oil. The fashion caught on, and African farmers successfully adjusted production to the new demand. Exports expanded to a phenomenal figure —from an estimated 1,000 kilos in 1841 to almost 5 million kilos in

1854.[3] The French economic stake in Senegal grew steadily bigger; but the colony now had to meet a dangerous long-term threat from a militant Muslim movement, one of the many warlike Mohammedan revivals which played such a large part in the history of the nineteenth-century Sudan.

One of the greatest leaders in this part of West Africa was Al Hadj Umar, whose career was in many ways characteristic of these movements. Umar, a Tukolor notable, had gone on a pilgrimage to Mecca and had also visited Egypt, Bornu, and Sokoto, becoming familiar with the thought and social conditions in the African portion of the Muslim world. A man of outstanding ability and strong religious conviction, Umar built up a powerful military machine, part crusading order, part trading enterprise, and part army, which stood for a reformed egalitarian and puritanical form of religion. He relied on a militant elite of disciples (most of them also Tukolor), who served as governors and generals. Occupied areas were controlled from stone forts, where his chosen lieutenants ruled rather like feudal barons, conscripting soldiers and levying taxes. Much of the resulting revenue went to purchase firearms from the coast, so that conquests provided the fuel for new conquests. Umar thus managed to seize control over the upper basins of the Niger and Senegal; he built up a vast empire which kept encroaching on its various neighbors, including the possessions of more orthodox Muslim princes.[4] He met with numerous revolts against the religious and financial exactions imposed by his governing theocracy. The French thus found themselves in a difficult position. Not only did Umar's empire hold the key to future commercial expansion toward the Niger, but his religious authority might also be used one day to threaten their security in the lower Senegal itself.

The French, however, found a brilliant leader in Louis Faidherbe, an engineer officer who had distinguished himself in Algeria (and subsequently gained additional laurels in the Franco-Prussian war). Faidherbe assumed charge of Senegal in 1854, and his appointment was perhaps one of the most successful ever made by the Second Empire. Within a decade he vastly extended the borders of Senegal, checked Umar's advance, agreed with the prophet on a demarcation of spheres of influence on the upper Senegal, and brought the French possessions in touch with the Niger. Faidherbe was as outstanding an organizer and administrator as he was a soldier. He created the

[3] Martin A. Klein, "Sine-Saloum, 1847–1914: The Traditional States and the French Conquest" (doctoral dissertation, University of Chicago, 1964), pp. 64–65.

[4] John D. Fage, *An Introduction to the History of West Africa* (3d ed.; Cambridge, Eng., 1962), pp. 148–149.

Tirailleurs Sénégalais, an African elite formation which played a major part in subsequent French advances; he promoted the cultivation of peanuts and encouraged educational work. When he finally left in 1865, his colony was the only dependency in tropical Africa where the colonizers had made any penetration in depth, and Senegal became the Frenchmen's main point of departure for subsequent conquests.[5]

South of Senegal the British held a narrow strip of territory along the Gambia River, where they had established a settlement in 1816 to check the slave trade. In 1857 they had also acquired Albreda, previously a French enclave, so that the Union Jack now floated over the entire navigable portion of the river. On paper the British thus owned a magnificent asset. The Gambia is the only water course in Africa where oceangoing vessels can steam up for more than two hundred miles beyond its mouth; the Gambia thus commanded a strategic ingress into the western Sudan. But what nature gave with one hand she took away with the other. Bathurst, the capital, stood in the midst of mangrove-fringed marshes. Malaria infected the river valley and tidal creeks, and disease formed a deadly barrier to European penetration. The interior, much of it rolling country covered by coarse grass, suffered from periodic droughts, like most of the western Sudan. There were no minerals. By the middle of the last century the country exported some peanuts through Bathurst; African dealers inland also did a little business in kola nuts and other produce. But the volume of trade remained small, and the British found their insalubrious possession so unprofitable that in the late 1860s and early 1870s there were serious, though unsuccessful, designs to hand the country to the French in exchange for concessions elsewhere.[6]

A trading vessel sailing south from Bathurst would pass Bulama, a small Portuguese settlement on the West Coast, and after a journey of some four hundred miles would make land at the port of Freetown. Freetown, the capital of Sierra Leone, had a curious origin. It owed its existence to the activities of British humanitarians and, like the neighboring Negro Republic of Liberia, might be described as part of the "philanthropist frontier." In 1791 a British association received a charter for the purpose of settling freed Negro slaves from the New World in their continent of origin, and soon a strangely assorted lot of

5 See John D. Hargreaves, *Prelude to the Partition of West Africa* (London, 1963), especially pp. 9–13, 99–103, 122–126. See also the article by Robert Louis Delavignette on Faidherbe, in Charles-André Julien (ed.), *Les techniciens de la colonisation (XIXe–XXe siècles)* (Paris, 1946), pp. 75–92.

6 For a general history of the Gambia see Lady Southorn, *The Gambia: The Story of the Groundnut Colony* (London, 1952), and Harry A. Gailey, Jr., *A History of the Gambia* (London, 1964).

settlers made their home in this new haven. The colonists included Negroes who had fought under the British flag in the American War of Independence; there were ex-slaves, who had obtained their liberty after Lord Mansfield's famous judicial decision of 1772 declaring slavery illegal in the United Kingdom; there were also Jamaicans and a collection of blacks taken off slave ships by the Royal Navy and dumped on the coast. The newcomers met conditions of great severity.

Most of Sierra Leone's coastline and creeks are lined by unhealthy mangrove swamps, and large areas in the interior are covered by brushwood and forest; disease conspired with climatic conditions to make the colonists' lot exceptionally hard. Sierra Leone's hot, moist coastal climate turned the settlement into a white man's grave and a black man's purgatory; torrential rainfalls were followed by a long dry season, punctuated sometimes by tornadoes or by desiccating northeast winds carrying clouds of fine Sahara dust known by sailors as "smokes."

After many setbacks, however, the colony slowly expanded. At Freetown sailing vessels dropped anchor in West Africa's finest harbor. In addition, the Church Missionary Society in 1827 founded Fourah Bay College, which in 1876 was affiliated to the University of Durham, England. Fourah Bay was the first, and at the time the only, institution of Western higher learning in West Africa, giving Sierra Leoneans an advantage from which they were quick to profit. Sierra Leone became an important base for the British navy's operation against the slave trade; Freetown also became a center for trade in palm oil and peanuts. Merchant ships of many nations—after many initial restrictions, especially against American vessels—sailed in and out with their merchandise. The Sierra Leone Creoles, English-speaking Negroes of mixed descent, benefited to some extent from this slowly expanding economy; they pushed outward along the coast and inward into the hinterland as dealers, clerks, government employees, mission agents, and sometimes as farmers.[7]

Freetown, with its shops, agencies, and newspaper offices, became one of the few places where a modified form of the British Victorian tradition struck roots in Negro Africa. Many British travelers regarded these anglicized Negroes with a good deal of contempt. There seems to be some kind of psychological law which makes apparent corruptions of one's mother tongue sound ridiculous; many German speakers regard Yiddish as ugly; Dutchmen frequently look down on Afrikaans; most nineteenth-century Englishmen regarded Creoles and their form of English with a similar contempt. The Creoles nevertheless supported British rule, especially since colonization sometimes

[7] For a general history see Christopher Fyfe, *A History of Sierra Leone* (London, 1962), *passim*.

led to clashes between Creoles and the tribes of the interior. The administration was gradually drawn into inland expansion, both to safeguard commerce by putting a stop to intertribal fighting and to prevent the French from reducing the colony to a small enclave. In the early 1870s Edward Blyden, a black scholar of great competence, visited Falaba and Timbo, two partly Muslimized countries inland; he helped to bring Falaba under British protection and stood out as a striking representative of that early generation of Negro intellectuals who did so much to further the imperial cause.

South of Sierra Leone, Anglo-Saxon philanthropy created yet another black-settlement colony. Many American humanitarians wished to better the American Negro's lot by sending him back to his assumed country of origin. Others saw repatriation as a convenient device for ridding the United States of free Negroes, whose vague legal status was a constant source of friction and whose very existence seemed a threat to Southern slaveholders. In 1816 American well-wishers of the Negro formed the American Colonization Society, which acquired some land at Cape Mesurado, Liberia, and promoted the emigration of American Negroes to this tropical frontier. The United States government provided some financial and naval support, but for some time the future of the colony remained in doubt. Contrary to current thought on the subject, black settlers were just as susceptible to fever as whites; they suffered from the tropical climate in the same way as Europeans. There was the usual pioneering story of lack of capital and unfamiliarity with local conditions. The fortunes of the settlement took a turn for the better only when Jehudi Ashmun, a white American, assumed command of the colony, wiped out two local slaving centers, and put an end to the local traffic. Liberia subsequently absorbed some additional black Americans; in 1847 the small state declared its independence under President Joseph Jenkins Roberts, a Virginian octoroon of outstanding ability. But Liberia's problems were far from solved. By the early 1870s the small state numbered no more than perhaps 20,000 American Negroes. Numerous quarrels broke out with the tribes of the interior, especially with the relatively civilized Mandingo. There were bitter internal dissensions among the colonists themselves; there were boundary disputes with the British and French; there was a good deal of graft and incompetence; there was little enterprise and less money. The Civil War emancipated the American Negroes and thereby lessened Liberia's attraction for them, so that only a trickle of newcomers made their way across the Atlantic. It was not until 1862 that the United States officially recognized its stepchild.

In 1871 the small state, a very poor financial risk, secured a loan on the London market at onerous terms, and President Edward J.

Roye was subsequently deposed on the grounds of having personally made money from the transaction. The Liberian settlers became a small, closely knit oligarchy which asserted far-flung claims over the interior, without possessing much in the way of technological, administrative, or economic resources to develop their patrimony. The Liberian experiment in some ways actually injured the Negro image in the white man's eyes; advocates of European imperialism never tired of pointing out Liberia and Haiti as object lessons concerning the black man's assumed incapacity to take charge of his own affairs. Liberia did not provide an inspiration to American Negroes in the way that Israel became a glorious example for so many Jews. The Liberian venture owed its initiative to white Americans; the colonists lacked the financial and scientific resources as well as the moral cohesion of the early Zionist settlers. Liberia held no religious appeal; Cape Mesurado was not the promised land to which exiles had looked back with immeasurable longing for centuries. The Liberians nevertheless managed to hold on under extremely tough conditions and finally took a modest part in the scramble for Africa by extending their hinterland and thereby unwittingly saddling themselves with a considerable "native problem."[8]

The Gambia and Sierra Leone were only outposts of British trade. The bulk of Britain's West African commerce centered in lower Guinea, the focal point of the trader's frontier in the area. Gold and slaves attracted dealers from England, Holland, France, and elsewhere; the newcomers built a network of forts along the coast, from which they sold guns, cloth, liquor, and trinkets to the interior. One of their chief suppliers of prisoners of war for sale to the New World was Ashanti, a powerful tribal confederacy. European influence was confined to the shores of the Atlantic Ocean, but even so, this limited form of colonization remained an expensive affair. Upkeep of forts, garrisons, and local staff cost a great deal of money; at first, only chartered companies could face the outlay involved. British trade throughout the eighteenth century thus rested on mercantile associations such as the Royal African Company and later the African Company of Merchants. The abolition of the slave trade struck a crushing blow to this system of exchange; in addition, many of the alluvial gold deposits in the area became exhausted, so that the Europeans were forced to look for alternate goods such as palm oil. The Ashanti, from the British point of view, thereby lost their usefulness as suppliers of

[8] One of the best works for the nineteenth-century history of Liberia is still, despite its prejudices, Vol. I of Sir Harry Hamilton Johnston, *Liberia* (London, 1906). For a good summary of the country's current problems see J. Gus Liebenow's article in Gwendolen M. Carter (ed.), *African One-Party States* (Ithaca, N.Y., 1962), pp. 325–386.

forced labor. Worse still, they were now well supplied with guns; they invaded the coastlands, fought against the local Fanti, and ultimately claimed suzerainty over the European forts. From about the 1820s, Britain supported the Fanti, who sought to ensure or recover their local independence; but the Ashanti were determined opponents. In addition, the forest belt proved almost as effective a barrier to British Redcoats as it did to Muslim cavalry from the savannah in the north, and the British found that the bush and the malaria mosquito combined were stronger than the white man's cannons.

In 1824 the Ashanti defeated Sir Charles Macarthy, a British governor who had espoused the cause of the Fanti. Macarthy was killed on the battlefield, and his skull ended as a royal drinking cup in the Ashanti capital. The British recovered from this disaster only with difficulty and in 1831 concluded a compromise peace. However, British power was in the ascendant. The British merchants in control of the coastal forts found a governor of exceptional ability in George Maclean, who steadily cooperated with the tribal communities hostile to the Ashanti and gradually built up British influence on the coast.[9] Affairs went so well that the Colonial Office in 1843 decided to resume control of the coastal forts, which for the previous fifteen years had been left to the administration of British traders. The British subsequently also acquired the Danish and Dutch settlements in the area and thereby rid themselves of various foreign complications. They also held a strong economic position. By the end of the nineteenth century, British traders along the Gold Coast did not rely on African middlemen as much as they did in the Niger delta farther east; they usually took goods to the interior themselves or employed black agents.[10] In earlier centuries, the Gold Coast had produced powerful middlemen states such as Akwamu, Akim, and Denkyera, but by the eighteenth century all these powers had crumbled before the might of Ashanti.

In the end, the British could not confine their own interests to the coast. In 1865 a Parliamentary Select Committee, disgusted with the expenditure entailed by Britain's West African obligations, advocated a partial and gradual British withdrawal. But traders throughout British West Africa wanted more, not less, protection, and the committee's resolutions had only a limited impact on British policy. The British would not pull out; nor could they escape the complications of

[9] See George E. Metcalfe, *Maclean of the Gold Coast: The Life and Times of George Maclean, 1801–1847* (London, 1962).

[10] Kenneth Onwuka Dike, *Trade and Politics in the Niger Delta, 1830–1885: An Introduction to the Economic and Political History of Nigeria* (Oxford, 1956), *passim*. Much of the above section is based on this work.

the turbulent frontier. Friction with the Ashanti continued, and in 1873 a strong Ashanti force advanced to the vicinity of the Gold Coast. But the Ashanti army suffered heavily from smallpox, and the British retrieved the situation. General Sir Garnet Wolseley hurried out from England and in 1874 occupied Kumasi, the Ashanti capital, after bitter fighting. Kofi Karikari, the Ashanti sovereign, wisely retired to the bush, and now it was the British who found themselves in a quandary. Fever stalked their ranks; provisions were scarce; the rains were about to break. Wolseley had to retreat, but the Ashanti were eventually forced to make peace. The British failed to follow up their success. They aimed at keeping Ashanti power divided, yet Kumasi managed to reconsolidate its power, and effective British rule remained confined to a strip of territory skirting the Atlantic coast.[11]

Farther east, along the Bights of Benin and Biafra, the pattern of European power was somewhat different. As the demand for slaves increased in the eighteenth century, European merchants extended their field of operations. Commerce fell into the hands of newer firms without means or men to set up coastal forts. The white traders worked in partnership with the small city-states along the Niger delta and relied for protection on the power of the British fleet and the diplomacy of Her Britannic Majesty's consuls. The delta communities successfully adjusted themselves to the changes occasioned by the gradual destruction of the transatlantic slave trade. By about 1830 the trade in palm oil was more important than the traffic in men. Demand for oils, fats, and soap steadily increased, and the local African communities were able to benefit from the command of natural waterways, which greatly reduced transport costs. Internally these trading states were organized into houses, consisting of the traders' own families, freedmen, and slaves; these operated both as political and as commercial units. They controlled great fleets of rowing boats; the mightiest houses would also employ people to reclaim wasteland and establish farms at strategic positions along rivers and creeks. The delta states were better armed than the tribal communities in the interior; they owned great war canoes, some of them capable of carrying 140 men and armed with a large-caliber gun in the bow. Coastal magnates married their daughters to inland chiefs; they protected their tribal customers and allies in peace and war; they appointed reliable family heads as produce buyers on commission and advanced barter goods for business ventures farther inland.[12]

The advance of European science and technology, however, slowly

[11] For a recent work on Ashanti military history see Alan Lloyd, *The Drums of Kumasi: The Story of the Ashanti Wars* (London, 1964).
[12] See Dike, *Trade and Politics*.

began to undermine the local monopolies held by the coastal states. In 1830 the Lander brothers, two outstanding English explorers, traced the lower course of the Niger. In 1852 MacGregor Laird, a great Scottish merchant, founded the African Steamship Company, a government-subsidized concern which ran a regular mail service to the West Coast. Laird's steamships enabled smaller traders to set themselves up in business, to compete with the established European firms, and to introduce new methods. In 1854 Laird, a convinced Christian and an enthusiast for legitimate commerce in the Livingstonian tradition, sent out a little steamer, the *Pleiad,* to develop navigation on the Niger. William Balfour Baikie, the vessel's medical officer, took charge following the death of the senior officer, and the expedition performed the astounding feat of completing its journey without the loss of a single man. This success was made possible by the prophylactic use of quinine and proved the turning point in the country's history. The malaria barrier had been broken; medicine and steam power between them destroyed the local monopolies of the city-states. After the middle of the century the British government and the more farsighted white traders looked to the hinterland rather than to the seashore. The old system of controlling the city-states through naval squadrons and treaties ceased to be adequate to the needs of British trade.

The African palm-oil brokers in control of the strategic river courses and creeks put up a determined resistance to keep out white interlopers. British vessels steaming upriver encountered well-directed gunfire from fortified points along the banks. The merchants then called on their government for protection, and the 1870s saw some stiff fighting. A series of expeditions left for the interior to destroy delta and hinterland towns which had attacked British lives and property. As long as vessels flying the White Ensign remained in the vicinity of trading posts, the traders did good business. When the dry period set in and warships could no longer ascend the river, Africans resumed their attack, so that barter and battle alternated with the regularity of the seasons. British commercial penetration, however, could not be stopped. By the 1870s four British companies were operating along the Niger valley; navigation extended up to 600 miles into the interior, and the way was open to direct political intervention. What subsequently clinched the matter was French interference. British merchants could, and did, fight black potentates. They could not, however, cope with the officials of a great European power intent on negotiating treaties with the African communities on the Niger and determined to restrict British trade. Commerce and prestige alike called for colonization, and a new chapter opened in Nigerian history.

The pattern of Portuguese settlement farther south, near the mouth of the Congo, and beyond, along the Angolan coast, bore some similarities to that of the small European enclaves in the Gulf of Guinea. In centuries gone by, Portuguese seamen had pioneered navigation from Europe to the Cape and to the Indies. The very names of major geographical features reflected Portuguese primacy of exploration. Sierra Leone (Serra Leôa), "the Mountain of the Lioness"; Lagos, "the Lakes"; Cameroun (Camarão), "the Prawns"; Gaboon (Gabão), "the Hooded Cloak"—all were linguistic reminders of past Portuguese greatness. The Portuguese also left their mark on Africa in a more substantial manner. Transatlantic crops such as maize, tobacco, chili peppers, peanuts, sugar cane, and sweet potatoes were brought to Africa by the Portuguese, who, in this respect, had done more to enrich Africa's diet than any other people except the Arabs. The Portuguese, however, played the major part in developing the African slave trade; Portuguese and other traders furnished the plantations of Brazil with black captives, and Angola became a major supplier. Angola in some ways became almost as much a dependency of Brazil as of Portugal.

The tenor of life in Luanda, Angola's chief city, followed that of Brazil.[13] The settlers cooked their meals in the Brazilian fashion, adopted some particularities of Brazilian architecture, and spoke a Brazilian form of Portuguese. Fashionable ladies perambulated through the streets accompanied by a train of slaves; educated men read books and pamphlets about the Brazilian revolution. Farther south, at Benguela, an influential party even instigated a brief rising in favor of federal union with the newly independent Brazilian empire. In the middle of the century Portuguese emigrants from Pernambuco settled in southern Angola; in the 1860s and 1870s some enterprising Brazilians started steam navigation on the river Kwanza and developed plantations.

Yet Portugal's possessions in Africa remained no more than a scattered network of ports and fortified posts, surrounded by ill-defined zones of influence. Most Portuguese settlements depended on sea and river communications (their original purpose had often been to serve as ports of call to the Indies, and their sites were chosen without regard to climate). Portugal, a poor and backward country, lacked the resources to develop its patrimony. Gone was the trade with the Indies; gone was Brazil; gone was the country's former naval power. Angola attracted few men of ability; the most energetic Portuguese emigrants usually preferred to seek their fortunes in Brazil. Angola

---

[13] According to a Portuguese expert writing in the 1840s, the whole of Angola then numbered only 1,832 whites, of whom 1,601 lived in Luanda. In addition, there were 5,770 *mestiços* (half-castes) in Angola.

received an unduly high proportion of convicts, or *degradados*. Slavery inhibited economic development, despite the good intentions of Lisbon. In 1836 the Portuguese government issued a decree outlawing the slave trade, but the Portuguese could not enforce their policy against strong local opposition; they lacked patrol vessels, and slave traffic continued until about the early 1870s.

Away from the coastal regions and the main river valleys the Portuguese generally exercised little control over the territories they claimed. There were a few bold frontiersmen like Silva Portô (a trader who came to Angola from Brazil), who in 1848 managed to reach Barotseland on the Upper Zambezi. The bulk of the inland trade, however, remained in the hands of indigenous merchants, many of them members of the Mbundu tribe. Mbundu caravans pushed deep into the interior, dealing in slaves and ivory as well as wild rubber.[14] Elephants' teeth were dispatched to Europe; slaves were shipped to Brazil and to the cocoa plantations of São Thomé. The Mbundu traders worked through native chiefs, whom they supplied with guns and powder, so that the trade in slaves and firearms alike spread outward like an epidemic.

In the 1870s, however, the Portuguese began to bestir themselves. Explorers such as Stanley and Livingstone passed through territory which the Portuguese claimed as their own; British writers declaimed against the failings of Portuguese rule; Lisbon understood that it either had to assert its government or abdicate from the colonial stage. In 1876 the Portuguese government raised a considerable loan to finance public works in Africa; engineers and technicians who in the ordinary course of events would never have dreamed of going to Africa were sent to Angola and Mozambique. Another important step was the foundation of the Lisbon Geographical Society for the encouragement of colonial studies; in addition, the Portuguese produced some outstanding missionary pioneers such as Antonio Barroso, who made a great name for himself inland. Slavery was at any rate formally ended; its abolition severed, at least psychologically, the last links with a discredited past.[15]

Dutch seafarers began to compete with the Portuguese and built up a great maritime empire in the East. On April 6, 1652, a small Dutch squadron, consisting of the *Goede Hoop,* the *Dromedaris,* and the *Reiger,* cast anchor at Table Bay, the magnificent harbor that domi-

[14] See Gladwyn Murray Childs, *Umbundu Kinship and Character* (New York, 1949).

[15] See James Duffy, *Portugal in Africa* (Cambridge, Mass., 1962), pp. 47–72; and for a distinctly pro-Portuguese point of view see F. Clement C. Egerton, *Angola in Perspective: Endeavour and Achievement in Portuguese West Africa* (London, 1957), pp. 54–81.

nates the southern tip of Africa. Their orders were to build a fort, plant vegetables, safeguard the cattle trade with the pastoral Hottentots, and set up a stores depot for ships on the long run from Holland to the Indies. The Dutch set out to make a market garden; unwittingly, they built a nation. The Dutch East India Company at first had no interest in colonization. The directors merely wanted a port where trading vessels might replenish their water casks and pick up fresh food to safeguard the sailors against scurvy. In time, however, the company realized that all manner of crops would flourish in the temperate climate of the Cape and that a permanent farming community was essential to assure the colony's future. Europeans received grants of land so that they might sell grain, beef, and wine to the Cape garrison and passing ships, but as the years went on the settlement expanded far beyond the directors' original intention. The whites gradually pushed deeper and deeper inland; as the road to Cape Town was extended, they took to pasture land rather than farming. The population increased; the numerous sons of Boer families often found difficulty in making a living at Cape Town, where much of the skilled work was done by imported Malay slaves. Subdivision of land, accompanied by more intensive cultivation, was not usually a feasible proposition under conditions where capital and labor were scarce and land was plentiful. Many poor men found that the best way to get on in life was to stake a claim on the frontier. The Boers kept trekking in order to avoid competition with their neighbors for pasture and to escape from boundary quarrels. The frontiersmen's intensive methods of cultivation sometimes exhausted the soil; the veld "got tired," and so they moved on in search of new pasture grounds, like the indigenous people whom they met inland. The colonists, of course, were never self-sufficient; even on the extreme edge of settlement they depended on imported guns and gunpowder and wagons, tea, coffee, and cloth, which had to be paid for.[16] The best way of making money was to drive cattle to the market; the towns were now a long way off, and herds possessed the great advantage that they could walk to the purchaser on their own feet. In addition, there were a few goods of small bulk and high value, like soap, candles, beeswax, and ivory, which paid the high expense of transport to the coast on slow-moving wagons.

First the trek Boers supplied the Cape market; later the center of

[16] For two differing interpretations see S. Daniel Neumark, *Economic Influences on the South African Frontier, 1652–1836* (Stanford, Calif., 1957), and Pieter J. van der Merwe, *Trek: Studies oor die Mobiliteit van die Pioniersbevolking aan die Kaap* (Cape Town, 1945).

economic gravity shifted more toward new ports that were opened on the East Coast. Port Elizabeth, East London, and Durban became the most advanced points of departure for inland expansion. By this time the trekkers themselves formed part of a new nation, no longer Dutch in the European sense of the word, but Afrikaners, speaking a new language, an African derivate from the Holland tongue. The trek Boer did not get a good press in nineteenth-century England. A succession of British missionaries and administrators applied the standards of Victorian middle-class morality to the Boers in much the same fashion as to the Bantu. The trekker often appeared as a poverty-stricken, shiftless loafer who stood in the way of progress. His very speech appeared as ridiculous as that of the Creole (another type of frontiersman who operated under specifically African conditions).[17] Subsequent generations, apt to romanticize the real and supposed virtues of peasants and preliterates, adopted a different stereotype. In contrast with his degenerate offspring in the towns of mid-twentieth-century South Africa—city slickers who drove automobiles and voted for apartheid—the old-style trekker was now described as a virtuous primitive, deeply rooted in the soil of Africa, like the Bantu, free from economic rationalism and other unpleasant features of urban civilization. Loving loneliness, divorced from the mainstream of Western thought, the bearded old Boer now emerged as a noble though tragic figure, who trekked through the ages as an eternal anachronism.[18] This interpretation, though picturesque, bore no more relation to reality than the late Victorian one. In their own day, the trek Boers, well steeped in a dour Calvinism and the lives of the ancient Hebrews, took their place among the world's foremost wilderness specialists, superior even to the hard-bitten *sertanejos* of the Angolan and Brazilian hinterland. The Boers adjusted their way of life to frontier conditions that would have baffled their Dutch, North German, and Huguenot ancestors. They could handle a span of oxen

[17] In 1929 the magisterial *Encyclopaedia Britannica* could define Afrikaans as "a meagre *patois* limited to a few hundred words," whose adoption in place of High Dutch was occasioned by the Boers' illiberal and inefficient system of administration in the past. With the same inaccuracy, the writer accounted for the trekkers' "deep distrust of European civilization" by the character of the parent stock who had left their places of origin "in circumstances tending to weaken the natural ties of kinship and pride of race that bind the average emigrant to his mother country." "Cape Colony," in *Encyclopaedia Britannica*, IV (14th ed.; 1929), 782.

[18] See Sheila Patterson, *The Last Trek: A Study of the Boer People and the Afrikaner Nation* (London, 1957), for a good example of this modern stereotype. For a characteristic lampoon of the Victorian variety see S. Erasmus (pseud. of D. Blackburn), *Prinsloo of Prinsloosdorp* (London, 1899).

in the roughest kind of country; they were knowledgeable as "soil prospectors" and wise to the ways of finding the best land in the wilderness. They also became crack shots and first-class horsemen and hunters. They engaged in frontier farming of a kind which required enormous tracts of land. Afrikaner society thus possessed an inbuilt tendency toward territorial growth. This found military expression in a highly specialized system of tactics adjusted to the Afrikaners' mode of economic production. They learned how to defend themselves behind closed circles of wagons; these served both as means of transport and as mobile pivots for mounted sharpshooters. The Boers' fighting potential was therefore greatly superior to that of Bushmen and Bantu. The Boers became southern Africa's most distinguished "empire builders," engaging in a form of expansion that owed nothing to the search for investment opportunities and therefore no mention of it is to be found in the early twentieth-century tracts on imperialism.

Left to themselves, the Afrikaners would have become the undisputed masters of South Africa. The exigencies of maritime strategy and the discovery of mining, however, brought a new and more powerful competitor—the British. In 1795 the Redcoats occupied Cape Town and established a military government representing the Prince of Orange, who had remained faithful to the British alliance, whereas the Dutch Republic, in league with the French revolutionary government, was at war with Britain. In 1802 the colony was restored to Holland, but four years later the British came back, and this time they stayed. The Cape became the base for British naval might in the South Atlantic, and the British inherited all the governmental problems of their Dutch predecessors. Boer and Briton soon came into conflict; inner white tensions in turn contributed to the expansion of the South African frontier. The Afrikaners criticized the activities of British missionaries and humanitarians; they objected to the emancipation of the Hottentots. The frontiersmen considered themselves insufficiently protected against the depredation of Bantu cattle raiders. The British authorities, for their part, stuck to rigid administrative economy, which influenced their policy even more than humanitarian, missionary, or commercial factors.[19] Further trouble arose when in 1833 the British freed the slaves throughout the British Empire, and additional bitterness was caused by the inadequate man-

[19] The literature on the subject is extensive. The best recent book on the question is C. F. J. Muller, *Die Britse Owerheid en die Groot Trek* (2d ed., rev. and illus.; Johannesburg, 1963). For the British humanitarian side of the story see William M. Macmillan, *Bantu, Boer, and Briton: The Making of the South African Native Problem* (rev. and enl. ed.; New York, 1963).

ner in which former slave owners were compensated for the loss of their property.

Slavery, of course, was not the main issue. A pastoral frontier economy of the type which dominated most of South Africa needed only a limited number of hands. The Boers did not require the same amount of manpower as the cotton plantations of the American South or the clove estates of Zanzibar. The internal slave trade never achieved any importance south of the Zambezi. But in South Africa two wholly different sets of customs and beliefs came into conflict. Egalitarian as the Boers were among themselves, they would accept neither political interference from overseas nor equality with the blacks at home. The Great Trek of 1836 and succeeding years formed the Boer frontiersman's Declaration of Independence. Admittedly its effects should not be exaggerated. Many Boers stayed where they were; the Western Cape, with its wealthy wine farmers, continued to follow a different tradition, partly because there were no warlike Bantu to threaten the farms. Nevertheless, the Afrikaners' center of gravity swung north. The trekkers occupied the highveld; great solid Boer wagons steadily lumbered inland, beyond the Orange and then across the Vaal rivers.

The Afrikaners set up several states of their own, rigidly excluding non-Europeans from the franchise. The British at first argued that the pioneers would continue to be British subjects; but the Queen's sovereignty inland was not upheld for long. In 1852, by the Sand River Convention, the imperial government formally guaranteed the emigrant farmers beyond the Vaal the right to run their own affairs; two years later a similar treaty at Bloemfontein admitted the full independence of the Orange Free State, and two white-frontier communities now held sway in the interior.

At the same time, the pattern of settlement had become even more intricate through the infusion of a substantial English-speaking element. The Great Trek had led to the occupation of the inland plateau, a relatively sparsely populated region. The position was very different on the Eastern Cape. Most of the land between the great escarpment and the sea was occupied by numerous Bantu tribal communities. There were constant border clashes, and in 1820 settlers were brought out from Britain to relieve the motherland of surplus people and to strengthen the European hold on the area. The colonists met with terrible hardships; drought, floods, torrential rains, and blights ruined many farmers, but then the tide turned. Merino wool developed into a valuable export, and Grahamstown and Port Elizabeth developed into thriving little townships.

The Cape evolved a complex ethnic caste pattern, with English-speaking people mainly at the top, dominant in the administration as well as business, Dutch farmers in the middle, and Colored and Bantu peoples at the lower end. The whites were strong enough to insist on a form of self-government, and in 1852 the Cape legislature became purely elective. The settlers, split between the poorer Dutch people who mainly lived in the countryside and the English with a much stronger stake in the towns, were divided. The former desired a suffrage based on low property qualifications; the latter would have preferred to exclude the poor. The Popular Party won; the Dutch were enfranchised, but so were Coloreds who could meet the qualifications of the voters' roll. Afrikaner nationalism did not, however, become a major political force for another generation. The British party, with its links to trade and its resultant interest in an active frontier policy, dominated the Cape; its parliamentary supremacy came under assault only in the 1880s, with the emergence of Afrikaner nationalism and an Afrikaner nationalist party.

In the meantime, for strategic and commercial reasons the British had also annexed Natal to the northeast in 1843, and in 1856 the region was formed into a separate colony with representative institutions. The settlers imported indentured coolies from India and developed tropical crops such as sugar and coffee. Political insecurity, however, remained. Boer and British colonists alike had to cope with the internal Bantu "proletariat"; in addition, there remained some relatively powerful indigenous states whose influence played an important part in shaping the local pattern of imperial expansion. Basutoland, a composite tribal monarchy welded together by the genius of Chief Moshesh, derived some protection from its mountainous terrain; the Basuto forces, mounted on hardy little ponies, possessed considerable mobility; Basuto diplomacy excelled at playing off the different white groups against each other. The Basuto looked to the British for protection. Zululand, farther north, formed a highly centralized military monarchy of a different kind, a black Sparta which relied on cattle farming, raiding, and war—the greatest of several "spear kingdoms" scattered over southern Africa from Natal to Tanganyika. The Zulu quarreled with the Transvaalers; they backed their territorial claims with a strong force of well-drilled foot soldiers armed with spears and oxhide shields. The Zulu state continued to be a formidable factor in local politics until 1879, when the British crushed the black impis at Ulundi.

To make an involved situation even more complex, European pioneers began to discover minerals, and a mining frontier was superimposed on a farming frontier. British settlers drifted into the far interior, which the Boers considered to be their own, and all hopes of a spatial separation between the Boer and the British spheres of influence came to nought. In the 1860s travelers brought back highly colored reports of enormous gold deposits beyond the Limpopo River, in the northern hinterland of the Transvaal. In 1867 diamonds were discovered near the Orange River, and prospectors of many nationalities flocked to the river diggings. These finds were thrown into the shade when in 1870 precious stones were found on the open veld. Kimberley developed into a tough border town, attracting pioneers from Europe, America, and Australia. Overseas capital began to move into an area hitherto dependent on a few agricultural exports, and the whole basis of South Africa's white economy began to shift. The diamond fields also became a magnet for the inland tribes, anxious to work for the white man in return for guns and other goods. African workmen returning from the diggings on expiration of their contracts brought back rifles to their native villages. The Bechuana tribes, willing to work for the white men, acquired modern arms, so that the diamond discoveries led to a revolution in the military balance of power in the interior. The new dispensation favored tribes like the Bechuana against more conservative military communities like the Matabele, who in the main preferred to stick to the accustomed pursuits of herding cattle and making war. The diggers and owners, meanwhile, found themselves face to face with a vast and little-understood problem of labor migrancy.

The British tried to resolve these difficulties by political unification. They aimed at a united South Africa, firmly attached to the imperial cause without being a charge to the imperial taxpayer. An economically prosperous South Africa would be able to buy British goods, secure its borders, and provide the Royal Navy with a firm strategic pivot in the South Atlantic. Lord Carnarvon, the British Colonial Secretary, thought in terms of a transatlantic example. In 1867 he had successfully steered the Dominion of Canada Act through the British Parliament. English and French Canadians had reached a political *modus vivendi* acceptable to both; perhaps the same might be achieved in South Africa. The Transvaal was in bad straits; the country was plagued by financial distress and internal dissensions, the Zulu remained a serious border threat, and the last straw was an unsuccessful war waged in 1876 by the burghers against Secocoeni, a northern chief. In 1877 the British annexed the Transvaal. Two years later the Redcoats wiped out the Zulu kingdom, and British might in South Africa seemed to have reached a new peak. Carnarvon's scheme for confederation turned out to be unworkable. The Cape, having obtained self-government in 1872, remained jealous of its privileges; the Transvaal brooded over its lost independence. From the social point of view, South Africa, with its huge African population, had nothing in common with Canada, a country devoid of any serious "native problem." In 1878 Carnarvon resigned over an issue involving Disraeli's foreign policy; his policy broke down, and the confederation scheme became a matter of discussion for constitutional antiquarians.[20]

In the great interwhite struggle for southern Africa the Afrikaners claimed priority of occupation. There were, however, claimants of even more ancient standing—the Portuguese. At the beginning of the sixteenth century Portuguese navigators opened the sea route to the Indies and broke into the triangle of trade which linked the East African coast to India, southern Arabia, and the Near East. For a time Portuguese garrisons and warships dominated much of the East African coast, but repeated attempts to establish their influence in the gold-bearing regions of the interior had little permanent effect. In the second half of the seventeenth century, moreover, the Portuguese establishment on what is now the coast of Tanzania and Kilwa met with a determined Muslim counterattack. By the end of the century the revival of Islamic might in the area had eliminated all traces of Portuguese influence beyond Cape Delgado. Portuguese power centered on the port of Mozambique; in addition, the Portuguese held on to a few coastal stations farther south.

Vast areas inland were controlled by Portuguese or Goanese adventurers who acquired semi-independent fiefs (*prazos*), some the size of English counties. Here they lived like feudal lords, surrounded by bands of armed retainers, footmen, and handsome black concubines. These great magnates traded in slaves and other commodities; they offered regal hospitality to their friends and waged war against their enemies. The Portuguese authorities lacked both the administrative and the military machinery to control these estate owners effectively or even to extract substantial revenue from their possessions. Ingenious attempts to promote white settlement all came to nought. Few Portuguese were willing to emigrate to fever-ridden East Africa. Many of the great estates passed into the hands of Goanese or mulattoes; many were controlled by absentee landowners who frittered away their substance in distant Goa. The great holdings themselves fell on evil days, partly as the result of disastrous tribal wars and partly because of the slave trade, which induced many *prazo* owners to sell the very tenants on whom their prosperity depended.

The slave trade, often financed by Indian merchants, became more

[20] For a good general reference work see Eric Anderson Walker, *A History of Southern Africa* (3d ed.; London, 1957), *passim*.

profitable as local industries, such as the production of gold dust, declined. Professional cutthroats in the nineteenth century raided deeply inland through the valleys of the Zambezi and the Luangwa. Many slaves went to Brazil, and later to Mauritius. In addition, slaves found a local market in the *prazos,* and the Portuguese administration could not or would not put an end to the traffic. Economically, the Portuguese in most of their possessions had as yet failed to make the decisive transition from forced to wage labor, the great change which characterized African colonization in its secondary stage. Climate and disease alike prevented the Portuguese, and also their Arab competitors, from using draft animals. The colonizers lacked both the means and the markets to construct railways; trade with the interior thus largely depended on carriers and remained restricted to a few commodities which could bear the high cost of head porterage. In addition to all these difficulties, the Portuguese had to cope with serious internal threats to their rule; the southern part of Mozambique was drawn into the great backwash of Zulu or Zulu-related hosts who swept north from Natal in the first half of the nineteenth century and established one of their kingdoms in Gazaland (eastern Mozambique).

The Portuguese nevertheless managed to hold on, and even succeeded in making good some ancient claims on the southern confines of their territory. The Transvaal was a landlocked state, and from its early beginnings Transvaal politicians covetously eyed the shores of the Indian Ocean. The British also put forth claims, and the future of Portuguese rule in the area south of Lourenço Marques, the chief port, was in danger. The whole region was weakly held; by the early 1870s Lourenço Marques was but a mean little settlement with narrow streets lined by flat-roofed houses and grass huts, protected by decayed fortifications and rusty cannons. Portuguese diplomacy, however, proved fully equal to the challenge. In 1869 the Transvaal acknowledged Portuguese sovereignty in the whole area. The British were induced to submit the dispute to arbitration, and in 1875 Marshal MacMahon, the French president, decided in Portugal's favor.

Mozambique might be fever-ridden and weakly held, a sphere of influence more than a colony, but the position of the Portuguese in this respect was not essentially different from that of other white colonizers in tropical Africa. The writings of British missionaries and explorers like Livingstone tended to obscure the essential characteristics of Portuguese rule. Portugal, a protectionist and Catholic power, could expect little sympathy from earnest Bible-reading Englishmen, who also firmly believed in free trade. In British literature the Portuguese were the first to stand out as the prototype of the vicious, immoral, and corrupt colonialist, who exploited the natives for his own good and stood in the way of progress. The real weakness of Portuguese imperialism, however, resulted not from too much, but from too little, governance. Portugal, a small and poverty-stricken state riddled by internal dissensions, was in some ways itself an Anglo-French economic colony, dependent on foreign capital. The partition of Africa between the great powers jeopardized the Portuguese *imperium* almost as seriously as that of the sultanate of Zanzibar and the kingdom of Ashanti. The Portuguese, infinitely more familiar with the power relationships of Europe, showed much greater skill in playing off one European power against the other. However, Portugal's economic resources proved unequal to its diplomatic ability; the Portuguese could not develop what they kept, and until the first half of the present century, they failed to launch colonial development on any serious scale.

North of the Portuguese sphere, Arab influence reigned supreme on the coast. In the seventeenth century the Imams of Muscat built up a commercial empire on the ruins of Portuguese power, and Muslim-owned trading vessels continued to ply between the ports of East Africa, India, and the Red Sea. In 1840 Sultan Seyyid, one of the greatest of these rulers, established his headquarters at Zanzibar and turned the island into an important commercial center.[21] He introduced clove cultivation and developed his kingdom into the world's most important producer of this valuable spice. While Seyyid's navy controlled the coast, his Arab caravans made their way deep into the African interior, where they cooperated with the Nyamwezi, the Bisa, and similar indigenous peoples in building up an extensive trade in slaves, ivory, and other commodities. "When you play the flute at Zanzibar," said an Arab proverb with some exaggeration, "all Africa dances down to the Lakes." Politically, the Sultan's word did not count for a great deal away from the coast. In the economic and the religious spheres, however, Muslim influence was substantial. Arab and Swahili traders brought new goods and helped to link the inland tribes to a wider world economy. They spread a modified form of their faith, which was adopted by trading and raiding communities such as the Yao in what is now Malawi. By the second part of the nineteenth century the coastmen had penetrated into the interior, meeting up with Mambari traders in present-day Zambia, while

[21] The standard histories of the Arabs in the area are Sir Reginald Coupland, *The Exploitation of East Africa, 1856–1890: The Slave Trade and the Scramble* (London, 1939) and *East Africa and Its Invaders, from the Earliest Times to the Death of Seyyid Said in 1856* (Oxford, 1938).

ivory hunters and slave raiders from the Sudan got as far south as Uganda. Muslim traders wielded considerable influence in centralized Bantu kingdoms such as that of Kazembe on the Luapula River, and among "stateless" peoples like the Nkonde of northern Malawi, Muslim adventurers established miniature sovereignties.[22] Had East Africa had been left to its own devices, Muslim power would almost certainly have become supreme over many parts of the East and Central African interior.

The profits of the inland trade at the same time helped to build up Zanzibari prosperity. Zanzibar also attracted many Indian merchants, who helped finance the Muslim slave caravans to the interior. In addition, an ever-increasing number of ships from the Northern Hemisphere cast anchor at Zanzibar. Much of this early commerce was in the hands of Americans; the name *merikani,* denoting cotton goods and blankets in the area, still stands as a linguistic monument to the Yankee traders' enterprise. Subsequently, merchants from Hamburg, Lübeck, and Bremen came to the island, importing articles as varied as hardware, mirrors, soap, and items of haberdashery. Neither the Germans nor the Americans had political ambitions; the Sultan's main problem was pressure from France on the one hand and interference from Britain on the other. The British wanted trade, not territory; they were determined to keep out the French and at the same time put an end to the traffic in slaves. Faced with a political choice, Seyyid preferred to trust the British and subsequently cooperated, albeit unwillingly, with the Royal Navy's antislavery campaign.

Zanzibari power, however, rested on even more slender foundations that that of Portugal. Seyyid's death in 1856 removed a ruler of outstanding ability who could not be replaced. Zanzibar's hold on the coast remained weak; the unstable union between Oman and Zanzibar soon broke up, and innumerable dissensions rent the island. Politically, Zanzibar became more and more dependent on Britain. London would have preferred to do business with a stable and independent sultanate, wedded to free trade and leaving the British free of direct administrative commitments. Britain therefore tried to bolster up Zanzibari power in much the same way as it supported the Sultan's rule at Constantinople. But at Zanzibar, as in Turkey, British policy rested on a contradiction. On the one hand, the British wanted to steer clear of internal commitments; on the other, they stood for reform. In East Africa they wished to wipe out the slave trade, one of the island's main economic foundations, with the result that they

[22] See, for instance, Lewis H. Gann, "The End of the Slave Trade in British Central Africa, 1889–1912," *Rhodes-Livingstone Journal,* No. 16 (1954), pp. 27–51.

had to interfere more and more in the country's affairs. British interest in the area increased even further when, in 1869, the Suez Canal opened for traffic, and steamers from Western Europe, bound for India, could avoid the long haul around the Cape. In 1873 Britain, relying on its overwhelming sea power, succeeded in closing the slave markets in the islands, so that the Sultan became more dependent on the Royal Navy's support against his discontented subjects. In 1877 Sultan Barghash of Zanzibar, convinced of his weak position on the African mainland, offered a concession to Sir William Mackinnon, an outstanding British businessman, to develop the territory between the coast and Lake Victoria. In return he asked for a share in the profits and customs revenue, which seemed a safer speculation than reliance on the revenue obtained through an ill-defined suzerainty along the shores of the Indian Ocean. London, however, had no interest in direct territorial commitments; the offer was rejected, with the result that the way remained open for a subsequent German irruption into East Africa.[23]

[23] See Kenneth Ingham, *A History of East Africa* (London, 1962), pp. 36–114. For the more characteristically African aspects see Roland A. Oliver and Gervase Mathew (eds.), *History of East Africa,* Vol. I (Oxford, 1963).

13. The Scramble for Africa

By the end of the 1860s a considerable portion of Africa's shoreline was under some form of European influence. However, coastal suzerainty did not necessarily mean a forward policy. For many years to come, British statesmanship in most parts of Africa continued its policy of caution. The bulk of French opinion looked askance at adventure overseas. Until 1881 the French colonial department formed part of the Ministry of Marine, with its traditional aim of maintaining French honor and rights rather than serving the interests of local traders. French statesmen gave first priority to the maintenance of prestige in Europe. After the disastrous Franco-German war of 1870–1871 most French soldiers gazed toward the blue line of the Vosges and dreamed of recovering Alsace-Lorraine. French Radicals dreaded a colonial debacle which might shake the Republic's reputation. French Royalists resented any glory which colonial successes might bring to the hated Third Republic, though by a strange contradiction they flocked into the officer corps and the colonial civil service and thereby helped to carry the Tricolor farther afield.

The great mass of German bourgeoisie wanted no part in colonial adventure. German imperialists of a later vintage used to complain that in 1871 the Reich had arrived too late among the great nations of the world and had thus failed to get its just share in the partition. Nothing can be further from the truth. If, from its inception in 1866, the North German Confederation, and five years later the unified German empire, had embarked on an active colonial career, the Germans would still have had many opportunities for overseas conquests. They were not, however, interested in such ventures at the time. Even Bismarck had to swim with the anticolonial tide.[1] When in 1880 the Kaiser's government tried to underwrite a new company

[1] William O. Henderson, *Studies in German Colonial History* (London, 1962), p. 116.

for the purpose of acquiring the Samoan rights owned by the bankrupt firm of Goddefroy in the South Seas, Ludwig Bamberger, a
doughty lawyer and one of Germany's best financial and banking
experts, defeated the project.

Expansion, however, was inherent in a situation where inequality
of technical and social equipment between the metropolitan and
native peoples was so marked as in Africa. The British attempted to
use African political institutions to further trade. They felt convinced that freedom of commerce was the best policy, not only for
themselves but also for foreigners. This idea was shared by many
other Europeans, such as the merchants of the Hanseatic cities in
northern Germany. African institutions, however, were not geared
to this purpose. "Indirect influence" all too often foundered on the
inability of rulers such as Lobengula and Lewanika to safeguard
white enterprise within the existing political framework of their
states. Informal empire did not operate successfully under conditions
marked by turbulent frontiers and extreme disparity of power and
culture between the white and black; hence most attempts at indirect
influence soon collapsed.

Much depended on the ability of African states to adjust themselves to rapidly changing conditions. This capacity varied considerably. The powerful Fulani states of Northern Nigeria had little in
common with the scattered Tonga clans of Northern Rhodesia. The
Amhara of Ethiopia represented a military power infinitely greater
than the small Yao communities of Nyasaland. Many African Muslim states managed to put up a desperate fight against Western
encroachment. The Islamic world had a long tradition of popular
puritanical movements which arose on the periphery of the Mohammedan world and tried to do battle against alien influence by reviving
Islam in its ancient purity. In the eighteenth century, Indian examples
thus inspired an attempted Wahabi revolution against Ottoman power
in Arabia. In the nineteenth century, Islam produced a whole crop
of militant religious movements in Africa, on the extreme circumfer-
ence of Muslim civilization, where Western power began to impinge
on the most backward parts of the Islamic world. Abd-el-Kader
fought the French in Algeria (1832–1834); in West Africa great
leaders such as Dan Fodio, Ahmadu Shehu, and Samori stood for
militant and puritan forms of Islam; the Mahdi for a time rid the
Sudan of Turko-Egyptian domination; the "Mad Mullah" did battle
against the British in Somaliland; the Senussi waged long-drawn-out
campaigns against the Turks and later against the Italians in Libya.[2]

[2] Bernard Lewis, *The Middle East and the West* (Bloomington, Ind., 1964),
pp. 95–105.

AFRICA in 1879

Madeira [p]

Ceuta [s]   [s] Melilla

ALGERIA   TUNIS

Canary Is.
[s]

MOROCCO

TRIPOLI

EGYPT

SENEGAL

L. Chad

Assab [i]
Obok [f]

GAMBIA

PORT. GUINEA

ETHIOPIA

SIERRA
LEONE

Porto Novo [f]   LAGOS
Cotonu [f]

LIBERIA

Grand Bassam [f]   Fernando Po
Assini [f]   [s]

GOLD COAST   S. Thomé   GABOON
                        [p]

L. Victoria

L. Tanganyika

SULTANATE
OF ZANZIBAR

ANGOLA

L. Nyasa

Mayotte [f]

Nossi Bé
[f]   [f]
St.
Mary

MOÇAMBIQUE

MADAGASCAR

TRANSVAAL

O.F.S.   BASUTOLAND

CAPE
COLONY   NATAL

Turkish [t]

Portuguese [p]

British [b]

French [f]

500   0   500   1,000 miles

But by and large, the power potential of African, and especially of Bantu, states remained small. In fact, it was often those very communities which had operated most successfully in the past that showed the smallest capacity for successful readjustment. The Matabele warrior state, for example, had a highly developed system of infantry tactics which for a time assured their local supremacy and enabled them to live a parasitic existence at their neighbors' expense. But they could not cope with revolutionary change. The European advance into Mashonaland in 1890 threatened to deprive them of their most cherished raiding grounds. If the Matabele had continued to make war on the tribal communities to the south and east, they would have gotten themselves into a war with the whites, which their king wished to avoid. If they had tried to escape from their difficulties by migrating to the north of the Zambezi, their herds might have perished from the dreaded tsetse fly in the lowveld, for Matabele medicine men had no means of coping with such a veterinary problem. Alternatively, Lobengula might have attempted to come to terms with the white man's new economic dispensation by taking an active part in mining enterprise, but he did not dare attempt any real reforms in the Matabele system of government or even in their fighting methods. Matabele generals, like so many senior European officers at the time, continued to believe that "cold steel" would take any defense. They would not change the accustomed ways which had so often brought victory in the past. Lobengula had some inkling of the problem; he piled up rifles, but could neither service nor effectively repair these new firearms. He also made some tentative inquiries into the possibility of securing ponies from Basutoland. But to all intents and purposes, the armies that opposed the chartered company in 1893 were little different from those that had occupied Matabeleland two generations ago, and they perished in withering small-arms fire from mounted troops.[3]

Lobengula's state was an extreme example. The Bechuana, under their great chief Khama, pursued a more diplomatic policy. They acquired guns by working for the white man; they adopted Christianity and successfully employed white missionaries as experts. But even so, Khama had to rely on British support against the Boers; his own kingdom lacked a sufficiently stable power basis for a genuinely independent existence.

The most successful adjustments occurred on the West Coast, in regions such as the Oil Rivers, where the African peoples could look back on centuries of trade with the West. Waterways helped to solve

[3] Lewis H. Gann, *A History of Southern Rhodesia: Early Days to 1934* (London, 1965).

the problem of transport, and Africans turned to cash crops and developed a rudimentary urban life, with the first elements of a farming and commercial middle class. Africans became palm-oil producers. Toward the end of the last century black pioneers in the Gold Coast took to cocoa farming, moved into the forest belt, acquired land from indigenous people, and on their own initiative built up a major industry.[4] From the military point of view, the West Coast states were not insignificant. By African standards the war canoes owned by the Oil Rivers cities were formidable instruments. But even these communities could not make the switch from rowboat to gunboat, and all failed to become powers in the European sense.

In theory the Europeans might have accepted a self-denying ordinance to abstain from interference in the African interior, but no matter how honestly intended, such a scheme could not have been enforced. Any freezing of white spheres would also have required an effective stabilization of black power relationships, and this was not possible. Whatever treaties Western governments might sign, rifles and other trade goods could not be prevented from filtering into the interior. Indigenous or immigrant warlords, using new military and economic techniques, could not be stopped from upsetting traditional arrangements. Africa was a continent in flux; the gun frontier had rolled inland, and on all sides new claimants for power were stepping in to seize their share.

In addition, there were other groups of unofficial Europeans from overseas who spread into what they regarded as one of the world's last open frontiers. There were merchants, exemplified by pioneers like Adolph Woermann.[5] There were petty adventurers without political aspirations, men like Carl Wiese, a German Jewish elephant hunter who became a political power in the Angoni country of what is now Zambia. All these newcomers helped to upset the existing balance of power; they produced new friction on the peripheries of the European spheres and in turn helped to push the various European powers to interfere inland. A noninterventionist policy could hardly be maintained in those circumstances. Noninterference, moreover, ran counter to the whole ethos of Western society in the late nineteenth century. The whites were convinced that, in some way or other, their own form of civilization was bound to spread throughout the continent. They were all cultural diffusionists; they all believed in their

[4] Polly Hill, *The Migrant Cocoa-Farmers of Southern Ghana: A Study in Rural Capitalism* (New York, 1963).

[5] Woermann, in 1882, established the first regular steamship service between Hamburg and West Africa and built up a great commercial empire which helped to lay the foundations of German Kamerun.

manifest destiny. True enough, not all European merchants or missionaries necessarily looked to the protection of their own country's flag. Some Frenchmen preferred to live under the Union Jack; some Britons liked to work under the Tricolor. But nearly all Europeans, be they traders, scholars, or soldiers, concurred in regarding Africa as a sociological museum, stocked with curious or disgusting exhibits produced by cultures either childish or decadent. Traditional Africa, in their view, had no future; some African potentates, men like Lobengula, seem to have agreed and often displayed a curious defeatism in their attempts at resistance.

The whites held the ideological initiative. They also had the physical means to make their power felt. The technological gap between their own society and that of Africa continually widened. The prophylactic use of quinine helped to raise the mosquito barrier, which had shut off the interior. The steam engine was successfully applied to land and water transport and brought about a complete transformation in the logistics of trade and war. The steam locomotive penetrated continent after continent. Goods could be carried overland cheaply; passengers could travel more swiftly and in greater comfort; mass armies could mobilize at great speed. The steam engine similarly revolutionized naval strategy. In the old days the remoteness of a region depended more on winds and currents than on distance; a sudden change of wind could alter the outcome of the battle. Steam introduced a new precision into the movements of a fleet; the turns of a ship's screw could be counted even more accurately than the paces of a soldier. Distance became a more predictable quantity.[6] Ships soon increased in size and were able to carry larger cargoes. Naval trade no longer needed to be confined to goods of small bulk and high value; merchants could now send commodities such as grain and coal around the world. The steamship thus changed the whole course of trade and diplomacy by increasing the profits from overseas commerce, especially in areas previously hampered by adverse winds. The Mediterranean once more assumed something like the preeminence it had enjoyed in antiquity. Vessels bound from

---

[6] In the sailing days, for instance, the Cape Agulhas current made rounding the Cape of Good Hope from west to east a difficult enterprise, except with a strong wind. The weak and variable winds of the Mediterranean were unfavorable for sailing vessels, whose captains used to joke that there were only four good Mediterranean ports—June, July, August, and Port Mahon. The northeast and southeast trade winds in the Atlantic rendered a voyage from the Northern to the Southern Hemisphere a singularly zigzag affair. In the Indian Ocean, navigation had since time immemorial depended on the peculiar system of monsoons and countermonsoons. The Red Sea, with its uncertain winds and rocky coasts, was particularly difficult to navigate.

Europe to the Cape of Good Hope could steam a straight course without making a long westerly detour in the South Atlantic. Without the steamship, moreover, the Suez Canal would never have been cut. The steamship made Africa and Asia alike accessible to Europe in a way that would have seemed fantastic to merchants and shipowners of an earlier generation. The employment of steam engines also changed the nature of naval warfare. Steam propulsion vastly increased the tactical mobility of fleets. But from the strategic point of view, admirals encountered new and unforeseen limitations. A sailing fleet in the days of Nelson could cruise for several months; fresh water and provisions could be secured almost anywhere. The steam engine, however, made ships dependent on coaling stations and vastly decreased their cruising radius. Naval power now rested on coal; maritime countries required a worldwide system of coaling stations. The change at first worked to the special advantage of Britain, which until about 1880 produced more coal than all other countries combined. The British became fuel exporters on a massive scale; they also built up a great network of bunkering stations which became vital pillars of their imperial supremacy and helped to make Africa accessible to the West as never before.[7]

There were similar changes in the technique of fighting on land. Here again science and military technology advanced hand in hand. Hiram Maxim, a famous American inventor, in 1888 started to experiment with explosives and subsequently built an arms factory at Maxim, New Jersey. The Maxim gun, the Gatling gun, and similar automatic weapons helped to bring about another decisive change in the nature of colonial warfare. Whereas the steam engine in its various uses had altered the logistics of imperial penetration, automatic weapons revolutionized its military tactics. Bechuana, Ashanti, and Yao warriors could acquire and use modern rifles, but they could neither purchase nor service quick-firing guns. The whites acquired a temporary monopoly of automatic infantry arms, and Lobengula's warriors massed in vain against the devastating rate of fire of a Maxim gun.

The initiative thus lay with the European powers, and European pressures began to determine the future of the continent. Current African historiography, influenced by the reaction against Victorian imperialism, sometimes fails to take sufficient account of the overwhelming political and technological disparities between the European powers on the one hand and the various African communities on the other. An older generation of imperial historians, inspired by a

---

[7] See, for instance, Bernard Brodie, *Seapower in the Machine Age* (Princeton, N.J., 1941), pp. 105–123.

mood of boundless self-confidence, wrote of the scramble for Africa almost purely in terms of negotiations conducted in the chancelleries of London, Paris, and Berlin. Anticolonialism and decolonization caused the pendulum to swing the other way. Some academic writers began to overcompensate; they saw the partition and the pattern of subsequent imperial rule too much in African terms, as European reactions to local African situations. Neither of these interpretations is complete in itself. Tribal politics did play their part in determining the shape of imperial enterprise. Lewanika, the calculating sovereign of the Barotse, had excellent reasons of his own when he asked for British rather than Portuguese protection. His intervention in the politics of the scramble was a matter of considerable local importance and helped to determine the geographical configuration of what is now the Republic of Zambia. The chartered company, the original colonial power, could no more ignore the political and social structure of the peoples with whom it came into contact than any other colonizer, but African influence in the encounters was limited. Even the strongest of African kingdoms wielded relatively little power. The main decisions were usually made in Europe or on the spot by ambitious colonial generals or administrators.

The partition provided only a few instances of major miscalculation concerning the strength of local states on the continent. The French failed to allow for the resilience of Muslim Algeria, and in the nineteenth century they had to fight much harder to hold the country than they had ever anticipated. The British gravely underestimated the fighting potential of the Afrikaners. The Italians made an even more disastrous mistake about the military capacity of the Amhara.

Otherwise the partition of Africa must be explained more in terms of European than of African factors. The British in 1890 had to humor Lewanika. Fifteen years later, when conditions had changed, an Italian arbitrator could settle a Portuguese-British boundary dispute by assigning a vast part of Lewanika's western provinces to the Portuguese. The Barotse grumbled but obeyed. The diplomatic and political initiative, in other words, generally remained with the whites. Even the best-organized African communities were rarely in a position to enter the Western political system on terms of anything like equality.

There were, of course, some exceptions. The Amhara carried out quite a successful foreign policy and carefully picked their way between conflicting British, French, Russian, and Italian interests. The Zanzibari, used to dealing with both Muslims and Franks, took up diplomatic contacts with Western countries and even once sent an embassy to the United States. Given different circumstances, the

Fulani kingdoms, part of an older Muslim state system, might perhaps have adjusted themselves to changing power realities more successfully than they did. But even well-organized Bantu states such as Barotseland or Buganda could not maintain ambassadors in European capitals or join the play and counterplay of Western alliances. The greatest Bantu communities lacked the technical, cultural, administrative, or diplomatic resources of the smallest Balkan states. They could not maintain their independence once the West decided to advance. Partition was only a matter of time; its ultimate shape was primarily determined by Europeans.

The exact starting point of the scramble has since become a subject of hot debate. Historians still disagree on many aspects, but two major landmarks emerge from their controversies. The first of these is the year 1869, which is a milestone on the road to partition. In South Africa a huge diamond, the "Star of South Africa," weighing 83½ carats, was discovered near the Orange River. There was a rush of fortune hunters inland; a few men made tremendous profits, unparalleled in the previous history of South Africa. These gains helped to finance gold mining in the Transvaal and subsequently provided funds for territorial expansion beyond the Limpopo River. The year 1869 also witnessed important changes on the coast of North Africa. The Suez Canal was completed. Merchant ships from Europe no longer needed to go round the Cape on their way to India; the East African coast became more accessible to Western Europe. Egypt soon acquired a decisive importance in British imperial planning. In the same year the finances of Tunis, a quasi-independent Muslim state nominally under Turkish sovereignty, were brought under the control of a tripartite commission of British and French representatives. The powers did not at first wish for annexations. They simply tried to protect their investors against the extravagance of the Bey and his ministers. But the British policy of shoring up existing Muslim states like Turkey, Tunis, Zanzibar, and Morocco in order to maintain some sort of law and order inland did not work. In North Africa and the Near East, European penetration produced bitter indigenous reactions, and the precarious balance of power among the various interested white parties could not be maintained.

The fight for a new sphere of influence in North Africa became strongly linked to the fortunes of the declining Turkish empire in the Balkans and the Middle East. Here the British tried to support Ottoman power against Russian imperialism. But after an unsuccessful war with Russia, the Turks had to make extensive concessions in the Balkans. The European powers intervened and at the Congress of Berlin in 1878 redefined the extent of Russian, Bulgarian, Montene-

grin, and Serbian gains. The Turks, threatened by the emergent nationalism of their remaining Christian subjects in the Balkans and
frightened by Russian encroachments in Asia, agreed in 1878 to hand
over Cyprus as a *place d'armes* for British use. Britain in turn promised France a free hand in Tunisia. Colonization in Africa thus suddenly became intertwined both with the aspirations of the Western
powers and, indirectly, with those of the small emergent nationalities
of Southeastern Europe. French intervention in Tunis, undertaken
somewhat reluctantly, originally aimed only at a protectorate with
limited objectives. The Bey's surrender to the unbelievers, however,
raised a militant Muslim reaction. The French army received its
marching orders, and the invaders of Tunisia were now compelled to
conquer and rule a people whom they could no longer manipulate by
diplomatic and financial means.[8]

The second major historical break came in the early 1880s, when
European penetration began to pick up speed. Scholars still do not
quite agree which state was responsible for this sudden acceleration
of white expansion. One school of thought stresses what might be
called the Belgo-German interpretation. The final partition of Africa,
according to this view, came about through the appearance of two
new powers which had not previously shown any interest in the continent. The newcomers upset the existing balance of power and
brought about a state of international hysteria in which all powers
rushed in to claim their stakes.[9] The first of these upstart competitors
to enter sub-Saharan Africa was not, strictly speaking, a power, but a
minor sovereign. Leopold II of Belgium, a man of great ambitions,
had for many years been interested in all kinds of colonization projects; he scanned the world for possible openings in countries as distant
as Formosa, Fiji, and Sarawak. His policies lacked a mass backing at
home. In Belgium, as in Britain, commercial and industrial interests
outweighed agrarian pressure groups in political importance. Belgian
factory owners had no desire to see their trade reduced by a protectionist policy. Nothing was further from their minds than to found a
full-fledged colony, linked to the mother country by protective tariffs
but costing the taxpayer a great deal of money. Belgian colonization
thus began as a royal speculation, initiated by King Leopold II, a
"projector" of an almost archaic cast of mind, in some ways more
like the entrepreneurs responsible for the Mississippi and South Sea

[8] For the best and most stimulating short account of the partition see Ronald
E. Robinson and John Gallagher, "The Partition of Africa," *The New Cambridge Modern History:* Vol. XI, *Material Progress and World-wide Problems,
1870–1898* (Cambridge, Eng., 1962), 593–640.

[9] See Roland A. Oliver and John D. Fage, *A Short History of Africa* (Harmondsworth, Middlesex, Eng., 1962), pp. 182–185.

"bubbles" of the eighteenth century than a modern capitalist. Leopold, however, took advantage of the growing interest of Western European businessmen in the potentialities of tropical Africa and of strong humanitarian feelings against the slave trade. A conference called in 1876 at Brussels discussed the best method of opening up the Dark Continent and founded the International Association for the Exploration and Civilization of Central Africa. This group, which soon became Belgian in character, sent out Henry Morton Stanley in 1879 to act as its agent. The drive for the Congo, one of the great gateways to Africa, was on. Belgian action, goes the argument, stimulated French enterprise, so that Leopold's diplomacy set off the partition.

The Belgians thus played an important part in the scramble, but their role should not be exaggerated. Leopold was out for profit more than power; his venture started as a commercial enterprise. A treaty concluded by his agents with the chiefs of Vivi on the Lower Congo in 1880 did not, in fact, provide for the surrender of sovereignty, though a falsified version was subsequently presented to the United States Senate to justify political dominion *ex post facto*. Leopold set out for sovereignty only in response to French action on the Congo. The race for territory in this part of Africa began with a treaty concluded by Savorgnan de Brazza with Chief Makoko north of Stanley Pool. In 1882 France ratified the treaty. Almost the entire French press, in a mood of patriotic fervor, put its weight behind a policy which promised grandeur and riches as well as a chance for scoring against the British for their power in Egypt. The French, tired of compromise in a previous Senegalese–Sierra Leonean boundary dispute, sought glory; Brazza's exploits and colorful personality had made the colonies a popular issue. French expansion came to hinge on three main lines of advance, the Senegal, the Congo, and the West African coast; from the later 1870s to the early 1890s the French made vast additions to their African empire.

The French government did not at first aim at a radical revision of policy. Paris meant to make prudent concessions to French naval and colonial lobbies in areas where France would not meet with immediate British hostility. The new course nevertheless upset the traditional balance. Leopold, faced with the prospect of foreign competition in the Congo, turned toward the acquisition of sovereignty as a means of keeping his stake in the Congo. The British tried to keep the French out of the Congo and to safeguard their mercantile interests by making a treaty with the Portuguese. The French, by 1879, had already embarked on a new course of empire building on the West Coast, which responded to their desire for international prestige as well as to pressure from special economic interest groups desirous of a privileged position in the West African market. The final scramble was on.[10]

The second factor in Africa was Germany, and historians have spent much time in assessing the driving forces which caused Berlin to turn to Africa. The orthodox Marxist view has already been discussed in a previous chapter. Marxists of a more eclectic type tried to put their finger on individual pressure groups, such as the Diskontogesellschaft, a big financial group; Marxists stressed the way in which German steel prices fell and asserted that German big business looked around for compensation overseas.[11] But the faceless-men theory will not carry a historian very far. Bismarck, like Salisbury, knew his own mind, and the idea that such men were secretly manipulated by anonymous pressure groups is a romantic myth of the Byronic kind. Once the Iron Chancellor had, for reasons of his own, set the course, mercantile interests did play their part in detailed execution. But the mainspring of German policy was more complex. One school of writers argues that Bismarck was deliberately provoking a minor quarrel with Britain to further reconciliation with France. Others stress internal policy; they claim that the diplomatic purpose was secondary and that Bismarck's main concern was to preserve his personal dominance over German political life. A colonial policy, with patriotic appeal, could rally support in an insubordinate Reichstag and in the autumn elections of 1884; more specifically, Bismarck gained a handle against the radical Freisinnige Partei, with its pro-British leanings and its dangerous connections with Crown Prince Frederick and his English wife.[12]

These two interpretations are not mutually exclusive. Most writers now agree that Bismarck's system of government was too authoritarian to allow African merchants and German Colonial League theoreticians to dictate policy and that local African considerations played only a very minor part in these decisions. Bismarck annexed Kamerun as he had annexed Lauenburg or Hessen-Kassel, as part of a diplomatic game in which economic factors or matters of local policy took second place. Moreover, he imagined that he could colonize inexpensively. But like so many of his French and British counterparts, he miscalculated badly. He intended to run colonization on the limited-

[10] Jean Stengers, "L'impérialisme colonial de la fin du XIXe siècle: Mythe ou réalité," *Journal of African History,* III, No. 3 (1962), 469–491.

[11] See George W. F. Hallgarten, *Imperialismus vor 1914: Theoretisches, soziologische Skizzen der aussenpolitischen Entwicklung in England und Frankreich; Soziologische Darstellung der deutschen Aussenpolitik bis zum Ersten Weltkrieg* (Munich, 1951), Vol. I, especially pp. 197–204. This is a monumental work with a wealth of sociological detail.

[12] John D. Hargreaves, *Prelude to the Partition of West Africa* (London, 1963), admirably explains these arguments; see especially pp. 316–321.

liability principle, exercised through chartered companies, without committing the full resources of the Reich. This policy in fact did not work, but Bismarck could not foresee the cost of colonization. A protectorate in South-West Africa was set up in 1884; others followed in Togoland and Kamerun and on the East African coast in what later became Tanganyika. In 1886 the Germans changed their course. Russia and Austria-Hungary quarreled over Bulgaria in the Balkans. Austria, Bismarck's ally, stood in need of British backing against Russia. Bismarck, who considered Eastern Europe infinitely more important to Germany than the whole of Africa, began to adopt a much friendlier attitude toward Britain, and the colonial drive was called off.

The British, for their part, had meanwhile become entangled in Egypt, and an important school of historians considers the Egyptian problem the key to the African partition.[13] Turkish power, once supreme over the country, was visibly declining. The "sick man of Europe" no longer seemed capable of keeping together his vast empire in Europe, the Near East, and northern Africa. In 1876 the Turks defaulted on their debts. Egypt's financial fate fared no better. The American Civil War led to a serious crisis in the vital textile industry; the interruption of transatlantic imports produced a great cotton famine. The valley of the Nile proved the ideal spot in which to grow cotton, and the Khedive Ismail, Egypt's ambitious ruler, attempted to modernize the country by using the proceeds of this most profitable cash crop. Postal services, railways, lighthouses, and military establishments were built; and more important still, the construction of the Suez Canal was completed owing to French initiative. In addition, Ismail endeavored to pursue a policy of territorial expansion in Africa. However, his plans were far too ambitious for his limited resources and inefficient administration. The peasants were squeezed dry by taxation. More and more foreign loans had to be taken up, and after the cotton boom collapsed, Ismail in 1875 was compelled to sell his shares in the Suez Canal to Britain. A year later he went bankrupt. France and Britain now assumed financial control over the country. Intervention led to an ineffective nationalist uprising, headed by Egyptian army officers, the country's partly westernized military intelligentsia. The French would not intervene; the British therefore acted by themselves and in 1882 crushed the Egyptian nationalist forces at Tel-el-Kebir.

The British did not originally wish to stay permanently, but having

[13] See Ronald E. Robinson and John Gallagher, *Africa and the Victorians: The Climax of Imperialism in the Dark Continent,* with Alice Denny (New York, 1961), for a classic statement of the "Egyptocentric" thesis of the partition.

once entered the country, they found withdrawal impossible. Imperial strategists no longer regarded Constantinople as the key to the Middle East; they now looked upon Alexandria and the Suez Canal as the pivot of Mediterranean policy. The experts regarded the Suez Canal as the spinal cord of the empire; Egypt seemed essential for the control of the naval route to India. British influence in the country was consolidated by Sir Evelyn Baring, who came out as British agent and consul general. British policy, according to some historians, hinged on the double pivot of the Cape and Cairo. It was determined by the general needs of imperial strategy and by Britain's desire to protect its older possessions in India and the East. British intervention in Egypt in turn involved the British in the troubles of the Sudan and Uganda. Their action also forced other countries to look for compensation elsewhere in Africa and thereby played the main part in determining the time and manner of the scramble.

The "Egyptocentric" thesis, well argued by Robinson and Gallagher, has great merits. It stresses the continuity of British imperial policy; it underlines the importance of Egypt for the continent as a whole; it demonstrates the way in which the colonial policies of conflicting powers came to interlock; it provides a great deal of insight into the mind of the British Establishment at the time. It is, however, too all-embracing in character. The partition as a whole can be explained more convincingly in terms of a polycentric approach. By the late nineteenth century there were many points of Afro-European contact, all with their own logic and all capable of generating expansive policies of their own. The partition of Africa was not determined from one or two geographical centers, any more than it arose from just a single set of causes, economic, military, or political. Each major European acquisition might upset the local balance of power; each new colony was likely to provoke expansion on the part of its neighbors. This had long been obvious to the most farsighted colonizers. The British seizure of Cape Town in 1795, undertaken at first for limited strategic motives, was fraught with far-reaching long-term consequences. "The new possessors of Table Bay," argued an outstanding Luso-Brazilian administrator in Mozambique at the time, "require very careful watching, or our want of energy will enable them to extend themselves northwards."[14] The writer, Lacerda e Almeida, was convinced that the British would be drawn inland, that Portuguese commerce and dominion alike could be secured only by the creation of a contiguous belt of territory from the east to the west

[14] F. J. M. de Lacerda e Almeida, *The Lands of Cazembe: Lacerda's Journey to Cazembe in 1798,* trans. and annotated by Captain R. F. Burton (London, 1873), pp. 14–21.

coast, which would shut out the British from the interior. Lacerda's attempt to build such an empire came to nought, but the Portuguese never quite forgot such grand projects and in the late 1880s once more tried their luck. They also had ancient claims to the Congo. The British, the leading commercial power in the area, backed the Portuguese claims and in 1884 signed a treaty with Portugal which recognized Portuguese demands on the Congo against Leopold.

The British and Portuguese, however, had failed to reckon with the strength of European opposition to such designs. As a result of a temporary Franco-German entente in Europe, a conference was called at Berlin in 1884 to discuss the future of Africa. All the major powers were represented, and their deliberations led to the General Act of the Berlin Conference of 1885. This stood out as a peaceful compromise between the major European states on the African continent, where they had enough in common to make some limited agreement possible. The signatories agreed on freedom of trade in the Congo basin and on the rules governing the partition; they recognized Leopold's claims to the Congo. In 1885 Belgium authorized its king to become sovereign of the Etat Indépendant du Congo.[15]

Balked in their Congolese ambitions, the Portuguese revived their claims to a belt of territory stretching from coast to coast and in 1886 came very near getting the big European states to accept Lisbon's main contentions. The Portuguese had two main assets: a quixotic pride which rejected any major concession to foreigners not exacted by superior force and their ability to maneuver one great power against another. But a good understanding between the major maritime powers always formed a potential threat to Portuguese ambitions in Africa. In the 1880s Austria-Hungary, Germany's ally, came into conflict with Russian policy in the Balkans. Bismarck, who originally had been prepared to back the Portuguese claims, now required British support in Southeastern Europe. In 1887 Britain and Bismarck's two partners in the Triple Alliance, the Hapsburg empire and Italy, agreed to safeguard the status quo in Southeastern Europe. Though Portugal could no longer count on German support, the Portuguese sent an expedition in 1889 to occupy the Shire Highlands in what is now Malawi. British opposition proved too strong, and in 1889 the British declared a protectorate over the disputed area.

By now, however, Portugal's local conflict with Britain was no longer an isolated affair, and the whole question merged with the wider South African one. British expansion in East Africa was linked

[15] Roger Anstey, *Britain and the Congo in the Nineteenth Century* (Oxford, 1962), *passim*.

to the enterprise of missionaries, of traders, and later of planters from the United Kingdom. But in addition, there was now a new power center, situated on the African continent itself, with an expansionist drive of its own—the South African mining frontier. When diamonds were discovered at Kimberley, southern Africa suddenly moved into the forefront of the world's economic stage.. So great were the profits from diamonds that producers could largely pay for the initial expansion of the industry from their own earnings and still accumulate sufficient funds for investment in other enterprises and new territorial acquisitions.[16] The chance for additional expansion came in 1886, when gold was found at the Witwatersrand in the Transvaal. Most of the concerns that were formed on the Rand during its pioneering period were connected in some way with people prominent in the diamond industry.

Outstanding among these financiers was an English parson's son, Cecil John Rhodes, who had come to South Africa for his health and who became the greatest of the nineteenth-century empire builders. In 1887 Rhodes acquired control over the whole of the De Beers mine at Kimberley; in the same year he also founded what later became the Consolidated Gold Fields of South Africa Limited. Rhodes's position on the Rand was not as strong as it was at Kimberley, but he regarded his great business achievements merely as steppingstones to a vast Anglo-Saxon empire in Africa. The Rand, he was convinced, represented only a fraction of southern Africa's mineral wealth, and some of the profits from the available mineral resources should be used to finance the exploitation of those additional reserves yet to be found inland. Rhodes linked the quest for minerals to further territorial expansion. He mistakenly imagined that a second Rand would be uncovered beyond the Limpopo River. Here, in what became Southern Rhodesia, Rhodes's financial control would rule supreme, as it did not do in Johannesburg.

His guess at the time seemed by no means an unreasonable one. The far north was reputed to be the Biblical Ophir, the land of King Solomon's mines, and these speculations were confirmed by colorful and greatly exaggerated tales, brought back by travelers such as Carl Mauch and Thomas Baines, of the vast new gold deposits to be found inland. Gold at this period was "trumps," far more than it is today, for at the end of the last century most of the currencies of the countries engaged in world trade were still based on the gold standard. Industry and commerce were expanding rapidly, but a good many years had passed since the last great gold discoveries in California

[16] S. Herbert Frankel, *Capital Investment in Africa: Its Course and Effects* (London, 1938), pp. 52–58.

and Australia gave a much-needed stimulus to the world economy. Southern African gold was thus of key importance.

Rhodes did not think mainly in economic terms. Inland expansion, he believed, would also lay the foundations of a new empire that would one day stretch from the Cape to Cairo and rival the British raj in India in its splendor. South African northward expansion would unite Briton and Boer in the common task of settling South Africa's half-empty hinterland, bringing civilization to the frontier. Empire building would also make the Cape, where Rhodes became Prime Minister in 1890, the gateway to the interior and the most prominent state in southern Africa. The Transvaal would be isolated, and later incorporated, together with the remaining South African colonies, into one united country, independent of direct British control though linked to the British Empire.

To achieve these plans competition from Portugal and Germany had to be eliminated. First the Transvaalers had to be prevented from joining hands with the Germans in the interior, thus cutting off further advance from the south. Imperial intervention secured Bechuanaland, the "Suez Canal into the interior." Then in 1888 Rhodes obtained by the Rudd Concession a monopoly over all the minerals in the countries under the sway of Lobengula, the Matabele king. He joined with various financial interests and, with the Matabele concession in his pocket, asked for a Royal Charter to secure powers of government north of the Limpopo River. The British government of the day was little inclined to finance territorial expansion out of taxation, but had no objection if an association of private investors would shoulder the risks and expenses under imperial supervision. There was, after all, nothing to stop private entrepreneurs from going it alone in the interior, and if colonization could not be avoided, it had best be carried on under official control.

A charter was issued to the newly formed British South Africa Company in 1889. The following year Rhodes dispatched a small, but efficient, privately paid and equipped force from South Africa, which successfully occupied Mashonaland. During the same period, rival trekkers from the Transvaal were firmly prevented from setting up any competing political authority beyond the Limpopo. President Kruger, the head of the Transvaal, cautiously decided not to intervene. In 1891, after lengthy negotiations, Rhodes's charter was extended beyond the Zambezi up to the Congo, though the rich copper deposits of Katanga fell into Belgian hands. The foundations had been laid for permanent British settlement in Rhodesia.

Rhodes's enterprise also helped to secure Malawi (Nyasaland) to the British flag. Rhodes provided financial assistance; this enabled the

British government to intervene more actively, without having to apply to Parliament for funds at a time when there was still a good deal of active opposition to further British expansion in Africa. Portugal was forced to relinquish many of its claims, and Portuguese projects of a great Central African empire were brought to an end. In 1890 an amicable agreement was reached between Britain and Germany, now steering an anti-Russian course. In 1890 the British position was recognized in countries as widespread as Uganda, Kenya, Zanzibar, and Nyasaland; the outlines of empire in East Africa assumed something like the shape which still determines the layout of present-day frontiers in the area.

In the meantime European penetration had also made headway in West Africa. In 1885 the British, faced with competition from the French, constituted the territories between Lagos and Cameroun into the Niger protectorate. A year later they issued a charter to what became known as the Royal Niger Company to administer the area and keep out foreign claimants. In 1889 the British and French concluded a fairly comprehensive boundary settlement, but French imperialism had lost none of its impetus, and advance into the French Sudan was resumed. The Tukolor empire could not resist French arms, and in 1890 French troops marched into Segou, the capital. The French then penetrated down the Niger and into the area south of the great bend, threatening British claims in that area.

In 1895 Joseph Chamberlain became British Colonial Secretary, and the British now also embarked on a much more active and determined policy. He strongly supported the Niger Company's insistence on keeping the French off the navigable part of the Niger below Bussa and out of the main portion of Hausaland. The French would not risk a conflict with Britain over such an issue; in 1898 they agreed to the main points of the British demand, and this agreement largely completed the diplomatic partition of West Africa.[17]

The year 1898 also saw the last great Franco-British encounter in the eastern Sudan. For years the French had been trying to get the British out of Egypt. Having failed to attain this objective, they sent out an expedition under Captain Marchand to the Upper Nile in 1896 in order to put new diplomatic pressure on the British. "Go to Fashoda," Hanotaux, the French foreign minister, told Marchand as the latter left Paris. "France is going to fire her pistol." The French move seemed extremely serious. Italy, Britain's ally, sustained a crushing defeat at Aduwa. French and Russian diplomatists collaborated at the Ethiopian court, and the French tried to associate the Abyssinians with a common anti-British endeavor. The Sudan, Egypt's

---

[17] Hargreaves, *Prelude to the Partition of West Africa*, pp. 338–349.

hinterland, was controlled by a fanatical religious-revolutionary movement which gained wide popular support among the local Muslims, though it failed to conciliate the pagan black people of the south. The Mahdists wiped out the last vestiges of Egyptian sovereignty in the area. General Gordon died a hero's death in Khartoum, and the British imperial and evangelical cause alike acquired a martyr of impressive stature. The Sudan experienced a short period of Mahdist rule, bloodstained in the extreme, but in the end the British struck back. In 1898 an Anglo-Egyptian force totally destroyed the Mahdist army a few miles north of Omdurman and reconquered the Sudan. Marchand's small force, operating at a great distance from its base, was helpless before the British. The Russians failed to give much diplomatic support to their French ally. The French neither could nor would risk a naval war with Britain. After a serious international crisis, the French swallowed their pride and evacuated Fashoda. In 1899 Lord Salisbury and the French ambassador in London signed an agreement whereby France abandoned the basin of the Nile, and the French dream of linking their West African empire to the Red Sea came to an end.[18]

The European state system of the time was able to cope with colonial issues by diplomatic means. In 1904 France and Britain liquidated their last outstanding differences; Paris promised not to ask for any future time limits to the British occupation of Egypt; London recognized French primacy in Morocco. The Germans subsequently tried to overthrow the Anglo-French entente and also to obtain some territorial advantages. The Germans failed in their diplomatic objective, but in 1911 they succeeded in obtaining a strip of French Equatorial Africa in return for relinquishing further claims in Morocco. A year later France declared a protectorate over Morocco, and an agreement with Spain limited the boundaries of the Spanish zone on the North African shore. The Italians, determined to seek compensation, made war on Turkey in 1911; in 1912 they annexed the vilayets of Tripoli and Benghazi and thereby helped to set off a grand assault on the Sultan's possessions in Southeastern Europe on the part of the Christian Balkan peoples. In 1913, just before the outbreak of World War I, Britain and Germany reached agreement on the future of Portuguese Africa. The British did not object to German expansion in the economic field, and the 1913 agreement recognized most of Angola as well as the northern part of Mozambique as part of Germany's economic sphere. Before the new agreement could be ratified, however, war had broken out in Europe over

[18] William L. Langer, *The Diplomacy of Imperialism, 1890–1902* (2d ed.; New York, 1960), pp. 538–544, 551–553, 564.

issues unconnected with Africa. The Germans failed in their hopes of neutralizing their African empire. The Peace of Versailles at last deprived the Reich of all its colonies, and for the first time in history a great European power was forced to relinquish all its possessions in Africa. Versailles thereby ended the partition and closed a major historical chapter in Africa as well as in Europe.

This bald and impressionistic account cannot do justice to the full complexity of the partition. A great deal more might be said about the Italian empire, or the Portuguese, or the intricate relationships between diplomatic, commercial, and military factors, or the interplay between white and black in the different parts of Africa. But a few simple conclusions can be drawn even from this incomplete summary. The partition centered as much on Europe as it did on Africa. The partition by itself did not occasion any major European wars. Even the greatest European powers observed a good deal of self-restraint. During the Morocco crisis of 1905 Germany could have forced a war of colonial conquest upon France, at a time when the Third Republic's Russian ally was reeling under the blows received at Japanese hands in the Far East. The Germans, however, would not risk Armageddon over a colonial issue. The British, in alliance with Germany, could have stripped Portugal of its empire, but London, as we have seen, never used its bargaining strength to the full. The British had diplomatic reasons for restraint. Up to 1910 they also wished to spare Portugal a major humiliation so as not to bring down the monarchy at Lisbon, thereby endangering—as they thought—the social and political stability of the Iberian Peninsula as a whole. World War I itself did not break out over African issues, but was precipitated by Austro-Russian conflicts in the Balkans and by the challenge posed by Serbian nationalism to the multinational empire of the Hapsburgs. France and Britain settled all their remaining colonial disagreements over Egypt and Morocco in 1904. Germany did not seriously covet the British or French possessions in Africa. Before 1914 German diplomacy did not even have any consistent designs toward annexing the Belgian Congo; the German Foreign Office was far too concerned with European questions and did not wish to drive Belgium into the arms of the Entente.[19] Subsequent German designs for a great *Mittelafrika* were not the cause of war in Europe, but rather were one of its effects, the natural result of a situation in which Germany had made enormous sacrifices and therefore wanted compensation for its sufferings.

[19] See Jacques Willequet, *Le Congo belge et la Weltpolitik, 1894–1914* (Brussels, 1962).

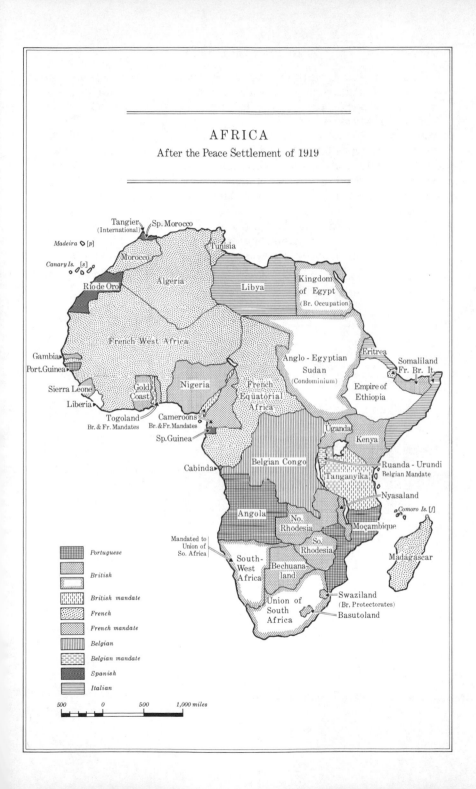

AFRICA

After the Peace Settlement of 1919

Tangier
(International)
Sp. Morocco

Madeira ◊ [p]

Canary Is. [s]

Tunisia

Morocco

Rio de Oro

Algeria

Libya

Kingdom
of Egypt
(Br. Occupation)

Gambia

Port. Guinea

Sierra Leone

Liberia

French West Africa

Gold
Coast

Nigeria

French
Equatorial
Africa

Togoland
Br. & Fr. Mandates

Cameroons
Br. & Fr. Mandates

Sp. Guinea

Anglo - Egyptian
Sudan
(Condominium)

Eritrea

Somaliland
Fr. Br. It.

Empire of
Ethiopia

Uganda

Kenya

Cabinda

Belgian Congo

Ruanda - Urundi
Belgian Mandate

Tanganyika

Nyasaland

Comoro Is. [f]

Angola

No.
Rhodesia

Moçambique

Mandated to
Union of
So. Africa

South-
West
Africa

So.
Rhodesia

Madagascar

Bechuana-
land

Swaziland
(Br. Protectorates)

Union
of
South
Africa

Basutoland

▨	*Portuguese*
▦	*British*
☐	*British mandate*
▦	*French*
▦	*French mandate*
▥	*Belgian*
▦	*Belgian mandate*
▨	*Spanish*
▤	*Italian*

500   0   500   1,000 miles

In summary, the partition had its origins in the weakness of most African political systems and their inability to cope with direct or indirect European pressures. The scramble reflected the existing balance of power in the West, and leading diplomatists in Europe were always more concerned with the general political equilibrium on the Continent than with local African issues. The imperial powers on the whole collaborated with some success in the division of Africa; this period of troubled understanding continued, until Europe went to war over purely metropolitan issues in the Balkans and Belgium.

The partition was the last great achievement of the concert of Europe; the boundary arrangements created during this period are among the more important legacies which the Western colonial system bequeathed to its indigenous successors on the African continent.

14. Dual Mandate

The empire, British Radicals used to scoff, was founded to provide outdoor relief for the upper classes. Continental critics of colonialism often belabored the same point, but an inquiry into the social origins of both empire builders and humbler administrators lends limited support to this theory. Rhodes and Lugard came from clerical households. Jameson's father was a lawyer. Sir Harry Johnston, Her Majesty's first Commissioner in British Central Africa, was the son of an insurance agent. Sir William Mackinnon, the founder of the British East Africa Company, started off in life as a grocer's apprentice. In the French colonial empire the military and aristocratic element played a somewhat larger part. Savorgnan de Brazza, a naval officer, came from an ancient patrician family. Marshal Lyautey was descended from a long line of soldiers, but the Lyauteys were bred in a tradition of simple tastes and strict religious observance of the kind that would have appealed to the most straitlaced Methodist merchants in England. European administration in Africa was therefore largely a middle-class achievement. Efficiency, reliability, and economy became its hallmark. Emphasis lay on function rather than on status. Officials did not look upon their jobs, in the manner of so many eighteenth-century English Whig lords, as sinecures befitting their high birth and connections, but rather as vocations. Despite all the charges of favoritism, family links rarely played a significant part in securing official advancement. Expatriate officials, unlike so many of their African agents, were not dependent on ties of extended kinship whose claims would take priority over the needs of an impersonal administration. Financial corruption was thus rare among white civil servants. African colonies secured an administration with regular and predictable financial requirements and obtained a valuable social investment of trained men who took a considerable part in the continent's development.

The best type of European official displayed as well a sense of social purpose characteristic of nineteenth-century middle-class reform-ism. His outlook on life and his terminology might differ according to his national and social background. The British were on the whole rank-conscious and monarchist, pragmatic, and respectful of estab-lished chieftainly authority, while the French were more egalitarian and legal-minded, bound to the Continental traditions of centralized administration. But no matter whether a civil servant spoke in terms of transmitting the benefits of French civilization to the "natives" or of guiding indigenous tribes toward a better life by making use of their accustomed institutions, the rationale of French and British administrators often had something in common. The colonial state ma-chinery was weak; hence much depended on the district officer's per-sonality. His job, as he saw it, was to teach the backward and uplift the poor. "Improvement" should be the keynote of government.

Lyautey, as a student at Saint-Cyr, thus founded a group for social action and took part in the activities of workers' circles, created by Albert de Mun, a royalist deputy. The British developed a similar form of paternalism. The great majority of colonial officials absorbed their ethos in public schools and at "Oxbridge"; the old-time district commissioner's office commonly suffused a faint air of the prefect's study.[1] Some British administrators gave clear expression to this bent. Robert Edward Codrington, charged with organizing a civil service for the British South Africa Company in northeastern Rhodesia, thus specifically asked for young recruits from England with a middle-class background and good physique, giving special preference to uni-versity men with teaching experience, locally known as "bum switch-ers." Codrington himself, tall, with a commanding presence, sporting a neatly clipped mustache, and gruff of speech, was just the sort of man who would have made a stern but respected headmaster at a British public school, and it was in many ways the schoolmaster's out-look which he brought to Northern Rhodesia. White government, he argued, had to be based on prestige, for the amount of military force available was small. The "natives" were but children. He felt con-vinced, therefore, that officers who could produce testimonials certi-fying the ability to keep British schoolboys in order would do equally well as district officers in remote outstations.

For all their regional and national differences, colonial administra-tions in the diverse parts of Africa generally developed along a roughly

[1] For a more detailed assessment of the educational and class background of the British colonial service see Robert Heussler, *Yesterday's Rulers: The Mak-ing of the British Colonial Service* (Syracuse, N.Y., 1963). For the French service, which included many sons of *fonctionnaires,* see Marcel Blanchard, "Administrateurs d'Afrique noire," *Revue d'Histoire des Colonies,* XL (1953), 377–430.

similar course. From Mauritania to Mashonaland, the story generally began with an initial period of pacification. The imperial powers suppressed all independent centers of local resistance, sometimes with the support of the weaker communities on the spot, who tried to play the white man against their more powerful neighbors. The administration more or less successfully secured to itself a monopoly of armed force; the "means of destruction" were brought under effective public control. In this initial phase habits of independent command, physical courage, and endurance stood at a premium. Officials generally enjoyed a good deal of freedom and often lived much like local dignitaries. A district officer's superior might be stationed several hundred miles away, and mail runners were often the only means of contact with distant headquarters. In some remote regions like the Northern Rhodesian or Tanganyikan backveld as many as nine months might pass until an isolated official would meet another white man. Under these conditions a few succumbed to drink or drugs. Some became local tyrants who abused the villagers and their women. But the great majority adjusted their mode of living fairly successfully, asserted their authority, and usually earned their subjects' more or less grudging respect.

In most parts of Africa this initial stage passed fairly quickly, and the pen soon succeeded the rifle as the main instrument of government. Taxation, for instance, required census work and detailed financial returns. The formalization of court work produced an ever-increasing number of legal documents. New problems arose when European enterprise entered the country, and colonial administrations had to put new laws on the statute books for subjects as diverse as veterinary control, safety precautions on the mines, and labor regulations. Gradually the familiar process of bureaucratization got under way. Government assumed more functions; more officials had to be employed; the growing administration in turn had to engage additional personnel to administer its expanding staff. In order to cope with the increase in clerical work, typewriters came into use; but some argued that these laborsaving devices created as many new tasks as they eliminated. Documents could be turned out more quickly; carbon copies could be reeled off for circulation to other offices, where they had to be read and acknowledged. The art of filing and of information retrieval were now essential skills in government. Offices thus acquired a permanent memory embedded in their records; administration became both more impersonal and more predictable. District commissioners at the same time had to spend more time at their desks and less on tour. Year after year complaints increased within the ranks of the administration itself that district officers were losing touch with "their people" and becoming nothing but glorified accounting clerks and tax collectors.

Disgruntled memorandum writers in government offices often exaggerated the extent of their desk work. Up to about the 1930s the functions of government in Africa on the whole remained limited, and bureaucratic commitments stayed small. "Whatever faults the European administrations in tropical Africa may have had—and they have had plenty if we are to believe all that their critics have said—complexity has certainly not been one of them. [Seldom in human history were] so many people governed by so few with so little fuss as during the heyday of African colonialism."[2] Even on the eve of its independence, when the civil-service list was swollen with expatriates busy "Sudanizing" the country, the Republic of Sudan had no more than 1,000 British civil servants in its administration, and this in a country of almost 1 million square miles with a population of no less than 9 million people. These figures, moreover, were unusually high for the period as a whole. During the later 1930s the Gold Coast, a country nearly as large as the state of Oregon and with a population of some 4 million people, was run with 91 British administrative and 100 military and police officers. The balance of the 842 British colonial administrators in the country were agricultural, veterinary, education, and medical specialists, or they served in the railway or public-works administration.[3] The French and Portuguese differed from the British in employing a somewhat larger proportion of European officials, but throughout colonial Africa the state machinery remained very simple. The British administration in a colony hinged on the governor's office and on a central secretariat, with a somewhat larger number of specialized departments, each provided with branch offices and field staff in the outlying districts. Colonies were generally divided into provinces, each headed by a provincial commissioner, assisted by district commissioners at the lower level. The French colonies were divided into provinces, subdivided into cercles, each in charge of a commandant de cercle. Each cercle was split into subdivisions, or districts; these in turn were broken down into cantons, and then into quartiers.

This simple state machinery placed obvious limitations on the colonial rulers. Governments, whatever their inclination, had to be extremely circumspect; a tremendous weight rested on the shoulders of individual administrators; large-scale oppression was physically

[2] George H. T. Kimble, Tropical Africa: Vol. II, Society and Polity (New York, 1960), 306.

[3] For a detailed table see Lord Hailey, An African Survey: A Study of Problems Arising in Africa South of the Sahara (London, 1938), p. 226.

impossible. Even had the rulers been ill-disposed toward their subjects, they lacked the physical means of power. The British especially
made do with an incredibly small military establishment. In Northern
Rhodesia, a territory larger than Britain, Germany, and the Low
Countries combined, they kept order between the 1920s and the early
1950s with no more than a single askari battalion, commanded by a
handful of white officers. The very paucity of the military potential
forced administrative officers to rely on tact, diplomacy, force of personality, and local influence.

Military force played a somewhat greater part in the French empire. The French regarded their overseas possessions as a reservoir
of manpower for home defense, never anticipating that one day the
balance might swing the other way and great masses of French conscripts might have to be withdrawn from the Rhine to fight a colonial
war beyond the Mediterranean. During World War I the French empire made a substantial military contribution, and in 1919 the French
introduced a limited form of compulsory service for the African subjects of West and Equatorial Africa.[4] But compared with the burden
borne by European conscript states, the defense load on Africa remained light.[5] Colonial government also managed with a very small
ratio of policemen to citizens. This was true even in countries like
Kenya, where racial complications between white and black added to
the difficulties of the administration.[6] Police and defense, in other

[4] During World War I, 181,000 Senegalese, 175,000 Algerians, 50,000
Tunisians, 41,000 Malgaches, 34,000 Moroccans, and 2,000 Somali served in
the French army. In 1928 the French army as a whole consisted of 415,000
soldiers and officers, national guards, and gendarmes from France, 16,500
Foreign Legionnaires, 103,500 North African troops, and 100,000 colonial
native, regular and irregular, and auxiliary troops. French West Africa furnished about 10,000 conscripts, who had to serve for three years but comprised only a limited proportion of the men theoretically liable to serve.
Belgium at this period maintained 16,810 troops in the Force Publique, an
African force largely conscripted and underpaid; it combined police with
military duties in a manner not satisfactory from either point of view. The
system was much inferior to the British system, which divided police and
military duties as soon as possible and thereby achieved the advantages of
division of labor. The British colonies in Africa were defended by some 12,000
African soldiers, commanded by European officers. This figure excludes small
territorial and reserve units. Data in this and the following two notes are abstracted from Raymond L. Buell, *The Native Problem in Africa* (2 vols.; New
York, 1928).

[5] In the Belgian Congo in the 1920s there were about 15 soldiers to every
10,000 inhabitants, compared with 10 soldiers and policemen in Tanganyika
and 12 in Uganda per 10,000 people. The average European conscript state
maintained some 150 policemen and defense personnel per 10,000 people.

[6] In 1927 Kenya had a proportion of 1 policeman to every 1,148 people. The
proportion in the London metropolitan police area stood at 1 to 367.

words, were bought at a relatively inexpensive price; law and order depended to a very considerable extent on the tacit consent of the governed. The colonial achievement in the constabulary sphere was, however, often ignored by humanitarian and philanthropic censors of the imperial system, who all too often accepted the absence of internal strife as part of man's natural state and considered any kind of military or police expenditure as money poured down the drain.

Throughout the 1920s and 1930s the various colonial administrations all remained bound to some extent to a nineteenth-century philosophy of government. In this, as in so many other respects, the European Establishment in Africa—governments, missionaries, and settlers alike—acted in some ways as repositories of ideologies that were weakening in the metropolitan countries. The state was conceived as a night watchman rather than as an entrepreneur. Trade, farming, and industry were generally left to private initiative, although in Kenya as well as in several French and Portuguese colonies special lobbies continued for a time to manipulate the state authority for the purpose of mobilizing obligatory labor and enforcing the cultivation of specified commercial crops. Social services for Africans remained largely the parson's preserve. In many parts of colonial Africa governments limited their efforts to subsidizing missionary schools and hospitals with public funds. France, with its *étatiste* and *laïque* tradition, again formed an important exception and built up a rudimentary system of state-run schools in West Africa, where lay teachers, working with small salaries and great devotion, acted as secular agents of enlightenment.[7]

Under these conditions, one man, the governor, could generally supervise the affairs of one territory quite effectively, and governors were left with a great deal of power. In the British colonies the laissez-faire doctrines of the period found expression in the ideal of financial self-sufficiency, a doctrine which helped to strengthen the position of local governments as against the center in London. Newly acquired protectorates might start off with small subsidies, but in the normal course of events they were expected to balance their own budgets thereafter. Richer territories like the Gold Coast thus pushed ahead, while the poorer colonies could hardly afford the most essential services, and spent a disproportionate share of their revenue on official salaries. The British Colonial Office rarely interfered, and the last word usually lay with the man on the spot. This was especially true at a time when the British public took little interest in imperial affairs —colonial matters were debated before a half-empty House of Commons and even the most ardent Negrophiles were concerned with pre-

---

[7] An example of this kind of school was the Ecole Normale William Ponty near Dakar.

venting abuses rather than initiating development. French and Belgian administrators found themselves subject to somewhat stricter control from Paris and Brussels. But in French-speaking as in English-speaking Africa, administrative realities usually differed a great deal from the elaborate theories enunciated at home. Moreover, colonial portfolios changed hands with surprising rapidity; ministerial control was rarely strict, and to some extent the colonial empire became a state within a state.

During the 1920s and 1930s also, colonial government from Dakar to Dar es Salaam was based on the rarely examined assumption of "indefinite time ahead."[8] White rule supposedly would last for many generations, perhaps for centuries. Africa could be modernized slowly by the creation of a viable export economy, depending mainly on the production of raw materials for the world market, which would ultimately pay for better public services. Civil servants concentrated on administrative rather than economic issues. They were also much more concerned with rural than with urban questions, for their whole training was usually acquired "up-country," and their ideal of service was "Sanders of the River," a British fiction hero, rather than the successful city manager. These generalizations, of course, should not be carried too far. There were governors like Sir Gordon Guggisberg in the Gold Coast who initiated a good deal of development. The 1920s and 1930s saw considerable change; district commissioners had to collaborate with a growing number of technical experts. The old type of proconsul, a man like Johnston in Nyasaland, an autocrat restrained only by financial stringency, gradually gave way to a more modern type of governor, who could be described as a "moderator" between opposing pressure groups rather than a ruler in his own right. Still, the constabulatory approach remained deeply ingrained in government, and gradualism continued as the unacknowledged doctrine of colonial rule.

Social and economic changes in the various colonies nevertheless brought about a shift in administrative attitudes. Public spending increased. All powers had to give more attention to the incipient problem of transforming peasants into proletarians and to providing rudimentary welfare institutions, labor services, and so forth. All had to reconcile administrative practices to an extremely uneven rate of economic change in their African possessions, and all to some extent pursued contradictory policies in different colonies. The solutions sought to the "native problem" all lay somewhere between the two extreme ends of a spectrum, with the "schoolmaster" concept of ultimate Europeanization at one end and the protective "game warden" outlook at the other. British missionary evangelicalism of the old-fashioned

8 Sir Andrew Cohen, *British Policy in Changing Africa* (London, 1959), p. 26.

kind and the democratic egalitarianism of the French Revolution both stood for Europeanization of one sort or another, but their ideals rarely became reality. British Europeanizers, by now a small and dwindling group, hoped to turn their subjects into black Englishmen, complete with middle-class standards and Methodist morality. French Europeanizers, by now also a weak section confined to the Left, hoped to transform tribesmen into French-speaking citizens of the "republic one and indivisible." Portuguese Europeanizers dreamed of their country's Lusitanian mission and envisaged their future empire as an overseas extension of Portugal with a social pattern resembling Brazil's.

The Europeanizers never got very far. The colonizers often had racial prejudices against black people, and in some areas, such as Kenya and Rhodesia, there was pressure from European settlers who could not envisage a policy of identity between themselves and their black neighbors. Africa's wealth and income were much smaller than Europe's. No colonizing power ever planned a transfer of wealth from the metropolitan countries to the colonies sufficiently large to make assimilation a practical possibility. Such a concept was politically impossible and also went counter to the whole laissez-faire outlook in colonial affairs. Most important of all, Europeanization would work only in areas where the old linguistic and ethnic links had been completely smashed, as they had been in the West Indies and Brazil. But in spite of all the fashionable talk of "detribalization" in the 1920s and 1930s, this happened only in a few marginal areas. The Cape Verde Islands, for instance, formed one of the rare exceptions. When the Portuguese first discovered the little archipelago in the fifteenth century, it was uninhabited. The bulk of the population was transported from the African mainland, with a sprinkling of white men. The islands developed a creole culture of their own, based on a mulatto and Negro population speaking a Portuguese patois. The Cape Verdeans were Portuguese citizens and looked to Portugal. The creoles of Sierra Leone developed a similar culture. So did the *Quatre Communes* of Senegal, which, in the tradition of the 1848 revolution, enjoyed full French citizenship, representation in the French National Assembly, and municipal self-government. The French colonial service, unlike that of the British, also contained a handful of highly educated Negroes who considered themselves black Frenchmen and were accepted as such. But assimilation of this kind was confined to a few individuals. France could never Gallicize the masses. The French lacked both the physical resources and the time required for such a policy. Even after several centuries, the French never fully Gallicized the German-speaking people of Alsace, and in Africa assimilationist policies faced infinitely larger obstacles. French rule in most areas

lasted only a few generations. Failure was therefore a foregone conclusion; personal assimilation, a highly selective process, made little
progress in Africa. In the French colonies assimilation worked on a
territorial rather than an individual basis. French theorists tried to in-
tegrate the colonies with the metropolitan country on a parliamentary
basis, through limited representation in the French Chamber of Deputies. The French attempted to link Africa with the mother country
through economic bonds, especially common tariffs; they tried to introduce metropolitan methods of centralized administration in "overseas France." The French stood for a policy of "identity," but even
this was of a selective kind.

The French thus based their governance on centralized rule from
Paris and on the same administrative concepts that dominated their
outlook on government at home. French civil servants emphasized the
virtues of coherence and uniformity in administration; they strongly
stressed what might be called the "stimulatory" function of government in economic life. French officials played an active part in mobilizing labor and in enforcing the cultivation of economic crops.
They relied on orders more than on persuasion. They generally saw
themselves as the new chiefs, and the French service produced a
whole generation of *rois de la brousse,* who governed their districts
with an iron hand. French rule was hierarchical in character; French
governor-generals exercised a much tighter control over local governors than British governors over their local residents, or British residents in turn over their district commissioners. African chiefs were
generally treated as subalterns rather than as partners in government,
though even here practice often differed from theory. The French
(and the Portuguese as well) after all encountered the same problems
of government as did the British. Men and money were short. Administration required local African agents, familiar with the local languages and mores. In Senegal, Faidherbe had based his rule on
indigenous chiefs. Lyautey followed a similar policy in Morocco and
described himself as the Sultan's first servant. Elsewhere in black
Africa the French initially concluded treaties with chiefs and at first
confined their intervention in local matters to a few major issues. As
time went on, many French administrators became convinced that
tribal authorities should be more closely controlled. They argued, not
always justifiably, that under the white man's peace the exactions of
local dignitaries were no longer tempered by the fear of rebellion.
Chiefs were said to abuse their power and to have become corrupt.
Many tribal heads were deposed; titles were discontinued; some
emirates disappeared altogether, and tribal areas were regrouped
into larger units.

This native policy occasioned a great deal of friction, and many

French administrators were persuaded that traditional chiefs could do a better job. In 1917 J. van Vollenhoven, the French governor-general of French West Africa, decreed that traditional chiefs should be appointed, wherever possible, to act as intermediaries between the *commandant du cercle* and the people. Chiefs, however, remained nothing but the agents of the administration, without independent judicial or executive power. Former soldiers or clerks with a knowledge of French were put into office, only to be dismissed if they did not carry out their duties in a manner acceptable to the French. There were exceptions. The kings of Mossi in the Upper Volta or the Fulani rulers of northern Cameroun, for instance, retained many powers. In the French Congo, Governor-General Eboué, a brilliant black West Indian, set up a system which strengthened indigenous institutions such as the *chefferies*. During World War II, Eboué tried to seek out traditional chiefs, train them in new methods, and preserve their dignity as natural leaders of the people. But by and large, chiefs played a much smaller part in the French than in the British administration. The French political officer retained a much greater influence in his district than his British counterpart. French remained the medium of instruction even in primary schools, and the French tried to educate their chiefs in French practice by sending selected candidates to special training institutions. The French did not stress the individual character of each territory; a uniform organization was fastened upon all.[9]

The French claimed that their system made a greater appeal to the emerging Africans and argued in favor of native courts not subject to the vagaries of tribal custom. A few Gallicized Africans reached high administrative positions and were received more or less as equals in French society. French officers, like the Portuguese, found less difficulty in mixing with educated black people than did British officers, or for that matter, Belgian and South African officials. The French bequeathed a tradition of unitary government to their African successors. The French system also helped to undermine the powers of traditional chiefs and thereby had the unintended effect of facilitating the ultimate abolition of chieftainly rule under independent African governments.[10]

[9] For more detailed accounts of French policy see Hubert Jules Deschamps, *Les méthodes et les doctrines coloniales de la France du XVIe siècle à nos jours* (Paris, 1953), and Robert Louis Delavignette, *Freedom and Authority in French West Africa* (London, 1950).

[10] For two contrasting points of view concerning British and French practices, respectively, see Michael Crowder, "Indirect Rule—French and British Style," *Africa*, XXXIV, No. 3 (July, 1964), 197–205, and Hubert Jules Deschamps, "Et maintenant, Lord Lugard?" *Africa*, XXXIII, No. 4 (October, 1963), 293–306.

Belgian policy stood halfway between French policies and the British practice of relying on traditional chiefs. The Belgians, like the French, believed in extreme centralization; Léopoldville ruled the provinces and Brussels ruled Léopoldville. The inhabitants of the Congo, both white and black, remained strictly excluded from all influence in government. The system rested on a firm alliance between three interlocking groups—the state administration, big business, and the Catholic Church—which controlled the bulk of African administration. But the Belgians, like the British, never tried to assimilate the indigenous people. The Belgians themselves were divided into French- and Flemish-speaking people and lacked an agreed cultural pattern which they could have imposed on the Congolese. Belgian administration, perhaps more than any other, considered its subjects "economic men"; they aimed at creating an African petty bourgeoisie which would enjoy the benefits of industrialization and therefore remain content with a subordinated political status. The Belgian government was much more empirical in its approach than the British, not to speak of the French, and administrative methods were switched without much concern for theorizing.[11]

The Congo Free State had initially appointed African agents, primarily for the purpose of getting Africans to produce as much rubber as possible. The system had led to terrible abuses, and when the Belgians began to reform their administration, they increasingly relied on chiefs. The new system, however, was almost as destructive of traditional authority as the old. Local headmen, traditionally subject to more important chiefs, were recognized as independent dignitaries, so that chiefdoms multiplied. After the end of World War I the Belgians began to reduce the number of recognized chiefs and subsequently, like the British, started to set up native treasuries. In Ruanda-Urundi the Belgians supported the dominant Tutsi class against their serfs and accorded to the rulers a position resembling that of the Northern Nigerian emirs in the early days of British rule. Throughout the Congo as a whole, however, chiefs did not receive the same judicial and executive powers that they obtained under the British flag. They were dismissed with much greater ease, and white district officers took a much more important share in local matters than on the British side of the border.

On the West Coast the British did make a real and sustained attempt to develop African municipal corporations, with partially elected councils and the power to raise rates. In most other parts of British Africa, however, municipal government remained strictly a white man's

[11] For a Belgian version of trusteeship principle and a Belgian governor's interpretation of the "black soul," see Pierre Ryckmans, *Dominer pour servir* (rev. and enl. ed.; Brussels, 1948).

affair. In Northern Rhodesia, for instance, British theories of government assumed that black workmen should come to the Copper Belt only as temporary residents. The administration until after the end of World War II resisted the "stabilization of labor," white or black, on the grounds that copper was subject to extreme fluctuations of price. A permanently urban black population would be liable to unemployment whenever copper prices slumped; permanent urbanization should therefore be avoided. The Belgians, on the other hand, deliberately aimed at producing African townsmen. Whole villages were encouraged to migrate to the neighborhood of the mines. The Belgians at the same time evolved a special administrative procedure for the government of what they called *centres extra-coutumiers,* which were governed by nominated councils under the strict control of district officers.

Belgian political and labor practices closely conformed to this system. In the Congo, as in Kenya, the first demand for representation on a local legislature came from colonial white, not from black, people. The Belgians, unlike the British, strongly resisted the colonists' clamor. The Congo settlers, unlike their Rhodesian and Kenyan neighbors, failed to gain any voice in determining policy in the country of their adoption. The Belgians thereby avoided many of the political disputes that subsequently shook the adjacent British territories. The same policy, however, also prevented representation for black people, with the result that the Belgians' very paternalism later incurred the accusation of failure to prepare their black subjects for self-government. In the industrial sphere, the Belgians, unlike the British companies in Northern Rhodesia, gave long-term contracts to their skilled white workers and made arrangements for their subsequent repatriation. Belgian workers found themselves in a more secure personal position than their British colleagues. At the same time white labor unions played a much smaller political and industrial part in the Katanga than in the Copper Belt. Belgian copper companies met with much less resistance from white miners in advancing black workmen into skilled positions than did their competitors in the Rhodesias. Nevertheless, all key positions in industry and government remained firmly in Belgian hands, and the Belgians, like the French or the Portuguese, never envisaged even a limited transfer of power to their African subjects.[12]

The British theory of indirect rule represented a different doctrine. The system owed a good deal to British experience with indigenous princes in India and also to British methods of governance in Nigeria,

[12] The best comparative survey for this period is still Hailey, *An African Survey,* 1938 ed.

which—in theory, at any rate—came to serve as a model for the rest of British Africa. In Northern Nigeria the imperial power found itself face to face with well-organized emirates which they hoped to modernize by a slow process of evolution. Lord Lugard, an outstanding administrator and writer, played a major role in building up the new system. Lugard justified colonial government through the theory of dual mandate. The governing power, in his view, owed a responsibility both to the indigenous races and to the world at large; the colonizers should educate their charges and at the same time develop the economic potential of their colonies for the benefit of all mankind.[13] He hoped to conserve all that was good in traditional institutions, to develop existing native authorities, and to use them for the purpose of slowly improving the community. The theory of indirect rule met with support from the most variegated schools of thought and soon hardened into an unchallenged orthodoxy. Conservative administrators dreaded the emergence of an uprooted intelligentsia of the Indian type, troublemakers, out of touch with the masses, who would drift into the towns and stir up trouble. Treasury officials approved of indirect rule as an economy measure, for chiefs were supposedly cheaper than bureaucrats. Anthropologists, frightened of the real or supposed evils of detribalization, wished to strengthen existing institutions. Liberals hoped to apply contemporary theories of national self-determination on the tribal level and to promote the emergence of local authorities in touch with the people and sympathetic to local aspirations. Advocates of *Realpolitik,* not a very numerous group, privately stressed the merits of "divide and rule." Missionaries, whose investment lay primarily in the countryside, wished to protect their charges from the ungodly influence of the cities and saw great merits in what they described as an "Africa for Africans." In addition, the postwar mood of disillusionment, with its increasing stress on cultural relativism, also helped to add popularity to a doctrine interwoven with so many different strands of opinion.

The British desired legitimate chiefs and, unlike the French or the Portuguese, rarely deposed the dignitaries they appointed. They accepted a great variety of chieftainly rule; they attempted to retain, though to modify, traditional legal institutions. They delegated both judicial and executive powers, such as the right to raise local taxes, maintain police forces, and issue administrative orders. Chiefs were treated with much respect in public, and the British tried to gain their way through persuasion rather than command. The British saw the native state as a basis for the political future of their African empire

[13] See Lord Lugard, *The Dual Mandate in British Tropical Africa* (Edinburgh, 1922).

and thought in terms of federating chiefdoms in order to form large
political units which, in some indefinite period ahead, would be able
to rule themselves.

Still the British, like the French, also displayed assimilationist
tendencies. Municipal government in West Africa was set up on the
British model to cope with the problem of the new towns. The number
of educated Africans employed in the central administration slowly
went up. Nevertheless the British always stressed traditional rule.
Indirect rule indeed represented a reaction against the older mechanis-
tic view of African society, which had considered the natives just so
many bricks to be rearranged in any order to suit the colonizers' will.
Yet the practitioners of indirect rule often made assumptions almost
as unhistoric as those of their less sophisticated predecessors in the
pioneering days of African empire. White civil servants understood,
or thought they understood, the machinery of government evolved in
larger African kingdoms. Hierarchical arrangements of power were
in tune with their own administrative experience. Overburdened administrators preferred to deal with individuals rather than with councils. Many district officers, moreover, could make little of "stateless"
African societies, which often appeared to them to be a deviation
from the normal pattern of society. Administrative reports were full
of complaints that the power of the chiefs "had declined" or "kept
declining," even where such observations made no historical sense.
Among communities such as the Tonga of what is now Zambia, or in
southern Nigeria, chiefs were "restored" who had never had any traditional authority and were, in fact, government nominees. Indirect
rule also had other weaknesses. The system could not be applied to
urban areas and developed at the very time when economic changes
were beginning to alter the traditional structure of society. Chiefs
received subsidies, but these did not suffice to meet accustomed obligations of hospitality to fellow tribesmen. Many a returning labor
migrant or village trader might have more money in his pocket than
his chief. The traditional rights of councilors were often disregarded.
Native authorities gradually assumed the right to raise local revenue.
However, chieftainships in the more developed areas could collect
more cash than native authorities in the backwoods. Indirect rule thus
reflected, and to some extent accentuated, the uneven rate of economic development within the different provinces of the same territory.

The imperial power moreover expected the native authorities to
shoulder all kinds of new tasks unknown to traditional government;
rainmakers might be turned into roadmakers. Many chiefs and their
councilors could not cope with such tasks on their own. They had to
engage paid secretaries or assistants. This meant that tribal govern-

ment in fact had to rely on educated people, clerks and interpreters, the very men whose influence the government wished to circumscribe. Indirect rule in practice depended on poorly remunerated local bureaucrats, many of whom had to eke out their salaries with government pensions or with small-scale farming. The half-time administrator was necessarily inefficient. Many posts went to the councilors' kinsmen, and in many local treasuries peculation was rife. Indirect rule was no more economical of European staff than direct rule. District officers had to conduct lengthy anthropological inquiries; they still had to spend a great deal of time as advisers and consultants; in many cases the real executive work still remained in their hands. The new course often led to a curious feeling of aimlessness among the white administrators; the doctrine might degenerate into a policy of passivity, aggravated by the overfrequent rotation of a numerically inadequate district staff. Labouchere's famous poem about the Uganda Railway, written in 1896, in some cases exactly reflected the district officers' own feelings about the new line of policy:

> What it will cost, no words can express;
> What is its object, no brain can suppose;
> Where it will start from, no one can guess;
> Where it is going to, nobody knows.
>
> What is the use of it, none can conjecture;
> What it will carry, there's none can define;
> And in spite of George Curzon's superior lecture,
> It clearly is naught but a lunatic line.

Indirect rule was in many cases more a theoretical than a practical departure from previous policy. The old-style British administrator, innocent of Oxford summer schools and amateur anthropology, had always tried to manipulate local authorities where he could do so with convenience. Traditional systems of jurisdiction had seldom disappeared entirely, even in European-settled areas. Indirect rule in many cases simply gave legal recognition to existing realities. The system moreover was rarely applied thoroughly. Indirect rule still required a numerous, well-trained European staff for its effective application. A great deal always depended on individual district or provincial commissioners whose personal outlook and intellectual caliber might vary widely. In practice both the British and the French rarely had enough qualified men on the spot to turn their diverse theories into administrative reality; conditions continued to have great variation even within the same territory.[14]

Indirect rule also failed to give advancement to "educated natives"

[14] For a detailed study see Lord Hailey, *Native Administration in the British African Territories* (5 vols.; London, 1950–1953).

in the central echelons of government. Colonial-trusteeship theoreticians at Downing Street might contrast the beauties of indirect rule with the supposed disadvantages of direct rule in settler-administered Southern Rhodesia, where the native commissioner held undisputed sway. Yet Southern Rhodesia, with its more tightly meshed administration, provided more outlets for the "new men," agricultural demonstrators, dispensary assistants, clerks, and African police sergeants, than its northern sister colony under Colonial Office rule beyond the Zambezi.

Nevertheless, indirect rule did imply a genuine, if limited, devolution of power. Native authorities received legally recognized powers of judicial decision. They obtained a real training in financial and executive responsibility. Chiefs and their councilors might find themselves caught between governmental pressure and popular criticism; many native authorities nevertheless carried out their tasks with ability and learned how to cope with all kinds of unaccustomed administrative problems unknown to their ancestors.

The Southern Rhodesians, and in a different way the South Africans, held onto the philosophy of direct rule. The Southern Rhodesians had adopted both the administrative procedures and the "color-blind" franchise of the old Cape Colony. They envisaged their territory essentially as a white man's country and used African chiefs only in minor administrative capacities. The settlers regarded their native neighbors as backward people whose inherited methods of governance were either barbarous in nature or dangerous to their white overlords. The Southern Rhodesians would not permit the reemergence of the Matabele monarchy which their forefathers had overthrown in battle. Settler leaders such as Sir Charles Coghlan, the colony's first premier, also had in their political makeup an assimilationist strain of the kind which Colonial Office administrators were beginning to lose. Coghlan felt convinced that white government would liberate Africans from the age-old tyranny of custom and permit the creation of an African petty bourgeoisie. Coghlan and his successors thus believed that advanced Africans should be encouraged to acquire land on individual tenure and to pass their property on to their sons in the European fashion, without having to conform to tribal patterns of inheritance. The settlers' outlook, itself ambivalent in nature, sharply clashed with the British missionary and philanthropic tradition of the period which generally stood for the preservation of indigenous black traditions according to trusteeship principles.

Direct rule in Southern Rhodesia centered on Salisbury, not on London. Decisions were made on the spot; civil servants moreover stayed in the same territory and often in the same district throughout their working lives. Administration was therefore speedy and efficient, much more so than north of the Zambezi. Southern Rhodesian theories of direct rule nevertheless underwent serious modifications in practice. The imperial government, in drafting the colony's constitution, had insisted on giving a considerable degree of administrative autonomy to the colony's native department. In many ways the native department thus operated as a state within the state; native commissioners acquired a more sympathetic outlook toward indigenous institutions than their white citizens, and chiefs continued to wield a limited degree of power, albeit much less than in Northern Rhodesia.

This brief and incomplete survey of colonial administration in Africa reveals an extraordinary but not surprising diversity. The rulers differed from one another in nationality and training, in personal idiosyncrasies, and in general outlook on life. The white man's colonial subjects also varied a great deal in their social structure and their response to various colonial situations. Yet Western empire in Africa displayed certain underlying uniformities. Government in its higher reaches depended on a thin layer of white officials, a tightly knit, generally well-educated group, with a great sense of *esprit de corps* and technical competence. Many of these people devoted the whole of their working lives to administration in Africa. On the upper levels of administration the African colonies thus acquired a highly specialized administrative labor force and, from this standpoint, received an indirect subsidy from the governing powers. The white administrators regarded themselves as an elite and believed themselves to be profoundly different from their black subjects and often also from their white fellow countrymen at home. Their social position was generally high. They remained the most envied social stratum and became what sociologists call a reference group, "the Joneses" whom their subordinates wished to imitate.

Colonial government was, however, always a multiracial affair. All white powers attempted, in some way or other, to make use of traditional African dignitaries. All colonizers also began to train a new elite of literate black men as the "noncommissioned" officers of empire. The "bush-bashing" district commissioner of the old school needed only a handful of messengers and policemen to supervise the villages in his charge, raise revenue, and apprehend malefactors. Economic development and administrative reforms, however, soon imposed a host of new tasks on government. The state generally became a relatively important employer of labor and, perhaps unwittingly, a training agency which transmitted all kinds of skills. The more developed colonial authorities required a whole army of qualified Africans —interpreters and accountancy clerks, forest rangers and laboratory assistants, public works foremen, telegraphists, police constables, schoolteachers, and agricultural demonstrators—all of whom learned how to converse in the language of their rulers and acquired at least a limited grasp of public administration. The new class looked to the state rather than to private enterprise for promotion and usually acquired an *étatiste* philosophy. Educated men also moved around a good deal. Senegalese and Dahomeans sought employment in more backward regions like Niger and Upper Volta. Malawians, educated at the Scottish missions by the lakeside, went as far as the Copper Belt and Barotseland to fill clerical and supervisory jobs, often exciting the envy of local people.

The upper reaches of government, however, continued to be the white man's preserve. A handful of Africans managed to reach high positions in the French services; Goanese secured senior appointments in Portuguese Africa. The supply of highly qualified administrative labor, however, remained infinitesimal. Even those colonial powers that, like the French and Portuguese, were willing to promote people of color in the central administration obtained few African recruits with sufficient educational qualifications. No European colonial power therefore succeeded in creating a substantial group of senior African administrators, capable of being posted from colony to colony, with a permanent stake in the future of empire. The African state employee, subject to a double pressure from the rulers above and the ruled below, thus acquired a curious duality of outlook. He looked to the state for promotion and perquisites; yet he could not afford to alienate his employer by outright resistance. The new African, moreover, became to some extent an object of envy to his unlettered countrymen. He found himself subject to a double pull—the state asked for individual loyalty to an impersonal and alien organization and kinsmen and friends expected services and favors which he could not provide without being accused of corruption by his superiors. The African state employee often envied his white seniors, whose conditions of service contrasted so strongly with his own and whose functions in the upper echelons of the administration he did not always fully grasp. In many colonies, such as Northern Rhodesia, public employees were thus among the first to agitate for better promotion prospects and generally to criticize the real or alleged failings of white government. The new African, however, rarely became an outright revolutionary. He criticized the state, and yet looked up to the state. He censured white government, and yet adopted some of its standards. He called for development, and yet charged the white man with exploitation.

15. Development or Exploitation?

African statistics are sparse and unreliable. Even modern sources on the subject are often of questionable accuracy. Official reports and yearbooks can easily produce an impression of accuracy which the facts do not warrant. Southern Rhodesia, closely administered and efficiently run from the early days of the occupation, stands out as one of the African territories best provided with statistical data, yet until comparatively recently even much of this material had to be taken with a grain of salt. Statistical work in Southern Rhodesia began under the government of the British South Africa Company, which required accurate figures for its administrators and shareholders. Overworked native commissioners, in charge of areas as big as English counties, had to compile population reports and provide figures concerning the number of farm animals owned by tribesmen in their area; they often solemnly informed headquarters that their district comprised 21,526 goats and 23,982 sheep—no more, no less. To this day nearly all African states lack reliable censuses of population. Many of the most publicized and apparently authoritative statistics rest on little more than informed guesswork. In 1934 Southern Rhodesia for the first time appointed a professional statistician; his department soon acquired an envied reputation in Africa for the excellence of the information provided. But even so, mistakes continued to be made; it was thus only recently that experts discovered that their predecessors had underestimated the number of Africans in the territory by about one-third.

Information concerning European trade or investment in Africa is equally hard to assemble. An economist could fill a whole book concerning just the obstacles. Statistics are often unreliable or incomplete; they are drawn from dozens of different countries and hundreds of different sources; types of classification may vary, and comparisons are often impossible. Yet these difficulties are nothing compared with those facing an investigator interested in African eco-

227

nomic life. We know, for instance, that around 1910 some African peasant farmers in Southern Rhodesia began to invest money in plows and carts, in boreholes, and in new kinds of European breeding stock. African-grown cocoa became big business on the Gold Coast, and in 1927 cocoa accounted for nearly 83 percent of the colonies' exports. Nigerian peasants became major palm-kernel producers; Africans in Uganda cultivated cotton on a large scale.

Until very recently, however, statisticians have not accumulated much reliable information on local capital formation anywhere in Africa, especially for agriculture. Perhaps the most valuable contribution is to be found in S. Herbert Frankel's massive work *Capital Investment in Africa*. Frankel's book, however, deals only with foreign capital, and this only in some countries. He explains that there is no information on the amount of capital repaid or lost during these years; he therefore had to ignore the question of capital wastage and could not estimate the "outstanding" capital in African territories at any particular date. Nevertheless, his statistics lead to some interesting conclusions. Africa experienced great difficulties in securing capital compared with other, more favorably placed parts of the world. Foreign capitalists, far from pouring their money into the newly founded colonies, were chary of placing funds in the Dark Continent. The rate of interest on overseas capital had been rising steadily for some years before the outbreak of World War I, and between 1914 and 1918 the supply of outside funds virtually ceased. After the war the rate of interest continued to remain high. In fact, Frankel explains, much of African economic development took place at a time when money was expensive in comparison to the last quarter of the nineteenth century, when large sums were made available for investment in other parts of the world.

The rate of interest varied considerably from territory to territory. From 1935 on self-governing Southern Rhodesia, with its cautious financial administration, managed to borrow money at only 3.85 percent, the lowest rate for any British territory in Africa. South Africa obtained loans on conditions not much worse than Southern Rhodesia's, but Nigeria had to pay more, while Kenya, at an interest rate of 5.06 percent in 1935, carried the highest rate of any British territory.[1] Even so, money was hard to get. Africa was not the reputed El Dorado of the Stock Exchange, and many leaders could secure more favorable conditions elsewhere. Yet there was economic progress. Frankel calculated that the total foreign investments in Africa, up to the end of 1936, amounted to some £1,322 million.

[1] S. Herbert Frankel, *Capital Investment in Africa: Its Course and Effects* (London, 1938), p. 178.

Between 1914 and 1936 probably more money flowed into Africa than during the whole period from 1870 to 1913. The 1920s and 1930s, in other words, were not a period of total economic neglect, but saw considerable development. The rate of investment, however, remained uneven; only certain countries benefited to any great extent, and most of the money loaned went into the mining industry.[2]

In the race for development, the Union of South Africa had many advantages. The country contained more people of European ancestry than all the rest of the continent together; the young dominion therefore commanded the greatest reservoir of human skills and capital existing in Africa. South Africa had a developed transport system. There was an efficient public service and, by African standards, a fairly productive agriculture; there were some excellent ports; there was a developed system of trade and finances. South Africa moreover possessed great mineral riches; the country's gold resources kept their value during periods of depression, when the price of commodities such as copper, maize, or peanuts rapidly dropped. Not surprisingly, South Africa attracted more than twice as much money as all the rest of British Africa.[3] From the mid-1920s to the mid-1930s South Africa thus nearly doubled the value of its gold output.[4] Mining supplied the government with an enormous amount of revenue and also provided funds for development of other industries.

In addition, South Africa generated capital for investment in other parts of Africa. In the 1880s Rhodes already had hoped to find a second Rand beyond the Limpopo, which would rival the riches of Johannesburg and attract more British immigrants to southern Africa. The pioneers who hoisted the Union Jack in Mashonaland in 1890 expected to find an El Dorado. From the commercial point of view, Southern Rhodesia turned out to be a comparative disappointment. There was some gold, but the settlers never found anything like the wealth Rhodes expected. In the early 1920s, however, the mining frontier suddenly moved north. Experts discovered a new method of working the low-grade sulfide resources of the Northern Rhodesian Copper Belt; the industry made spectacular progress; Rhodes in the end was proved right, except that the wealth of the far north rested on

---

[2] Frankel, *Capital Investment in Africa,* especially pp. 151–153, 174.

[3] According to Frankel's calculations, a total of £1,221,686,000 was invested in sub-Saharan Africa between 1870 and 1936. Of this, £523,017,000 went to South Africa; £941,307,000 went to British Africa (including South Africa) as a whole. Of the money invested in South Africa, about two-thirds found its way into mining. Frankel, *Capital Investment in Africa,* pp. 156, 158–161.

[4] The value of South Africa's gold output increased from £42,285,000 in 1926 to £79,495,000 in 1936. Frankel, *Capital Investment in Africa,* p. 114.

copper instead of the expected gold. American, as well as British and South African, investors put money into the mines.

Copper production in the Belgian Congo made similar progress. Development began in a small way during the first decade of the 1900s. Organized mineral production was incompatible with a "robber economy" based on the export of ivory and wild rubber. The original abuses practiced under the Congo Free State administration disappeared, and after 1908 a more orderly Belgian colonial administration enforced a more sensible policy of economic development. In 1910 a southern railway reached Elisabethville, provided the mines with an outlet for their products to Beira in Portuguese East Africa, and enabled the Belgian mines to import coal from Southern Rhodesia and stores and mining equipment from South Africa. World War I stimulated activities, and in 1918 over 20,000 tons of copper were turned out. The slump occasioned a serious setback, but world capitalism surmounted the crisis. In 1936 output reached well over 100,000 tons, and by 1958 copper output amounted to 237,000 tons. The Congo also became the world's greatest producer of industrial diamonds and one of Africa's largest suppliers of hydroelectric power. Mining development went with improved social legislation; the Belgians proved intelligent employers, and after thorough investigations during the late 1920s, the Belgian administration came out with model labor laws for its territory.[5]

South and South Central Africa thus developed into major mineral exporters. Mining dominated the local economy, and minerals from the southern portion of the continent accounted for most of sub-Saharan Africa's foreign trade.[6] In addition, other territories as well made advances. The proclamation of imperial rule over the Gold Coast encouraged an influx of European capital. Foreign entrepreneurs imagined that deep-level mining might also create a second Rand on the West Coast. British and South African investors, however, suffered many disappointments. The gold-bearing strata proved insufficiently rich, and the African people were too numerous and tenacious to give up long-established rights. Gold mining nevertheless made some advance; by 1935 about 41 percent of the country's exports consisted of minerals, mainly gold and diamonds. Gold mining, together with the need to secure a firm hold over the Ashanti, also caused the government to embark on railway building. The opening

[5] See Granville St. John Orde Browne, *The African Labourer* (London, 1933), especially pp. 133–140.

[6] Frankel thus calculated that by 1935 the special mining territories of South Africa, South-West Africa, the two Rhodesias, and the Congo accounted for 67 percent of the international trade of Africa; minerals accounted for 78 percent of their exports. Frankel, *Capital Investment in Africa*, p. 213.

of the forest by railways and later by motor roads in turn gave great stimulus to the production of cocoa on the part of individual peasant owners.[7] But from the standpoint of Africa's mining economy as a whole, the West Coast cities no longer played a major part. Commercially speaking, the axis of Africa had shifted to the southern portion of the continent.

Most of this mining enterprise rested on huge foreign-owned combines, able to mobilize vast amounts of capital and to pay for expensive machinery and equipment. The Northern Rhodesian companies thus carried out extensive geological research and conducted large-scale aerial surveys completely beyond the means of the old-fashioned prospectors who had pioneered the search for minerals. Big companies put up model townships; they provided health services, cleared the mining areas of malaria, and constructed mining hospitals and training establishments. Amalgamation into large units also brought major financial and political advantages. Production could be planned over longer periods of time. The companies acquired a stronger position for getting their share in the world market. Marketing became more economical. Overhead expenses diminished, and the companies as a whole could deal with the administration to greater advantage. Big concerns, moreover, could wait much longer for their money than the small entrepreneurs who had pioneered the gold industry of Southern Rhodesia and diamond production at Kimberley. In Northern Rhodesia, for instance, serious copper development began in the early 1920s. The companies earned nothing at all until 1932 and reached the full profit-earning stage only in 1937; but after an extended "dead" period gains rose, and Rhodesian copper shares, like South African gold stock, became a magnificent form of investment.[8]

Large-scale mining enterprise unlocked a tremendous amount of new wealth inaccessible by traditional methods of production in Africa. But almost from the start the big mining companies faced a barrage of criticism, sometimes from quite unexpected quarters. In Northern Rhodesia, for instance, the first attacks on the system came not from the Africans, but from the very settlers who had been drawn to the Copper Belt by the big mining concerns. Alien capitalists, the colonists claimed, were drawing superprofits from the territory and were stripping the protectorate of its natural wealth. The

[7] John D. Fage, *Ghana: A Historical Interpretation* (Madison, Wis., 1959), pp. 64–65.

[8] By 1941 some £22 million had been invested in the Northern Rhodesian copper industry. Gross trading profits over the previous eighteen years amounted to £25 million; of this, £7 million went into taxes and less than £7 million went into dividends.

country's economic development was lopsided; secondary industries were being neglected. The bulk of the country's wealth went into the pockets of investors abroad; what little was left within the colony's borders benefited a small group of privileged people rather than the workers. White-settler leaders in Northern Rhodesia (and also in Kenya) therefore advocated all kinds of *étatiste* solutions—state-planned location of industries, marketing controls, and state enterprise to speed up economic growth. Soon black leaders put forward similar arguments; in many ways they shared the economic misconceptions of white mine workers, or even of European farmers, but they gave a specifically African slant to the settlers' reasoning and stressed that white miners and employees were both part of a privileged minority.

European socialists, arguing in a similar fashion, elaborated these strictures. The Communists especially saw the development of these mining territories as a deliberate conspiracy, designed to retard the colonies in question and keep their peoples enslaved to alien monopolies. They stressed the high rate of profit and implied that these profits were in some part due to the imperial connection. The colonial system, in their view, provided the metropolitan countries with terms of trade much more favorable than would have been enjoyed between countries of equal political status. The big mining men formed a specially privileged stratum even among their fellow capitalists; their superprofits played an essential part in shoring up Western capitalism as a whole. Mineral exploitation, the argument continued, was not in any way a progressive form of enterprise. Extractive industries took all of Africa's natural wealth and benefited none but the imperialist exploiters. Large-scale mining with its superprofits was a particularly objectionable form of enterprise which either failed to stimulate or, indeed, actively restricted development in all other sectors of the economy. The fault lay with a system which depended on foreign investments. Balanced economic growth was impossible without massive saving at home. This must be achieved by a centrally planned economy which would control both labor and domestic investments and put an end to the activities of foreign capitalists. Only a revolution could better the condition of the people; the existing system must be smashed and consigned to the trash can of history.[9]

The Communist argument has, in one form or another, become accepted in most of the emergent states of Africa. Foreign-owned

[9] This case has been pleaded in a large number of both Marxist and non-Marxist works. For an unusually succinct and well-written statement of the Communist case see, for instance, Jack Woddis, *Africa: The Way Ahead* (London, 1963).

mammoth mining enterprise is widely regarded as the most characteristic and also the most dangerous form of colonial or neocolonial
exploitation. This is therefore a good opportunity to insert a broader
discussion of the arguments involved. A general *caveat* regarding the
Marxist-Leninist case must, however, precede this excursus, so as to
make the Communist dialectic more intelligible. Social studies, in the
Communist view, serve two distinct but interrelated functions: science
illuminates their world; more important, science must change it. An
analysis of mining enterprise in Northern Rhodesia should tell us
something about that country; in addition, however, such an intellectual enterprise should also form a weapon in the African class struggle. British imperialism stands arrayed both against the Zambian
proletariat and against the whole Soviet bloc. British capitalists therefore merit total condemnation. Such censure, however, can never be
absolute. If, for the sake of discussion, a British Conservative government were to form an alliance with the Soviet Union against the
United States, British capitalism would, in the Soviet view, play a
temporarily progressive role, however unworthy the subjective motives of British negotiators might be. These two elements, the analytical and the instrumental, cannot always be easily distinguished
in Marxist-Leninist interpretations. Scholars, however, must always
look at the two faces of the Soviet Janus—the distinction between
what Communist theoreticians believe to be objectively correct and
what they regard as fit intellectual sustenance for short-term allies.
Thesis turns to antithesis in a never-ending flow; practicing Communists may have to deny tomorrow what they assert today. Communist "objective" analysis, by a curious dialectical somersault, can
have no absolute value outside a given political context.

Marxist theory moreover contains an inbuilt protective device which
safeguards its conclusions, whichever way the facts happen to go.
Marxists believe that goods derive their value from the labor which
they incorporate, not from the demand which they satisfy. Capitalists
supposedly do not perform any socially necessary work, hence all
profits automatically derive from exploitation. If, on the other hand,
capitalists do not make profits, or garner only small gains, they also
find themselves on the wrong side of history. If profits fall, the capitalist system must contract and will thus be ultimately overthrown.
The Marxist is thus proved right in either event. In spite of these
various contradictions, Marxist concepts enjoy a wide appeal, not
only among Communists, but also among thinkers bitterly opposed
to the teachings of Marxism-Leninism. Many Marxist strictures of
colonial capitalism have become part of the standard intellectual fare
both in the emergent states in Africa and among many outstanding

scholars in the West. The gold- and copper-mining industries of southern Africa, with their high rate of investment and profits, are commonly cited as the most characteristic and also the most onerous form of colonial exploitation. All too often, however, this censure rests on certain unacknowledged assumptions which deserve further discussion in the context of African mining development.

The first of these preconceptions concerns the respective roles of primary and secondary industries. All Marxist and many non-Marxist economists believe that a country which makes a living by selling raw materials to foreigners necessarily stays poor. Prosperity supposedly cannot be gained without factories, especially steel mills and machine-tool manufactures. There is, however, no justification for this belief. The doctrine rests in the highly ethnocentric assumption that the chronological pattern of the British industrial revolution must prevail all over the world. Yet Denmark and New Zealand, which lack heavy industries, are a great deal more prosperous than, for instance, East Germany, with its massive industrial complex in Saxony. The question of priority also needs to be considered. Modern Zambia may well make money in manufactures, but this does not mean that Northern Rhodesia would have done better in the 1920s and 1930s, at an early stage in its development, by directing funds into factories. Thirty years ago the country lacked an economic infrastructure; manufacturing would have been expensive in social as well as economic terms and might merely have led to a dead end.

The next point concerns the general relationship between colonial capitalism and secondary industry. Marxist arguments notwithstanding, a capitalist economy does not necessarily preclude industrial development in colonial or ex-colonial territories. South Africa and Southern Rhodesia both started as mining and farming countries. In time they built up factories and steelworks with money made in primary industries, an economic policy which they shared with countries as diverse as Australia and the United States. South African and Southern Rhodesian capitalism should, in strict Marxist logic, be regarded as the most progressive forms of bourgeois economic organization in Africa, yet they continue to be cited as the most reactionary form of colonial exploitation, an assumption which makes nonsense of the secondary-industries argument.

The third argument concerns the method of development. Many critics, both white and black, assumed that imperial administrators should, as part of their trusteeship obligations, have accelerated progress in countries such as Northern Rhodesia by setting up state-owned or state-supported industries. The colonial government could, of course, have set up factories of that kind, but either such enterprises would have had to compete with foreign firms on a free market or else manufactured goods from abroad would have had to be excluded by high tariffs. The former course of action might well have led to the speedy collapse of such industries; the latter would in all probability have compelled local inhabitants to buy products of lower quality at higher prices than would have obtained in a free market. Neither course of action would have benefited Northern Rhodesia.

Looking at this controversy from the metropolitan point of view, it is difficult to see what type of commercial policy the imperial power should have adopted at home. Free trade, the anticolonial reasoning asserts, milks the dependent territories of their resources, but protective barriers raised by the mother country against imports deprive the colonies of markets. Both courses would therefore have incurred equal censure. The problem of foreign loans puts the colonial power into a similar quandary. Large-scale foreign investment supposedly robbed Africa of its economic wealth, but had the colonial governments kept out foreign funds, they would have incurred even harsher criticism. The imperial powers would rightly have been accused of running their dependencies in a "game-warden" spirit. Such a policy would have been taken as proof that capitalism had become incapable of generating new investment funds, that the system had therefore reached its last stage of decadence, and that its internal breakdown prevented the development of Africa's natural resources. Such arguments, which damn the colonialists if they do and damn them if they don't, must be accepted for what they are—bastions to defend a position taken up in advance for political or ethical rather than economic reasons.

Many Marxist writers assert at present, and imperialist writers argued in the past, that Great Britain needed colonies to improve its terms of trade. Colonial domination supposedly enabled the imperialists to sell at high prices and to buy at low ones. An examination of the figures concerning the British terms of trade does not bear out this contention.[10] The argument also ignores the fact that up to the early 1930s, that is to say during the heyday of British imperialism, the British Empire was built on free trade. Northern Rhodesian mining magnates, for instance, did not give any special preference to British purchasers. They sold where they got most for their copper. The Northern Rhodesian government, for its part, did not give special favors to lenders from the United Kingdom. Anybody who would

[10] For detailed figures, see John Strachey, *The End of Empire* (London, 1961; New York, 1964), pp. 146–153. Strachey adds that terms of trade figures, as given by him, are always difficult to assess accurately and, for the nineteenth century especially, should be regarded as merely approximative and illustrative of general trends.

invest was at liberty to do so. South African, American, and even some Continental investors bought Northern Rhodesian mining shares; hence the territory could borrow where money was available at the most favorable rates at the time.

The robbery-of-resources argument has a more obvious appeal. Large-scale mining, according to this case, stripped countries such as the Congo and Northern Rhodesia of irreplaceable wealth; the indigenous people lost their heritage; foreign mining enterprise should therefore be entered on the debit side of imperialism. The case cannot, however, be easily sustained. The foreign investors did not in fact take away from African tribesmen a form of wealth which they had previously enjoyed. Foreign capitalists did not, like the Soviets in Manchuria or Eastern Germany, dismantle machinery or strip the country of existing equipment. The mining companies created a new form of enterprise; they mined ores which communities such as the Lamba and Lala could not have exploited with the technological means available to tribal society. The Northern Rhodesian mining companies, moreover, showed considerable courage and capacity for long-range planning. In the early 1920s financial journals such as the London *Economist* regarded Northern Rhodesian copper as a very risky form of investment. The Northern Rhodesian government was equally skeptical of large-scale development; the authorities at Livingstone believed that foreign investors might well lose much of their money. A government-directed economy would not, in the early 1920s, have gone ahead with large-scale development work even if the administration had possessed the men and the money to embark on such a program. In Marxist language, the Northern Rhodesian mining concerns therefore performed a progressive function.

Large-scale mining, moreover, was not confined to purely extractive processes, but also set off development in what might be called the "nonmetallic" sectors of the economy. Here a distinction must be made between simpler forms of enterprise, such as alluvial gold washing, and complex ventures, such as the deep-level excavation of copper, vanadium, or gold. The technology of alluvial gold production is comparatively simple and requires little capital. Many African communities in countries as widely separated as Ghana and the ancient kingdom of Zimbabwe knew the art of washing the yellow metal and worked this natural resource. That does not mean that mining of this type, needing little capital and often stopping short of processing the extracted raw material, did not contribute to economic well-being. In East and Central Africa, indigenous miners sold their gold to Arab or Portuguese traders and thereby acquired more consumer goods than they would otherwise have enjoyed. Large-scale mining, however, made for much greater changes. The mines created markets for more agricultural produce. The flow of investment was not confined just to sinking shafts and driving tunnels. Smelters and electrolytic plants went up in the bush. Mining gave rise to railway development, to road construction, and to the provision of port facilities. Money went into workshops, electric power plants, waterworks, and cement factories. The concentrations of population created a demand for permanent housing. The emergence of townships, large and small, required public utilities and public services. Development in turn attracted a multitude of people eager to meet the growing demand for building material, food, fuel, clothing, and all kinds of services. Banks and trading stores opened their doors. White and black farmers alike found new opportunities for selling their grain and cattle, and "the basis was thus laid for a multiplier-accelerator process of economic growth."[11]

The African mining territories paid the price of development in the form of profits to overseas investors. These were high, and as John Strachey, a moderate British socialist, has put it, "It is impossible to become aware of them without understanding the sense of outrage which possesses a subject people as soon as it comes to know what is happening to it under imperialism." In support of his case Strachey quotes figures for expenditure by the Northern Rhodesian mining industry in Northern Rhodesia and argues that of the £36,700,000 realized in 1949, only £12,500,000 was spent in Northern Rhodesia at all. He concludes that "a gross profit or surplus, call it what you will, or some £24 million, or two-thirds of the total, was transferred to the United Kingdom and America," implying that foreign investors pocketed two-thirds of the country's mining wealth.[12] The realities are, however, not so dramatic. Strachey fails to mention the expenditures

[11] S. Daniel Neumark, *Foreign Trade and Economic Development in Africa: A Historical Perspective* (Stanford, Calif., 1964), pp. 103–104.

[12] Strachey, *The End of Empire,* p. 177, 178. The figures are derived from Phyllis Deane, *Colonial Social Accounting* (Cambridge, Eng., 1953), p. 37, which provides more extensive detail. Her figures give the following estimated expenditure (in thousand pounds) for the Northern Rhodesian mining industry in 1949:

European salaries, wages, and bonuses	4,100
African wages and bonuses	1,400
African rations	600
Payments to contractors	1,000
Payments to Rhodesian Railways	1,800
Income tax, customs	3,600
Total expenditure	12,500
Gross value of output	36,742

incurred by mining companies on imported raw materials, imported services, and depreciation. The investors' net gains were thus only a fraction of what he believes them to have been.[13]

Strachey also expresses indignation over the figures devoted to African wages. He points out that only £2 million in money and rations went to Africans working on the mines, out of a gross value of output amounting to £36,742,000. The mineowners, however, also had a case. The mines, according to Miss Deane's figures, paid £3,600,000 into the public coffers. The government spent some of this on projects benefiting Africans on the Copper Belt, a contribution to African living standards ignored by the conventional Marxist argument. Wages for unskilled men were small because the supply of such labor was large and its competence was low. But African copper miners went to work because they wanted to; in Northern Rhodesia there was no compulsory labor of the type practiced under the fully collectivist system that then prevailed in the Soviet Union. The Central African mines, with their high level of technology and their paternalistic outlook, also eschewed the kind of underground labor on the part of women and children that was utilized during the early industrial revolution in Great Britain. The African proletariat in some ways, therefore, paid a lower price for incipient industrialization than did the British workers in the eighteenth century. African mine workers on the Copper Belt enjoyed a higher standard of living than they did in their native villages; they received better housing and food than at home, so much so that their average physical well-being consistently improved in employment.

African workmen also experienced some disadvantages. They kept one foot in the rural areas and retained their land rights in the African villages. Wages, however, were generally assessed in terms of the

---

[13] See Deane, *Colonial Social Accounting*, p. 270. Miss Deane gives a detailed breakdown for the years 1945 and 1946 only. The figures for 1946 for the output of the mining industry (in pounds) were as follows:

Value of metal sales	15,111,600
Less value attributable to foreign companies (i.e., operating surplus and royalties)	5,316,800
Remittance to cover operating costs	9,794,800
Remittances to cover capital expenditure	937,400
Total company remittances	10,732,200
Less imported raw materials and equipment	3,641,800
Less imported services (i.e., realization costs and outside refining)	1,710,300
Less local purchases of goods and services (i.e., payments to contractors)	180,000
Less depreciation	955,200
Net national output of mining	4,244,900

needs of single men, not in terms of family needs. African mine laborers, with their traditional obligations to an extended circle of relatives, had to carry a burden much heavier than that which a British workman would be expected to bear on behalf of his kinsfolk. In times of slump, African mine workers could always go back to their villages, which gave them some form of protection. Moreover, the African subsistence economy perforce acted as a buffer, shielding the money economy from fluctuations; this provided what in fact amounted to unemployment and old-age benefits, and, of course, saved the companies and the state large welfare costs. Cash wages remained stabilized over long periods, and the problem of raising real wages hinged on the provision of fringe benefits, such as better housing and ration scales. Nevertheless the new wage economy did allow for a certain amount of spread in wages. Surprisingly enough, by the beginning of the present century a skilled black Rhodesian laborer may in certain cases have been better off than an unskilled English workman.[14]

African living standards were thus by no means uniformly bad. Black wages and economic progress, on the other hand, were almost certainly retarded to some extent by the restrictive practices of white trade unionists. European labor unions throughout southern Africa successfully obstructed the entry of black people into various branches of highly skilled employment. Admittedly, these restrictions affected only a limited group of African workmen at the time; they did, however, significantly contribute to the development of apartheid. But this raises issues which, though extremely important, are different from those usually discussed under the heading of colonialism.

The problem of the artificially managed wage did not originate in the colonies and was not confined to them.[15] Strachey's attack must thus rest on a more general basis. Like so many other critics of Western enterprise in Africa, he assumes in the manner of a medieval

[14] In 1902 an agricultural laborer in Lincolnshire made £3.0.0 a month, and a Tyneside laborer about £4.8.0. An African driver during this period might earn about £2.0.0 in Southern Rhodesia, and a highly paid African miner about £3.0.0, in addition to board and lodging, that is to say, fringe benefits not available to his English colleague. An English domestic cook during this period would earn about £2.0.0 a month, with "everything found." These figures, of course, do not take into account the different price levels in England and Rhodesia, respectively. These are difficult to compare, especially as English and African laborers purchased different kinds of food. The figures given can therefore be regarded only as illustrative and approximative.

[15] For two discussions on the subject see Peter T. Bauer, "Regulated Wages in Under-developed Countries," in Philip D. Bradley (ed.), *The Public Stake in Union Power* (Charlottesville, Va., 1959), pp. 324–349, and Sheila T. van der Horst, *Native Labour in South Africa* (London, 1942).

Schoolman that there is a "just price" for labor as for any other commodity. But he does not say what this price ought to be. Nor does he specify what he would consider a just return on capital invested, or to what extent financial risks and services should be properly remunerated, if at all. Again, there is no attempt to analyze the kind of situation which would have occurred if the mines had paid an uneconomic wage high enough to create a privileged group of African as well as European mine workers. In the absence of any such objective standards, the economist has nothing more to say, and the pamphleteer must take over.

For many decades mining dominated the cash economy of sub-Saharan Africa. From the first decade of the 1900s, however, agricultural exports began to rise sharply, and agriculture rapidly increased in relative importance.[16] Much of this development centered on South Africa, by far the most advanced country and the most important pioneer on the African continent. Yet economic growth in many other parts of Africa also went forward at a rapid pace. There is, accordingly, no justification at all for the view, fashionable among critics of the colonial system in the 1920s and 1930s, which saw Africa as nothing but a stagnant pool, whose people, under the imperial aegis, either stood still or were retrogressing. Africa's agricultural progress was all the more surprising in view of the many natural obstacles faced by cultivators black and white alike. Many parts of Africa suffer from alternating cycles of drought, followed by heavy tropical downpours which leach the soils. Erosion forms an ever-present threat to inexpert farmers. The peoples of Africa faced all kinds of human, plant, and animal diseases peculiar to tropical areas. Development was desperately hampered until Western research found means of coping with afflictions such as malaria, sleeping sickness, and parasites attacking cattle. The lack of transportation facilities further impeded development. Most parts of Africa lacked good riverine communications; because of the great distances, inland pro-

16 Tables of the value of domestic exports of sub-Saharan Africa, excluding Ethiopia, Liberia, and Madagascar, worked out in Neumark, *Foreign Trade and Economic Development in Africa*, p. 153 (based on Frankel, *Capital Investment in Africa*), give the following figures (in million pounds):

	1907	1924	1935
Union of South Africa:			
Minerals	39.2	57.6	78.3
Nonminerals	6.4	25.9	22.1
Other areas:			
Minerals	42.6	68.0	102.7
Nonminerals	24.0	81.2	75.8

ducers in the past could rarely market their crops. The imperial impact vastly changed this situation. The period from 1880 to 1920 was the great age of railway building in Africa. By the end of the 1930s about 32,000 miles of railroad track were in operation, about two-thirds of which served South Africa, the Rhodesias, the Congo, and the Portuguese colonies.[17]

The steam locomotive helped bring about a social revolution. An ordinary freight train used nowadays in Africa will do the work of 15,000 to 20,000 carriers for one-fifth to one-tenth the cost. The steam engine thus relieved the sweating African porter from his age-old labors; for the first time in the continent's history farmers could produce economic crops away from coastal and river ports. Africa's scarce manpower could at last be used in pursuits more profitable to the economy than head porterage. In the 1920s and 1930s motor-trucks and bicycles also began to make their appearance in the bush. The new means of locomotion might in some ways be called "markets on tires," providing backward farmers with new incentives for turning out more and better crops.

Agricultural development in twentieth-century Africa stood, so to speak, on three legs. There was cultivation by African peasants; there was farming by European settlers; there were some large-scale plantations run by big concessionary companies. Of all these, African enterprise was by far the most important, but it was also the form of enterprise that varied most extensively in methods, technical skill, and output. African peasants faced many obstacles. They had to contend not only with the difficulties of nature, but also with lack of physical and social capital. Throughout most of Africa their work continued to depend on hoes and axes and on the unaided power of the human muscle. In most parts of Africa tribesmen lacked incentives for intensive cultivation. Land was plentiful; whenever cultivators had exhausted the fertility of their gardens, they moved on, allowing nature to restore the fertility of the soil. As long as the supply of land seemed unlimited and storage facilities and markets few or nonexistent, African cultivators would only have wasted time and effort by producing more specialized crops. Where conditions became favorable, however, African farmers did make use of new opportunities and in some areas made astonishing progress.

One of the best-known success stories concerns the development of cocoa in the Gold Coast (now Ghana). The Gold Coast had an ancient tradition of overseas trade. The commerce in palm oil and other commodities had created a certain amount of capital. Long-standing links with the Western world and improved railway and port

[17] Frankel, *Capital Investment in Africa*, p. 374.

facilities created under British aegis put bush farmers in touch with metropolitan customers. Contacts with other countries also introduced new cultivable plants, including the cacao tree. *Theobroma cacao,* a native of Central and South America, was first carried to the islands of São Thomé and Fernando Po by the Portuguese. In 1879 Tete Kwashi, an enterprising Accra man, brought the plant to the mainland; government and mission agriculturists popularized the crop, and by 1891 the Gold Coast exported its first cocoa crop, amounting to just eighty pounds. The plant prospered in the hot and humid atmosphere of the West Coast, and its cultivation quickly caught on. African peasants soon understood the potential of the crop; they displayed precisely those gifts of foresight, calculation, and economic acumen that their detractors so often deny. The cacao tree requires four to five years until it bears a crop and produces maximum yields only between the ages of ten and fifteen years, though it will continue to bear fruit long thereafter. African growers therefore had to invest a good deal of capital in relation to their resources and had to wait a considerable time for their profits. This they managed to do, and within a few decades the output of the Gold Coast multiplied several thousand times. The colony's agricultural department provided valuable help, and by 1935–1936 output amounted to 285,351 tons, that is, nearly half the world's supply.[18] Cocoa enabled the Gold Coast to pay for substantial imports of cement, machinery, flour, and so forth, commodities unknown to the country in the 1890s. Carriers and canoes gradually gave way to steam locomotives, trucks, and bicycles, and conditions of life underwent a major transformation.

The achievement of black cultivators in the Gold Coast was by no means unique. Around 1820, peanuts were introduced to Senegal from Central America. African peasants first grew the new plant as a food crop and later accumulated surpluses for export. The suppression of the slave trade, the decline in the exploitation of wild rubber, and improved communications gave a great stimulus to peanut cultivation. Marseilles soapmakers bought large quantities of peanut oil. African cultivators quickly responded to the new demand, and between 1841 and 1854 the export of Senegalese peanuts jumped from 1,000 to nearly 5 million kilos. The French administration tried to stimulate production further. Government agronomists developed superior seeds, which were distributed to farmers through Sociétés Indigènes de Prévoyance, government-controlled cooperative societies with compulsory membership. After 1932 these bodies were used to educate farmers in better methods of cultivation; they supplied modern equip-

[18] Lord Hailey, *An African Survey: A Study of Problems Arising in Africa South of the Sahara* (London, 1938), pp. 906–909.

ment, stored produce, and in some places transported and sold crops in officially controlled markets. The world depression dealt French West Africa's exports such a severe blow that France for the first time came to the rescue of a colonial crop and, at least temporarily, sacrificed the interests of metropolitan consumers and oil millers to those of African producers. After the early 1930s the principle of guaranteed price and marketing for peanuts was generally respected, though pressure from opposing French interests sometimes succeeded in either limiting peanut imports to France or setting the guaranteed price at such a low level as to provoke bitter protests from Senegalese producers and exporters.[19]

The effects of French policy are difficult to assess. French officials, like the British, were often convinced that private middlemen must be "parasites." They tried to control trade by various means, but official marketing control may well have hurt the peasants by reducing competition for their products and thereby reducing their incomes. French official pressure on Africans to cultivate "industrial crops" induced farmers to expand the area under cultivation and to exhaust the soil. In Senegal millet became a subsidiary crop, and its people were increasingly dependent on imported rice. Africans augmented their purchasing power, and thus were increasingly dependent on guaranteed prices and markets artificially sustained by the French government. Famines became exceptional occurrences in French West Africa, but its people continued to remain at the mercy of droughts, plant diseases, and locusts, while the rural population remained undernourished. The French, again like the British, almost certainly underestimated the black peasants' ability to adjust themselves to market fluctuations and to respond to economic motives; enforced cultivation constituted exploitation in the true sense of the word in that it did away with the producer's free choice. French West Africa nevertheless saw some real economic progress and became a substantial producer of tropical export crops. Senegal was one of the world's great production centers of peanuts and by 1937 exported more than half a million metric tons. Black farmers thus succeeded in a task that later foiled a heavily capitalized but top-heavy British public corporation, whose attempts at large-scale mechanized peanut production came to grief in Tanganyika after World War II.

African cash farming, like any other kind of economic development, brought many new problems in its wake. The Gold Coast, for instance, now depended largely on a single crop; traditional crops were neglected, and the country became a major importer of foreign

[19] Virginia Thompson and Richard Adloff, *French West Africa* (Stanford, Calif., 1957), pp. 311–314.

food. As long as cocoa prices held, this did not matter; black culti-vators enjoyed a higher income than they could have achieved with traditional crops. But when prices fell, cocoa farmers found them-selves in grave difficulties. The cocoa growers' predicament was also made more difficult by technical deficiencies. Farmers generally turned a deaf ear—sometimes not without justification—to expert advice that plots should be weeded, manured, and kept free of insect pests. In many areas land became scarce, and what was worse, the early cocoa farms began to die out.

African society at the same time experienced a new kind of social differentiation. The old pattern of a small family farm, run entirely by the labor of the peasant's own kinsfolk, gradually disintegrated. The majority of growers came to rely on hired labor; some accumulated great wealth, but others fell into poverty. West Africa as a whole now had to face the problem of migrant labor, with the additional disadvantage that small proprietors could not afford welfare facilities remotely comparable to those provided by big European-owned min-ing companies. The growers also believed that foreign buyers com-bined to keep down cocoa prices. In 1937 most of the big European firms entered into an agreement to restrict competition and to prevent local prices from rising above the world market level. The African growers, to their good fortune, were not then tied down by any official distribution monopoly, and they retaliated by refusing to sell to the buyers' combine. Some European firms, moreover, remained aloof from the restriction scheme, and in the end the two parties to the dis-pute concluded a truce which once again allowed cocoa to be sold abroad. There were many other difficulties, but by and large African agricultural enterprise made considerable progress, especially on the West Coast; the black farmer became what he had never been before in the history of his continent—a factor of some importance in the world economy.

In relation to the enormous size of the African landmass, white agricultural enterprise remained restricted in extent, being confined to a few relatively limited areas. Nigerian nationalists assert in jocular fashion that the *Anopheles* mosquito merits a symbolic place in their country's flag for having kept white settlers out of their country. The facts were, however, more complex. The hardships of a tropical cli-mate, lack of communications, natural obstacles, and the counter-attractions of healthier and more accessible lands in the New World and the Antipodes all combined with disease to discourage white men from taking up land in Africa. The great nineteenth-century *Völkerwanderung,* from Europe to the American West and the Rus-sian East, to Latin America and Australasia, largely bypassed Africa.

European farming in sub-Saharan Africa generally remained confined to the lands south of the Zambezi, and even here progress was slow. More than two centuries elapsed after the initial Dutch settlement on the Cape before the white population of South Africa passed the 200,000 mark. Farming in South Africa attracted little foreign capital; although Europe's wealth increased, its investors preferred countries like the United States, Australia, and New Zealand, which did not offer the same climatic difficulties and which, except for the latter, did not have to worry about an extensive "native problem," with all the accompanying military and administrative complications. As with capital, so it was with labor. Unskilled white workmen could not find jobs in South Africa. The Cape used to import slaves, and the local whites developed a marked contempt for unskilled work, which became associated with tasks fit only for men of color. In the early nineteenth century the British abolished slavery and lightened the lot of the Hottentot, but the Bantu of the interior provided white South Africans with an additional source of cheap unskilled labor. The indigenous people of Australia and North America had been mainly hunters and food gatherers, whom white settlers could employ only to a limited extent as trackers, herdsmen, or suppliers of fur. The Bantu, on the other hand, were an Iron Age people, familiar with agriculture and pastoral farming of a simple kind; they could easily be trained to work on farms, especially at a time when the frontiersmen's own methods of production were fairly elementary.

South Africa accordingly never experienced any large-scale white immigration, and economic progress remained relatively slow. Cape farmers turned out limited quantities of grain, fruit, vegetables, wine, and livestock for local consumption and for ships plying the Indian trade. But the settlers who pushed inland had to rely largely on grazing of a simple type, requiring many acres. Territorial expansion in most parts of South Africa thus owed its primary impetus to cattlemen rather than to capitalists, with land as the prize of victory. Technically backward as the settlers might have been, their economic and military potential nevertheless remained far superior to that of the Bantu. The black tribesmen thus lost control over most of the available land, and South Africa became the only region on the continent where the overwhelmingly greater part of the available acreage passed into white ownership.

After about the middle of the nineteenth century, moreover, European farmers at the Cape strengthened their economic potential and found a modest kind of prosperity. Growing ports and expanding mining compounds furnished farmers with additional markets. Engineers put up roads, bridges, railways, and dockyards. The growth of shipping and banking helped to put the country in touch with new customers overseas. Some farmers began to work out more intensive methods, and various technological improvements made their appearance in the countryside. Landowners experimented with new products such as mohair and ostrich feathers, while South African Merino wool acquired a recognized place on the world markets. In the twentieth century, technological change acquired increasing momentum. Agricultural mechanization and progress in agricultural processing industries such as fruit canning, tobacco manufacture, and meat refrigeration vastly added to the country's wealth. Farmers developed better methods of plant selection, stockbreeding, and soil management. Veterinary surgeons learned how to cope with various kinds of animal diseases. Despite large remaining islands of backwardness, South Africa developed into the most skilled and most versatile of Africa's agricultural exporters.[20]

From the end of the nineteenth century on, European farmers also penetrated beyond the confines of South Africa into what are now Rhodesia and the railway belt of Zambia. Throughout a large part of this tremendous region the European agriculturist usually followed in the miner's footsteps. The widely scattered mining townships and marketing centers required food; European farmers thus settled on the highveld, usually along the railway lines constructed to serve the miner's needs. As on every other frontier, grazing and tilling normally started as a scratch affair. There was the old story of vast distance and scanty markets. Both immigrant cultivators and stockmen could buy land and native cattle at low prices, yet at first they found great difficulties in making ends meet. Pioneering brought hardships; settlers frequently had to eke out their livelihoods by selling firewood, by transport riding, and by prospecting.[21] In addition, they had to shoulder numerous experimental risks. A newcomer might spend a large amount of money to improve his herds, only to have his pedigreed beasts struck down by some little-known disease. The properties of the soil were often unfamiliar to strangers, and a farmer might lose all his capital by planting the wrong kind of crop.

European farmers in Kenya met difficulties of a similar kind, and the story of their endeavor is typified by the career of Lord Delamere, their most distinguished representative. Delamere made his home in Kenya in the early 1900s. He obtained a vast land grant and settled down to farm. Delamere's ideal was to transplant the social patterns

[20] See, for instance, Cornelis W. de Kiewiet, *A History of South Africa, Social and Economic* (2d ed.; Oxford, 1950), for an excellent general history.

[21] For example, see Percy F. Hone, *Southern Rhodesia* (London, 1909), pp. 193–199.

of English country life, with its paternalistic relations between gentry and laborers, to the highlands of East Africa, but reality turned out very different from such romantic ideals. He tried first to breed sheep, but his animals proved unsuitable. He then turned to cattle, but the beasts died. He next took to the cultivation of wheat and inaugurated research into rust-resistant varieties. Later he turned to ranching and finally succeeded in breeding high-grade Merino sheep. Partly as a result of Delamere's efforts, more European settlers—many of them with aristocratic names or military backgrounds—went to East Africa. They all experienced similar setbacks. Much capital was lost and many experiments failed, but in the end the settlers created an efficient export economy producing tropical crops such as coffee, tea, sisal, and pyrethrum.[22]

Rhodesian farming methods, like those of Kenya and South Africa, improved in similar fashion. Transport facilities became more adequate; the administration provided better agricultural and scientific services. Another great boon was the introduction of tobacco, a cash crop of relatively small bulk and high value, which made notable progress from the 1920s on. Many of the huge old farms were gradually subdivided. Farmers employed improved methods of cultivation; they could afford more fertilizers and machinery. The use of native labor slowly became a little more efficient, and the pattern of agriculture gradually began to resemble more that of older countries overseas. The settlers, of course, continued to meet many obstacles. The battle against cattle disease took a long time to win. Rhodesian farmers also had to spend more on machinery, fertilizers, transport, and repair services than, say, an American working within the framework of a highly developed and integrated economy.

In terms of technical performance, European forms of agriculture achieved considerable success. European farmers produced vast quantities of flue-cured tobacco, a commodity which required more skill and capital than indigenous black cultivators possessed. They developed dairy farming and introduced various specialized crops unknown to traditional African farming. They put up dips and dams, tobacco barns, fences, and windbreaks, thereby improving the value and productivity of their land. European settlement even changed the very appearance of the landscape by bringing in new trees such as wattle and eucalyptus, with beneficent ecological effects on the countryside.

European farming also had profound social effects. In Southern Rhodesia something like half the available acreage gradually passed

[22] See Elspeth Huxley, *White Man's Country: Lord Delamere and the Making of Kenya* (London, 1953).

into European ownership. Black men found themselves confined to a much smaller area than in the preoccupation days. In many parts of Rhodesia, European settlement brought about heavy pressure on the land; white landownership in many cases produced an intractable African tenant-farmer problem, as well as a system of absentee ownership popularly known as "kaffir farming." Worse still, the world slump led to government intervention. The smaller white maize farmers made up for their inadequate capital resources with their voting power; they secured featherbedding measures to shield themselves against competition both from the more efficient large-scale white producers in the country and from African peasants working at lower cost. Nevertheless, in other ways white occupation helped to stimulate African farming enterprise. In Southern Rhodesia the Europeans moved into a country nearly twice the size of Great Britain and inhabited at the beginning of the present century by considerably less than a million indigenous people. Southern Rhodesian Africans, unlike the Indians of North America, the Araucanians of Chile, or the Maori of New Zealand, in the end managed to retain something like 40 percent of the total acreage and kept a base sufficiently large to develop a more intensive kind of agriculture than that practiced before the white occupation.[23] They learned new techniques of agriculture and benefited from government stock- and agricultural-improvement programs.

In many areas, such as the Northern Rhodesian railway belt, white farmers acquired their holdings in districts only thinly settled before the arrival of the white man. European-initiated development, in fact, sometimes attracted black newcomers from other parts of the country. The effects of white land occupation were often contradictory, and the debit and credit sides of the account are not always easy to draw up from the African cultivator's point of view. White conquest often displaced black people from their ancestral acres, yet pacification also allowed the weaker African communities to use their remaining lands more effectively. Tribesmen no longer had to construct their villages with an eye to tactical defense possibilities, hence black peasants could move out farther afield in search of tilling and grazing grounds without having to worry about raiding parties. There was an end to the interminable stock lifting and crop thefts engendered by tribal

[23] In 1911 the "European" area in the country amounted to 49,149,000 acres. By 1962 it had been reduced to 36,834,000. The native areas in 1962 stood at 44,386,000 acres, with the balance devoted to forest area, game reserves, and so forth. The country's total acreage amounted to 96,610,000. R. W. M. Johnson, *African Agricultural Development in Southern Rhodesia, 1945–1960* (reprint from *Food Research Institute Studies,* IV, No. 2 [1964]; Stanford, Calif.), p. 173.

wars. The European impact for the first time created a market for indigenous as well as white farm products. Not only white townsmen, but also white dairymen and tobacco farmers, bought African-raised beef and maize to feed their workmen. African farmers bought new implements such as plows and carts, and later on even motortrucks, from their white neighbors. The white farmers' lobby was on the whole sufficiently intelligent not to oppose government-directed improvement schemes in the reserves; the administration constructed dips and dams in the native areas; agricultural instructors gave advice on improved methods, with the result that the numbers of African-owned cattle and of acres under African cultivation vastly expanded under the new regime in Rhodesia.[24]

Black and, to a lesser extent, white farmers carried the main burden of agricultural development in Africa. The third, and on the whole least important, instrument of progress was company enterprise. Big business preferred to put its resources into mines and railways and, in South Africa, into factories. There were, however, some notable exceptions. Unilever in the Congo and the Cameroons Development Corporation in West Africa promoted extensive agricultural enterprises. Liberia also owed much of its development to similar foreign initiative. In 1926 the Finance Corporation, a Firestone subsidiary, concluded an agreement with the Liberian government and advanced money to the small, financially unstable republic under very onerous conditions. The Liberians accepted Firestone's terms, partly because they wished for American diplomatic support against their colonial neighbors and partly because they anticipated a substantial infusion of American investments. To a certain extent, Monrovia got what it wanted. Long-standing boundary troubles with the French came to an end. The Liberians secured sufficient cash to satisfy some of their creditors and attained the unusual distinction of being one of the few nations to repay their war debts to the United States in full. Firestone received extensive land and tax concessions and in turn initiated the world's largest rubber undertaking. Furthermore, the company acquired a good reputation as an employer. It paid its workmen much more adequately than the government and other local entrepreneurs and also subsidized wages by bonuses for increased output and by selling low-priced food to its employees. Plantation laborers could work their own plots in spare-time hours; debt peonage was strictly avoided. The company put up hospitals, built roads, and established a public radio service and other undertakings. Firestone had sufficient perception to encourage independent

[24] For more recent developments see, for instance, Johnson, *African Agricultural Development, passim.*

rubber production in Liberia, proving thereby that company enterprise need not necessarily conflict with private initiative. The company provided free rubber seeds to independent growers, as well as high-yielding clones, or buds, and trained instructors to advise on methods. "The Firestone Plantations Company," wrote a standard handbook some twenty years after the start of these operations, "represents the one concrete evidence of economic progress in Liberia since 1926."[25]

Company enterprise, on the other hand, led to a great deal of friction. The Firestone enterprise, in fact, produced all the tensions that come with the impact of a great capitalist concern on a weak and underdeveloped country. Liberians complained that leading positions in the enterprise were reserved to Americans. There was much resentment with regard to the company's exemption from corporation taxes and other public charges. The company disputed the Liberian figures and asserted that its contributions amounted to about one-third of the country's revenue. Firestone's profits came under attack; Liberians spoke of exploitation, even though the wages paid on Firestone estates were much higher than elsewhere in the country. A much more substantial criticism concerned the size of the concession. Firestone received a grant of 1 million acres, a very large area for a country no bigger than the state of Ohio. The company actually worked only a small portion of the available land, but its very presence may possibly have discouraged other foreign investors from putting money into the country. Liberians also accused Firestone of wielding undue political influence, though the country's ruling stratum displayed considerable skill in pitting the company, the American government, the League of Nations, and various foreign powers against each other. Firestone thus aroused a great deal of antagonism, some of it justified and some of it ill-founded, but all typical of the kind which a successful foreign corporation, whether a British firm like Unilever or an American concern like Firestone, so often arouses in an underdeveloped country dominated by an economically weak but self-conscious and sensitive ruling class.

In summary, the interwar period saw tremendous economic growth in Africa. There is, accordingly, no justification for the view of this period of African history as one of imperial neglect in contrast with Communist progress.[26] True enough, development was uneven. Large

[25] Raymond L. Buell, *Liberia: A Century of Survival, 1847–1947* (Philadelphia, 1947), pp. 49–50. The book also reproduces the main concession agreement during the period (pp. 100–111).

[26] See, for instance, Leonard Barnes, *Soviet Light on the Colonies* (Harmondsworth, Middlesex, Eng., 1945), for an interpretation of this kind.

areas of Africa were little affected by change; only South Africa, the oldest white-settled area on the continent, managed to build up substantial industries, while the continent as a whole remained a primary producer which devoted its resources to the export of minerals and crops. Africa did, however, see vast additions to its real resources in the shape of railway lines, roads, mines, plantations, hydroelectric plants, and other assets. These economic changes came about without large-scale liquidations and without forced labor of the Stalinist variety. Imperial rule indeed shielded sub-Saharan Africa from other foreign pressures and prevented internecine struggles; colonial Africa bore but a minor military burden; it operated with a relatively small and inexpensive state machinery, so that comparatively few resources were diverted into civil service and defense expenditure (the Gold Coast had fewer than 150 civil servants in the 1930s).

The new enterprise, by the very speed of its impact, created a host of social tensions. The clash of black peasant agriculture, white farming, and company ventures, for instance, might engender sharp competition for labor and natural resources. Competition, on the other hand, might also imply cooperation. Firestone's activities to a certain degree assisted indigenous Liberian rubber producers; white Rhodesian tobacco farmers bought native-grown maize. The various new enterprises in some ways complemented one another. Critics of existing colonial practices often erred, therefore, when they advocated reforms in terms of a rigid either-or choice and contrasted black with white farming or primary with secondary industries as mutually exclusive categories.

Contact with the white man, whether as merchant, mineowner, farmer, or manufacturer, also brought about economic changes of a more intangible kind. Europeans taught African villagers the art of storing ideas. In the past, tradition had depended on memory and word of mouth; the old knew most and the young least. Now missionaries and others showed how words might be committed to paper and permanently preserved. Not only were labor migrants enabled to communicate with their fellow villagers back home by means of inky marks on paper, but also they were enabled to read books and newspapers. Of equal significance was the creation of a vernacular literature which began, as in Europe, with translations of the Scriptures and the compilation of hymnbooks in indigenous languages. Cashbooks and catechisms both demand literacy of their users, and these skills in turn helped to speed up economic transformation.

In addition, economic change spread new ways of measuring time and space. The Africans, of course, could reckon time quite adequately for their purposes; they divided the year into months and seasons, or they used the growth cycle of a crop, with the day further subdivided by the sun's position or what people would normally be doing at that hour. But in villages there were neither printed calendars nor mechanical clocks. Time was an everlasting stream. The white man's beliefs, however, were very different. Time to the European was something that could be minutely subdivided, a commodity for sale. Time was money, punctuality a virtue. This was the first lesson learned by a labor migrant working off his labor "ticket" or certificate indicating the monthly period worked. New terms for months of the year and times of the day began to enter the Bantu languages, often, characteristically enough, in their English dress. Linked to these novel concepts was a new sense of space which slowly began to percolate down to the Africans in towns and by the side of settled railway lines. Outside the more densely settled regions of Africa land to the tribesman was a continuum; land was unlimited in supply and went on forever, like time. The Europeans, on the other hand, conceived of land in terms of individual tenure; space was apportioned with an imaginary square grid, with each of these little bits a marketable piece of merchandise. These ideas found a ready response wherever land came to be in short supply. The new space-time concept slowly influenced African thought in general and in turn contributed to the great economic transformation that was beginning to change the face of Africa.

16. Businessmen and Bureaucrats: The Growth of State Control

There are certain parallels in history, and some of the most striking instances occur in the social situations and the social thought of backward economies. In countries where machines are scarce and unskilled hands are plentiful, the statesman's greatest problem is not so much unemployment as underemployment. Farming requires a great labor force which is not always used to its best advantage. There is often underemployment in the administration; it is not just "jobs for the boys," but "too many boys for the job." Domestic service similarly employs great numbers of retainers whose presence lends luster to their respective establishments but who do not do much work. There are too many workers, yet the employers always complain about a shortage of labor. Eighteenth-century England, for instance, was in many respects a backward country. Labor productivity was low by modern standards. The countrymen who drifted into the new industrial towns frequently found great difficulties in adjusting themselves to the unaccustomed discipline of mine and factory. A considerable labor force was employed for the purposes of conspicuous display, as footmen, lackeys, and kitchen maids in great country houses—always a sure symptom of an economy furnished with scanty mechanical means.[1] The British employer's outlook under these circumstances was essentially a moralistic one. He distinguished sharply between

[1] Domestic-service conditions in modern Africa closely reflect the degree of a country's economic development. European householders with comparable incomes will be able to afford at most one "boy" in Johannesburg, a highly industrialized metropolis in South Africa. In Salisbury, in Rhodesia, a similar employer may engage perhaps one permanent servant and a young lad to help him in the garden. In Blantyre in Malawi a white merchant or a senior African government official will employ perhaps four men to do the same amount of work; each of these four servants will insist on doing only a few specified services, with bitter "boundary disputes" over job prerogatives.

253

the "deserving" poor who worked for wages and the "idle" poor who kept a few cows on the village common and worked on their own account or who, worse still, presumed to live on charity when they were physically fit to seek work. The unemployed or the underemployed incurred moral censure for their supposed laziness and inability to respond to economic motives.

The early stages of colonization often produced a similar outlook among the new rulers in Africa. Missionaries, settlers, and administrators widely agreed—though for very different reasons—that black people supposedly lived vicious, idle, and immoral lives in their kraals, where they sat on their haunches, guzzled beer, and watched their wives working in the blazing sun. Africans were described as "a nation of unemployeds." European concepts of chivalry and Western beliefs in work as a form of prayer mingled curiously with the economic self-interest of particular employers' lobbies and the administration's demand for revenue. Usually the various pressure groups on the spot united in demanding state action of various kinds to get tribesmen to work. European farmers, mineowners, and concessionaires believed that the administration should intervene in the economy on their behalf. In addition, public authorities themselves frequently enforced *corvées* and compelled villagers to maintain local roads, repair bridges, furnish carriers, and the like. Throughout early colonial Africa the talk was of labor shortage. Machines of any kind were few; human muscles had to make up for the scarcity of capital. Labor, moreover, was used inefficiently; the employers' very reliance on state intervention discouraged the introduction of laborsaving devices and prevented adequate labor management. The British South Africa Company's early administration in Southern Rhodesia compelled Africans to work for European farmers. Forced labor was rife in the Congo Free State. As late as 1919 the imperial authorities in Kenya issued a circular instructing district officers to bring Africans into employment. The French in Equatorial Africa resorted to even worse practices; these excited the anger of humanitarians such as André Gide, who denounced the great concessionary companies and played an important part in ending the concessionary regime.[2] The Portuguese similarly resorted to forced labor, and so did the Liberians.

Gradually, however, the emphasis shifted to the "economic man." Employers discovered, as had their predecessors in nineteenth-century Europe, that workers did indeed respond to economic incentives. Laissez-faire doctrines in time acquired more popularity, with the British usually leading the way; the French followed much more

[2] Virginia Thompson and Richard Adloff, *The Emerging States of French Equatorial Africa* (Stanford, Calif., 1960), pp. 16–20.

slowly, with the Portuguese and Liberians, economically the most backward of governing powers, bringing up the rear. Southern Rhodesia made an early start by getting rid of forced labor at the beginning of the present century; here missionary, humanitarian, and imperial pressures all combined to put a stop to compulsion. In Kenya the circular of 1919 aroused strong opposition from local clergymen, from the Conference of Missionary Societies in Great Britain and Ireland, and from the Aborigines Protection Society. In 1921 the Colonial Office gave way and issued a White Paper forbidding officials to take any further part in labor recruiting for private employment. The Belgians introduced similar reforms in the Congo. The French in West Africa stuck to various forms of compulsion, including the use of military conscripts, for a much longer period. The final break came in 1946, when the Constituent Assembly passed a law abolishing forced labor in all its forms throughout French black Africa.[3] In the Portuguese colonies forced labor continued until Portugal's adherence to the Abolition of Forced Labor Convention of 1957, which took formal effect in 1960. From then on the Portuguese did away with a system whereby Africans could be compelled to work, at approved wages, in a manner desired by the administration.

From the 1920s, Africa thus slowly moved away from the more oppressive kinds of economic compulsion. The speed of this development varied considerably, reflecting to some extent the uneven rate of economic development throughout the vast continent. Moral and political issues influenced the situation; so did humanitarian pressure in the metropolitan countries. In addition, economic and administrative exigencies played a major part. Throughout most of sub-Saharan Africa the state machinery remained weak. Labor services could be only sporadically enforced. White employers in the early days might talk about the mobilization of manpower for productive purposes with the same enthusiasm as Marxist-oriented theoreticians of a later generation, but the district commissioners and policemen in the field were few. Many Africans successfully evaded their obligations. Unwilling draftees did little work. Concessionary regimes based on forced labor were just as likely to end in bankruptcy as to be economically successful.

In 1903 the French discovered that at least one-third of the capital sunk into the French Congo by investors, that is to say, nearly 12 million francs, had been lost without a trace. Although by 1906 a number of the better-run companies had made profits aggregating some 10 million francs, nine others had disappeared and twenty-one

---

[3] Virginia Thompson and Richard Adloff, *French West Africa* (Stanford, Calif., 1957), pp. 491–492.

had a deficit totaling more than 9 million francs.[4] In any case, conscript labor could play only a part in a simple "robber economy," based on the export of uncultivated produce such as wild rubber, or in farming or mining enterprises of the most rudimentary kind. But draftees were useless for growing more highly specialized crops or for servicing complicated machinery. Motortrucks, for instance, did away with conscripted carriers. Motor transport also required skilled drivers who would work willingly and look after their vehicles. Villagers, called out by their local chiefs at the government's behest, were quite capable of maintaining simple bush tracks, but the construction of great macadamized highways and of railways and bridges was a skilled art, requiring not unwilling conscripts, but properly trained gangs working under highly skilled specialists. Obligatory labor services moreover went counter to the interests of the wealthier and more progressive employers, who could secure hired hands without compulsion and who saw no reason that their more backward competitors should secure special advantages at public expense. Even wartime attempts to conscript labor for public services usually failed to give much satisfaction. During World War II the Northern Rhodesian government, for example, introduced legislation to compel African laborers to serve for two months' time at normal rates of pay. Conscripts worked on white farms, but pressure from the European agriculturists themselves persuaded the authorities to do away with compulsion and to set up a voluntary labor corps instead. Even this expedient proved unsatisfactory, and G. B. Beckett, a spokesman for the white farmers in the legislative council, explained to the legislature that the real remedy for the farmers' troubles was to be found in better pay and conditions, in improved incentives, and in heightened labor efficiency. The agricultural work force, he added, should be stabilized, for mechanization could not be achieved with casual drifters.[5]

Another type of state intervention resorted to compulsion for the purpose of making black farmers grow specific cash crops. This policy, sporadically enforced in various parts of tropical Africa, similarly assumed that villagers would not respond to ordinary economic incentives. The authorities therefore tried to substitute the governmental stick for the economic carrot. In 1917, for instance, an ordinance was passed in the Belgian Congo obliging Africans to cultivate specified acreages for food or export crops; in the Ubangi district Africans were made to grow ten *ares* of cotton and twelve palm trees each. But in

---

[4] Thompson and Adloff, *The Emerging States,* p. 16.
[5] Lewis H. Gann, *A History of Northern Rhodesia: Early Days to 1953* (London, 1964), pp. 333–334.

1919 the Congo Commission for the Protection of the Natives criticized this form of enterprise in terms that stood out as a model of good sense. These *corvées,* the commissioners argued, proved wasteful of labor and resources, obliged Africans to desert their regular occupations, and should therefore be terminated.[6] Systems of forced cultivation moreover compelled the state to guarantee commodity prices over a fixed number of years against market fluctuations and thereby raised all kinds of administrative difficulties which sometimes threatened to make the system uneconomical. French experience was similar in many respects. The French in Equatorial Africa began with a mischievous system of concessions which involved the compulsory collection of forest produce. They subsequently introduced various reforms and in 1930 specifically limited compulsory cultivation for hoarding against times of scarcity or for purposes of agricultural training. This policy continued to meet with approval even among many reformist intellectuals, who still envisaged Africans as thriftless children in the grip of a "prelogical mentality," whose lot should be improved despite themselves. Nevertheless, even more limited degrees of pressure were likely to be disappointing in their results. The large extension of peanuts in French West Africa was partly occasioned by the activities of Sociétés de Prévoyance rather than by direct state action. The tremendous expansion of cash crops, especially cocoa and peanuts in the Gold Coast and Nigeria during this period, was the result of African enterprise and owed little to governmental pressure.

The several colonial powers during the interwar period thus moved toward various forms of laissez-faire policies, albeit at greatly differing speeds. Progress was often slow and hesitant, encountering sometimes as much resistance from the moralistic outlook of the administration as from economic pressure groups. Paternalistic civil servants, as well as merchants with axes to grind, complained that the free play of the market would undermine the black man's moral stamina. "The native in the cotton-growing areas of the [Uganda] Protectorate is at present far from being hard worked. . . . All around him he sees competition for his cotton, and there is no doubt in my mind that there is a certain amount of bribery and corruption to induce him to sell his cotton. This cannot have a good effect on him." The writer, a representative of the Empire Cotton Growing Association, therefore pleaded for state control:

> If, for a term of years, the Government had exercised an even closer control, and had themselves bought all the cotton from the natives, or

[6] Raymond L. Buell, *The Native Problem in Africa,* II (New York, 1928), 500–501.

had grouped all buying within an organization which they could influence, such measures would have had considerable administrative advantages. Prices would have been stabilized and profits would have been diverted towards general development and education. The natives would not have been rich it is true, but they would have been very reasonably prosperous, and the dangers to them of getting rich too quickly would have been obviated.[7]

The British administrators in Uganda fortunately did not act upon these recommendations. They lacked both the men and the means to interfere in marketing on any major scale; Uganda developed an independent peasantry as well as a substantial class of black traders, who began to compete with Indian merchants on their own ground and who, by the end of the 1950s, carried on nearly half the country's retail business. The ideas underlying the above report, however, continued to influence a good deal of official thinking. Later they became part of a new orthodoxy which, in a somewhat different form, helped to shape economic thought throughout postcolonial Africa. The white official and his successor, the black party functionary, both shared the same moralistic outlook. Both generally assumed that the middleman, especially the small hawker of alien extraction, must be an economic parasite.[8] In this respect the British administrator's economic reasoning frequently ran parallel to that of Marxist-oriented critics of imperialism, who also felt that distributors could not create value. Most British administrators were convinced, as Sir Andrew Cohen, a great imperial civil servant, put it, that "the evils of agricultural debt which have been known in many parts of Asia must be kept away from Africa; if land is pledged as security, it must be for loans from Government-owned credit banks" or banks operating under public supervision.[9] Cohen and his fellow officials all wished to encourage the emergence of small peasant agriculture. Small farmers, however, stood in urgent need of credit facilities. For a long period there were no land banks. Existing credit institutions in Africa were more suited to undertaking larger transactions than to providing loans in penny packets. Cohen failed to realize that in the field of small-scale lending the old-fashioned Indian moneylender (like his Jewish equivalent

---

[7] C. N. French, *Report on the Cotton Growing Industry of Uganda, Kenya, and the Mwanza District of Tanganyika* (London, 1925), quoted in Buell, *The Native Problem in Africa,* I, 623.

[8] There were, of course, exceptions to this rule. The British South Africa Company's early administration in the two Rhodesias was often inspired by a degree of economic realism commonly absent from many other administrations under Colonial Office care.

[9] Sir Andrew Cohen, *British Policy in Changing Africa* (London, 1959), pp. 96–97.

in the Rumanian and Galician villages of old) might well have been more flexible in his methods, more accessible to and more familiar with his clients than a state-run credit institution which, in backward countries, is all too often run by an expensive, cumbersome, and overbearing bureaucracy directed by political appointees and which often operates at higher overheads than those incurred by private lenders. In a society of small producers there is indeed much to be said for a Shylock, but the imperial official and his successor all sympathized with Antonio.

British and French officials put similar obstacles in the way of small traders. In many parts of West Africa the immigration of peddlers, especially Indian or Lebanese, was restricted. This policy always met with strong support from local pressure groups afraid of competition and often went hand in hand with racial or national sentiments. In Southern Rhodesia, for instance, white Christian and Jewish traders both combined to keep out Indian newcomers; only a relatively small number of Indians managed to enter the colony after it received "responsible government" in 1923. Established Indian merchants in turn would often give their silent approval to legislation designed to exclude other Indian competitors from the country. Again, in areas such as West Africa, Africans similarly agitated against the entry of black people from other parts of their country into established preserves. In Nigeria, Yoruba and Hausa often resented the arrival of Ibo from the east. Ashanti traders in the Gold Coast berated competition from Gao merchants.

Unfortunately, colonial authorities at times shared the fundamental attitudes which underlay these various complaints. The white administrator (again like his postcolonial successor) frequently saw the local demand for mercantile services as a fixed and predictable quantity. One man's gain, in his view, must therefore be another man's loss. Immigration barriers against Indian or Lebanese planners thus operated as a crude kind of economic planning, comparable to the devices of eighteenth-century German princelings who sought to limit the number of Jewish families within their principalities by bans on marriages and other means, on the grounds that local trade would bear only a specific number of shops.

These assumptions, however, rested on a number of serious misconceptions. The volume of commerce was neither fixed nor exactly predictable, least of all with the inadequate means of economic planning available to the colonial authorities. Restrictionist policies moreover tended to ignore the economic realities of trade in underdeveloped countries. Cultivators in Africa, as in all backward areas, usually produced on a small scale; they had little storage capacity and less cash. They were thus obliged to sell their produce in small quantities and at frequent intervals. Producers often lived many miles away from the nearest market, and the cost of assembling and conveying a large number of small packets for trade was heavy. Distribution raised similar problems. Buyers might also live a long way from the next store, but they wished, or indeed were forced, to buy goods in very small quantities. Three lumps of sugar, half a cigarette, or a few sticks of matches might form the last links in a distributive chain beginning with a large consignment of merchandise shipped to a Nigerian port. Commercial distribution, an essential link in the huge enterprise of raising and maintaining a backward economy above the subsistence level, therefore necessarily absorbed a great deal of manpower and resources.[10] Many imperial officials failed to understand these economic realities and concluded that the territories in their charge must be overrun by useless middlemen. They often did not understand the way in which increased competition might lower the cost of production and that a scarcity of small hawkers in fact might injure the very producers, black or white, whom they wished to benefit.

The argument is worth laboring, for time and again the rulers of Africa, be they backveld farmers in Rhodesia, high-ranking Colonial Office administrators in Uganda, or African party functionaries in Guinea, all adopted similar modes of economic reasoning. During the 1930s, for example, many white cultivators on the Northern Rhodesian railway belt found that they could not diversify production on their farms because opportunities for trade remained restricted. There were only a limited number of commercial firms in the country. These businesses commonly did not wish to be bothered with small parcels of diverse products from widely scattered farms; merchants naturally preferred to restrict their operations to larger and simpler transactions concerned with just one or two commodities like maize. Indian traders, willing to deal in small quantities, ready to accept low profit rates, and endowed with the qualities of endurance, thrift, and economic foresight, were well qualified to fill the gap and thereby to increase the farmer's turnover. European pressure, however, combined with official prejudice and African preconceptions to keep Indian newcomers out of the country. White farmers favoring economic restrictionism thereby unwittingly emptied their own pockets.

The British authorities in West Africa adopted similar measures. They maintained severe controls on the immigration of Levantine

[10] See Peter T. Bauer, *Economic Analysis and Policy in Underdeveloped Countries* (Durham, N.C., 1957), pp. 67–70.

traders. This was based on the assumption, partially correct, that the presence of a substantial non-African minority might create political complications and also on the much more dubious precept that the activities of petty expatriate traders would stand in the way of African economic development. While the administration admitted foreign industrialists without trouble, the bigger European firms encountered all kinds of obstacles to recruitment of Levantine employees overseas; the setting up of new expatriate enterprises in semiwholesale or retail business was all but stopped. British colonial thought (and, for that matter, the thought of other white colonizers) thus oddly mirrored the economic concepts of German nationalists of the period, who sharply distinguished between *schaffendes,* that is to say, creative, and *raffendes,* or exploitive, capital. The desirable capitalist, according to this interpretation, engaged in manufacturing. The undesirable businessman devoted his energy merely to distribution and therefore made no new contribution to his country's wealth. This economic logic, however, finds little support in the economic history of Africa, or indeed that of any other continent. The annals of Rhodesia and of East Africa are rich in examples of how mercantile capital is transformed into manufacturing capital. Grandfather—to construct an economic model—landed in the new country with his little pack. He spoke English with a Scottish, Yiddish, or Gujarati accent, but he soon got to know the ways of the colony and set himself up as a petty trader. He carefully husbanded his resources; he refused to spend his money on slow horses, fast women, or similarly uneconomic kinds of expenditure and thereby accumulated a substantial credit balance in the bank. His son extended the shop into a chain store. His grandson opened a factory and ultimately became a substantial manufacturer. Trade often created industrial capital in a way which imperial officials, their intellectual critics at home, and their postcolonial successors in Africa commonly failed to understand.

The official's preconceptions, sometimes blended with a snobbish distaste for petty traders, produced an outlook favorable to economic restrictionism. This operated with particular force against ethnic minority groups devoid of political influence. In French West Africa, for instance, Syrian and Lebanese traders played a major role in pioneering trade in the backwoods, where life was tough and profits were small. The big French trading companies eagerly sought the Levantines' services, for they were less expensive to employ than Europeans and usually more efficient than Africans. During the world slump French firms had to close many of their hinterland branches, but the Levantines clung to their savings and stayed to fill a commercial vacuum. However, there were so many complaints of their allegedly unscrupulous practices and their "unhygienic and clannish way of living" that the government stringently curtailed their immigration. After World War II the French lost their mandates in Syria and Lebanon, and Levantines were treated as foreigners. French official attitudes further hardened as Syria and Lebanon came to espouse the cause of Arab and Cameroun nationalism and as the Syrian and Lebanese traders showed themselves adept at evading foreign-exchange regulations.[11]

The British in West Africa acted in the same way. They tried to strengthen indigenous black traders by keeping out Lebanese competitors. The British authorities thereby reduced the volume of trade and unwittingly benefited existing British firms in the country, the very companies whom African nationalists would censure for their monopolistic practices. The protected firms were able to operate in a less competitive market; their profit margins therefore remained higher. Opportunities for price-fixing and market-sharing arrangements increased. Impediments placed in the way of foreign merchants reduced opportunities for African customers to pick and choose between different suppliers. Restrictions, oddly enough, also diminished opportunities for African employees to gain business experience in somebody else's firm before setting up shops of their own.[12] In addition, restrictionist policies tended to be self-perpetuating. They fortified existing vested interests. They also supported the belief, widespread among Africans, that the amount of trade in any particular country must be fixed in its aggregate amount, that commerce normally yielded high profits not commensurate with the value of the services rendered. These convictions soon hardened into articles of faith which a subsequent generation of African civil servants, party functionaries, and journalists all adopted with the same fervor as their imperial predecessors.

Advocates of laissez faire thus never enjoyed very good innings in colonial Africa. Imperial government at its best was protective in outlook, and officials usually believed that the state must play an active part in regulating the economy for the public good. In the earlier stages of colonization, however, the state machinery remained weak and could not handle complicated jobs. There were few statisticians

11 Thompson and Adloff, *French West Africa,* p. 430.
12 Peter T. Bauer, *West African Trade: A Study of Competition, Oligopoly and Monopoly in a Changing Economy* (London, 1963), especially pp. 156–171. This is a basic work for the understanding of African economic history and the problems of underdeveloped countries in general.

in government service; there were only a limited number of technical experts of any kind on the public payroll. Governments perforce had to limit their activities to a restricted number of tasks. The gradual growth of wealth, however, facilitated the creation of a more elaborate bureaucracy. Prosperity also created new pressure groups. These new lobbies in turn called for state interference, mixing welfare with economic arguments to protect their own stakes.

The pace of public intervention thus slowly speeded up. It gained increasing momentum with the world slump; in British Africa it developed with the greatest speed in territories such as Southern Rhodesia, where economic development had become most diversified and where local economic interests could most effectively sway the legislature through the power of the vote. The Southern Rhodesian constitution, in the fashion of most early nineteenth-century constitutions in Europe, allotted the franchise according to property and income qualifications. Most, though not all, electors were white. When they began to feel the economic pinch, they tried to safeguard their livelihood through state action in just the way their counterparts were doing in the more highly developed countries of Europe and North America. Many liberal observers from abroad interpreted the white Rhodesians' behavior in terms of racial prejudice. In fact the territory's political community thought in economic more than in color terms; the various pressure groups all tried to protect their interests against the weaker or less organized sections of the community, whatever their ethnic ancestry. During the slump white Rhodesians embarked on a relief program, entirely empirical and uncoordinated in nature, but one which in some ways bore an odd resemblance to the "new deal" and which, in a different racial setting, subsequently found many parallels in black Africa.

Southern Rhodesia followed Britain and the United States in going off the gold standard. There was a public-works program which employed workless whites for road making at higher wages than they could have obtained under free-market conditions. The unionists, most of them white but a few of them colored artisans, shielded themselves against undercutting from nonunion labor by enforcing a complicated system of regulated wages. The so-called Industrial Conciliation Act of 1934 set up boards with powers to prescribe rates of renumeration for skilled trades. Urban employers, in other words, had to pay agreed wage packets to whatever skilled workmen they employed, white or black. This conformed to inherited trade-union principles but in practice gave a privileged position to white artisans, for employers had no reason to engage black people unless they could thereby undercut white workers. Critics overseas described the law as an anti-African measure, but from the economist's point of view the artisans' color would not have mattered. A privileged section of the working class managed to raise the price of labor for itself, and thereby depressed real wages for all those outside the charmed circle of the unionized. The Rhodesian townships became protected fiefs for unionists (the rural areas were excluded from the operation of the act), and the first prosecution under the new law was in fact directed against an employer who underpaid a white South African immigrant.[13]

The smaller European corn growers got corresponding advantages. The colony introduced a thoroughgoing system of maize control. This operated in a very complicated fashion, but the underlying idea was simple. The world's grain market was overstocked. The colony exported maize at a loss, while local purchasers within the territory had to pay an artificially high price for the farmer's produce. The smaller white growers, a numerous and politically influential group, obtained the lion's share in the profitable local pool. Their competitors, the bigger white producers working with more efficient methods and the small African cultivators operating at lower overheads, received smaller quotas than they would have been able to secure in a free market. Again liberal critics censured the law for its allegedly antiblack bias. In fact the state-run maize-control machinery discriminated against a whole range of people of all colors—the well-capitalized white farmers capable of turning out maize in larger quantities, black peasants, and, of course, Rhodesian consumers of whatever race, an unorganized and heterogeneous collection of people who had no one to speak in their behalf.

In addition to these and other measures, white Rhodesians, like the citizens of other British dominions, firmly resolved to keep down their own number by limiting the entry of newcomers to the colony. This restrictive policy owed a great deal to national considerations. Southern Rhodesians wished to live in a British country; they accordingly put various obstacles in the way of foreign-born immigrants, a policy oddly paralleled in white Algeria at the other end of the African continent. Rhodesians moreover believed that their authorities would be able to pick immigrants for their suitability; they wrongly imagined that government selection boards could predict what kind of applicant would suit what kind of job, how much capital an immigrant would

[13] For the Rhodesians' "new deal," see Lewis H. Gann and Michael Gelfand, *Huggins of Rhodesia: The Man and His Country* (London, 1964), especially pp. 96–99 and 122–133.

need, and what sort of man would be able to succeed in business under Rhodesian conditions. Rhodesian requirements became so stringent that the young Rhodes himself, a sickly man with neither money, diplomas, nor degrees to his credit, would never have been able to enter the country. The settlers, of course, felt convinced that these restrictive policies would enhance their prosperity. Their economic logic was that if eggs are scarce, eggs become dear. If men are scarce, men become dear, and wages must go up. In fact, however, the settlers acted against both their long-term political and their own economic interests. They kept down their own numbers, and thereby weakened their position in a way which not even their most convinced opponents dared to suggest at the time. White painters may have gained higher wages for painting other peoples' houses than they would have gotten in a free-market economy, but the painters would also have to pay artificially high rates to the electricians when their lights needed fixing; wage regulation, in fact, may well have diminished the total number of jobs which artisans of any color could mark up on their order books. The smaller white maize growers similarly attained a privileged position. The European farming community generally applauded, disregarding the fact that not only black cultivators, but also the more efficient white producers, the bigger maize growers, and even white dairy and tobacco farmers, highly skilled people not faced with African competition, helped to foot the bill.

War gave a new impetus to state intervention in both industry and commerce. During World War I, German East Africa was cut off; the Germans in the colony developed the same ingenuity at developing ersatz products that they displayed in the beleaguered Reich. A planter invented a gasoline substitute made from copra. The German authorities provided a substitute for its manufacture, but the factory fell into Allied hands before gasoline could be delivered in any quantities. Experts in a government-research institute turned their hands to the production of commodities previously imported from overseas—medicines, rubber products, oil, candles, and so forth.[14] Engineers in Rhodesia and other colonies furnished other kinds of war material. The Allies, however, commanded the world's seaways and, unlike the Germans, had no need to turn out high-cost substitutes of inferior quality. In the meantime, the Union of South Africa, economically the most progressive country on the continent, had begun on a dramatic course of industrialization. The war and postwar years

[14] William Otto Henderson, *Studies in German Colonial History* (London, 1962), p. 92.

saw rapid development; growth continued, albeit at a somewhat slower pace, after the end of hostilities. World War II again gave a tremendous impetus to South African manufactures, and the Union attained one of the most astonishing rates of industrial expansion in world history.[15] After a time lag Southern Rhodesia followed suit. Between 1938 and 1958 the colony increased the gross value of its manufacturing output by more than twenty times; the settlers thereby achieved what may well have been the highest industrial growth rate ever to have been attained in any backward country, capitalist, socialist, or Communist.[16]

The development of Rhodesian factories was mainly the result of private enterprise. During World War II, however, the Southern Rhodesian government began to take an increasingly important share in the manufacturing process. The colony urgently required steel for the manufacture of armaments. Existing facilities were inadequate; new investors would not come forward in sufficient numbers. Sir Godfrey Huggins, then Prime Minister, feared also for his country's future economic independence—ISCOR (Iron and Steel Corporation), the great government-controlled South African steel trust, held a sizable share in the Rhodesian Steel undertaking at Bulawayo, and in any postwar slump the trust might concentrate production within the Union's borders. In addition, Huggins formulated a rudimentary "takeoff" theory. The colony must diversify its production; where private entrepreneurs would not do the job, the government should step in with

[15] Growth of industries, private, governmental, and municipal; gross value of output (in pounds):

Year	Number of employees	Gross value of output
1911	65,916	17,240,000
1920	175,520	92,913,844
1930	218,298	111,799,115
1939	352,500	199,617,262
1945	488,661	375,344,485
1950	713,151	774,718,000
1954	855,295	1,229,793,000

From *State of the Union: Economic, Financial, and Statistical Year-Book for the Union of South Africa, 1960–61* (Johannesburg, 1961), pp. 418ff.

[16] Gross output of manufacturing and repair establishments in Southern Rhodesia, according to the Central African Statistical Department, Salisbury, Southern Rhodesia, was (in thousand pounds):

Year	Gross value of output
1938	5,107
1945	14,062
1949	31,316
1955–1956	76,220
1957–1958	105,096

public capital. The government would then manufacture semiraw materials such as steel ingots, which private capitalists would work up into finished goods. After World War II, the Southern Rhodesian government did a good stroke of business by acquiring their country's railways at a comparatively low price.

But white Rhodesians would go no further in the direction of socialism. The white Rhodesian working class, mainly skilled people, might criticize capitalism. Many of their arguments, in fact, percolated down to African workers and became absorbed into African nationalist thought. The European artisans, however, were never strong enough to wield power on their own. They would not collaborate with African unskilled workers, whom they envisaged as a potential threat; they could never think of seizing power on their own, as their South African colleagues had unsuccessfully tried during the Rand Rising of 1922. The European workers, a relatively prosperous group, thus merely acted as a powerful lobby of the American type, extorting as many concessions from the Establishment as they could. They succeeded in safeguarding the interests of their own unions. They also obtained a number of industrial reforms concerned with safety regulations in mines and factories and restrictions on working hours which, by the very nature of things, also benefited their unfranchised black colleagues. But the white worker remained a reformist at heart. White Rhodesians continued to follow orthodox financial policies; they normally balanced their budgets and never made any attempts at expropriating private enterprise without compensation. Throughout the 1940s and 1950s they therefore managed to retain the overseas investors' confidence and were able to borrow money at comparatively low rates of interest, an achievement which made up for their subsequent inability to secure international aid on philanthropic or political grounds.[17]

The settlers also enjoyed the additional advantage of stable administration, having resisted all temptations to "Rhodesianize" the existing civil service by turning government jobs into a preserve for

[17] Southern Rhodesia obtained "responsible government" in 1923 under a constitution which in practice gave autonomy to the European settler population. The territory was the only British Commonwealth country which, so to speak, had to pay cash for the privilege of responsible government. Rhodesians in 1923 paid £2 million toward the amount payable by the Crown to the British South Africa Company for administrative deficits accumulated in the past and for public works put up under its charter. In 1932 they purchased the country's mineral rights from the company for £2 million. In 1947 they bought the Rhodesian Railways in a deal involving a loan issue of £32 million. The white Rhodesians' adherence to orthodox financial methods involved them in a good many internal disputes over policy. In the end, however, their prosperity did not suffer.

unqualified locally born whites with political pull. They did, however, help to pioneer many different kinds of state intervention in the economic life of Africa. The European colonists in Kenya followed a similar policy. They believed in government regulation of agricultural production, of industrial location, of marketing, and of the labor supply. Their initiative played a major part in producing a strong and efficient governmental machine and also a habit of looking to the state in economic matters, subsequently taken over by African politicians in independent Kenya.[18]

The postwar period saw, too, government intervention of other types, especially various attempts in territories under British Colonial Office rule at heavily capitalized, publicly administered agricultural enterprise. In 1947 the British started an extensive project in Tanganyika to grow peanuts. The Labour government in power at the time thereby hoped to provide Britain with ample supplies of fats and oils at a period when these commodities were short all over the world. The scheme also owed a great deal to an intense feeling of urgency about colonial development, by now a secular doctrine of improvement which had absorbed all the moral fervor that had once gone into the evangelization of pagan Africa. The project was in addition influenced by wartime attitudes, which led many policy makers to believe that heavy expenditure, large-scale planning, and massive mechanization could overcome obstacles. Further, the climate of opinion was influenced by the supposed successes of Soviet collectivized agriculture and the widespread, though unfounded, belief in the inefficiency of small-scale agricultural producers. The scheme envisaged the clearing of 3,500,000 acres. Money was no object, and by the spring of 1949 some £20 million had been spent. The project nevertheless ended as a resounding failure.[19] The authorities made all kinds of mistakes; few crops were produced, and by 1950 the planners realized that mechanized production on the scale envisaged would not pay. Had the British been willing to improve transport facilities and to offer sufficient monetary incentives either to white planters or to African peasants working on their own account, like the peanut growers of French West Africa, they would in all probability have been able to purchase all the peanuts they wanted. But the prestige of government-initiated enterprise was by now so firmly established that even the vast losses incurred by the British Overseas Food

---

[18] Michael McWilliam, "Economic Policy and the Kenya Settlers, 1945–1948," in Kenneth Robinson and Frederick Madden (eds.), *Essays in Imperial Government; Presented to Margery Perham* (Oxford, 1963), pp. 171–192.

[19] See, for instance, Alan Wood, *The Groundnut Affair* (London, 1950).

Corporation could not dim the reputation of publicly financed enterprise.[20]

Government participation in industry and agriculture, though important, was of direct concern to only a limited number of producers. Public control of foreign trade, on the other hand, was likely to affect every citizen with a stake in a market economy. In the late nineteenth century British humanitarians generally believed in free trade and bitterly resisted all attempts by chartered companies or other governmental agencies to dominate commerce. British free traders were not, of course, always successful in their efforts. Sir George Dashwood Taubman Goldie's Royal Niger Company, for instance, resorted to monopolistic trade practices not sanctioned by the terms of its charter. In 1900, however, the company's political rule came to an end, and throughout most of colonial Africa the authorities were either unable or unwilling to enter trade directly. The exigencies of World War I made some temporary breaches in the position of private traders. In Southern Rhodesia, for example, the mines department instituted a system of import licenses at a time when shipping was short and supplies were inadequate. After the end of hostilities the machinery of control was dismantled, and import regulations ceased to be enforced.

World War II brought changes of a much more profound nature which affected most of British Africa. The history of trade controls in Africa would make a fascinating book in itself, and only a few cases can be mentioned here. In British West Africa, for instance, real or supposed wartime needs led to the setting up of a massive system of import restrictions. In practice these benefited the older and better-established European firms against their smaller and less well connected competitors, particularly those of Levantine origin. Import controls continued for some years after the war, and the import trade remained extremely profitable.

Colonial governments, mainly for reasons of administrative convenience, preferred to deal with a few large firms and thereby succeeded in strengthening their position. This created a tense political situation, especially on the Gold Coast, where the authorities as well as the dominant Association of West African Merchants were heavily, though not always justly, blamed for the prevailing shortages and the

[20] The British Overseas Resources Development Acts of 1948 and 1956 established a Colonial Development Corporation for the purpose of assisting British colonial territories. The corporation obtained funds from the British treasury, but interest had to be paid on each loan. At the end of 1956 the corporation was running sixty-six development projects for which the total approved capital amounted to £75 million.

high level of prices.[21] More important still, the colonial power helped to strengthen an *étatiste* tradition in economic affairs. This outlook was taken over from the British imperial authorities by African politicians who, as they were not usually recruited from the merchant class, rarely wished to scrap these controls, being inclined to regard them as the natural prerogative of state authority.

The creation of government-controlled export monopolies had even more far-reaching effects. When French Equatorial Africa cast in its lot with Free France during World War II, for instance, trade patterns changed abruptly, giving the government a chance to exercise tight control over the country's commerce. The Allies insisted that the country's exports should be channeled through a government agency rather than be handled by private traders. Moreover, officially determined prices were imposed on goods sold in the domestic market. These controls were not lifted after the war, but instead were reinforced by additional measures imposed by metropolitan France for its own benefit. Tight control was maintained through currency allocations; there was an elaborate system of licensing which probably benefited none but a few favored firms at the expense of their competitors. What is more, the government lacked the means to enforce its decisions, and a large-scale contraband trade with neighboring countries inevitably developed. From 1949 on, the government somewhat relaxed its grip, but control of foreign-currency allocation remained with the French authorities, and the federation's purchases were largely confined to the franc zone, where prices continued to rise.[22]

In British West Africa the real or assumed exigencies of World War II led to stringent export controls. These in practice helped to freeze the patterns of trade and hindered the growth of new firms. In the late 1940s the control machinery was further extended, and all British West African colonies set up tightly regulated marketing boards which received the sole right to purchase crops destined for export and sell them abroad. They alone could fix prices paid to the peasant producers; they alone could determine what grades were judged fit to be sent abroad. Producers accordingly had to accept any prices which the boards chose to pay, and the countervailing force of independent merchants exporting goods on their own account was eliminated. Processors of agricultural produce similarly had to purchase their raw materials at prices laid down by the boards. The boards initially insisted that the reserves accumulated in this fashion be used to stabilize the prices paid to the farmers, while objectives of

[21] Bauer, *West African Trade*, pp. 145–155.
[22] Thompson and Adloff, *The Emerging States*, pp. 214–215.

more general interest, such as the financing of development and re-search, had only secondary claim on the marketing boards' re-sources. In practice the boards soon used their power to impose what amounted to heavy indirect taxation on the peasantry. They accumu-lated large surpluses; these were not handed back to the producers, but were disbursed on other types of public expenditure.

The advocates of this system defended their policy by arguments which strangely blended the moralizing paternalistic concepts of old-fashioned, conservative district commissioners with more recent be-liefs in the virtues of state control as a means of socialist planning. Public bodies, according to this school of thought, would make better use of the farmers' money than the farmers themselves. If they ob-tained the full value of their output, they would waste their cash or sit back in idleness instead of producing more crops. The retention of surpluses would fight inflation. Useless middlemen would be eliminated. A rigid inspection system would cause the quality of the product sent abroad to go up.

The opponents of the system were often styled reactionaries, yet they based their case on the fundamental rationality of the African farmer. Black farmers, they argued, were completely capable of spending their income in a manner conducive to both their own and the public in-terest. They were quite fit to plan their investments. The purchases of thousands of scattered farmers all had a genuine economic rationale, even if this did not accord with the collectivized conspicuous con-sumption entailed in costly buildings, swollen salary checks for of-ficials, and prestige projects of the kind that make such an impressive splash in information handouts. A visitor to an African village, they pleaded, might see dozens of people squatting outside their huts and putting together garments on sewing machines. These sewing machines were bought from hard-earned income. In the aggregate they might form an important part of national investment. The hum-ble tailors, however, remained inconspicuous. Government statisti-cians did not assess the value of their output; yet these sewing machines in their totality might constitute a more economical and rational use of resources than an expensive industrial showpiece, put up with public funds at high cost. Critics of the marketing boards were also inclined to defend the much-despised middlemen. Petty traders who habitually cheat their customers and charge too much, they argued, are not likely to stay in business for long. A state-run organ-ization is not, however, subject to similar pressures. Monopolistic sales organizations moreover lack flexibility; in some cases marketing boards realized lower prices on the world market than independent exporters. Furthermore, critics of the system could see no reason that farmers should, through the operation of price control and the imposition of export taxes, be exposed to a higher rate of taxation than teachers, civil servants, or any other section of the population. If they were able to get the full value of their cocoa or their peanuts, the argument continued, expenditure on investment and consumption alike would extend into a wider field.

The opponents of compulsory marketing systems had the better case from an economic standpoint, even though their critique of state-run monopolies had its political aspects. Obligatory marketing arrangements under public supervision, they felt, provided the state with enormous powers over individual producers. The system makes peasants dependent for their livelihood on the good will of great state organizations and their local agents. Marketing boards require a considerable bureaucracy. Opportunities for graft and blackmail multiply. Marketing boards all too easily become a major source of patronage to the local ruling party and provide a ready-made, though not always a very efficient, means for *dirigiste* economies run by single-party dictatorships. The new dispensation may thereby greatly strengthen the bureaucratic element in society. It can also be used in a Marxist sense to prevent the emergence of a strong indigenous mercantile middle class and a prosperous, independent peasantry. Yet this very system grew up under the colonial aegis and has survived imperialism as one of Europe's most fateful legacies to the emergent states of Africa.

17. Teachers and Doctors
in Colonial Africa

"We want the reader to note these four things, among others, that the coming of European powers has brought to Africa," wrote a modern African nationalist leader in a book otherwise strongly critical of imperialism: "the coming together of different tribes, better communications, a new economic system, and the creation of new classes among the African people."[1] Foreign rule, the writer continued, did away with internecine warfare, introduced new methods of production, and in many ways eliminated the villagers' age-old isolation. "Colonialism has created a radio audience, and the next is most likely to be a television audience. It has created a travelling public by land, sea, and air. . . . It is only a blind man who will not appreciate that colonialism has fertilized, stimulated, invigorated, and shaped African nationalism. The twentieth-century African nationalism is indeed the child of European colonialism." In this great social transformation missionaries played a major part and served as Europe's first assault force in the struggle for the mind of the people of the African continent. In most parts of sub-Saharan Africa white clergymen pioneered all modern schooling and medical services, but education posed problems which far transcended those of imparting literacy. The pioneer missionary saw himself not merely as the apostle of a superior faith, but also as the representative of a new way of life. He believed in individual salvation instead of tribalism hallowed by belief in ancestral spirits. He stood for a creed of individual economic effort and for European techniques of production rather than primitive methods. He represented the values of the Christian and monogamous family as opposed to the ideals of extended kinship groups practicing polygamy. The African, in the missionary's view,

[1] Ndabaningi Sithole, *African Nationalism* (Cape Town, 1959), pp. 65–74, especially pp. 68, 71, 74.

273

had to acquire a conviction of sin, but this sense of sin could not arise until the shackles of tribalism were broken. As an Afrikaner clergyman saw it, a tribesman might see the light and confess his wickedness, but if he did so, the man whom he had wronged would sue him. In that case the sinner's clan would pay the fine but reproach their kinsman for not keeping his shame hidden.[2] Africans, in other words, must turn to the Gospel and be regenerated in a higher faith. The new religion, however, also had a social message and necessitated the creation of schools, hospitals, and workshops as adjuncts to the Church. The missionary stood for literacy; the white preachers were, after all, in a very special sense, "people of the Book," and most of their converts came from mission schools.

Evangelization thus went hand in hand with educational work, and the political scramble was followed, and in some places preceded, by a spiritual scramble for Africa, with a host of competing societies staking out spheres of influence in the interior. The missionaries built up networks of bush schools, with an occasional teachers' training institution, or more advanced centers of instruction. Black teachers or evangelists became a familiar sight in many villages; a considerable number of Africans picked up the rudiments of reading, writing, and arithmetic.

White missionaries and their black subordinates often displayed an astonishing degree of fervor and faith. Yet the initial results of their work were generally limited. European and American mission societies depended on voluntary subscriptions on the part of overseas well-wishers. This kind of international aid was likely to fluctuate or even to dry up in times of war or economic difficulty. The early missionaries faced disease; they had to cope with living conditions of the grimmest kind, and a great proportion of them perished in the bush of blackwater fever and other deadly sicknesses. The missions suffered from inadequate coordination and mutual suspicion. They were also subject to perennial pressures which led them to overextend their efforts. Missionaries on the spot might feel obliged to answer calls for schoolteachers from local chiefs and move in while the going was good; they would try to forestall competitors and occupy a virgin field before some other denomination might step in. The early history of many mission societies in Africa oddly resembled that of the political partition, with the men in the field urging a policy of swift evangelical advance, while the "foreign secretaries" in charge of headquarters at London or Paris commonly advocated caution. The

2 J. M. Cronjé, *En daar was Lig: Die Sending van die Ned. Geref. Kerk in die O.V.S. in Noord en Suid Rhodesië gedurende die Jahre 1899–1947* (Bloemfontein, South Africa, 1948).

interplay of rival sects, complicated by varied local reactions from different African groups, resulted in dispersal of effort and an extremely uneven rate of educational development.

From some parts of Africa, such as portions of Northern Nigeria, Christian missionaries were excluded altogether. The Muslim peoples of Northern Nigeria thus suffered serious disadvantages in the race for advancement, while their pagan or formerly pagan countrymen in the south moved ahead. Regions like Malawi or Basutoland found themselves especially favored and became bases for new evangelical and educational advance into other areas. The uneven speed of economic and educational expansion also produced another kind of migration. Youngsters from more backward regions like Zambia had to go abroad, to South Africa, to benefit from more advanced courses, and South Africa or Dahomey in turn would export teachers to areas more poorly served from the scholastic point of view.

The missionaries were not usually much interested in learning for its own sake; they regarded the school as a recruiting ground for the Church, and most early mission instruction remained on a low level. "The method of teaching young children in the nineteen-twenties," records the present president of the Republic of Zambia, "was to gather them under a tree on which was hung a cloth painted with the letters of the alphabet. I well remember sitting for hours under a shady tree chanting 'a-e-i-o-u,' then forming the letters with my fingers in the sand. We would smooth out a little area near where we were sitting and the teacher would wander round among the children correcting our letters. Each cloth was called *Nsalu* and when we had *Nsalu* one, two and three, we were promoted to the first class, where we were allowed to use slates."[3] In out-of-the-way bush schools, missionaries and teachers perforce had to employ a great army of African auxiliaries, people familiar with the ways of the villagers and able to speak their language. Many of these black teachers themselves had barely passed beyond literacy; they were often nothing but part-time intellectual workers who had to supplement their meager incomes with farming. The missions, moreover, faced the perennial problem of the "brain drain"; well-qualified teachers were tempted away by higher salaries to take up jobs in government service or with commercial firms as clerks and interpreters.

The resources of the mission societies were limited. Even if they had been more plentiful, backward communities could in fact absorb only a limited amount of training. At the outset of evangelical en-

[3] Kenneth D. Kaunda, *Zambia Shall Be Free: An Autobiography* (London, 1962; New York, 1963), p. 9.

deavor there was usually an initial period of resistance when missionaries had to overcome fears and resentments and few Africans wished to be taught. Learning usually started with a key group, often situated at either the top or the bottom of the African social hierarchy. In states such as Barotseland, where pioneer missionaries labored with the consent of an intelligent and adaptable aristocracy eager to acquire the intellectual techniques of the West, the upper classes at first wished to monopolize education for themselves and excluded the slaves. In "stateless societies" or among people with weakly defined political authority, the missionaries would often make their first converts among outcasts, runaway slaves, exiles, or old women without relatives, the *déracinés* of tribal society. Gradually the new learning would catch on. African headmen realized the value of the imported skills in their dealings with the white administration; labor migrants picked up the art of writing letters to their relatives at home. The missionaries helped to create a new class of literate Africans who came to see education as the passkey to prestige and privilege.

The great mass of the population, however, was at first little affected by the new learning. School syllabuses usually bore scant relationship to the needs of village society. Few African farmers could afford to keep their children at school for any length of time when the youngsters were needed to weed the parental gardens or look after the family cattle. Distance might present an insuperable problem. Poor peasants might not be able to afford school fees, however low these might be. Children could not do homework in crowded, poorly lit huts at home; there was also a universal lack of inexpensive reading material. The rate of educational turnover remained high; few children managed to go to more advanced grades; and those who did were much older than their European classmates overseas.[4]

On the economic plane too missionary teaching was limited in its results. Industrial training sometimes managed to enrich native economies that had already reached some degree of diversity. In Barotseland, for instance, early missionaries built improved houses or canals and popularized the use of iron nails. Elsewhere the new skills taught by Christian instructors made slow progress, for unless the whole way of life was changed in a village, together with its technology, the new arts could find little scope.

In the spiritual field missionary progress was equally slow. The mission churches made a number of sincere converts and produced some martyrs of true moral stature. But missionary teaching did not

---

[4] Similar difficulties, of course, were faced by the children of the less prosperous white settlers in mining townships with a fluctuating population and on lonely farms situated at great distances from the nearest schools.

usually strike deep roots in most Africans, who continued to live in their traditional environment. The tribesmen became acquainted with stories from the Bible and biblical terminology; the Bible was the one and only great literary production which Europeans made known over most of black Africa. Africans began to adopt biblical phrases to express their hopes and often also their political and social resentment of the new order; but it is uncertain how far African religious ideas were fundamentally changed by the new creed. The old gods continued to wage a tenacious underground battle; accustomed beliefs in the powers of ancestral spirits and the efficiency of witchcraft survived among vast numbers of converts. The missions, moreover, rarely succeeded in breaking down the family systems of rural Africans. Mission records were always full of complaints that even highly trusted teachers or evangelists had secretly taken a second wife or mistress or, as the whites put it, relapsed into sin. Polygamy remained the desired way of life among rural Africans, even though the great majority by necessity stayed monogamists.

In most parts of Africa the "heroic" period of missionary work ended some time during or shortly after World War I. Above all, there was a shift in the missionaries' own attitude. The early pioneers of the Gospel were men of an inflexible cast of mind, willing to make enormous personal sacrifices because they were convinced that they were fighting Satan and all his works and such a battle brooked no compromise. Geographical isolation may have helped to shield many missionaries in the bush from the more critical movements in contemporary Protestant theology. As time went on, living standards improved. It is perhaps not entirely fanciful to see some connection between a more liberal attitude toward the "heathen" and better communications and easier living conditions enjoyed by missionaries and other academic workers in Africa. The Pax Belgica or Pax Britannica became an established fact. The grimmer aspects of precolonial Africa gradually fell into oblivion. A new generation of missionaries came to Africa who no longer, like François Coillard, had to witness the plight of political offenders being thrown to the crocodiles in the Zambezi or their pupils' families being liquidated by the victorious faction in a civil war.

After World War I, missionary subscriptions from overseas began to drop, and missionaries became more anxious for financial support from the colonial administrations. The imperial administrations at the same time became more willing to support education for Africans. Here again the speed of advance differed greatly from one area of the continent to another. Much depended on the local metropolitan power or on the quality of the missionary societies in question. An equally important part was played by the social structure of the local African communities. Education thus made greater progress among people like the Ibo and the Ganda, where traditional society had already given many opportunities for individual advancement, than among rigidly stratified peoples.

On the Gold Coast the first education ordinance was enacted as early as 1882, only twelve years after the first British Education Act.[5] Although for many years the missions continued to provide the bulk of all schooling, the ordinance set new standards; in time an increasing proportion of educational cost was borne by the government, with the result that the system made steady advance, and the Gold Coast obtained an educational lead over many neighboring territories. After World War I public revenue began to rise in many territories; trusteeship ideas spread among administrators and even among a section of the European settlers in Africa. White men and black alike became more conscious of the economic and administrative value of mass literacy. Storekeepers wished to engage black clerks able to read and write and do simple sums; agronomists desired literate African demonstrators to help in conservation work; policemen asked for African detectives capable of drafting reports. Public subsidies to approved mission societies steadily increased; the colonial administration met a growing proportion of the missionaries' educational expenditure and insisted at the same time on more efficient performance. There was a more deliberate effort to adapt elementary education to local African conditions. Primary instruction spread more widely, with the more highly developed territories such as Southern Rhodesia, southern Nigeria, and Cameroun taking the lead, and backward regions such as Ethiopia and Mali at the end of the line.[6]

[5] John D. Fage, *Ghana: A Historical Interpretation* (Madison, Wis., 1959), p. 66.

[6] For comparative educational distribution maps of Africa see Guy Hunter, *The New Societies of Tropical Africa: A Selective Study* (London, 1962), pp. 240–241. In the field of primary education Southern Rhodesia had a particularly good record. By 1938 already more than 30 percent of African children between five and fifteen years of age attended schools of some sort. In many imperially administered colonies such as Nigeria and the Anglo-Egyptian Sudan, the average attendance was then under 5 percent and in Kenya and Bechuanaland between 10 and 15 percent. A generation later, in 1964, Southern Rhodesia had one of the highest ratios of children in primary schools on the continent of Africa. The following ratios of children at school to total population give an approximate comparison: Rhodesia, 1 in 6; Ghana, 1 in 8; Algeria, 1 in 12; Guinea, 1 in 24; Liberia, 1 in 40; Mali, 1 in 61; Ethiopia, 1 in 108. In 1964, 640,000 African schoolchildren were enrolled. Figures from *African Advancement in Rhodesia* (Salisbury, Southern Rhodesia, 1965), p. 14.

Educational philosophies differed widely from one country to another. The French aimed at creating a small Gallicized elite; they emphasized intellectual achievement and urban values. The Portuguese also believed in assimilation; they shared the preference of the French for teaching in the metropolitan tongue, but otherwise set their sights much lower and differed from the French in always using religious instruction as an integral part of scholastic education. The Belgians concentrated on primary and industrial training. The British adopted a more pragmatic approach and, subject to some general guidelines, allowed each of their dependencies to formulate its own policy. Their theory of education for Africa stressed the values of rural life and local rule. Primary school children carried on their studies in the vernacular. The real or supposed needs of the countryside received more emphasis than in the French-speaking colonies, though in practice the British colonies, especially those in West Africa, produced a larger number of partially Europeanized Africans, imbued to some extent with metropolitan values, than the supposedly assimilationist-minded French.

Despite these differences, there were broad similarities. Primary school education vastly expanded throughout Africa—especially after World War II—so much so that teachers could rightly speak of an educational revolution on the African continent. European languages became widely known; the printed word spread and put Africans in touch with new ideas. The schoolmaster, trained to literacy and accustomed to speaking in public and to organizing others, became a person of recognized standing. In many parts of Africa the first nationalist leaders were teachers. Education acquired great prestige as diplomas and degrees appeared to offer the only opportunity to a better future.[7] Secondary schooling, however, advanced more slowly and in many parts of Africa developed only after World War II. Progress after that was rapid, though again extremely uneven. Secondary schools grew up most rapidly in the more advanced portions of Africa, regardless of their forms of political rule. The wealthier territories on the West Coast, with their more ancient traditions of trade and urban life, headed the list, with the Gold Coast in the lead. Settler-ruled Southern Rhodesia went forward more quickly than Northern Rhodesia under the Colonial Office. The British colonies in the aggregate did best of all; the Belgians and French came second, with Ethiopia,

[7] In Sierra Leone, for instance, an overwhelming majority of African informants in a social survey agreed that education was the "best" thing the Europeans had brought to Africa, followed by radio, electricity, and so forth. Slavery, guns, bombs, and war were regarded as the "worst" things imported by the whites. See John Dawson, "Race and Inter-group Relations in Sierra Leone," Part I, *Race*, VI, No. 2 (October, 1964), 83–99, especially 93.

Somaliland, and the hinterland states of the western Sudan at the bottom of the chart. Generally speaking, the proportion of post–primary school pupils formed a small percentage of the school-going population. Nevertheless, by about 1957 the African territories between the Limpopo and the Sahara collectively could count well over 180,000 students in secondary and technical schools, a figure which would have both delighted and astonished educational pioneers of an earlier generation and which represented a major achievement in an area completely devoid of modern schools at the beginning of the imperial era.[8]

Education is an industry that consumes much of its own product. Schools train boys for the scholastic profession, among others, so that educational advance is apt to generate its own momentum. After World War II the cause of advanced education for Africa also gained massive support in the metropolitan countries and gathered to itself some of the idealism that had inspired missionaries to evangelize Africa in the Victorian age. Higher education in English-speaking Africa had begun earlier in a small way under ecclesiastical auspices. In 1827 the Church Missionary Society had founded Fourah Bay College in Sierra Leone. The school originally concentrated on the training of ministers and devoted most of its attention to the teaching of liberal-arts subjects. By 1875 Fourah Bay was presenting candidates for degrees at the University of Durham, England, and the small college thereby exercised a considerable influence on West Africa as a whole. In 1916 the South African Native College opened its doors at Fort Hare and offered courses for external degrees at the University of South Africa. During the interwar years the British founded additional

---

[8] Exact statistical comparisons are difficult, as classification and methods differed from territory to territory. According to the calculations contained in George H. T. Kimble, *Tropical Africa:* Vol. II, *Society and Polity* (Oxford, 1960), 107–133, the number of secondary school students more than tripled in Commonwealth tropical Africa during the first postwar decade, reaching over 75,000. In the Belgian Congo and Ruanda-Urundi there were some 50,000 pupils in postprimary schools of one sort or another by 1957. In French West and Equatorial Africa some 28,000 students attended secondary and technical schools. The figures for Mozambique and Angola stood at 23,000. In Liberia 2,600 students were enrolled in secondary and technical schools in 1958. The Ethiopian figure stood at less than 5,000. Between 1959 and 1960 Nigeria, with an estimated population of 37 million, had 48,398 pupils in secondary schools and 3,750 in technical schools. The corresponding figures for Ghana, with a population of perhaps 6,600,000, were 11,874 and 2,522; Senegal, with a population of perhaps 2,573,000, 8,356 and 2,207; Southern Rhodesia, with an African population of some 3,600,000, 3,300 and 1,406 African pupils; Northern Rhodesia, with an estimated African population of 3,500,000, 1,890 and 1,432.

colleges at Achimota near Accra on the Gold Coast, at Yaba near Lagos in Nigeria, and at Makerere in Kampala, Uganda. These institutions, however, could accommodate only a few students; most Africans in search of advanced courses went either to Britain or to South Africa, and not many Africans obtained a university education. The postwar advances in secondary education vastly increased the number of African students studying abroad. The colonial governments provided more bursaries; the British Parliament gave massive financial support under the Colonial Development and Welfare Acts for the expansion of existing universities or the creation of new ones.[9] London University took the lead in opening up this new academic frontier. The last decades of imperial rule in Africa, in fact, produced an intensive effort at academic colonization. Metropolitan institutions carved out new spheres of influence for themselves in tropical Africa, and wits scoffed that the more the empire contracted, the more London University expanded.[10]

In the French and Belgian territories university education developed at a slower pace, but there was a similar pattern of expansion under the patronage of metropolitan institutions. In 1953 the Institut des Hautes Etudes at Dakar received university status; its examinations were presided over by professors delegated from the universities of Bordeaux and Paris. The Belgians opened an institute of higher learning in 1954 at Lovanium near Léopoldville, affiliated with the Catholic University of Louvain. More and more European scholars looked for research and teaching jobs in Africa; experience in Africa became a recognized qualification for a growing number of posts in European and American universities, and returning academic expatriates helped to bring about changes in metropolitan ways of thought concerning Africa.

All the new African universities owed their origins to Western initiative. They generally displayed both the strengths and the weaknesses of the liberal European intellectuals who filled most of their teaching posts and administrative appointments. All the new universities tried to carry European academic traditions to Africa. However

---

[9] Between 1945 and 1955 more than £3,700,000 was made available for institutions of higher learning in British tropical Africa. In addition, an allocation of £1,250,000 was made for the University College of Rhodesia and Nyasaland. For a more detailed account of these various problems, see Great Britain, *Higher Education: Report of the Committee . . . under the Chairmanship of Lord Robbins, 1961–63,* Cmnd. 2154.

[10] For a critical essay on British university expansion see Sir Eric Ashby, *African Universities and Western Tradition* (Godkin Lectures at Harvard University; London, 1964).

much expatriate university lecturers might criticize the alleged dangers of ethnocentric value judgments in other spheres of life, they were determined to preserve Western standards of scholarship and academic salaries in their own bailiwicks. University teachers generally sympathized with African independence movements and commonly argued in favor of rapid Africanization of administrative services at the expense of immediate efficiency. In the field of academic teaching, however, they insisted on maintaining the levels of Louvain and London. By and large they preferred quality to quantity; they valued academic more than on-the-job training; they often also looked down upon other academic precedents, such as the American land-grant colleges, which had played such an important role in the United States. The white academic pioneers firmly believed in the rights of free teaching and research as well as in academic autonomy, but they did not always realize how fragile such ideals might prove in many of the "leveling" new nation states which they hoped to set up.

Immigrant teachers naturally transmitted to Africa curricula largely modeled on those of their own parent institutions and inevitably produced elites who had little in common with the mass of African peasants. This in itself would not have mattered had not so many intellectuals made the mistake of too closely identifying academic development and economic and political development. Many university teachers mistakenly believed that a territory's capacity for self-government could be reckoned by the number of its graduates, an assumption that would have hardly been understood by European nationalists of an older vintage. They often failed to appreciate that the man who writes a brilliant dissertation is rarely equipped to run a factory. British academics in particular sometimes adopted the Victorian gentry's contemptuous view of "trade"; sometimes they passed on this anticommercial cant to their pupils, most of whom looked for advancement in civil service or political careers rather than in entrepreneurial or managerial capacities. The overwhelming majority of African students, moreover, managed to study only with the aid of scholarships provided by colonial governments. The new educational programs therefore commonly had the unintended effect of linking education with government patronage in the students' minds, thereby strengthening the *étatiste* outlook on life among a new generation of graduates.

Europe made an equally great impact in the field of healing. When the whites first set foot in Africa, the indigenous population was tended by medicine men—herbalists and diviners. The medicine man's work was not only to prevent, diagnose, and treat disease, but also sometimes to smell out witches and give advice on a multitude of other problems facing individuals, clans, or tribes as a whole. Among the Bantu, medicine men, gorgeously arrayed in strange costumes, acted as detectives to search out witches and bring supposed culprits to trial by ordeal. They were expected to contact the ancestral spirits of their patients to find out what ailed the sick and to cast spells on their clients' rivals. African medicine and religion were closely bound together; the early missionaries therefore found the task of preaching Christianity doubly difficult. The African doctor was a shrewd botanist, but much of his therapy, like Dr. Faust's, depended on sympathetic magic. A patient with a weak back would be treated with a mixture of the powdered bones of a python's back, injected at the site of his pain. The muscles of a lion's heart were used to strengthen soldiers about to go into battle. Bantu healers were imagined to possess a healing spirit who would find the right remedies and thus wielded tremendous psychological influence. They could not, however, cure their patients of malaria, sleeping sickness, bilharziasis, hookworm, or similar parasitic diseases. They had no remedies for river blindness, conjunctivitis, tuberculosis, leprosy, rheumatism, epilepsy, diabetes, or congestive heart failure or for acute infections such as typhoid, pneumonia, and meningitis, which in many parts of Africa are still referred to modern doctors only after they have been unsuccessfully treated by medicine men. Despite all tales from the pens of journalists or thriller writers about mysterious and wonderful cures, little of scientific value has as yet come out of the Bantu medicine man's pharmacopoeia.[11] Disease thus confronted Bantu society with an insoluble problem, and the image of the hale and hearty tribesman was often just a storywriter's dream. In tropical Africa a very large number of people were, and still are, chronically ill from the hour they are born to the hour of their death, and their life expectancy is still low— about thirty-five years.

The first pioneers in the assault on disease were mission doctors. Men like James Stewart, a Scottish clergyman who obtained doctorates in both medicine and divinity, played a major part in the medical history of Africa. Such mission doctors tried to use the art of healing as an adjunct to evangelization; physicians like David Livingstone also made a significant contribution to the practice of tropical medicine.[12]

11 Michael Gelfand, *Proud Record: An Account of the Health Services Provided for Africans in the Federation of Rhodesia and Nyasaland* (Salisbury, Southern Rhodesia, 1960), pp. 1–4.

12 See, for instance, Michael Gelfand, *Livingstone the Doctor, His Life and Travels: A Study in Medical History* (Oxford, 1957).

But the sum total of their early endeavors was limited. Mission societies lacked both the men and the money for an extensive medical
campaign; progress came only with government subsidies and active
official intervention. Colonial health reform on a broader scale drew
its strength from the same blend of idealism and self-interest, of growing knowledge of applied science and widening administrative competence, which had inspired similar changes at home.

Seventeenth-century British governments had worried no more
about conditions on British slave ships than had the African chiefs
and traders who supplied the human merchandise. The eighteenth
and nineteenth centuries produced a new social consciousness which
found expression in a magnificent literature concerning social evils in
England. "Capitalist self-criticism" and parliamentary inquiries produced a wealth of documentation concerning sickness and poverty of
the kind not available for backward countries like Montenegro and
Ethiopia. Departmental reports and medical returns gave their own
twist to social research. Social critics in Britain and industrial critics
in general made copious use of this material, often overlooking both
the evils in poverty-stricken rural regions that lacked published data
and the fact that the willingness and ability of British governments to
furnish such data were in themselves an indicator of social progress.

Proconsuls like Cromer and Milner were heir to this humanitarian
tradition and shared many assumptions of left-wing reformers at home;
conversely, many early Fabians were convinced imperialists. The
European imperialists exported their social conscience to Asia and
Africa, where sickness and poverty had previously been regarded as
part of man's unalterable fate. From its inception the new imperialism
contained an element of self-criticism incomprehensible to any traditional African ruler. By the early twentieth century all metropolitan
governments felt accountable to public opinion at home for social
conditions in their dependencies. They began to use established metropolitan techniques for eliciting information through departmental
returns, statistical abstracts, and commission reports. The more advanced governments not only promoted such research, but also paid
for its publication. The volume of official literature available on the
conditions of any one colonial territory thus itself became an indicator
of the ruling power's willingness to promote reform, yet this very
literature provided the critics of such a government with more ammunition. The British especially excelled at investigations of this kind.
Local administrators had to produce details on subjects such as mortality in African mines; archivists and filing clerks stored this information; government printing presses put the data into circulation.

Successive ministries in London, spurred on by parliamentary criticism, then proceeded to investigate, castigate, and legislate.

Belgian and French officials developed a similar paternalistic outlook, and throughout much of colonial Africa pressure from the metropolitan authorities became a major factor in promoting reforms, sometimes against the inclinations of the men on the spot. Large concerns like the British South Africa Company wished to avoid criticism; the directors themselves were open to the very humanitarian and trusteeship arguments which animated the company's critics. Financial magnates, moreover, realized that there was a link between profits and productivity, that disease-ridden, ill-fed African workmen were not a cheap source of labor. By and large the bigger concerns, with their metropolitan connections and their greater capital resources, had a consistently better record in health matters than small and under-capitalized ventures. Before World War I the British South Africa Company, for instance, exerted pressure on overseas subsidiaries to correct poor conditions. In addition, substantial local European populations formed influential pressure groups.

The history of white settlement in Africa has frequently been written in terms of simple class struggles between white men and black locked in combat for the good things of life. The realities of colonization were a good deal more complex. The Europeans soon came to realize that infections would not stop at the boundaries of native compounds; they did not want to hire sick people as cooks or nursemaids and wielded sufficient influence to make their voices heard. The Rhodesian whites produced their own form of trusteeship. Settler paternalism profoundly influenced medical development in Southern Rhodesia, where for a period of twenty-three years the Prime Minister was also the country's most distinguished surgeon.[13]

Colonization in Africa, moreover, proceeded at a time when Europe was producing a surplus of well-qualified, scientifically trained people willing to try their luck abroad. A perusal of the early medical registers in the Rhodesias and Nyasaland reveals a surprisingly large number of doctors with high qualifications, often men without sufficient capital to buy a practice at home; doctors such as these preferred to make their living in the colonies rather than "wait for dead men's shoes" in hospitals in London or Paris. White doctors and nurses, entomologists, chemists, and other scientific specialists carried out a long and little-publicized battle in African compounds and in the bush. They faced deadly diseases like sleeping sickness or leprosy

---

[13] See Lewis H. Gann and Michael Gelfand, *Huggins of Rhodesia: The Man and His Country* (London, 1964).

as a matter of course and collectively stand out as one of the most remarkable groups of people who ever left their home countries to shoulder the "white man's burden" overseas.

The Europeans' campaign against disease proceeded in several distinct phases. Colonial governments slowly increased the curative services. During the interwar years the number of hospitals gradually went up. The years following 1945 saw much swifter progress. Medical development in most cases was at first concentrated in the larger towns, but in time the campaign was extended to the backveld. In 1935 Southern Rhodesia inaugurated a new program of rural clinics in the reserves, where African patients received regular visits from government doctors and surgeons could perform minor operations in properly equipped theaters. With their red- or green-tiled roofs visible for miles away in the bush, these clinics formed the front line of medicine in the backveld; their presence itself helped to effect a major psychological revolution in the villagers' outlook on disease.

Other territories made similar progress. In 1924, for example, French West Africa was divided into medical districts with a chief medical officer at the head of each. The French built central hospitals in each colony for the purpose of supervising and supplying dispensaries and maternity clinics in outstations. These were served by European and African doctors; the more complicated cases went to central hospitals. By the beginning of World War II this system was fairly complete in the coastal colonies, though still seriously deficient in the hinterland, where the dispersed population often resisted treatment. In 1934 the French therefore set up their first mobile units; other colonizers, such as the Rhodesians, followed suit in motorizing medicine. The white man's skills in healing became more highly respected. In addition, medicine opened new professions to Africans. Educated men and women found employment as dispensary assistants, nurses, and laboratory technicians. In time numerous Africans completed their medical training and themselves took part in the assault on disease. The general impact of these curative services varied widely. An economically advanced settler territory such as Southern Rhodesia, animated in the medical sphere by a true sense of social responsibility, did comparatively well. Backward areas such as Nyasaland, where the European population was scanty, lagged behind. Even so, the bulk of colonial territories had an infinitely better record than India or China, with Southern Rhodesia well in the lead over independent states of older standing, such as the United Arab Republic.[14]

[14] According to the United Nations *Compendium of Social Statistics, 1963* (Statistical Papers, Ser. K, No. 2; New York, 1963), pp. 155–158, the following was the proportion of inhabitants per hospital bed in 1957 to 1959:

Without attempts at prevention the colonizers' efforts in curative medicine would have had little success. The growing number of hospitals and rural dispensaries might be impressive by relative standards, but in absolute terms the provision of medical facilities was uneven and varied greatly from territory to territory. Most hospitals remained concentrated in the cities; many villagers never saw a doctor throughout their lives. Worse still, the revolution in African life, the growth of townships and mining compounds, brought a host of new problems, so varied, and sometimes so disastrous in their impact, that a modern geographer has spoken of a great counterassault of disease in Africa.[15]

Newcomers—European, Indian, Arab, and Levantine—brought in sicknesses from abroad. Africans traveling by railway and motortruck spread respiratory and venereal infections from the city to the village. The spread of disease was not a new story. Africa had already witnessed considerable population movements in precolonial days; disease had never been stationary. When the Kololo, a conquering horde from the healthy uplands of South Africa, moved into the fever-ridden Zambezi valley, they were struck down by malaria and its concomitant, blackwater fever, which they probably could resist little better than Europeans. But the construction of roads and railroads made people infinitely more mobile, and the geography of disease probably changed much more rapidly than in earlier days. Within the memory of living man, bilharziasis, a waterborne infection carried by a snail, has spread into Southern Rhodesia and now menaces South Africa. Sleeping sickness has similarly spread from Uganda to the Congo and from there to the two Rhodesias.

United States	110
Southern Rhodesia	230
United Arab Republic	510
Tanganyika	590
Nyasaland	790
Mali	1,110
Ghana	1,700
China (Mainland)	1,800
India	2,200

According to more recent figures from *This Is Southern Rhodesia* (ISP No. 7; Salisbury, Southern Rhodesia, 1964), comparative figures for other African countries are as follows:

Southern Rhodesia	250
Kenya	660
Ghana	1,100
Sudan	1,100
Sierra Leone	1,550
Ethiopia	3,500
Liberia	4,000

[15] Kimble, *Tropical Africa: II, Society and Polity*, 172–174.

Until the advent of modern science, technology, and administrative skills, the city has always been one of mankind's greatest potential killers. Tudor London, or for that matter medieval Timbuktu, may have been picturesque to look at, but Tudor London was a cesspool of disease, where probably more people died than were born. When Tudor statesmen unsuccessfully tried to stem the interminable growth of the capital, they were not acting as romantic proponents of the rural way of life; they clearly realized that the city was a danger to health and that London consumed human lives. Pioneering townships in Africa took an equally grim toll from both white and black inhabitants. Salisbury, an early European settlement in Southern Rhodesia, started off as a collection of shacks, where the pioneers suffered from dysentery, malaria, and all sorts of other afflictions. Poor sanitation and inadequate drainage similarly made early white settlements in Northern Rhodesia a paradise for the anopheline mosquito; Europeans suffered even more heavily from disease than Africans, and the white death rate was comparable to the losses an army might sustain in wartime.[16]

Africans were not incapacitated by malaria and blackwater fever to the same extent as Europeans, but they encountered a host of other problems; they lacked the white man's resistance to tuberculosis and fell victim to all sorts of respiratory diseases. New food habits, acquired in urban surroundings, proved deleterious to health. African beer, brewed from corn, sorghum, or similar ingredients, and a diet of beef, maize, and relish contained protective elements and had greater nutritional value than imported white bread, buns, syrup, and lemonade. Rapid urbanization created an ever-present housing problem. Conditions in the villages were, of course, far from ideal. African kraals provided a ready shelter for malaria-bearing mosquitoes and for the tampans responsible for relapsing fever, but beehive-shaped huts, made of mud and thatch, were at least easy to construct. There was less overcrowding than in the towns; people spent more time in the open air and sunshine and were less exposed to tuberculosis than in urban slums. Newcomers to the towns, on the other hand, usually had to crowd into a small space, and health problems got even worse as labor migrants tried to eke out their scanty incomes by subletting accommodations to kinsmen and friends.[17] Cities also introduced

[16] According to the figures compiled by Michael Gelfand, the European death rate in northwestern Rhodesia stood at 64 per 1,000 between 1904 and 1905. The figures greatly improved subsequently; by 1908 the death rate had dropped to 25.71 per thousand.

[17] But this extra source of income also enabled the householders to buy more food and to build up resistance to diseases. Tuberculosis sometimes increased in new hygienic African townships because the family had less money for food.

sanitation problems of tremendous proportions. Health now depended on such unromantic factors as sewage, toilets, and clean water supply, on the provision of adequate heating, and on preventive measures such as the spraying of ponds to wipe out mosquitoes.

In many ways the history of modern Africa centered more on the provision of drains than on showier subjects like political parties and parliaments. Public health depended on the creation of a complex administrative and medical framework which proved beyond the abilities of all pioneering administrations. Most early mines and townships were a standing menace to health and, like early London, produced a biological deficit by destroying more lives than they produced.[18]

The battle began with measures against individual diseases, and the first major breakthrough was the victory over malaria. Throughout the nineteenth century the anopheline mosquito posed a much greater threat to white penetration in Africa than any number of spears and muskets. Success came in sight only when, in the late 1890s, Ronald Ross, a famous British medical man, discovered how mosquitoes transmitted the protozoa responsible for the disease. Starting with the main urban and mining centers, the colonial authorities began to clean up stagnant pools, eliminate breeding places of the anopheline mosquito near the main settlements, and spread more knowledge concerning general hygiene.[19] The main battle was subsequently extended to suppress afflictions such as smallpox, and by the end of World War II the colonizers could look back to a record of considerable achievement in the struggle against communicable sicknesses.[20]

In a wider sense, however, health depended on an infinitely larger number of factors, especially on general labor conditions of Africans both on the move and in employment. Migrant workers are always exposed to health risks, no matter where. Polish farmhands doing seasonal labor on East Prussian estates and Mexican *braceros* harvesting crops in California create all kinds of problems for the medical administrations of the countries concerned. But industrially advanced nations like Germany and the United States possessed medical infra-

[18] According to the figures provided by Raymond L. Buell, *The Native Problem in Africa*, II (New York, 1928), 35, the population of Dakar in 1925 stood at 34,000. The death rate then amounted to 32.79 per 1,000 and the birthrate to 31.08 per 1,000.

[19] See, for instance, Michael Gelfand's two works *Tropical Victory: An Account of the Influence of Medicine on the History of Southern Rhodesia, 1890–1923* (Cape Town, 1953) and *Northern Rhodesia in the Days of the Charter: A Medical and Social Study, 1878–1924* (Oxford, 1961).

[20] For example, the Northern Rhodesian Copper Belt was "cleaned up" from the early 1930s on; similar progress was achieved in many parts of the Congo and the West Coast.

structures of a type completely absent in Africa. Many African labor migrants, moreover, had to cover great distances to get to their places of work. In the early stages of colonization there were no mechanized means of transport; there were no rest houses. Would-be miners might have to face hostile tribesmen, robbers, or wild animals along the way. Even so, the lure of foreign employment proved strong, and as early as the late 1870s the diamond mines at Kimberley, for instance, attracted adventurous men from areas as far away as Barotseland. For many years conditions were bad in the compounds and worse on the road to work. Black migrants seeking work with African farmers in Uganda or in West Africa met similar difficulties; there were no welfare provisions; there were no facilities for people in transit; disease and hardship took a heavy toll of life.

Improvements began at the bigger mines. South African capitalists in the early 1900s organized bodies such as the Witwatersrand Native Labour Association, which provided transport, food, and medical inspection for recruits and also organized saving schemes. Southern Rhodesia soon followed suit; so did the mines in the Belgian Congo, with the purely agricultural countries consistently lagging behind in their care of workers on the move. The larger mines similarly pioneered improved health conditions for the men placed in jobs. They had more money to look after their employees; vast aggregations of people in the compound were more visible to social and health reformers than scattered groups of farmhands, whether they were working on white-owned estates in Rhodesia or on black-owned fields in Uganda. The early mines in Africa usually had a horrendous death rate. In the pioneering days of Rhodesia, for instance, compound managers wrongly thought that African laborers living in pole-and-daga huts and eating the same kind of food as in the villages—maize with relish and some occasional meat—would keep as fit as they had in their kraals. The sudden influx of large numbers of men, working much harder than before, living under strange conditions without their wives' care, and crammed into overcrowded quarters with poor ventilation and inadequate washing facilities, resulted in mortality figures that shocked the most hard-boiled. Food might be adequate in quantity, but since the men had no one to collect herbs, it turned out to be deficient in vitamin content, and many men reported sick with scurvy. The biggest killer of all was pneumonia, which resulted in one-third of all deaths. During the first decade of the 1900s, however, the Rhodesians managed to effect a major revolution. The administration insisted on improved scales of food and proper hospital and sanitary facilities, as well as medical inspection, safety precautions, and compulsory rest days, with the result that the black workers' death rate showed a dramatic drop.[21] Southern Rhodesia also developed an efficient system of labor inspection and provided a much better system of safeguarding its workers than was available in the French and Portuguese colonies, in Kenya, Uganda, and the Gold Coast, not to speak of economic backwaters like Liberia.[22] Improvements gradually spread north; the copper mines of the Belgian Congo and Northern Rhodesia similarly proved model employers, the Northern Rhodesian mining magnates going to much trouble to avoid the errors made during the earlier stages of industrialization in South Africa.

The total effect of these measures on Africa as a whole is hard to assess. Conditions differed from one town to another, from city to countryside, and from territory to territory. A great deal depended on municipal policies, urban legislation, and welfare laws, subjects too broad to be included here. There is no doubt, however, that mortality figures greatly decreased. In the more highly developed territories African life expectancy began to go up, with Southern Rhodesia leading over an established Latin American country like Mexico, and Mexico in turn doing slightly better than Ghana and Northern Rhodesia. The net reproduction rates of the more advanced territories also showed a tremendous upswing.[23] Africa experienced a vast rise in population, with some of the more favored territories doubling their numbers each generation. This demographic expansion constituted a major increase in economic potential. More hands became available to do additional jobs in backward countries, usually in great

[21] In Southern Rhodesia mortality figures dropped from 73 per 1,000 in 1907 to 28 per 1,000 in 1911 and 15.39 in 1925.

[22] In Uganda, for instance, imported migrant laborers had a death rate of 180 per 1,000 in 1925, primarily because they were not medically screened, nor were food and blankets given to African workmen in transit. For further comparisons see Peter J. Duignan, "Native Policy in Southern Rhodesia, 1890–1923" (doctoral dissertation, Stanford University, 1961), pp. 257ff.

[23] The following are comparative life expectancies at birth, calculated by C. A. L. Myburgh, quoted in Gelfand, *Proud Record,* pp. 52, 53:

Southern Rhodesia	48
Swaziland	48
Mexico	39
Ghana	38
Northern Rhodesia	37

Myburgh's estimates for net reproduction rates of selected African countries were:

Southern Rhodesia	2.0
Northern Rhodesia	1.7
Swaziland	1.6
Ghana	1.5
Mozambique	1.1
Angola	1.0

need of more people. The growth in numbers also entailed a growth in what might be called the African people's real income. Modern economists have often failed to keep account of this factor and have measured economic progress only in terms of cash earned per head of population. This procedure, however, implies an important and generally unrecognized value judgment; it measures wealth in terms of cash. The vast increase in population brought about under the colonial aegis was caused by a striking fall in mortality figures, and this itself is a form of wealth. Africans obtained a longer average life expectancy, and hence a real increase in terms of man's universal proclivity to pay for the satisfaction of prolonging his existence. Whatever political disadvantages colonialism might possess, from the biological standpoint its record is one of the great success stories of modern history.[24]

[24] Peter T. Bauer, *Economic Analysis and Policy in Underdeveloped Countries* (Durham, N.C., 1957), p. 53.

18. African Townsmen

Cities are of ancient origin in certain parts of Africa, and problems of urbanization have long beset the continent. From early times the region south of the Sahara between Cameroun and the Ivory Coast saw the emergence of numerous towns as centers of states. The typical settlement pattern within this region was one of towns, often walled, and large villages, rather than one of dispersed homesteads. In addition, the trans-Saharan trade, riverine communications, and growing agricultural surpluses helped shape the pattern of urban life. Timbuktu's greatness rested largely on trade in such goods as gold, salt, kola nuts, and cloth.

> The great feature which distinguishes the market of Timbúktu from that of Kanó is the fact that Timbúktu is not at all a manufacturing town, while the emporium of the Háusa fully deserves to be classed as such. Almost the whole life of the city is based upon foreign commerce, which, owing to the great northerly bend of the Niger, finds here the most favored spot for intercourse, while at the same time that splendid river enables the inhabitants to supply all their wants from without; for native corn is not raised here in sufficient quantities to feed even a very small proportion of the population, and almost all the victuals are imported by water-carriage from Sansándi and the neighborhood.[1]

The cities of Hausaland made a great name for themselves as centers of handicraft, and the products of Hausa smiths, metalworkers, dyers, tanners, and shoemakers found customers all over the western Sudan and as far afield as North Africa. Ancient East Africa developed a maritime civilization dependent on ocean commerce. By the time Portuguese navigators had penetrated into the Indian Ocean at the end of the fifteenth century, cities like Kilwa and Mombasa had be-

[1] Henry Barth, *Travels and Discoveries in North and Central Africa: Being a Journal of an Expedition Undertaken under the Auspices of H.B. Majesty's Government by Henry Barth, Ph.D., D.C.L.,* III (New York, 1896), 357.

come important entrepôts whose people carried on a far-flung trade with Arabia, Persia, and China.

Another type of city was the "tribal" capital, for example the kibuga of Buganda. The kibuga formed the royal seat, the administrative and ritual center where the sacred fire and drums were kept and where matters of dispute were brought before a court of appeal. The kibuga had an impressive agglomeration of buildings, constructed of cane and rattan, divided by well-maintained streets, and centering on the royal palace. From the economic point of view, it was neither quite a village nor a town. At the height of its splendor the capital may have contained something like 40,000 people, but the city dwellers still depended on agriculture. Chiefs built high fences around their estates. Within these enclosures retainers cultivated gardens, but urban crops had to be supplemented by food brought in from country estates.[2]

Settlements such as these, however impressive in their setting, housed only tiny proportions of the population in precolonial Africa. Most African societies lacked sufficient surplus to maintain urban life; communications imposed enormous problems, and even the most prosperous cities remained limited in size. European technology brought about a major change. In many parts of Africa agriculture became more productive than before. Steamships, railways, and motortrucks facilitated the movement of people, of manufactures, and of food. Medical science gradually reduced some of the more serious health hazards. The new rulers had the means of deliberately planning new settlements; they imported new techniques of architecture, city building, and administration. They could also supply settlements over long distances. The colonial era thus saw a swift expansion of urban settlements both along the African coastlines and in the hinterland; the city in many ways became the colonizers' most characteristic contribution to the new Africa.

The new cities, like the more ancient settlements, can be divided into three major types. There were trading posts, created by the needs of maritime or overland commerce. There were mining communities, whose importance arose from the proximity of ore bodies in payable quantities. There were administrative centers, whose main industry was government. There was a fourth type of settlement—the military post, set up to protect a trading center or to guard a remote frontier against barbarian incursions. This type of settlement assumed some importance in West Africa, where European slave traders built strong castles such as Elmina or Gross Friedrichsburg on the coast. The

[2] Peter C. W. Gutkind, *The Royal Capital of Buganda: A Study of Internal Conflict and External Ambiguity* (The Hague, 1963), pp. 9–21.

South African and Algerian frontiers also produced their species of army settlement. But over the greater part of sub-Saharan Africa, pacification came relatively swiftly; the Europeans did not face as many turbulent frontiers as their predecessors in medieval Europe. The citadel city never attained the same historical importance as it did, say, on the ancient Anglo-Welsh border, and in the typical colonial center plain clothes always predominated over the military uniform.

On the West Coast of Africa, Dakar stands out as an example of a new trading center. Geographically, the city holds a commanding position on the route from Western Europe to Brazil and to South Africa, and its harbor affords a safe anchorage for the largest ships engaged in the South Atlantic trade. The main French center here was Gorée in the harbor area of Dakar, an ancient slave-trading post situated on an almost waterless island. In 1857 the French decided that they needed proper port facilities, and marines landed from the *Jeanne d'Arc* on the peninsula where Dakar now flourishes. There were only a few indigenous villages in the area, and the inhabitants eked out a meager existence from fishing and pastoral farming. The French compensated the local people for the loss of their pasture rights and constructed a fort. In 1862 they set to work on a port; four years later the Messageries Impériales opened a regular steamboat service.[3] Dakar subsequently became the center of an important railway system which connected the port with Saint-Louis in the north and the hinterland of Senegal and Mali to the east. Dakar also developed into a major base port, an "African Gibraltar," as well as one of the greatest commercial ports in the French empire, ranking after Le Havre and Marseilles. In 1902 the French designated Dakar the capital of French West Africa in succession to Saint-Louis. The city grew rapidly, and just over a hundred years after its initial occupation the settlement had expanded into a great, bustling seaport with a population of nearly 400,000 people, a living monument to French imperial enterprise and African cooperation.

Johannesburg, Africa's greatest mining city, lies south of the Limpopo River in the Transvaal province of South Africa. Technically, the growth of Witwatersrand falls outside the geographical scope of this book. Johannesburg, however, stands out as the most characteristic example of a Western megalopolis in Africa—with all its virtues and its vices. The experiences of the Rand profoundly influenced city planning as far away as the Northern Rhodesian Copper Belt, so that Johannesburg merits inclusion in this brief review.

[3] Claude Faure, *Histoire de la presqu'île du Cap Vert et des origines de Dakar* (Paris, 1914), pp. 101ff., and Jacques Charpy (ed.), *La fondation de Dakar (1845-1857-1869)* (Paris, 1958).

In 1886 a traveler passing across the Witwatersrand saw nothing but the bleak undulating veld, with a few Boer homesteads in the dips and a small group of prospectors' tents on the ridges. Then the gold seekers struck it lucky. In the following year chemists perfected the McArthur Forrest process of treating tailings by the cyanide process, and gold from the deep-level mines could now be profitably extracted. By another fortunate chance, coal was found in abundance on the Rand itself, and the diggers were saved the prohibitive cost of carting coal inland. The mining settlement soon turned into a bustling, gold-hunting city, ill-controlled by the archaic Boer administration of the Transvaal. White miners and merchants, teachers and technicians, pickpockets and prostitutes flocked to the settlement; within a few years the windswept camp had metamorphosed into the financial center of South Africa. The city also acquired a huge population of migrant black workers. Englishmen, Australians, Zulu, Americans, and Indians poured in, and Johannesburg became the most polyglot community of southern Africa.

The city grew rapidly, and today numbers more than 1 million people and covers more than 90 square miles. Johannesburg is a city of stark contrasts, of wealth and poverty, of a sophisticated intellectual life and of crime, with some of the worst *bidonvilles* of Africa and also some of the finest and most progressive black African housing schemes on the continent. Gold mining attracted a large white and black labor force; in addition, Johannesburg became the greatest trading, manufacturing, and banking center in Africa. For political reasons Johannesburg never attained the status of a capital. The Transvaal continued to be governed throughout most of its history from Afrikaans-speaking Pretoria, whose people usually looked down on the *uitlanders* in the mining metropolis. The Union of South Africa subsequently adopted a queer arrangement which reflected the internal division between English-speaking and Afrikaans-speaking white South Africans. Cape Town became the seat of the Union's Parliament; Pretoria turned into the center of government for South Africa as a whole.

For another example of an artificial capital we must turn north to what is now Zambia. After 1900 small groups of European farmers, traders, and prospectors made their way from Southern Rhodesia and South Africa into the thinly populated plateau of northwestern Rhodesia, then the extreme northern limit of the South African settlement frontier. Livingstone, a small railway center on the Zambezi River, became the natural port of entry and the seat of the local administration. With the opening of the Copper Belt in the 1920s, the territory's whole center of gravity shifted to the north. Livingstone became more and more unsuitable as a capital. His Excellency the Governor was conducting the affairs of the country from a converted billiard room in a former backwoods hotel roofed with corrugated iron which caught the rays of the tropical sun and turned the place into an oven. The British might have been expected to put the center of government into the Copper Belt, into the economic heart of the country. Instead they often segregated government from trade, a practice which in Nyasaland had led the country's first commissioner-general to set up his headquarters in the beautiful mountain country at Zomba, away from the quarrelsome missionaries and businessmen at Blantyre. After lengthy investigations by Stanley Adshead, a prominent British town planner, the Northern Rhodesian authorities decided to create an artificial capital at Lusaka, in the heart of a European farming district, on the relatively cool, windswept plateau between the Zambezi and the Copper Belt. Lusaka was planned from the start as a government town; the city became a kind of backveld Canberra, centering on a big unattractive secretariat, which—as in so many British territories— stood out as the symbol of colonial power. Planning was based on the assumption that Lusaka would be the country's administrative, social, and cultural center, where industrial development would be strictly limited.[4] The new capital nevertheless pushed ahead and subsequently attracted a number of industries, displaying that pervasive tendency of so many modern cities to acquire momentum of their own and to attract more and more people once basic services have been established.

On the surface the new cities put up by the colonizers had little in common. They varied in geographical location and economic purpose; they differed in appearance and character. The British-created cities generally displayed a marked tendency to sprawl; the French and Portuguese often held onto the older Latin tradition of a closely planned township. But the vast majority of these urban settlements displayed one major characteristic. They were new creations; they arose where nothing had been before. They differed sharply, therefore, from older settlements like Kano or Timbuktu in West Africa. The walled cities of the Sudan, like those of medieval Europe, had grown up slowly over the centuries; the majority of their people had lived all their lives within its bastions. Their inhabitants made their living as small-scale artisans and traders or served the local courts and drew their incomes from provincial tributes, but the scale of enterprise, economic or administrative, was always limited. Many West African townsmen, like the citizens of Western medieval centers, kept a stake

[4] Diary, 1930, by Professor Stanley D. Adshead (copy in AD 1; Historical Manuscripts Collection, National Archives of Rhodesia, Salisbury).

in the country and farmed their gardens for part of the year. The new townships were rarely built on indigenous foundations; few of the older centers managed to become the nucleus of a great modern city like London or Frankfurt. There were, of course, exceptions. Zanzibar, an ancient port, still conducts a valuable maritime trade. Ibadan, the largest indigenous city in black Africa, has become a modern provincial capital in Nigeria, housing government departments and a university as well as offices for cocoa brokers, transport contractors, and insurance firms.[5] But African cities are in the main of recent origin. Chicago was a flourishing town more than fifty years before the first prospectors struck gold at Johannesburg; Detroit is older by a century and a half than Dakar.

The new African cities had a tremendously high rate of growth.[6] The number of people, in fact, generally exceeded the number of available houses and jobs. Secondary industries remained confined to a few centers such as Salisbury or Dakar; most of the new urban settlements, like revolutionary Paris at the end of the eighteenth century, thus suffered from what might be called "underindustrialization." Work was often hard to find, and wages were low because unskilled labor was abundant. The new cities were ringed with shanty towns, hurriedly thrown together out of planks, corrugated iron, or anything else that came to hand. Municipal services such as lighting, sanitation, and sewage disposal often remained inadequate, and social-welfare services were nonexistent. Whores, touts, and thugs found their way into the new cities. In addition, the towns developed another kind of parasitism as rural people came to live with a wealthier relative in the city for varying periods of time and in fact became his dependents. This form of clientage had in a sense some social utility. It served as a rough and ready method for redistributing African incomes in favor of the very poor and furnished some kind of social assistance for those most in need. But private patronage often served as a substitute for social services which the governing powers failed to provide in an adequate fashion. Ties of extended kinship at the same time threw a great burden on those most likely to invest their money in new enterprises and may have acted as a brake on the emergence of an indigenous African bourgeoisie.

[5] For a general discussion see Lucy P. Mair, *New Nations* (London, 1963), pp. 128–159.

[6] See, for instance, Thomas L. Hodgkin, *Nationalism in Colonial Africa* (London, 1956), p. 67. Between 1935 and 1955 Léopoldville in the Congo grew from 26,622 to 340,000 people. Elisabethville grew from 22,858 to 120,000 people. Dakar in 1936 had 92,000 inhabitants; in 1955 the figure stood at 300,000.

The new cities usually retained this makeshift character for a considerable length of time. Few of the original newcomers, white or black, looked upon the colonial townships as home. The early white miners on the Northern Rhodesian Copper Belt, for instance, simply wished to make enough money to return to Johannesburg or London at the end of their contract. They did at any rate mean to stay in wage employment, for European workmen had no other means of livelihood. The African newcomers, however, were exposed to an even greater pull. The vast majority looked upon mine work as a temporary job and resumed work on their ancestral fields when their spell in town was over. Hence African townsmen for long retained a stake in both the city and the countryside; they remained wanderers between two worlds, at home in neither.

Many factors combined to produce this social instability. The wage-workers who during the nineteenth century had drifted into the factories of Birmingham, Bordeaux, and Berlin had usually lost all their land; they rarely possessed any family acres to which they might return in their old age. Not so the black workers who manned the mines in Nkana or drove trucks in Kampala. The supply of land in the rural areas might be gradually diminishing, but in most parts of Africa many urban workers still retained some traditional rights in the villages, rights which they were loath to surrender. In many cases government policies also helped to delay the stabilization of labor. Throughout the 1930s and 1940s, for instance, the Northern Rhodesian authorities wished to prevent the growth of a permanent labor force on the Copper Belt. There was always the danger of a slump, and if a depression hit the country, miners—white and black— would do best by going back to their respective homes instead of saddling the administration with an unmanageable problem of providing unemployment insurance and other services. This policy contained two contradictory aspects. It was a protective device, and as such was for many years supported by paternalists in the British Colonial Office and by the bulk of the missionaries, who wished to shield the black people from being exploited and debauched in the cities. It also had an economic aspect. Rhodesia, like most other African territories, possessed neither the administrative machinery nor the material resources to care for large numbers of unemployed Africans in the towns; in the rural areas the workless at least would keep alive. It seemed less troublesome and less expensive, therefore, to let the system of migrant labor continue.

Many governments or municipal administrations tried to limit the number of immigrants. White-settled territories like the Rhodesias developed an elaborate system of passes, designed to control the number of black newcomers in the towns. Africans had to carry all sorts of documents to identify the bearer. Useful as these might be in some cases as a means of protection against the withholding of wages on the part of dishonest employers, passes nevertheless became a bitter sort of grievance. The system, of course, was not in any way peculiar to Africa. In the beginning of the last century French workers had been obliged to carry the *livret,* a kind of police visa, which recorded the bearer's changes of address, his wages, and his reason for leaving his job. Germans still have to register with each change of residence; workers in Soviet Russia carry internal passes. But passes were no more acceptable to Africans than to their fellow workers elsewhere; passes moreover restricted the mobility of labor and in that sense might form an instrument of exploitation.

Furthermore, most colonial administrations insisted on residential segregation between white and black. In Southern Rhodesia this policy had originally derived from the firm conviction that white-created cities like Salisbury should be regarded as European enclaves and that African laborers should be nothing but temporary sojourners in these communities. Residential segregation is not a system peculiar to colonial Africa; the independent West African cities of old used to set aside areas a little distance from the main settlement—outside the walls if there were circumvallations—where foreign traders had to live.[7] In Africa, residential segregation was not felt as a grievance so long as the social and economic gaps between white and black remained almost unbridgeable. The system, however, led to bitter opposition once African businessmen or professional people began to rise in the social scale. Forced to live cheek by jowl with illiterate migrant laborers, African schoolteachers and traders found difficulty in maintaining the very middle-class standards which the Europeans had introduced. African and European traders alike could not freely invest in land and business sites; the residential color bar continued to interfere with the free operation of the market, and Africans especially found just cause for complaint against this exploitation.

In a city like Salisbury the African migrant laborers' problems were made worse by social and industrial obstacles to their advancement. Urbanization in general acted as a solvent of traditional social distinctions. The states of Sine and Saloum in Senegal had been traditionally divided into different classes—warriors, free peasants,

---

[7] In fifteenth-century England, Hanseatic merchants in London occupied quarters of their own, called the Steelyard, where they administered their own affairs and found refuge in case of trouble.

artisans, and slaves. Members of the artisan caste could not marry outside their status group; the warrior class held most of the positions of honor.[8] In a city, however, such distinctions made little sense; the artisan might rise in the social scale and leave the nobleman behind. The city thus produced a host of new social tensions. The new administrative creations rarely evoked a common patriotism or a sense of municipal pride. The different racial groups—Europeans, Indians, Lebanese, and Africans—were for the most part determined to pursue their accustomed ways of life in the new setting. The great majority sought their friends, and to an even greater extent their wives, only within their own racial groups.

Economic conflicts often strengthened these new tensions as favored national groups tried to hold on to positions of vantage once gained. Resistance on the part of established communities to the absorption of more recent immigrants is again not something peculiar to a colonial situation. A modern sociologist investigating the position of foreign white labor migrants on the European Continent has come to the sorrowful conclusion that "there is no country of reception in Europe which does not report considerable resistance to migrants on the part of the host community. The 'no coloured' stipulation in accommodation advertisements in Britain finds an echo in the rider 'no Italians' in similar columns in the Swiss press."[9] Be this as it may, the African labor migrant, unable to do what he liked on his own, became subject to both physical and psychological exploitation. The Rhodesian African who made money could not invest his savings in urban land on the same terms as his European competitor; the worker who was prevented from taking his family to the township suffered psychologically.[10]

In many parts of Africa these tensions became immensely magnified. In the white-settled areas of Rhodesia, for instance, it was European artisans who came as urban pioneers and filled the skilled jobs. Most of them had a difficult time in the early days. They belonged to a labor force that was unstable; they drifted from mine to

[8] See Martin A. Klein, "Sine-Saloum, 1847–1914: The Traditional States and the French Conquest" (doctoral dissertation, University of Chicago, 1964).

[9] Nadine Peppard, "Migration: Some British and European Comparisons," *Race,* VI, No. 2 (October, 1964), 103.

[10] Again this situation was by no means peculiar to Africa alone. "Dr. J. L. Villa found," the sociologist quoted above continues, "that 90 per cent of the maladjusted workers mentioned in his study [of Switzerland] had left their families behind in Italy and he made the point that the regulations in some countries, Switzerland in particular, restricting family immigration, were inhuman and should be relaxed." Peppard, "Migration," p. 104.

mine and from job to job; they were not entitled to unemployment benefits. Many years passed before the white immigrant came to look on the Rhodesian town as home, the place where he intended to spend his old age as well as his working life. The European reacted the same way workers all over the world had done in comparable situations; he tried to carve out a protected fief for himself on the labor market. He insisted on traditional workers' demands such as "equal pay for equal work"; he rejected the "fragmentation of jobs." In the Rhodesian situation this policy probably helped to slow down African industrial advancement and in the long run may well have restricted employment opportunities for white men as well. The gulf between white and black workers was further emphasized by sharp differences in their respective wages. Black unskilled labor was relatively easy to get; it was cheap, albeit inefficient, as long as the African remained a commuter between township and kraal. White skilled labor could be obtained only at relatively high rates; no one was willing to work in a colony where the cost of living was necessarily high and where many amenities of older countries were lacking unless he received a good deal more money. However, many employers were quite satisfied with this arrangement, since it was obviously cheaper to employ skilled men who came voluntarily from elsewhere than to train backward African villagers who were still tied to their old homes.

European immigration was, of course, double-edged in its effects. The newcomers stimulated enterprise by importing new skills and creating new opportunities. Well-organized European trade unionists in Rhodesia, moreover, enforced concessions such as the eight-hour day or improved safety devices in factories; these gains also benefited their black fellow workers. The expanding cities provided many new opportunities for Africans. The new towns, on the other hand, produced bitter social tensions which, on a lesser scale, were paralleled within African society itself. On the Northern Rhodesian Copper Belt, for instance, Nyasalanders had traditionally enjoyed a lead. Missionaries were at work in the Lakeside Protectorate much earlier than in the neighboring territories. Nyasaland, like Sierra Leone on the West Coast, became an exporter of literate labor. Nyasa clerks and interpreters emigrated to the Copper Belt and got better jobs than their less tutored competitors from, say, the Bemba country. Many Northern Rhodesian–born Africans thus complained of favoritism shown by Nyasa clerks to other Nyasalanders, even though this kind of ethnic favoritism never managed to congeal into legislation. To conclude, the greatest obstacle to permanent urbanization arose from the African's traditional stake in the village lands.

This was a factor of even greater importance than racial legislation or racial prejudice. Kampala in Uganda, for example, had no permanent white-settler population, no apartheid laws. But after two generations of town life most black workers still left their wives behind in the rural areas; concubinage and prostitution were rife in the city, and settled family life was as rare as in an old-fashioned California mining camp.[11]

For all its drawbacks, the town also acted as a liberating force. Wages were generally low, but the city provided an opportunity to earn money—enough to pay a bride price, help one's family out of difficulties, or buy a bicycle or a sewing machine. The city saw new forms of crime and vice, but it also provided a refuge for people tired of the limitations and the boredom of rural life. The city produced a new kind of anonymity, where a man would no longer have to worry to the same extent about witchcraft accusations from jealous neighbors or from talebearing about his private life. The city did produce slums, but many African town dwellers also became accustomed to houses far more durable and comfortable than those which their ancestors had fashioned from sticks, straw, and beaten earth. Housewives no longer took their washing to streams infested by crocodiles or bilharzia; they turned on a water tap or went to a well. Much of the new city housing might be of the most contemptible quality; but the better kind of dwelling at least had a chimney, and families no longer had to crowd around an open fire in a smoke-filled hut, as in the reserve. As national incomes rose, the more advanced territories such as Southern Rhodesia and the Belgian Congo made considerable progress in slum clearance and put up a number of model townships for Africans. Municipal sanitation made great advances. Even the worst slums ceased to be subject to epidemics of the kind that used to decimate European cities in the seventeenth century or even later.

African townsmen moreover fashioned a host of new organizations, ranging from burial societies to labor unions and political parties. Factories and workshops transmitted a vast new range of skills unknown in tribal days. The cities produced new norms of conduct and a new kind of public opinion. The city usually had the best schools; it generally provided the best hospital services. The city offered new kinds of entertainment—from the very best to the very worst. The city also put new ideas into circulation; magazines, newspapers, and radio talk helped to create new opinions and a new and more radical climate of politics.

[11] See Aidan W. Southall and Peter C. W. Gutkind, *Townsmen in the Making: Kampala and Its Suburbs* (East African Studies, No. 9; Kampala, Uganda, 1956).

The total effect of this revolution is difficult to assess in purely numerical terms. Tropical Africa remained the least urbanized part of the world, with the smallest number of cities.[12] By the mid-1950s only a few African territories, mostly those situated on the West Coast, could boast of a fairly substantial African bourgeoisie. The lower middle class had somewhat greater strength, but even independent master craftsmen, contractors, bus owners, and shopkeepers generally formed only a tiny segment of the African population as a whole. The urban working class was very much larger, but by the mid-1950s the whole of colonial Africa probably numbered no more than 5 million wage earners. Even this figure does not refer to workers in the European sense, that is to say, to people wholly and continuously dependent on wages or salaries for a livelihood. Many African workers were still part-time peasants, and even so they amounted to only a small percentage of the population as a whole.[13]

The long-range effects of these changes nevertheless turned out to be of momentous importance. Second-generation townsmen especially began to improve their social status, rising from unskilled to semi-skilled, skilled, and even specialist occupations. Some black people rose in the administration, like Governor Félix Eboué, a French-speaking West Indian. Some became men of wealth, like Nnamdi Azikiwe, an early nationalist leader in Nigeria who made his name as a banker, company director, and newspaper owner, or Sir Milton Margai of Sierra Leone and E. M. L. Endeley of the Cameroons, both of them political men of consequence and well-known physicians in their private lives. *Stadtluft macht frei* ("town air makes free"), said a medieval German proverb, and in the twentieth century similar sentiments passed through men's minds all over Africa.

[12] According to George H. T. Kimble, *Tropical Africa:* Vol. I, *Land and Livelihood* (New York, 1960), 97–98, less than 10 percent of the people in tropical Africa in 1955 lived in communities of 5,000 or more. The territories where the percentage of urban people thus defined exceeded 10 percent were Eritrea, French Somaliland, Ghana, the two Rhodesias, Zanzibar, and possibly Ethiopia. In the Philippines the corresponding figure was about 25 percent, and in the United States, 60 percent. Only five cities had a population of more than 200,000.

[13] See Hodgkin, *Nationalism in Colonial Africa,* pp. 118–119. Hodgkin's figures exclude the Portuguese possessions. According to Hodgkin, the territory with the highest percentage of wage earners was Southern Rhodesia, with 24 percent. Then came Northern Rhodesia with 13 percent and the Belgian Congo (with Ruanda-Urundi) with 8.5 percent. The Gold Coast had 4.5 percent and French West Africa about 2 percent.

PART THREE

Decolonization

19. The Rulers Waver

The African townsman had a better chance of getting to know Western political ideas and Western forms of political organization than his cousin in the countryside. In most parts of Africa townsmen were the first to fight for a new political order. The temptation is great to project present-day history into the past and to write the annals of colonial Africa in terms of a ceaseless struggle on the part of black Africans against their white overlords; the truth is more complex. Initially, the great majority of newly educated African townsmen sided with their rulers and for the most part disapproved of or actively opposed tribal resistance movements. In the nineteenth century educated English-speaking West Coast Africans such as Bishop Samuel Adjei Crowther or Surgeon Major James Africanus Beale Horton saw colonial rule as a progressive force which would give a new chance to the poor and would deprive corrupt aristocracies of ill-deserved power.

Even the lower ranks of the educated hierarchy generally looked askance at the older tribal systems. In 1893, when the Matabele kingdom stood at the brink of war with the white settlers in Mashonaland (in what is now Rhodesia), Micka Nxobbe, an expatriate intellectual of Matabele descent, wrote to the Matabele king from the Transvaal strongly advising against hostilities. The Matabele, Nxobbe argued, should follow the example of the Basuto and place themselves under British protection. In addition, the Matabele ought to westernize their system of administration. "Better for you must want a clark and put them into ann office to make your right [to assist in the judicial administration]," Nxobbe wrote, in halting English, but with the firm conviction that the future lay with European-educated men like himself. "I am one of them. . . . Then you let the people build a big house for office and coming work. . . . If you got a high case with the nother [another] people, you send the case to England. . . . If you do not that you lose your country indeed."[1]

[1] Micka Nxobbe to Lobengula, March 3, 1893 (copy in WI 6/1/1; Historical Manuscripts Collection, National Archives of Rhodesia, Salisbury).

The emergent class of black teachers, evangelists, civil servants, and clerks realized for the most part that they were not as yet in a position to control the new state machinery. European rule was opening new prospects, new jobs, new opportunities for education unavailable in traditional Africa. The new African wanted equality with the white man; he rarely meant to go to war with his rulers. There were, of course, exceptions. In Muslim Africa, leaders like Mohammed bin Abdullah, the "Mad Mullah" (who fought against the British in Somaliland during the first two decades of the 1900s), could rally many supporters who were both learned in Islam and familiar to some extent with Western thought. During World War I, John Chilembwe, an educated African influenced by American Negro thought, unsuccessfully tried to set up a revolutionary theocracy in Nyasaland.[2] But the surprising thing about these rebels is not that they took to arms, but that for the most part they could make so little impact on the structure of imperial rule. During World War I the Allies fought a series of bitter campaigns against the Germans in Africa; the combatants could spare very few troops for police duties, yet the overwhelming majority of their subjects, educated or otherwise, did not attempt to revolt.

The postwar years witnessed new stirrings. In the Rhodesias and the Belgian Congo, for instance, prophets arose who proclaimed the end of the world and the liquidation of the white man's evil trinity of Church, state, and big business. According to some versions, American Negroes would land in Africa to liberate Africa. According to others, Jesus Christ himself would set up a new kingdom of freedom and justice; the white man's wealth would be given to the poor, and all true believers would come into their own. The Messianic element continued underground and strongly colored subsequent manifestations of African nationalism, but the bulk of the more educated people held themselves aloof. Educated French Africans such as Blaise Diagne, the first black deputy in the French Chamber, asked for reforms, equal opportunities with white men, and an end to discrimination, but Diagne meant to live under the Tricolor and end his days as a black Frenchman.[3]

Educated English-speaking Africans generally thought in similar terms. Speakers at pan-African congresses called on the colonial

[2] George Shepperson and Thomas Price, *Independent African: John Chilembwe and the Origins, Setting, and Significance of the Nyasaland Native Rising of 1915* (Edinburgh, 1958).
[3] Rupert Emerson, "Colonialism Yesterday and Today," in Kurt London (ed.), *New Nations in a Divided World: The International Relations of the Afro-Asian States* (New York, 1963), p. 8.

powers to put trusteeship principles into practice. As we have seen, they clamored for protection against exploitation, for better schools, for reforms in local government, and for African advancement in industry and administration. There was no thought of immediately liquidating all Western empires. European liberals shared these views; only an insignificant minority thought in terms of granting independence to all colonies; self-determination might be the ultimate goal of colonial policy, but self-determination lay in the dim and distant future. In fact, independent black countries such as Haiti and Liberia incurred a good deal of criticism from humanitarians abroad, and few whites wished to spread what they regarded as mulatto misgovernment throughout Africa.

Even World War II did not make much immediate difference. France and Belgium were overrun, but white rule, whether directed from Vichy, from the Free French headquarters in London, or from Léopoldville, remained undisturbed. The British looked upon Africa as a vast bastion for the defense of the world against Nazi aggression. Once the Germans invaded Russia, the Soviet Union had no desire to embarrass its British ally and to weaken the Western war effort by anticolonial agitation. The Africans themselves remained loyal to the imperial connection; huge numbers of black people voluntarily enlisted in the British forces and fought stoutly under the direction of British officers, many of them white settlers from Kenya and the Rhodesias. South Africa, and to a lesser extent Southern Rhodesia, also raised large formations comprised only of white fighting men; these gained numerous battle honors in countries as widespread as Ethiopia, Libya, and Italy. The military planners responsible for mobilizing these white units were quite willing to denude southern Africa of most of its troops and worried little about the possibility of black uprisings while the soldiers were fighting in some distant theater of war.

The postwar years, however, saw great changes. The British withdrew from India, Burma, Ceylon, and Palestine, but Africa was not affected to the same degree. Few British Labour men—not to speak of the Tory opposition—foresaw that within two decades after the German armistice the Union Jack would have disappeared from every African capital except Salisbury in Rhodesia and that by then the white Rhodesians would also be under heavy pressure from the mother country to hand over power to an African majority. The British Labour government of the late 1940s was much more concerned with pressing domestic economic problems than with African policies. The British were then facing a desperate economic situation. War had consumed much of their wealth; their cities were bombed;

half their merchant fleet was at the bottom of the sea. Many of
Britain's colonial and foreign investments had been sold to pay for the
war effort; former British dependencies such as India and Egypt had
run up substantial sterling balances in London. Britain was importing
more goods than it could sell abroad; the British Labour government was therefore more interested in Africa as a source of much-
needed raw materials than as a laboratory for political experiments.
The British thus sank vast sums into Tanganyika in order to produce
peanuts by means of large-scale mechanized farming under state
management; the ill-starred groundnut scheme was designed to help
Britain over its deficiency in edible fats and owed nothing to decolonization policies. The British were forced to court South Africa,
which extended credits to the United Kingdom. In Central Africa
the Labour government made various concessions to the local settlers in order to expand the production of much-needed minerals
and to gain the cooperation of Southern Rhodesia in matters such
as railway transport and coal supplies. The British also emphasized
the differences between black Africa proper and the multiracial territories of East and Central Africa. There was no talk of "paramountcy
of African interests"; the problems of Britain and Kenya should be
solved by "partnership," and the governing power specifically rejected
all schemes whereby one race would monopolize political power at
the expense of other communities.

The French, like the British, were willing to make reforms in their
colonial empire; but few Frenchmen as yet thought in terms of granting full independence to their colonies. On the contrary, a more liberal
form of administration would strengthen the connections linking the
mother country to its possessions. Political federalism, administrative
decentralization, and social reform were the watchwords of France,
and leading Africans such as Léopold Sédar Senghor were willing to
adhere to a humanized French association.[4]

The colonizers' aspirations now appear to have been strangely
unrealistic. The Western European countries were all weakened by
war, but Britain at any rate basked in the glory of victory. Liberia,
Ethiopia, and Egypt, the only independent African states north of the
Limpopo, counted for little on the international stage. Liberia remained
a backward country, without influence or prestige. Ethiopia had
proved incapable of shaking off Italian rule by its own exertions and
owed its liberation mainly to British, Indian, African, and white South
African troops. Egypt wielded little military power. There was a good

[4] See, for instance, Robert Lemaignen, Léopold Sédar Senghor, and Prince
Sisowath Youtévong, *La communauté impériale française* (Paris, 1945), pp.
58ff.

deal of discontent in all the European colonies, but no territory in black Africa was threatened by a revolutionary situation of the classic type outlined by Lenin. Black Africa, for the most part, lacked an industrial proletariat; urban workers formed only a small portion of the population; the majority of unskilled laborers retained traditional links with the villages and were too backward to be mobilized for revolutionary action. The skilled workers and technicians in many parts of Africa were European immigrants who had no thought of combining with their black fellow workers; the majority of African skilled workers were as yet too insecure in their position to voice any very radical aspirations. Except for some West Coast territories such as the Gold Coast the African bourgeoisie generally lacked cohesion, numerical strength, and political self-confidence. The African lower middle class was more numerous but equally weak. In many parts of Africa, moreover, the bourgeoisie consisted wholly or partly of immigrants from Europe, India, or the Near East, that is to say, people without any thought of revolutionary action. Territories such as Kenya, Nyasaland, and Southern Rhodesia faced serious rural problems; there were clashes of interest between white farmers and planters on the one hand and African laborers or African tenants on the other.

Moreover, Africa as a whole lacked a substantial landless proletariat; most of the African continent remained under- rather than overpopulated; land pressure of the Southeast Asian variety was confined to only a few areas. The armed forces, the police, and administrative cadres continued firmly under the rulers' control and could not be penetrated by oppositional groups so long as the whites kept their grip. The imperial powers controlled a great network of naval, military, and air bases; European staff planners regarded Africa as a vast strategic buffer essential for NATO's defense. The European rulers' military might remained impressive. Throughout the period of decolonization the whites in Africa never at any time met with a successful armed challenge from black revolutionaries; uprisings such as the Mau Mau rebellion in Kenya and the anti-Portuguese revolt in northern Angola remained rare and were crushed or contained.

Throughout colonial Africa economic enterprise was making rapid progress. The imperial administrations were stepping up the pace in educational, social, and medical reforms. There was no suggestion that capitalism in Africa had reached that point of diminishing return where, according to Marxist theory, the ruling economic and political system would itself become a brake on production and collapse under the weight of its own economic contradictions. The rulers' position seemed relatively secure in the field of ideas. Western democracy enjoyed the prestige of victory; dictatorships were discredited. Critics of the imperial system in Africa itself generally clothed their demands in a democratic terminology. In British Africa it was only extreme conservatives and white settlers who argued that a devolution of power to African leaders would necessarily lead to the establishment of single-party dictatorships. British Africans called for self-govern-ment and equality of rights, but they spoke in terms of British parlia-mentarianism; they generally professed loyalty to Crown and Com-monwealth and supported their arguments by reference to the rulers' professed beliefs in Western democracy.

African nationalism moreover lacked a territorial focus. Liberia or Ethiopia could not become an African Savoy or an African Prussia. Furthermore, not a single African colony had been a nation state at any time in its history. None of the existing territorial boundaries coincided with those of any previously known state. No African as yet thought of himself as a Malawian, a Zambian, or a Tanzanian. African nationalist leaders therefore faced ideological disabilities much greater than those which beset European nationalists in Ger-many, Italy, or Poland a century before.

Yet within a space of two decades, the white man's flags were hauled down. Empire suffered from a number of fatal flaws which prevented its survival through the second part of the twentieth cen-tury. The full story of decolonization still remains to be written, but some conclusions emerge clearly. The colonial powers failed to co-operate with one another. Colonization in the 1880s had gone with a series of international congresses; there had been such a thing as the "concert of Europe." Decolonization in the 1950s and 1960s, however, was unplanned and uncoordinated; the colonial powers lacked both an effective doctrine of government and a consistent policy. The colonial cause no longer appealed to the people in the metropolitan countries. The colonizers' political and psychological weaknesses far outweighed their military assets, even though, from the arms standpoint alone, the imperialists were in fact stronger than ever before.

Since the early days of imperial expansion the gap between the rulers and the ruled widened rather than narrowed in the field of military technology. Between 1896 and 1897 the Rhodesian settlers, for instance, had to face a great African uprising. White mounted riflemen, equipped with some automatic guns, fought irregular black infantry, plentifully supplied with muskets as well as modern firearms. The settlers lost something like 10 percent of their total number, a staggering figure, much higher than the proportion of casualties suf-fered by white colonists in the Algerian national uprising or the Mau

Mau war in Kenya in the twentieth century. But the settlers had never doubted for a moment that victory would be theirs, that the whole of Europe stood behind them, and that they represented the forces of progress. The European clergymen and missionaries in the country, the nearest thing to a local intelligentsia, were as full of fight as their fellow whites; there was none to sympathize with the insurgents or call for concessions in the cause of peace. The settlers' estimate of themselves was generally shared by public opinion in Britain and North America; the intangible factor of morale had worked in the white man's favor.

In the 1950s the position was very different. The colonialist armies were better equipped from the purely technical standpoint; they had helicopters, radio equipment, tracked vehicles, fighter bombers, and transport planes. Partisan forces had to rely on homemade weapons at the worst and foreign-made automatic weapons, hand grenades, and light mortars at best. However, colonialist forces labored under severe political disadvantages which usually canceled out their military superiority. The British and Belgians, moreover, were increasingly unwilling to make use of their military strength. Abdicationist sentiments had by this time begun to spread, not merely among convinced socialists and pacifists, but even among a minority of colonial administrators and settlers. During World War II, for example, a British colonel like Sir Stewart Gore-Browne, an early settler and a *pukka sahib* of the traditional kind, became convinced that there must be something wrong with an empire that had collapsed so quickly under Japanese assault in the Far East; Gore-Browne later turned into a leading white liberal and ultimately a supporter of black nationalism.

Ardent advocates of empire came to feel that the metropolitan countries owed a debt of gratitude to their colonies for their military turnout; the Free French, especially, understood quite clearly that the road back to Paris started in Brazzaville in 1944. The war had also stimulated criticism of imperial rule in other ways. The British and French had tried to interpret world events to their subjects and had called for their cooperation. In Northern Rhodesia propaganda teams had gone to the villages to call for recruits to the army and to explain to the villagers why goods were in short supply and what the fighting was all about. The Allies professed to be battling for the rights of small countries to govern themselves; they spoke up against Nazi racism. But did not the Westerners' own empires suffer from similar flaws?

During and after World War II the ideological initiative thus passed to the critics of colonialism. The rulers in general now were more apologetic; they wavered; they compromised and gradually became more and more convinced of the necessity for their ultimate abdication. Each reform and each concession led to new demands. These in turn accelerated the progress of decolonization and further contributed to the rulers' loss of confidence. Decolonization was rationalized into a policy goal that had supposedly motivated the imperial venture from its very beginning. The devolution of power came to be looked upon as an inevitable process, and this belief in inevitability became a factor of historical importance. Only the Portuguese and the Afrikaners—militarily among the weakest of colonizers—were willing to hold on at all costs. So were the white Algerians and, to a lesser extent, the white colonists in Southern Rhodesia (though even white Rhodesia produced its own brand of restrained liberalism). The great majority of Westerners no longer had much faith in their imperial mission, and historians are still trying to explain how this reversal of opinion came about.

According to Marxist analysis, the natural allies of the colonial subjects should have been the most poorly paid section of the metropolitan proletariat, those white workers least corrupted by the spoils of empire. In reality the unskilled laborers in Western Europe were apathetic, if not actually hostile, to the aspirations of colonial peoples. British conscripts back from Egypt or India were not particularly sympathetic toward the local population; the Western working classes rarely labored under a feeling of imperial guilt. The majority of intellectuals, however, had very different ideas. Intellectuals, of course, do not form a cohesive class: they differ in their work, their professional attainments, their incomes, and also in their political ideas. There are intellectuals of the left, of the right, and of the center. But it is safe to say that a large proportion of the journalists, university teachers, radio commentators, and writers in Western Europe and North America took some pride in being dissenters; they saw themselves as the appointed critics of the established order. They stood for change, although they bitterly disagreed concerning the exact goals of social transformation and the methods employed to better the ways of humanity. In Great Britain especially, some intellectuals took over the intense preoccupation with status of Victorian gentlefolk, those members of the upper classes who had held no landed estates themselves but had made their living in the army, the Church, or at law, which they regarded as the only professions worthy of gentlemen. Many British, and also French, intellectuals developed their arrogant contempt for trade, an antimercantile ideology often strengthened by, but not necessarily born of, Marxist teachings. The great majority of Western intellectuals, moreover, now pinned their faith to secular rather than religious reforms. They wished to achieve justice and social equality in this world instead of the next. Hence foreign domination, or indeed social inequalities of any kind, seemed far less acceptable to the educated than ever before. The European settler in Africa came under particularly sharp attack. As the struggle between communism and Western democracy intensified after the war, the white colonist, with his claims to social and political superiority over the "natives," appeared as a political liability, though Slav colonists in Siberia and Sakhalin did not. The growing disdain for colonial commitments, and for the surviving colonialists, gained additional strength from the thermonuclear revolution in warfare, which was interpreted by some theorists as making obsolete the whole body of conventional strategy, with its insistence on bases and on the control of oceanic lines of communications. The image persisted, even though World War II was followed by a whole rash of new "conventional wars," which still required strategic assets and military skills of the traditional variety.

The trend against colonialism was accentuated by the vigorous and well-justified reaction against racist and strong-arm philosophies of the Nazi variety. This made both colonial domination and white color-bar practices in Africa and elsewhere seem infinitely more objectionable than in the past. But the reaction against existing values went even further. Wartime idealism, the prestige of the "permissive attitude," the passionate belief in the rights of small nations, all spilled over into the colonies. White colonizers and European settlers, not sufficiently remote to be romantic, sometimes incurred guilt by association in the public mind.[5] Above all, there was among many intellectuals widespread disillusionment with Western industrial civilization itself. The gap between the secular doctrine of progress and the realities of mid-twentieth-century Europe seemed to become unbridgeable. Two world wars, with the mass extermination and the mass expulsions of inoffensive people, torture, and terror, crushed the spirits of the most sanguine. Nuclear warfare seemed to threaten civilization with destruction on an apocalyptic scale; the world seemed torn from its orbit. Disaster always made the headlines, especially at a time when news could travel faster than ever before. Highbrow psychological analyses and lowbrow newspapers often converged in stressing the abnormal and the depraved. The hero disappeared from the novel; the Victorian empire builder, the pioneer of fiction, who supposedly had brought peace to the blood-soaked African veld, dropped out of popular novels and travelogues, except for children's books and film scripts, always the last refuge of archaic concepts.

The popularization of psychology proved another factor in this

[5] See Lewis H. Gann and Peter Duignan, *White Settlers in Tropical Africa* (Harmondsworth, Middlesex, Eng., 1962), pp. 9–19, and Lewis H. Gann, "The White Settler: A Changing Image," *Race*, II, No. 2 (May, 1961), 28–40.

ideological transformation. Scholars like Jung looked on primitive people in a way reminiscent of Rousseau and deplored the real or supposed vices of Western city-bred men. This type of thought then made its impact on popular literature.[6] Some intellectuals indeed projected their own dislike of the entrepreneur, or even of industrial civilization as a whole, on the settlers, the people who supplied the mechanized farmers, the factory managers, the technicians, and a considerable section of the skilled workers for the developing regions of South and Central Africa. The white emigrant on the boat bound for Africa ceased for some to be a culture hero; he became instead the moneygrubber of plebeian origins, the representative of "admass" and neon lights.[7] Psychologists like O. Mannoni in *Prospero and Caliban* argued that the white colonizers in Africa were distinguished by a special psychological makeup which supposedly made them more willing to rule over others; other scholars came to different conclusions, finding that Rhodesian whites, for instance, were no more inclined to be tough-minded than their fellow citizens in Britain.[8] Nevertheless, the stereotype of the ruthless settler persisted and became a political factor of some consequence.

The general climate of opinion was influenced further by the emergence of a new body of professional Africanists who did much to replace Western thinking on colonial problems in general and on African matters in particular. An especially important group among these writers were the anthropologists. From the 1920s on, scholars under the influence of Malinowski and others perfected their fieldwork, and the new approach resulted in major contributions to the study of man.

[6] As an example one might take V. S. Reid's book, *The Leopard;* this deals with the Mau Mau rising in Kenya and represents the central white character as a neurotic, while the black hero speaks in terms of pseudo-Biblical simplicity.

[7] See, for instance, Reginald Reynolds' poem, "The Emigrant Ship," *Africa South,* III, No. 4 (July–September, 1959), 4, especially the following lines:

> They talk of Wogs and Niggers, trash and treasure
> And bargaining. The urgent wail of sex
> And Tin Pan Alley stirs in strident measure
> The unfulfilment of our lower decks.

[8] In 1958 Cyril A. Rogers thus compared the attitudes of Rhodesian white and British electors according to Eysenck's "toughminded-tenderminded" scale, which tested attitudes on matters such as corporal punishment and the death penalty. He found that the right-wing white Dominion Party ranked very much like British Conservatives. The United Federal Party, the white middle-of-the-road party then in power in Rhodesia, was slightly more "tenderminded" than the British Socialists; white liberals in the United Rhodesia Party were rather like members of the British Liberal Party in their attitudes. See Cyril A. Rogers, "The Organization of Political Attitudes in Southern Rhodesia," *Rhodes-Livingstone Journal,* No. 25 (March, 1959), pp. 1–19.

The new learning also helped to put so-called primitive people into a much more favorable position. In abandoning older value judgments, many students of society began to make new kinds of implicit assumptions. The savage of old became preliterate man, a change in terminology which was itself likely to conceal an unrecognized value judgment. Under these conditions the very real achievements of the West were sometimes forgotten, and for some intellectuals protest became almost a Pavlovian reflex. Writers disgusted with modern wars forgot that, in terms of recuperative powers of the societies involved, the preindustrial wars waged by Rome against Carthage, the Thirty Years War in Germany, the campaigns of Jenghiz Khan or of Chaka's Zulu hosts in South Africa, were probably more destructive than any war waged in twentieth-century Europe. Intellectuals stricken with cultural guilt feelings often came to regard civilization and barbarism as one and the same, and this outlook colored pronouncements made from official information services. "We must not divide men into primitive and civilized, superior and inferior. Those labels only justify the cult of injustice, self-aggrandizement and exercise of power," argued a prominent American information expert.[9] Indeed, the exercise of power itself, a necessary element in any political community, now sometimes seemed a crime. Western civilization, by its command over nature and its great resources of intellect, had favored man by presenting him with an infinitely larger range of choices than he had ever possessed before. But this very quality of civilization sometimes seemed an evil to intellectuals doubtful or contemptuous of the idea of free and rational decision. In the same way, the superior wealth of the West was often interpreted not so much as stemming from superior skill, efficiency, and managerial ability or a different economic ethos, but as the result of exploitation, an interpretation which once more reflected the undervaluation of entrepreneurial capacity widespread among so many men of letters. At the same time the optimism of the intelligentsia concerning the underdeveloped countries sometimes made them blind to the real difficulties that faced the new states: the new countries' lack of internal cohesion, their general inability to adopt the institutions of Western democracy, the tendency of so many Balkan-type countries to exploit foreign-born minority groups, and the pervading corruption that made efficient government a matter of great difficulty in many backward lands.

During the 1940s this kind of thought affected Africa only to a limited extent. In the early 1950s, however, Africa increasingly began

---

[9] Quoted from a speech made by Edward R. Murrow, Director, United States Information Agency, November 5, 1961 (cyclostyled; Salisbury, Southern Rhodesia, American Consulate General).

to make the headlines. By this time Western dominion had largely disappeared from Asia, so that anticolonial thinkers were able to concentrate their attention on Africa. British socialism, moreover, had lost a good deal of its former emotional impact at home; nationalization of the means of production no longer possessed the old glamour; great victories had been won in the war against poverty. As British reformers attained many of their domestic objectives, crusaders looked for new objectives in the colonies. British, and also French, social idealism turned outward, in the same way that a century and a half earlier British missionary, abolitionist, and philanthropic sentiment had spilled over into the foreign field. Many Labour speakers became convinced that Britain's proletariat lived in Africa.

No one, of course, can say exactly how far this change in the climate of opinion actually influenced conduct of day-to-day affairs at Whitehall. Civil servants take account more of their departmental heads than of newspaper articles; professors rarely decide policy. The intelligentsia did, however, succeed in putting the colonial Establishment on the defensive; they exerted a good deal of influence on expatriate African students and politicians. They also succeeded in creating an anticolonial public opinion composed often of highly vocal lobbies which claimed to speak for the nation as a whole and which exerted an influence quite out of proportion to their numbers. During the early 1950s, for instance, there were lengthy debates in Britain over the possibility of linking the two Rhodesias and Nyasaland into an association. Amalgamation into a unitary state, the official argument went, was not acceptable either to the Africans or to public opinion at home. British policy makers therefore decided in favor of a looser federation; they did so despite the fact that at least 95 percent of the British people, whose "public opinion" was being thrown into the scales, had not the slightest idea of the difference between amalgamation and federation and cared less. The advocates of empire therefore faced serious handicaps; they were constrained not only by their own legal tradition, but also by press and Parliament. The intelligentsia played a dual role in tightening these constraints and in making decolonization more acceptable to a wider metropolitan public, one not initially always well disposed toward the cause of African nationalists.

In addition to these ideological arguments, the imperial powers faced considerations of a very practical kind. Was not empire ceasing to "pay" either in the military or in the economic field? The French, for example, seemed only to compound their wartime losses by expensive colonial campaigns. The war in Indochina imposed great sacrifices on the country. No sooner were the French rid of the Indochina commitment than they found themselves faced with a serious struggle in Algeria. By 1959 the French were said to maintain half a million men in North Africa. France was reduced to temporary military impotence in Europe and was no longer able to make its promised contribution to NATO. Yet the loss of Indochina in no way injured the French economy. The French got over the disappearance of their East Asian empire just as quickly as the Dutch got over the loss of their possessions and investments in Indonesia. In fact, the argument went, imperial might was not compatible either with a balanced budget or with true grandeur on the European Continent.

Similar discussions played an important part in Great Britain and Belgium, although the military argument in these countries never attained such importance. On the one hand, there were the spiritual descendants of Lenin and of Rhodes, who asserted—for very different reasons—that empire was a paying proposition for the metropolitan countries. They were opposed by liberals and the humanitarian socialists, who argued that empire yielded little or no profits or, alternatively, that profits rested on exploitation.[10] Provided the successor governments could maintain order at home and commerce abroad, decolonization, many reasoned, would be a profitable as well as a moral decision.[11] Of course, some of the new governments might go Socialist and, at the worst, nationalize big foreign concerns without compensation, but even the most predatory policy of confiscation, the argument continued, would not necessarily injure more than certain sectional interests. A Socialist successor government would still have to buy foreign goods, and if the investor suffered, the merchant and the manufacturer might still make a good living. The losses of decolonization might well be recouped in trade. Economic arguments were thus added to the anticolonial armory, and between 1954 and 1964 the colonizers withdrew from all parts of Africa except the Portuguese empire and the white-settlement colonies south of the Zambezi.

[10] See Andrew Shonfield, *British Economic Policy since the War* (Harmondsworth, Middlesex, Eng., 1958).
[11] See John Strachey, *The End of Empire* (London, 1961; New York, 1964).

20. The Subjects Organize

Colonization, as we have seen, acted as a kind of political and cultural blood transfusion. The imperial powers developed new systems of communications and new forms of education and social services; their economic policies wittingly or unwittingly led to the emergence of new African elites and new mass-communication media such as the press. The British and French, as distinct from the Belgians and Portuguese, however, went a good deal further. They created their own forms of representative institutions, endowed with sufficient power to make their control a great political prize. The British, on the lowest levels, promoted local councils to underpin indirect rule; they also fashioned bodies such as the African Representative Council of Northern Rhodesia, intended to advise the government on the central level. Still more important were the legislative assemblies, designed to make laws and control the finances of each territory under the Union Jack. These assemblies all developed on a very similar pattern. A legislative council would set out with an "official" majority comprised of senior civil servants, perhaps comparable in certain respects to the governmental voting bloc in a British eighteenth-century Parliament.[1] In addition, special-interest groups would be represented through nominated members. Gradually the nominated members would be replaced by elected members; these unofficials would steadily increase their powers at the expense of the officials. In the so-called multiracial territories like Kenya and Northern Rhodesia, the unofficials comprised a powerful white bloc who tried to obtain control of the council. But except for Southern Rhodesia, the European electorates never managed to dominate the legislature. Instead, the number of African elected members steadily increased, and African elected members ultimately obtained

[1] According to Sir Lewis Namier, *England in the Age of the American Revolution* (2d ed.; London, 1961), p. 228, the British House of Commons elected in 1761 thus contained some 50 ministers and civil servants and 157 court officials, sinecure holders, and officers in the fighting services.

320

a decisive majority on all British legislative councils north of the Zambezi.

The struggle for influence in the legislature went hand in hand with a battle for control of the executive. Again the British worked out a kind of repetitive pattern. In a constitutionally backward colony the governor's position corresponded in certain respects to that of an eighteenth-century British monarch; the governor was head of the executive and commander in chief; he was assisted by an executive council of senior civil servants whose position depended on the government. Gradually unofficials, white and black, would secure representation in the executive as well as in the legislative council. Executive-council members gradually evolved into ministers, and the British African territories developed some kind of cabinet system, in which ministers were dependent on a majority in the legislature.[2]

The British system, in other words, did not originally conform to the modern "Westminster" system of government. British legislative councils allotted seats to interests rather than to persons; they resembled the "estates general" more than modern legislatures. Defenders of the system argued in terms similar to those used by advocates of the unreformed British House of Commons in the early nineteenth century; they pleaded that all interests in the body politic were enjoying "virtual representation" which corresponded to their respective position in society. African nationalists and European colonists both strove to transform these councils into elected assemblies; the Europeans in Northern Rhodesia desired a highly weighted property franchise; the Africans in time became converts to the idea of one man—one vote. The British system thus faithfully reflected ethnic and economic conflicts within each territory. But it also made some provision for gradual reform. British Africans, more than black people in any other part of colonial Africa, obtained some experience in the exercise of executive power. The British system built up cadres of educated men knowledgeable in the art of political debate and capable of drawing up a budget or advising on departmental policy. The British created a constitutional machinery which ultimately allowed power to pass from London to local African governments in much the same way that power had previously been devolved from London to Britain's white dominions overseas.

The French constitutional scheme contained contradictions of a somewhat different kind. French policy in Africa embodied two contradictory assumptions, referred to by Kenneth Robinson, a

[2] For a general work on the emergence of conciliar government in the colony see Martin Wight, *The Development of the Legislative Council, 1606–1945* (London, 1946).

British scholar, as the "policy of identity" and the "policy of paternalism." The French Revolution stood for the "republic one and indivisible"; it did away with representation by estates and proclaimed the equality of all citizens. These principles were embodied in civic rights bestowed in the nineteenth century upon the people of the *Quatre Communes* of Senegal; these communities obtained, among other privileges, the right to elect a deputy to the French National Assembly. The extension of French power over vast areas in West and Equatorial Africa during the latter part of the century, however, gave increasing emphasis to the policy of paternalism, a policy which strongly appealed to the legitimist and authoritarian tradition of French politics. The Senegalese *communes* survived as equalitarian islands in an authoritarian sea. (It was only in the mid-1950s that municipal legislation on the French pattern was applied to other cities in black Africa.) Paternalism created a special regime for the mass of Africans who were looked upon as subjects instead of as citizens and who were administered by French civil servants but were subject to customary law.[3] In 1944 the French introduced a number of reforms, but pressure from French metropolitan parties of the Left and from new African parties in the colonies was strong enough to push the Fourth Republic further along the road toward identity— *not* toward the concept of dominion status for the colonies. In 1946 the Loi Lamine-Gueye, like a modern edict of Caracalla, proclaimed the civic equality of all French subjects. The French constitution of 1946 considered all "overseas territories" parts of the Republic of France.[4] But electoral assimilation was never taken to its logical conclusion. The premise of absolute civic equality, according to one fascinating statistical calculation, would have meant a mammoth legislature, numbering 1,040 deputies, of whom 496 would have been elected from overseas France.[5] For all its egalitarian terminology, the French system thus also came to rest on a form of "virtual representation."

The French likewise introduced major economic reforms. Forced labor went by the board. Public investment was encouraged. The French set up an important new agency, known as FIDES (Fonds d'Investissement pour le Développement Economique et Social), and did away with the older doctrine of territorial self-sufficiency.

[3] Thomas L. Hodgkin, *Nationalism in Colonial Africa* (London, 1956), pp. 33–40.

[4] Black Africa in 1946 elected 23 deputies to the French legislature. Ten years later, it had 33.

[5] Virginia Thompson and Richard Adloff, *French West Africa* (Stanford, Calif., 1957), pp. 44–82, especially 44–46.

On the lower levels the French created local councils, known as general councils, later renamed territorial assemblies, one for each of the eight territories of French West Africa and one each for the four territories of French Equatorial Africa and the two trust territories of Togo and the Cameroons. There was also provision for some degree of federalism; the West and Equatorial African colonies were grouped into loosely connected units, with a grand council for each. The general councils were patterned on French departmental councils, but assumed greater powers than their French prototypes. They could make decisions concerning the local budget; they had many rights concerning rates and the basis of taxation. They could not, however, debate political issues; they had no share in executive power, and their influence remained much inferior to that of a British legislative council. In each territory the administration continued to operate as a quasi-independent force, still much influenced by paternalistic concepts. The system as a whole nevertheless gave considerably more say to African politicians than they had enjoyed in the past. The constitution created an African lobby within the French Chamber of Deputies; it provided a valuable training ground for politically conscious Africans, who acquired a thorough knowledge of metropolitan politics, especially those of a left-wing variety. Educated French Africans similarly acquired a stake in local government. The new territorial assemblies were filled with functionaries and, to a lesser extent, African schoolteachers, not peasant majorities. The assemblies became the political mouthpieces of the emergent white-collar strata, and each turned into a focus for a separate territorial identity. French Africans, moreover, enjoyed certain civic rights; there was a lively press, so that French political ideas began strongly to influence French-speaking Africa.

The Portuguese and Belgians, by contrast, failed to create any central representative institutions where local Africans could acquire political influence. Portugal in 1932 became a dictatorship headed by Salazar. The União Nacional was the only authorized political movement in the country; there was neither freedom of speech nor freedom of the press. The anticolonial cause had no opportunities for benefiting from party struggles within the Portuguese Establishment itself. Portuguese preoccupations with prestige and national grandeur, as well as Portuguese insistence on protected overseas markets, precluded concessions either to white or to black separatists in the colonial empire. The Belgians also stuck to a highly centralized form of colonial government. The Congo was divided into five provinces, each in charge of a governor, with a governor-general at the head of the Congolese administrative hierarchy. The Belgian system rested on a triple alliance between the state, the Church, and big companies; there was no room for local representation. Demands for constitutional advancement within the Congo first came from European immigrants. The Belgians, however, were determined not to grant to white settlers political powers of the kind which the colonists had acquired in Kenya. The Belgian administration would not grant a legislative council of the British model; they tried to keep colonial affairs "out of politics" and strove to create a black lower middle class which would be satisfied with economic gains and content with paternalistic government run from overseas. This policy rested on the assumption that the Congo might be isolated from the remainder of Africa and that the currents of "subversive" thought could be kept out of the colony. The Belgian Charte Coloniale granted neither freedom of the press nor freedom of association. There were many newspapers and an efficient broadcasting system; but all were subject to effective political control. Belgian economic policy, however, required the creation of a considerable class of educated black people with a primary or a secondary school education. There were far more literate Africans in the Congo than, say, in Portuguese East Africa, or even in Kenya, and these educated people could not be prevented from picking up information from abroad. Congolese radio audiences could tune in on foreign broadcasts; labor migrants, itinerant traders, and students moved across the borders and spread new ideas, so that the Belgians' political hold also began to weaken.

African parties of a secular kind began their existence in the British and French colonial empires. The earliest groupings were often clubs, formed for educational, cultural, or recreational purposes, but capable of taking some part in the public life of their respective territories. Political scientists can trace some curious parallels between white-settler and African associations of this type. In the late 1890s, for instance, European colonists in Bulawayo, then Southern Rhodesia's economic capital, formed a literary and debating society; this was comprised of educated people such as lawyers and doctors, and the society soon began to make political as well as economic demands. About a generation later, educated Southern Rhodesian Africans banded themselves into clubs of a similar nature; in the early 1930s African schoolteachers, clerks, and junior civil servants founded welfare societies in various Northern Rhodesian townships. The "new men" transacted their meetings in English and discussed local issues of interest to their own class, but soon began to put forward requests for reforms of a more general, though still of a strictly loyalist, nature. Welfare societies did not at first attain much influence, for even in Northern Rhodesia the European colonists held all the key positions.

On the African West Coast the colonial rulers had to deal with a very different situation; there was an African middle class, and a number of political organizations were run by influential Africans. Associations of this kind included the Nigerian National Democratic Party, founded in Lagos in 1923 by Herbert Macaulay, a well-connected civil engineer; the National Congress of British West Africa, run by J. E. Casely Hayford, a distinguished Gold Coast lawyer; and the Senegalese section of the French Socialist Party, formed in the 1930s by Lamine Gueye, a Wolof attorney.

These groupings, white or black, usually owed a great deal to the efforts of lawyers. Charles Patrick Coghlan, a Bulawayo attorney, led the European settlers of Southern Rhodesia against the governance of the British South Africa Company; W. E. G. Sekyi, another lawyer, founded the Aborigines' Rights Protection Society on the Gold Coast. The predominant position attained by legal luminaries is easy to explain. Lawyers are trained to speak in public; they acquire much influence with their clientele; they must be familiar with the rulers' laws and legal loopholes. Lawyers, moreover, are able to build up a private practice which does not necessarily depend on government patronage—an unusual position in a backward country, where so many of the most desirable careers are found in the civil service. The influence of these early organizations was, however, limited: they were usually confined to a few important towns; their main attraction was for people with some degree of wealth or education; they generally held themselves to demands for constitutional reforms of a strictly limited kind.[6]

The next step in political organization usually consisted in the formation of congresses, with a wider popular backing. These congresses, or fronts, claimed to represent all the people within the country, and their membership was considerably larger than that of welfare societies. The more important of the congresses were usually organized on a "national" basis, that is to say, they accepted the boundaries of the existing colonial units, but wished to replace expatriate lawmakers and administrators by officeholders of their own color. Again there were certain parallels between white and black organizations in Africa. In Southern Rhodesia in 1917 the white opponents of chartered company government banded themselves in the Responsible Government Association, comprised of farmers, mine workers, railway men, and clerks, without distinction of economic interests. The Responsible Government Association agitated for an

[6] Hodgkin, *Nationalism in Colonial Africa,* pp. 139–168, especially pp. 139–141. For a general study, see Thomas L. Hodgkin, *African Political Parties: An Introductory Guide* (Harmondsworth, Middlesex, Eng., 1961).

end to chartered company rule. In 1923 the settlers obtained self-government; the Responsible Government Association became the ruling group under the name of the Rhodesian Party, but this white class alliance subsequently split up.

In most parts of Africa black organizations of the congress type sprang up only after World War II. These associations owed a great deal to the political fermentation engendered by the conflict against the Axis powers. Some hopefully looked to the example of the Indian Congress Party; others pointed out the real or supposed parallels between the sufferings of Occupied Europe under the Germans and those experienced by Africa at the hands of their colonial rulers. These congresses included the United Gold Coast Convention, set up in 1947, and the Northern Rhodesia African Congress, formed in 1948 from a Federation of African Welfare Societies. In French West Africa the Rassemblement Démocratique Africain was established at a conference in Bamako in 1946. These new organizations built up a popular following; they created some sort of organizational framework, with national, regional, and district secretaries; party emissaries traveled around the countryside on bicycles, in party vans, or in trucks, diffusing slogans and voicing local grievances. Thomas Hodgkin, a British writer, has ably summarized the difference between such congresses and parties of a more orthodox kind. Political parties usually represented a later and more elaborate form of organization. Congresses played their main part during the last stages of imperial rule; they tried to speak for all the people, and their organization was in general of a very loose kind, grouped around a nuclear executive or working committee. For the most part their strategy was aggressive; they used all sorts of pressure techniques, ranging from moderately worded petitions or deputations to boycotts, strikes, and civil disobedience.[7] Congress movements often had great difficulty in disciplining branch organizations. Many congresses built up youth movements, which frequently became more radical, more inclined to violence, and less susceptible to central control than their parent bodies. Congresses commonly also had serious financial problems; subscriptions would arrive in an irregular or unpredictable fashion. Sometimes dishonest officers would embezzle party funds. Some congress movements therefore used pressure tactics on the public; political activity would at times degenerate into a specialized form of protection racket, whereby people were forced to buy membership cards from one or even several political organizations as an insurance policy against being beaten up or having their huts burned down.

[7] Hodgkin, *Nationalism in Colonial Africa*, pp. 143–144.

Movements like the Northern Rhodesia African Congress tried to appeal to all the people in the territory. They proclaimed their opposition to imperialism in all its forms; they collaborated with other like-minded organizations such as labor unions, cooperation often being facilitated by the fact that a small nucleus of leaders might hold office in several different bodies. Most congress movements, however, had to cope with ethnic problems. The Northern Rhodesia African Congress, for instance, drew much of its original support from the relatively prosperous Tonga farmers on the railway belt.[8] In the late 1950s the movement split into two sections: a moderate wing retained the allegiance of the Tonga, while a more radical wing won mass support in the poor northeastern section of the territory. Other organizations derived their backing right at the start from one or another tribal group. The former Kenya African Union had its main base among the Kikuyu, politically the most advanced people in the country; the Uganda National Congress primarily relied on the Baganda. A third category confined its appeal specifically to one tribe. This was true, for instance, in the Belgian Congo, where governmental policy combined with the sheer size of the territory to prevent the emergence of well-organized national parties. In Léopoldville, for example, members of the Bakongo organized themselves into the Alliance des Bakongo (ABAKO), which aimed at the restoration of the ancient Bakongo state, divided by this time among the Belgian Congo, Angola, and the French Congo. ABAKO resembled many of the earlier congresses in combining the functions of a political pressure group, a mutual-aid society, and a social-protest movement. It tried to provide jobs for the workless, hospitalization for the sick, and alms for the poor, but it failed to extend its appeal beyond the confines of the Bakongo people, and in this respect it was like most other political organizations in the Congo.[9]

In the early 1950s the political initiative in British and French West Africa began to shift from congresses to political parties of a more tightly knit kind, run in a more systematic and centralized fashion, endowed with more specific programs, and intent on seeking wider popular support. Many factors combined to bring about this change.

[8] Lewis H. Gann, *A History of Northern Rhodesia: Early Days to 1953* (London, 1964), pp. 386–388, 423–427. The Northern Rhodesia African Congress derived special strength from local African opposition against the project of linking Northern Rhodesia, Nyasaland, and Southern Rhodesia into a federation, ruled by a mainly white electorate.

[9] For the Congo see Alan P. Merriam, *Congo: Background of Conflict* (Evanston, Ill., 1961), and René Lemarchand, "Congo (Leopoldville)," in James S. Coleman and Carl G. Rosberg, Jr. (eds.), *Political Parties and National Integration in Tropical Africa* (Berkeley, Calif., 1964), pp. 560–596.

A new generation of politicians entered public life, many of them university graduates, familiar with the techniques of mass parties overseas and impatient with the moderate outlook of the older leaders. The new men generally used a more militant phraseology and increasingly emphasized the "African" nature of the independence struggle. The early Congress leaders all courted support from liberal, humanitarian, and Socialist groups in the metropolitan countries; as a rule they spoke the language of Western liberalism and pleaded their case in terms of Western democracy. The new leaders continued to make good use of their metropolitan connections, but generally had more confidence in their own strength; they also pressed for social as well as political reforms and usually put their trust in a Socialist program of one form or another. Socialism, in their view, would not interfere with the African petty bourgeoisie, many of whom were their supporters, but would clip the wings of foreign investors, especially those who put their money into key industries such as mining. On the Gold Coast, Kwame Nkrumah successfully challenged the more moderate J. B. Danquah; in Senegal, Léopold Senghor wrested leadership from Lamine Gueye. The new leaders all pressed for constitutional reforms; constitutional reforms in turn helped precipitate the formation of mass parties. In the early 1950s, for instance, the British— half willingly and half under pressure—introduced new constitutions in the Gold Coast, Nigeria, and Sierra Leone. These instruments of state provided for the formation of predominantly African governments based on a party or a coalition of parties with a majority in the legislature. In Nigeria and on the Gold Coast these reforms went hand in hand with the introduction of taxpayers' suffrage. African political leaders thus had to press for mass support, and the birth of many important West African parties, like Nkrumah's Convention People's Party or the Action Group and the Northern People's Congress in Nigeria, can be correlated with different phases in constitutional advancement.[10] In the Belgian Congo, the Belgians in 1957 agreed to hold municipal elections. This concession similarly gave impetus to the formation of new parties, most of them based on ethnic loyalties. In addition, there were some groups that tried to represent all Congolese people as a whole. Of these the Mouvement National Congolais was the most important. Its leader, Patrice Lumumba, a former post-office clerk, tried to build up a tightly knit nationalist organization, modeled in many ways on the Convention People's Party. Lumumba, like Nkrumah on the Gold Coast, might be called a "black Jacobin"; he believed in the Congolese equivalent of the French revolutionary

[10] Hodgkin, *Nationalism in Colonial Africa,* p. 149.

"republic one and indivisible"; he tried to do away with traditional ethnic and caste distinctions and to forge a new nation.

Lumumba, an unstable and violent man, failed to solve the problem of uniting a multitude of different ethnic groups under one banner; in the end he was himself forced to play the tribal card, and the Mouvement National Congolais became a coalition of tribal forces. Many other African leaders, however, succeeded where Lumumba failed. Nkrumah in Ghana, Sékou Touré in Guinea, Julius Nyerere in Tanganyika, and Hastings Banda in Malawi created mass organizations with fairly wide support, united in a radical program of anticolonialism. These new parties often relied on the prestige of semideified leaders like Nkrumah and Banda, who were thought, in some sense, to express the national will and therefore to be beyond criticism. The new mass organizations commonly staffed their cadres with white-collar workers, clerks, and schoolteachers to whom politics often became a livelihood as well as a vocation and who frequently looked to control of the state machinery as a means of advancing their own careers. Yet the new movements at the same time engendered an immense amount of idealism.

African parties, like separatist churches, owed their existence to the efforts of black people. Parties gave a new pride to their members. Party militants also drew on great reservoirs of resentment—resentment against abuses, resentment against color bars in their various aspects, resentment, above all, against the inability to secure social acceptance from the white rulers. Traditional Matabele society had been infinitely more highly stratified than the settler society which took its place; the Matabele called their subjects dogs and proudly lorded over their dependents. But the Matabele never proclaimed any ideals of social and political equality. The whites did and thus were condemned out of their own mouths.

Many of the new parties built up a mass following and acquired an ideological appeal which the colonial powers could not counter. In addressing their fellow subjects the nationalist leaders frequently made extravagant promises that were likely to become political liabilities once independence was achieved. Party speakers in the villages often foretold that independence would bring freedom from all earthly woes; land and houses, education and social services, even train fares and bus rides would all become free. African nationalism sometimes became tinged with the very Messianic strains that had distinguished the millennial radicalism of the Kimbanguist kind in the Congo. In countries like Northern Rhodesia, African leaders were thus often forced to speak with two voices. Sometimes they talked in terms of modern states, ruled on the liberal principle of one man—one vote and equipped with all the white man's political and technological know-how. At other times they conjured up a golden past and cashed in on the conservative villagers' distrust of white-sponsored improvement schemes. Africans were warned against measures designed to improve agricultural techniques; contour ridging was said to be a labor-wasting scheme; in any case, white settlers were only waiting to take over improved African lands. There was propaganda against white clinics, where black women were supposedly being sterilized. Tales sprang up along the Northern Rhodesian railway belt of white vampire men, who sucked the blood out of their captives and turned human flesh into canned meat. There were stories of imperialists who poisoned sugar to make men impotent or to cause their wives to miscarry. The European administrators had great difficulty countering such rumors, and when in the early 1950s a British district commissioner held a public meat-eating demonstration in which he and his senior African clerk sampled suspected food, many of the audience simply concluded that the district commissioner must possess some especially strong medicine to resist the mysterious toxin.[11]

Tactics such as these might cause bitter resentment among the European administrators on the spot, but African nationalist propaganda, both of the respectable and of the virulent variety, did succeed in making nationalists. Countless numbers of African villagers or city laborers became conscious of political problems and began to search for secular solutions to the ills of their world. Many African political parties, like African churches and trade unions, began to some extent to transcend the ties of kinship and tribal allegiance. Above all, African political organizations became leadership cramming schools.[12]

Ambitious young Africans began to look to parties as the most suitable means to influence and power. The party structure, with its caucuses, committees, and district organization, served as an academy of political education. Party organizers had to become talent spotters; party functionaries found themselves called upon to use their gifts as administrators, planners, tacticians, and propagandists. Party work, like separatist church activities in earlier days, created a new outlet for talents and for untapped resources of idealism which the colonizers had failed to harness to their cause; it provided both psychological satisfaction and hopes for material advancement in the postcolonial state.

African political leaders also had to concern themselves with eco-

[11] Gann, *A History of Northern Rhodesia,* pp. 426–427.
[12] George H. T. Kimble, *Tropical Africa:* Vol. II, *Society and Polity* (New York, 1960), 297–298.

nomic ends; the same officials would often serve on the boards of labor
unions, welfare societies, and cooperatives, as well as those of parties.
A limited group of Africans thereby acquired valuable training in
many aspects of public life; African political activity itself thus helped
to create the indigenous cadres which would subsequently take control
of the colonial state machinery. Party work gave to many of its de-
votees a sense of release, the feeling that anything might be possible.
An African village schoolmaster who advanced, say, to the chairmanship of a party's provincial executive would soon believe himself the
equal, if not the superior, of the colonial provincial commissioner. But
more than that, a man with drive and ability could look forward to a
ministerial appointment in a newly independent state, a position his
father would never even have dreamed of. Many an African political
soldier was convinced that the new state would truly open a career
to the talented and that a loyal and hardworking party worker carried
a minister's portfolio in his knapsack. The new parties thereby became
capable of generating a powerful feeling of personal involvement and
of high idealism. Party work, however, also helped to destroy some of
the old certitudes of life. In economically backward territories especially political success became to many Africans a golden key to all
the desirable things in life, and each generation of leaders soon found
that they would in turn have to battle with younger rivals for the
triple goal of power, prestige, and prosperity.

The struggle for independence was therefore likely to develop
harsh tempers and bitter impatience of all opposition. The colonial
empires themselves had set an example of authoritarian government.
Even the more liberal systems such as those developed by the British
in West Africa had allowed only limited popular participation in government, and this itself was confined to a small elite. Colonialism frequently bred an *étatiste* outlook, one which was especially congenial
to poor countries where state employment was the most obvious way
to economic advancement. The struggle against the "imperialist
enemy" in turn seemed to put an extra premium on unity, on un-
swerving opposition to "traitors, stooges," or plain crooks. These
attitudes were often carried over into the postcolonial period and
profoundly influenced African political life even after the Union Jack
or the Tricolor had been lowered. Political activity moreover made a
tremendous contribution to the "revolution of rising expectations."
The widespread misunderstandings about the nature of independence
and the unrealistic expectations aroused in the population at large
were interestingly documented in a Cameroun African newspaper,
which in 1960 courageously decided to dispel these misconceptions.
Independence, wrote *La Voix du Peuple*, did not mean, among other

things, that people would no longer have to work; nor would freedom do away with bosses or with discipline at one's place of employment. Freedom did not mean the end of all laws or the disbandment of the police force. Women would not be able to seek a divorce as might suit their fancy. Customers would not be able to go into a shop and take what they liked. The Europeans would not automatically go home. White men could not be considered completely useless once Africans were able to do without their services. It would not be possible for travelers to go from Douala to Yaoundé without paying. Liberty did not mean that one could bash (*casser la gueule*) the first man, preferably a European, who stepped on one's toes.[13] The more level-headed Africans did not share these semi-Messianic expectations, but the independence struggle nevertheless created a political mortgage for the future, a liability that the new leaders would often find difficult to discharge.

[13] Quoted from *La Voix du Peuple,* January 1, 1960, reprinted in translation in Victor T. Le Vine, *The Cameroons, from Mandate to Independence* (Berkeley, Calif., 1964), pp. 216–217. The journal also tried to dispel the opposite fears, that freedom would mean license, that churches would be closed and all Catholics hanged, that freedom would mean corruption and favoritism, that racial hatred would replace hatred of colonialism, or that national sovereignty could be bargained away so as to bring Cameroun into the French Community.

21. Winning of the Political Kingdom

The British, wits used to say, acquired their empire in a state of absentmindedness. They dismantled their empire in an equally unplanned fashion. Decolonization came by fits and starts, by a series of *ad hoc* decisions designed to cope with interrelated pressures at home and abroad; concessions in turn acquired new impetus of their own, and within the space of a single decade Britain's African empire had broken apart into a galaxy of sovereign states. A full account of British decolonization would fill a book of its own, and this chapter will therefore concentrate on a few key areas which profoundly influenced the remainder of Africa.

Imperial devolution in "black Africa" began in the Gold Coast, a colony where indigenous cocoa farmers, traders, and professional men already wielded considerable power and where the British had built up a relatively highly developed system of education. By the end of World War II there was plenty of political ferment in the colony. Many Ghanaian soldiers had seen service abroad; the war had brought higher employment and wages and had put a premium on Ghana's agricultural exports. The British were in a generous frame of mind. In 1945 the British Parliament passed the Colonial Development and Welfare Act, which made £120 million available for improvements in the colonies over the next ten years. In 1946 the British introduced a new constitution which embodied much of the African nationalist program of the 1920s. But the first years of peace bitterly disappointed the expectations of the "new men," the cocoa farmers, clerks, mechanics, schoolteachers, and traders. The spread of education and the progress in cash farming and secondary enterprises had greatly increased their number, self-confidence, and political ambition. At the same time there was growing discontent. Consumer commodities remained in short supply, prices soared, capital goods were hard to get,

333

and the British encountered great difficulties in implementing their improvement schemes. In 1947 J. B. Danquah founded the United Gold Coast Convention, the first well-organized political movement in the country's history. Danquah called for self-government; he also hit upon the idea of reviving the traditions of the ancient Ghanaian empire and attaching the name of Ghana to the Gold Coast. It was Danquah too who invited Kwame Nkrumah, a young man trained in Britain and America, to become organizing secretary of the UGCC. In 1948 there were serious disturbances in the colony. By the standards, say, of Indian communal riots they were insignificant. But the Gold Coast troubles made a profound impression on the British Colonial Office. For one thing, the Gold Coast had always been regarded as a model colony with an advanced and sensible population. In addition, the British government had sent out a high-powered commission, headed by Aiken Watson, a distinguished legal man. Watson and his colleagues went far beyond their terms of reference and concluded that the underlying cause was a deep and justified dissatisfaction with the existing colonial constitution. The relevant Colonial Office records are not yet open to the scholar's scrutiny. But there is some evidence that the Colonial Office was now forced to take stock of the situation as a whole. If Watson was right, either the British would have to accept rapid constitutional advance to self-government or they would have to maintain the British position by force. The latter choice probably seemed unacceptable, both because of the expense involved and because policy makers must have assumed that British public opinion would not stand for such a policy. The Gold Coast riots thus helped to precipitate Ghanaian independence; Ghanaian independence in turn had a snowball effect on British policy in other parts of Africa and thereby perhaps on French and later on Belgian policy.

Danquah then made what, from his point of view, was a political mistake by collaborating with the government in the preparation of a new constitution. Nkrumah, a successful orator, stood aloof. In 1949 he founded his own group, the Convention People's Party, which cried out for "self-government now" and denounced the investigatory committee as bogus. Nkrumah's strategy was sound. The UGCC became a middle-class rump; the masses followed Nkrumah, and in 1950 the CPP organized a campaign of positive action of strikes and limited violence to force the authorities into an immediate grant of self-government. Nkrumah went to jail and thereby became a "prison graduate," a martyr for the cause of independence. But the British never attempted any real repression; elections were held in 1951, and the CPP won a smashing victory at the polls.

The Governor, Sir Charles Arden-Clarke, then carried out one of

those remarkable reversals of British policy which became characteristic of British statesmanship during the whole of this period of African history. Nkrumah was released from prison and invited instead to
become Leader of Government Business, a post equivalent to that of
Prime Minister. Opposition was now mainly confined to more conservative and traditional-minded people, especially the Ashanti, and
to some extent to the people in the northern territories and in Togoland. But this opposition was necessarily particularistic; it failed to
organize a nationwide movement capable of competing with a centralized popular party. The CPP firmly held onto the reins of power. The
ambitious young functionaries in the party's leading ranks displaced
the older professional people from whom the main critics of government had been drawn in earlier days. The British backed a unitary
rather than a federal solution: Arden-Clarke, a clergyman's son with a
fine military record in World War I and wide experience throughout
the African empire, established a working partnership with the CPP.
He cooperated closely with Nkrumah in the formation of an independent African government and probably contributed as much as any
individual Briton to the policy of decolonization in Africa. In 1957
Ghana became a free and independent member of the Commonwealth,
with Arden-Clarke its first governor-general.[1]

Ghana became an independent country, with an impartial civil
service, a flourishing economy, and a healthy budgetary surplus. But
there was no real agreement between government and opposition to
observe existing constitutional limits, and neither trusted the other.
The CPP, originally a fairly loosely organized party, evolved an increasingly monolithic party structure and took the lead in working out
an authoritarian one-party state, with Nkrumah as President, committed to a policy of militant anticolonialism. Ghana was a comparatively small country, with only some 6.5 million people, but its
independence profoundly influenced the remainder of black Africa.
Ghana acquired a temporary primacy among the new African nations;
the country became a center of pan-African propaganda and an inspiration for many African political men in the still dependent parts
of the continent. Nkrumah, with his emphasis on the seizure of political power as the prerequisite for social and economic progress, made
a profound impression on African intellectuals that went far beyond
the boundaries of his own country. He built up the legend of an increasing struggle against British imperialism and called on his countrymen to follow up this political victory by an offensive on the
economic strongholds of colonialism.

[1] This summary has been abstracted from John D. Fage, *Ghana: A Historical Interpretation* (Madison, Wis., 1959), pp. 81–85.

The British, for their part, had passed the point of no return. Ghanaian decolonization had provided a precedent, that vital point of departure for so many British ministers and senior civil servants. Once Ghana had achieved independence, there was no longer any reason to deny similar privileges to any other West African territory. The question was now simply when and how, and subsequently discussions of West African policy became concerned merely with the mechanics of decolonization.

Nigeria, the largest and most populous of the West African countries, attained full independence three years after Ghana. The delay was due not to British obstruction, but to internal disagreements among the Nigerians themselves. The country, with a population of some 35 million people, was highly diversified from the ethnic point of view. The north formed part of the Sudan's ancient Islamic civilization; traditional emirs continued to hold a powerful position. Northerners, moreover, feared competition from the more highly educated Yoruba and Ibo of the south and dreaded the influx of southern immigrants into government jobs. The new political ideas made their strongest initial impact among the Ibo, whose individualism had received an added stimulus from colonial experience. Educated Ibo made successful careers for themselves in commerce, semiskilled trades, and the professions; they also provided many political leaders, such as Benjamin Nnamdi Azikiwe, whose newspaper *West African Pilot* had revolutionized West African journalism. In the 1930s Azikiwe had founded the Nigerian Youth Movement, which aimed at dominion status for Nigeria and pursued a radical line. In 1944 he participated in the formation of the National Council for Nigeria and the Cameroons (NCNC), a congress type of organization whose main strength lay in the Eastern and Western Regions. After the war the NCNC forced the political pace; in 1947 the British thus granted a new constitution which at last extended the competence of the legislative council to include Northern Nigeria and provided for a majority of Nigerian representatives. Sir John Macpherson, who became Governor in 1948, embarked on a policy of further advance and called for a series of regional and national congresses to shape the new system. These discussions made the Nigerian leaders face up to the ethnic, cultural, and religious differences in their country. The northern emirs formed the Northern People's Congress; the rivalry of Ibo and Yoruba increasingly turned the NCNC into an Ibo instrument and led to the formation of the Action Group as a Yoruba party under Chief Obafemi Awolowo. None of these groups were in favor of a unitary state; the constitutional differences between them was essentially one of emphasis. In 1951 a new constitution established regional legislatures in Eastern, Western, and Northern Nigeria, but it fell far short of self-government. In 1954, after further conferences, the British finally agreed to establish a full federal system, with a central legislature and regional assemblies. From 1954 to 1960 the struggle for self-government turned into a conflict between Nigerian politicians rather than a Nigerian struggle against the British; the chief element of delay was the lack of mass political organization and administrative experience in the north.[2] The Nigerian leaders nevertheless displayed a high level of statesmanship. Complete fragmentation was avoided, and in 1957 the Nigerian central legislature called on Britain to set the date of independence. There were further negotiations, and in 1960 the country achieved full dominion status. Three years later the new federation followed in Ghana's path by adopting a republican form of government, though continuing to pursue a more moderate and pro-Western policy than its rival Ghana.[3] The smaller British West African colonies followed suit.[4] However, English remained the official medium of communication everywhere, and British economic enterprise continued to play a major role in these emergent nations.

Decolonization in British West Africa followed a path of strict legality. Imperial devolution in French-speaking Africa, on the other hand, began with a French revolution. In 1940 the Third Republic went down in military defeat. The French possessions overseas were temporarily left stranded, but soon the Vichy regime asserted its power, and by the end of June 1940 most of the French West and Equatorial African territories had sworn allegiance to Marshal Pétain. Two centers of political resistance, however, remained. In Chad, Governor Félix Eboué, a West Indian, held aloof from Vichy; he was supported by the French residents in Fort-Lamy, who were almost all hostile to Vichy and determined to resist the French metropolitan government. In the French Cameroun, the majority of French colonists and most of the African elite found the prospect of submitting to Vichy equally unacceptable. Capitulation to Pétain would surely mean the eventual incorporation of the territory into the Reich. Cameroun had been a German colony; Nazi prewar propaganda had stridently demanded the return of Germany's former colonies. In 1940 French De Gaullist sympathizers therefore staged a successful

2 John E. Flint, *Nigeria and Ghana* (Englewood Cliffs, N.J., 1966), p. 164.
3 For excellent recent studies see Dennis Austin, *Politics in Ghana, 1946–1960* (London, 1964); James S. Coleman, *Nigeria: Background to Nationalism* (Berkeley, Calif., 1958); Richard L. Sklar, *Nigerian Political Parties: Power in an Emergent African Nation* (Princeton, N.J., 1963).
4 Sierra Leone achieved independence in 1961 and Gambia in 1965.

coup; Chad followed Free France. In Brazzaville, Colonel de Larminat, aided by local sympathizers, similarly seized power on General de Gaulle's behalf; Gabon declared for the cause of Free France. The French Equatorial colonies became a base for resistance to the Germans. A new political spirit grew up, and this found expression in more progressive legislation. In 1942 De Gaulle, at Eboué's behest, promulgated new decrees concerning the status of the *évolué* and of the *communes indigènes*. Two years later, in 1944, the Free French assembled the Brazzaville Conference. The Free French required their African possessions as a political base. They still believed in political assimilation as a goal, but they were willing to pursue administrative decentralization as a policy. They agreed that the colonies should have a say in a projected new constitution; the conference thus advocated some kind of a colonial parliament, preferably a federal assembly, as well as various social reforms, including the abolition of forced labor.[5]

The French constitution of 1946 retreated somewhat from the Brazzaville position; the Fourth Republic stressed assimilationist doctrines and tried to reconcile federalist concepts with the realities of a French Union. But the reformers' work unwittingly favored the cause of imperial devolution. The constitution provided for the creation of legislative assemblies in the French territories and thereby gave great encouragement to the creation of parties. The constitution also guaranteed the right to vote and, for all its numerous brakes and safeguards, began to draw the masses into politics. At first there were numerous restrictions. French nationals enjoying civil status could exercise the franchise without qualification. Those citizens of other status had to be specifically enumerated. But the voter lists nevertheless grew steadily. The enumeration of 1946 included practically all people who had at any time held responsible positions in private or public enterprise, veterans, property owners, and holders of hunting or driving licenses. In 1947 the basic list was supplemented to include people literate in French and Arabic; later all heads of families were also included. Constitutional advancement mainly benefited the Rassemblement Démocratique Africain (RDA), a union of African parties led by Félix Houphouet-Boigny. The RDA, though petty bourgeois more than proletarian in character, at first cooperated with the Communists both in Africa and in France itself. However, when the Communists tried to turn it into a dependent fief, the RDA split. Houphouet took the greater part of the organization along with him in a new policy of full cooperation with the French. The moderate

[5] Victor T. Le Vine, *The Cameroons, from Mandate to Independence* (Berkeley, Calif., 1964), pp. 131ff.

RDA politicians encountered a good deal of criticism from more radical Africans; the French colonies, after all, remained politically tied to the mother country; there was little talk of independence, and even French Communists thought in some ways along assimilationist lines.

African politicians nevertheless wielded increasing influence. The new French citizenship laws made Africans legally equal to Frenchmen and subjects equal to their chiefs. The old-style French district officer, once king of the bush, lost more and more of his traditional powers. The proliferation of technical services, subordinate to their own directors, did away with the administrative simplicities of old. The appointment of independent judicial officers deprived local administrators of their accustomed function as local judges.[6] The French administration thus lost internal cohesion, and educated Africans obtained more say. In Paris, French party alignments were fluid, and party discipline continued lax. The African bloc in the Chamber of Deputies could therefore make its power felt by trading votes on French domestic issues for concessions concerning their African bailiwicks. Africans achieved ministerial positions in Paris, and in 1956 a Socialist government headed by Guy Mollet tried to work out a new compromise by means of the so-called Loi Cadre, passed at the behest of Gaston Deferre, then minister for France overseas. The various African territories received semiresponsible government; the two federations of French West Africa and French Equatorial Africa were weakened, a change much desired by wealthier African territories like Houphouet's Ivory Coast, which resented having to shoulder economic burdens for the more backward hinterland states. Houphouet still envisaged a Franco-African Community with federal institutions and a common executive; he opposed RDA politicians like Sékou Touré, who stood for African independence within something like a French Commonwealth of Nations.[7]

In 1958 Houphouet got his chance. Morocco and Tunis had both attained their independence in 1956. A desperate struggle was continuing in Algeria, where French settlers, the French army, the metropolitan government, and competing Algerian independence movements all pursued different aims. The guerrilla war waged by Algerian nationalists against the French had led to a bloodstained deadlock. In May 1958 De Gaulle assumed power as a result of the

[6] The authors are indebted to an as yet unpublished paper by Robert L. Delavignette for much of this information.

[7] For a good general study see Thomas L. Hodgkin and Ruth Schachter, *French-speaking West Africa in Transition* (International Conciliation, No. 528; New York, 1960).

Algerian imbroglio and appointed Houphouet as one of his principal ministers of state. The General was determined to bring the Algerian struggle to an honorable close and rebuild French military and political prestige in Europe. He had exalted notions of a great community of African peoples freely linked to France; he was resolved not to repeat the mistakes made in Africa north of the Sahara. The French Union gave way to a French Community, and each territory was allowed to vote on the question of status and membership within this new grouping. All French territories approved of the new instrument, with one decisive exception.

Sékou Touré controlled Guinea; he instructed his followers to vote no, and in 1958 Guinea obtained full independence. The French angrily withdrew all their personnel and technical aid; the course of imperial devolution was now decided by the speed of the fastest, not the slowest, ship in the fleet. Guinea was admitted to the United Nations and garnered all the prestige accruing to a sovereign power, however small. The more moderate African leaders had to be content with appointments to the French delegation; they had to meet the usual charges of being "neocolonialist stooges," and the various French-speaking territories thus rapidly drifted into full independence.

Territorial nationalism meant political fragmentation. Senghor and other like-minded men tried to reconstitute a French West African federation, but the Ivory Coast remained aloof and the scheme broke down. A much less ambitious project of linking Senegal and Sudan in a Federation of Mali came to grief both over personal disagreements between leading statesmen and over differences of opinion that arose from the economic disparity between the relatively well-off Senegal and the poverty-stricken Sudan. In 1960 the various French territories all obtained full independence. Togo and Cameroun, both of them former trust territories, as well as Dahomey, the Ivory Coast, Niger, Upper Volta, Mauritania, and Mali (the former French Sudan) remained outside the French Community. The Malagasy Republic, Senegal, Chad, the Central African Republic (flanking the Belgian Congo to the north), and Gabon stayed within the Community, but were also recognized as sovereign states, with their own representation in the United Nations.

There was a certain amount of unreality about a nation like Gabon, with its queerly shaped frontiers and with only half a million people. But vested interest in fragmentation was too strong; once a territory attained independence, no reigning president, prime minister, or parliamentary secretary had much wish to lose his status by joining a federal union and reverting to the position of a provincial potentate. The new French states also had many difficulties with their neighbors.

Mauritania had to resist Moroccan claims for annexation. Togo became locked in a bitter dispute with Ghana. Cameroun now insisted on a precarious unity defining its borders according to the earlier German Kamerun and had to cope with serious internal violence.

Fragmentation, however, had certain administrative advantages; none of the new states was too large for effective administration. The community of interests among the states of "French expression" was quite real. Their economies were closely linked to that of France, which continued to supply numerous exports and which, in relation to its income and population, provided more foreign aid to its former dependencies than any other country in the world. The French cultural imprint also remained profound. French culture was so pervasive that French-speaking African leaders often encountered great difficulty in meeting British Africans on a common ground; an attempted union between Ghana and Guinea, the two most radical African states on the West Coast, never got very far. The various French African leaders on the whole developed greater fellow feeling than their counterparts in British Africa. Not only had their countries been administered under a common system in the past, but the most prominent political men had often been to the same schools—for example, the William Ponty school in Dakar. They had shared the same experiences as members of the French Assembly or belonged to the same political movement, so that former French Africa continued to function as a political reality in the postcolonial world.[8]

The Belgian Congo, on the face of it, also belonged to Africa of French expression. The Congo, however, was to have a history very different from that of French West Africa. The Belgians had governed their vast African dominion in an autocratic and paternalistic fashion; they aimed at the creation of a conservative, well-satisfied African bourgeoisie which would act as the junior partner in a Belgo-Congolese partnership designed to develop the country's economic wealth. The Belgians built up excellent medical and social services; they encouraged technical education; they promoted African housing schemes. But they failed to associate the emergent African elite in the work of senior administration. They tried to keep the Congo isolated from the rest of the world, and they failed to provide a central legislature which might have acted as a focus of national unity. At the same time there was a good deal of discontent among the better-educated proletarians in the cities. The évolués resented exclusion from the more senior administrative jobs; they also envied the high

---

[8] For a summary see Stewart C. Easton, *The Rise and Fall of Western Colonialism: A Historical Survey from the Early Nineteenth Century to the Present* (New York, 1964), pp. 284–292.

standard of living enjoyed by white expatriates, who had to be tempted to the colonies with substantial salaries. In the countryside the dual impact of an exchange economy on a subsistence economy and of Christianity on paganism produced a host of new social problems, and rural radicals often became as resentful of the educated Africans as of the Belgian rulers. In 1940 Belgium, like France, was overrun by the Germans, and all links between the metropole and its colonies snapped. But the Belgian administration remained in command of the situation, and the Congolese made no attempt to throw off Belgian rule. After the war the Belgians for a time were intent on holding onto their colonies. The Belgians, like the British, voted massive funds for a vast development program.[9] Belgian solidarity in the Congo, however, began to disintegrate as a result of social and political changes within the motherland. The triple alliance of Church, state, and companies suffered its first blow in the educational field. There was a bitter struggle between Catholics and anticlerics over Church education; both groups tried to enlist African support, and many *évolués* proclaimed themselves anticlerics in an attempt to increase African influence in public life. By 1958 the old alliance between Church and state had broken down. Even the union between the state and the trusts had been somewhat shaken by a rather unpopular government decision to call in American capital to develop the hydroelectric resources of the lower Congo.[10]

The extension of Belgian political and social struggles promoted speedier reforms; it also created sharp shifts in policy. Between 1945 and 1947 the Belgians put through various social-improvement schemes. The *évolués,* however, stepped up their demands, and from 1947 to about 1954 the Belgians attempted to meet the new challenge by a policy of cautious assimilation. Advanced Africans received some privileges; at the same time the Belgians vainly tried to force the mass of Africans into a Western way of life by discouraging polygamy, suppressing certain traditional associations dedicated to the maintenance of pagan rituals, and taking action against various Messianic movements that responded to the social and spiritual aspirations of the poorly educated.

The 1954 elections brought a Liberal-Socialist coalition into

[9] For an excellent recent work see Alan P. Merriam, *Congo: Background of Conflict* (Evanston, Ill., 1961), especially p. 39. The plan was intended to cover the period from 1950 to 1959, and the Belgians projected a total expenditure of some 48,114,000 francs or $962,280,000.

[10] Ruth M. Slade, *The Belgian Congo: Some Recent Changes* (London, 1960), pp. 39–43. See also Crawford Young, *Politics in the Congo: Decolonization and Independence* (Princeton, N.J., 1965), a major study.

power at Brussels. The Belgians allowed more freedom of speech and publication to the Congolese. Africans obtained a greater share in local government. There was new social-welfare legislation, and two universities were founded in the country. The Belgians now aimed at "gradual emancipation," but instead began gradually to lose control of the situation.[11] The Belgian authorities found themselves under increasing fire from critics at home. In Belgium the colonial cause had commanded even less public support than in Britain or France. Now a large section of the academic intelligentsia entered the battle against empire; bitter struggles continued among Liberals, Socialists, and Catholics concerning colonial policy. The United Nations became a major force in the battle for imperial emancipation. More important still, Belgium's Western European allies were now embarked on a policy of rapid decolonization. Ghana achieved independence. In 1958 De Gaulle visited Brazzaville, just across the Congo River from Léopoldville, and announced that any French African territory desiring independence could strike out on its own.

De Gaulle's ringing words made a profound impression among educated Africans in the Belgian as well as in the French Congo. To make matters worse from the Belgian point of view, copper prices were beginning to fall. Although there was unemployment, more people kept drifting into the cities, where the population rapidly outgrew the means of production. The immigrants formed a host of voluntary associations—tribal, regional, and professional—but of all these voluntary groupings, tribal associations were not only the most numerous, but also the most dynamic.[12] At the same time Belgian internal dissensions helped to weaken the authority of traditional chiefs. In opposition at Brussels, the Social Christian Party, for instance, bitterly blamed the authorities for encouraging pagan superstitions and this was accompanied by a widespread campaign in the newspapers accusing traditional authorities of corruption, extortion, and even ritual murders. Many chiefs attempted legal proceedings, but they were not allowed to take their cases to the courts because the administration feared an open conflict between chiefs and missionaries. This was the beginning of a civil-disobedience movement which spread rapidly through the country and found enthusiastic support among the young. African confidence in the stability of European rule began to wane rapidly, and the language of politics became in-

[11] Georges Brausch, *Belgian Administration in the Congo* (London, 1961), pp. 62–72.

[12] René Lemarchand, "Congo (Leopoldville)," in James S. Coleman and Carl G. Rosberg, Jr. (eds.), *Political Parties and National Integration in Tropical Africa* (Berkeley, Calif., 1964), pp. 560–596, especially p. 569.

creasingly uncompromising. Congolese political manifestos, such as that of the *Conscience Africaine,* a prominent African journal, still spoke in terms of extreme moderation; in 1956 *Conscience Africaine* accepted a cautious scheme for a thirty-year plan leading to political emancipation. ABAKO (Alliance des Bakongo), however, issued a militant reply, asking for emancipation not in thirty years' time, but today.[13] After this no party could afford to come out with more modest demands. The campaign for full and speedy independence received further encouragement from academic well-wishers of the Congo overseas and from a great conference of pan-African national-ists held at Accra in 1958.

In Belgium itself there was a further shift in political power. The 1958 elections returned a Social Christian Party majority. Brussels appointed a parliamentary commission to formulate a policy of eman-cipation; from then on every decision in the Congo was to be subject to political discussion in Belgium. As a reaction, civil servants in the Congo would refer the smallest decision to their superiors, and the administrative machinery ground to a halt. Governmental inde-cision, political agitation, growing unemployment and labor activity, lack of schools for urbanized children, and news from abroad helped to spark off serious riots in Léopoldville in 1959. The Belgians re-stored order quickly and ABAKO was dissolved, but in Belgium itself the will to hold onto the colonies was disintegrating. By this time the Belgians could have reestablished their hold only by massive deployment of troops, by repression of political activity in the Congo, and by removing Congolese affairs from the influence of Belgian parliamentarians. However, the conditions for a Belgian counterrevo-lution did not exist, and the Belgians drifted into a policy of rapid decolonization. They had no wish to incur moral and political censure at home and abroad by holding on just for a few years, with ultimate abdication in view. Belgium thus issued a program for leading the country to speedy independence under a new system of government, with local, territorial, and provincial councils on the subordinate level and a chamber of deputies and a senate on the national level. By this time political parties were proliferating all over the Congo; competing political men were jockeying for positions of future power; separate ethnic groups and even corporate bodies such as the Force Publique all looked forward to self-determination.[14] Rioting became endemic in many parts of the country. The demand for independence in several

[13] Both documents have been printed in English in Merriam, *Congo,* pp. 321–336.

[14] For an interesting account see Colin Legum, *Congo Disaster* (Baltimore, 1961).

cases assumed a Messianic character, with promises of a new Heaven and a new Earth; many Congolese refused to pay taxes; civil authority started to disintegrate; and some Europeans began sending their dependents out of the country.

In 1960 the Belgians summoned a round table conference in Brussels, where members of the main Belgian parties met delegates from the principal Congolese groupings as well as traditional chiefs. The Belgians were faced with an African ultimatum: abdicate or fight. The argument was not about independence, but on the question of what form of government the new state should have. Contrary to a widespread myth, many of the new Congolese leaders were by no means devoid of education or practical knowledge. The Congolese delegates assembled at Brussels, for instance, included a substantial bloc of people with post–secondary school training or experience in business or administration.[15] The Congo could also draw on the services of a good many black *diplômés* with advanced qualifications in sciences or humanities.[16] But there was no sense of national unity or common purpose. The Belgian Congo, a country as large as Western Europe and inhabited by a vast number of different peoples, was larger and more difficult to govern than any other African state. Moreover, the Belgians, by having introduced politics at the local rather than the national level, gave an unintended emphasis to tribal loyalties in town and country alike. When national elections were held in 1960, they became in effect an "ethnic census." There was no one predominant nationalist movement with which the Belgians could have bargained over a phased transition to independence; no Congolese leader was strong enough to settle for less than "freedom now," but none enjoyed national status. The round table conference would therefore have done well to work out a federal or confederal type of constitution. Lumumba and his political allies, however, insisted on a strongly centralized republic. The Belgians also wished to preserve the existing administrative structure and dreaded the "Balkanization" of their former colony.

[15] Merriam, *Congo*, p. 100, states that the 72 Congolese delegates interviewed by CRISP, a Belgian research organization, included 12 people educated beyond secondary school level; 12 were chiefs or notables, 25 clerks, 1 a teacher, 5 accountants, 2 planters, 3 members of the legal administration, 6 merchants, 5 civil servants, 2 journalists, 1 an administrator of a cooperative.

[16] At the time of independence the Belgian Congo could draw on the services of some 4,000 *diplômés*, whose qualifications in subjects such as veterinary science, agriculture, teaching, and theology were equivalent to those of American college graduates. In addition, there were 30 Belgian university graduates whose qualifications were equivalent to those of American higher degrees. See Bernard B. Fall, "Education in the Republic of the Congo," *Journal of Negro Education*, XXX, No. 3 (Summer, 1961), 266–276, especially 272.

The round table conference thus pronounced in favor of a unitary constitution. After involved negotiations Lumumba became Prime Minister; his rival, Joseph Kasavubu, head of ABAKO, was made President, and in 1960 the Congo began its troubled career as an independent state.

The Congolese leaders, however, were unable to cope with a steadily worsening situation. Independence created new jealousies, as the spoils of office seemed to be divided in a very unequal fashion. Many African politicians obtained incredibly rapid preferment in the civilian sphere. Clerks became ministers, and junior employees took over whole departments. The soldiers of the Force Publique, a military formation which already had a bad record for brutality and mutinous conduct, therefore came out with similar demands for lightning promotion. In the end the soldiers mutinied, possibly with encouragement which came from outside; white officers were arrested, and some were killed; some white women were raped, often in the presence of their children. Violence did not erupt just because the troops had white officers. In neighboring Zambia, for instance, an African government took over in 1964; there were no black commissioned officers in Zambia at the time, but the Zambians were able to continue the engagement of white British and Rhodesian officers without trouble. In the Congo the "revolution of rising expectations" had gone too far. Wild disorder continued, and in 1960 the Belgians decided to reinforce the troops already stationed at the Kamina and Kitona bases, which themselves formed part of the NATO defense framework. Shortly afterward Moise Tshombe, head of the CONAKAT party (Confédération des Associations Tribales du Katanga), announced the secession of Katanga, the country's richest mining area. Tshombe received support both from the local Lunda people and from the European residents in the area. The central authorities at Léopoldville, on the other hand, pleaded that Belgian intervention formed a violation of the treaty and blamed Belgian instigation for Katanganese separatism. In the end the United Nations agreed to furnish troops, and Belgian colonization ended, as it had begun, with a short-lived attempt at international collaboration over an African trouble spot.[17]

Political development in East and South Central Africa took a somewhat different course. Kenya is in many ways the land of the

[17] See Ernest W. Lefever, *Crisis in the Congo: A United Nations Force in Action* (Washington, D.C., 1965). The Belgians subsequently granted independence to the trusteeship territories of Ruanda and Urundi; these became independent states in 1962.

might-have-beens. Of the many strange suggestions, the most remarkable entailed the creation of a Jewish Zion on the Kenya highlands. In 1895, the British began to drive a railway from Mombasa
to the shores of Lake Victoria for the purpose of destroying the slave
trade, advancing imperial influence inland, and opening a strategic
back door to the still-disputed Nile Valley. The railway, however, had
to be paid for, and the British had to assure their line of regular
traffic. This proved a difficult problem. In precolonial West Africa
many indigenous peoples had already developed a considerable export
trade in tropical crops such as peanuts and palm oil. In West Africa
a sizable trading class had emerged; overseas commerce had already
profoundly affected the hinterland before the British and French ever
parceled out the country during the African scramble. The East African inland trade, however, had depended mainly on commodities such
as ivory and slaves, goods of small bulk and great value. There were
no indigenous agricultural export economies, capable of supplying
trade in bulk. Sir Charles Eliot, the British commissioner for the East
African protectorate, suggested a policy of European colonization in
the salubrious highlands, where white farmers would supply the railway with freights. The British authorities became convinced that
settlement was feasible and that there were endless acres of unoccu-
pied land available for immigrants. In 1903 the imperial government
therefore offered an area amounting to some 5,000 square miles to the
Zionist movement as an autonomous homeland for the persecuted
Jews of tsarist Russia and other countries. The suggestion owed a
great deal to British humanitarian ideals. However, it aroused as
much consternation and dismay among orthodox Jews as among the
British colonists already established in Kenya. The former dreaded
the idea of forfeiting the Holy Land; the latter were incensed at the
idea of turning over British territory to an alien people and of offering
the privileges of self-government to foreigners while withholding
home rule to British subjects in the colony. No one in those days even
considered the African problem or doubted that the Kenya highlands
were in fact available for settlement.[18]

After much experimentation, after many trials, errors, and disappointments, the whites built up a relatively highly productive agricultural economy, based on large estates and specializing in the
production of tropical cash crops such as coffee and pyrethrum. The

[18] Elspeth Huxley, *White Man's Country: Lord Delamere and the Making of
Kenya,* Vol. I, *1870–1914* (2d ed.; London, 1953), 125. After bitter internal
disputes the Zionists rejected the offer for theological rather than political
reasons, and Kenya escaped the problems involved in creating a Jewish "free-
land" on African soil. Instead, British and South African farmers made their
homes in the highlands.

first demands for self-government came from Europeans rather than Africans; the colonists' main political bugbear was at first Indian immigrants rather than the voiceless and voteless indigenous population. The European population, however, remained small. The settlers drew their main strength from farming and trade; there was little industry. Indians rather than Europeans filled the more subordinate posts of clerks, artisans, and traders; the European demand for self-government under white auspices came to naught; the settlers managed to have a major say in local legislation, but they never controlled the executive as a whole. Kenya became the scene of a triangular battle, in which the stronger party always called for imperial devolution and the weaker party advocated the imperial presence. The initiative at first rested with the settlers, and Africans called for British support against the white colonists' protonationalism. In the early 1950s the settlers' political star began to dim; African political and social demands took on an ever-increasing momentum, and now it was the settlers who looked for support from London against their black fellow citizens.

The most politically conscious of all indigenous Kenyan peoples were the Kikuyu. Many Kikuyu managed to obtain an education; many of them gained advancement in the towns. But the Kikuyu tribe also suffered from extensive disruption and profound frustrations. Kikuyu reserves became incapable of yielding a satisfactory livelihood to a population no longer decimated by recurring raids or famines. The Kikuyu claimed extensive land areas alienated to European settlers, whose prosperity and privileges excited the envy of the landless. Kenya, moreover, lacked secondary industries; there were not enough jobs to go around, and the Kikuyu, who contained a larger percentage of educated and half-educated people than any other Kenyan tribe, grew increasingly radical in temper. Some Kikuyu therefore began to advocate the expulsion of European farmers; many turned against Christianity and called for the restoration of ancient customs such as female circumcision. The Kikuyu women especially opposed government-sponsored soil-conservation programs; they argued that the hard work of digging contour ridges and effecting similar improvements would be more profitably spent in the cultivation of their ancestral acres. After a lengthy period of unrest and after many missed opportunities on the government's side, the Kikuyu began the Mau Mau revolt, turning not only against the Europeans, but also against the loyalists of their own race. The Kikuyu rebels were not wholly backward-looking; the insurgents wanted bicycles and similar amenities just as much as their more peaceful neighbors. They were, however, convinced that the destruction of European farming enterprise and of European administration would restore what they imagined to have been a golden past. There was fierce gang fighting in city and countryside alike, and the insurgents combined all kinds of magical practices with the more humdrum business of partisan warfare. The British retaliated by massive arrests, large-scale resettlement, and reindoctrination programs. But above all they elaborated older methods of infiltration used against Communist partisans in the Malayan jungle. They formed pseudo-gangs, made up of captured and converted terrorists and led by European commanders. The pseudo-gangs infiltrated into genuine Kikuyu combat groups, and in the end the uprising was successfully smashed.[19]

The Mau Mau revolt was the only instance in modern British African history where the independence struggle was preceded by a military campaign. The British dealt successfully with the guerrilla uprising, but victory was due to the intervention of imperial forces from Britain. The settlers could not have dealt with the challenge on their own, and their political influence declined accordingly.[20] The aftermath of the Mau Mau uprising in some respects resembled the Boer War in that the victors, after winning their battles in the field, chose subsequent political abdication in preference to a policy of holding on. Success in arms in the end merely speeded the process of what white Kenyans called betrayal and what the advocates of decolonization considered an inevitable course in coming to terms with history.

The British at first tried multiracial government, in which no single racial group would be able to rule the colony on its own. The first advance was the Lyttleton Constitution of 1954, which set up a council of ministers, including a nominated African. After further political strife, Africans were granted parity on the legislative council under an arrangement designed to favor African moderates. The new constitution again proved unacceptable to the African opposition, and in 1960 the British decided on a radically changed course. The settlers lost their commanding position; Africans were allowed to form political parties on a countrywide basis, and the center of politi-

[19] See, for instance, Ian Henderson and Philip Goodhart, *Man Hunt in Kenya* (Garden City, N.Y., 1958). The official British version is contained in F. D. Corfield, *Historical Survey of the Origins and Growth of Mau Mau* (London, 1960). Another government-sponsored study was John C. Carothers, *The Psychology of Mau Mau* (Nairobi, Kenya, 1955). The point of view of a former African detainee is given in Josiah M. Kariuki, *"Mau Mau" Detainee: The Account by a Kenya African of His Experiences in Detention Camps, 1953–1960* (London, 1963).

[20] See George Bennett, *Kenya: A Political History; The Colonial Period* (London, 1963).

cal gravity shifted to the Africans.[21] Tribal antagonisms now burst into the open. The Kenya African National Union (KANU) emerged as a multiethnic group, with the Kikuyu and Luo its most important components; the rival Kenya African Democratic Union (KADU) was made up of various other tribes, including the majority of Masai leaders.

In 1963 Kenya finally obtained full independence under an African government run by KANU and began to face the massive social and political problems involved in land reform. Many European farmers, dreading expropriation of their holdings, the deterioration of administrative services, or personal insecurity, left the country. Others decided to stay on and brave the winds of change. The Europeans argued that they had been encouraged by successive British governments to invest their money and their labor in Kenya; they had bought their land in good faith and had developed at their own risk and with their own enterprise the cash economy on which the country depended. In the Europeans' view a take-over of large, well-run, and highly capitalized farms by an African government acting under popular pressure would merely produce clusters of African small holdings capable of sustaining only low-level subsistence farming. As a result, exports would sharply diminish, and a considerable number of African laborers would find themselves without jobs. This would mean that the land might in fact support fewer people than before, and the country's cash economy might break down. In any case, the settlers should be compensated for loss of their property by the British government, which had originally sold the vacant crown lands to immigrants. However, the imperial government would not in the main grant the settlers' demands. Some European farming activity continued after independence, but the country's future now rests with African agriculture. Africans also stepped into the intermediate positions previously held by Indians in trade and administration, regardless of considerations of economic cost or efficiency. The local burden of decolonization was thus borne by the immigrant communities rather than by the imperial power whose presence had played such an important part in producing Kenya's complicated racial pattern in the first place.

Tanganyika's road to independence was much smoother. In Tanganyika the Germans had encouraged some European farming, but white land settlement was never as extensive as in Kenya. After World War I, many of the German estates passed into the hands of British, Greek, or Indian purchasers, so that the character of settlement became much more cosmopolitan than in Kenya. The settlers were far fewer in number, and their farms intermingled more closely

[21] See, for instance, George Bennett and Carl G. Rosberg, *The Kenyatta Election: Kenya, 1960–1961* (New York, 1961).

with African holdings than in the north. Tanganyika's political future under the British mandate seemed insecure to many settlers; during the 1930s Nazi claims for the return of the former German colonies and fears of British appeasement in Africa helped to keep out other prospective British land purchasers. The white-settlement areas never achieved anything like the solidity of the "white highlands" in Kenya; Tanganyika never had a chance of becoming an "expatriate Ulster" in the tropics. In 1954 the British tried to give expression to their idea of multiracialism by introducing a system of equal representation for Africans, Asians, and Europeans in the legislative council; each race obtained an equal number of members. But the main African nationalist party, the Tanganyika African National Union (TANU), objected to the principle of parity as undemocratic.[22] The British placed great hopes in the supposedly moderate character of TANU, and in 1961 Tanganyika attained independence, beating out even Kenya in the race for full self-government.

White colonization in Kenya, Tanganyika, and neighboring Nyasaland was the product of the planter's frontier; the white community consisted primarily of farmers or estate owners, civil servants, and employees. A large proportion of these men retired to England at the end of their working lives, in much the same pattern as British settlers in India or Ceylon. The two Rhodesias had a somewhat different pattern of settlement. Southern Rhodesia formed part of the South African miner's frontier; the earliest immigrants came to mine gold; later on European companies also developed base minerals, and the mining frontier advanced beyond the Zambezi into what is now northwestern Zambia. The mining compounds in turn provided markets for farmers; white farmers subsequently built up an efficient tobacco industry in Southern Rhodesia and soon were exporting their produce in large quantities. After World War II, Southern Rhodesia began to set up secondary industries, as well as iron and steel mills. But the country's home market remained small; Southern Rhodesian manufacturers could not easily compete with the more substantial enterprises developed in South Africa. The Southern Rhodesians therefore looked to a larger protected market in what was then Northern Rhodesia and Nyasaland. Closer economic association with the black north, white factory owners argued, would facilitate further industrialization; nothing but new manufactures could absorb a rapidly increasing African population unable to find an adequate livelihood in the land. The economies of all three Central African territories were still weak and specialized; a common bloc would be able to borrow capital on more advantageous terms; it would also be

[22] For a detailed appraisal of TANU's point of view see Tom Mboya, *Freedom and After* (London, 1963).

able to carry out a more effective economic policy in matters concerned with railway transport and hydroelectrical development.

The Rhodesian advocates of federation were not, however, thinking in economic terms alone. They were patriotic Britishers who wished to add one more dominion to the empire and lend further luster to the Crown. Rhodesia had, in fact, become one of the world's last remaining repositories of old-fashioned imperial pride; it was in some ways a sociological refrigerator which, in the comparative isolation of Central Africa, preserved traditional British ways of thought that were passing away in the mother country. The British Rhodesians' protonationalism was originally concerned with the supposed threats from white Afrikaners rather than from black Africans. During World War II, British Rhodesians had experienced much hostility from some of their Afrikaner fellow citizens, who thought that South Africa and Southern Rhodesia were ill-advised to fight what they regarded as "England's war" and who objected to conscription in Southern Rhodesia. In 1948 an Afrikaner nationalist government came to power in South Africa; this victory further incensed Rhodesian protonationalists. Postwar prosperity in the Rhodesias attracted numerous Afrikaner immigrants to the lands north of the Limpopo. In Northern Rhodesia especially, British Rhodesians feared that the Afrikaners might gain a majority on the country's small electoral roll; British Northern Rhodesians thus looked to association with the southern sister colony to form a powerful British bloc in the heart of Africa.

Later the British colonists' focus of fear began to shift from Afrikaners to Africans. The West Coast was becoming a black man's country. Central Africa, in the Europeans' view, should avoid this fate. Western democracy, most white Rhodesians argued, could not be effectively naturalized in Africa; the newly independent African countries were all bound to become black dictatorships. The new rulers would have to satisfy the masses by economic concessions; these would be paid for by British settlers, who would lose their farms, their houses, and their jobs to the new ruling class. Since minority rule was inevitable, settlers argued, let it then be exercised by a white minority, more qualified from the technological, the entrepreneurial, and the administrative standpoint than a black party bureaucracy composed of former clerks, chief's messengers, and village schoolmasters. Had Southern Rhodesia, with its white-ruled government, not established a much better record in matters such as African health and educational services than Northern Rhodesia and Nyasaland under the Colonial Office—not to speak of black countries such as Liberia and Ethiopia? Was Southern Rhodesia not attracting numerous black immigrants from the north, especially from Nyasaland? Did these immigration figures themselves not point to the beneficence of settler rule? Were the settlers, unlike many privileged groups in other parts of the world, not willing to tax themselves heavily for the right to rule themselves? The African masses surely were as ignorant as they were apathetic. All they wanted, in the whites' view, was a higher standard of living, which could be provided only by industrialization under white auspices. Some further concessions might have to be made to the blacks, but even liberal Europeans usually thought only in terms of assimilating a limited group of able Africans, a policy which would in fact deprive the untutored masses of their effective or potential leaders.[23]

The Africans in the northern territories saw the issue in a very different light. Association with the white south would prevent African advancement; the industrial color bar would harden, and Africans would lose their land to white immigrants. White Southern Rhodesians would introduce their own form of direct rule in the north and do away with chiefs. The settlers, having gotten political concessions, would only ask for more. The Europeans would set up a white dominion on the South African model. Political association with Southern Rhodesia would prevent the emergence of independent black states and leave Europeans in possession of a political monopoly. The northern Africans, politically still on the defensive, thus looked to the imperial power for protection; potential decolonizers, by a strange but perfectly intelligible logic, asked for help from the Colonial Office.

The British imperial authorities, for their part, tried to yoke the white and the black ox before the same cart. The problems of multiracial territories, in their view, could be solved only by a partnership in which neither race could permanently dominate the other. An association of white Southern Rhodesia with the black north would gradually erode the European power structure south of the Limpopo. Economic advancement would soften political controversy. A united Central Africa, peaceful, stable, and pro-Western, would then become a third force on the African continent, capable of mediating between Afrikaner-ruled South Africa and the emergent black states on the West Coast.[24]

This was Britain's last chance, British experts argued in the early 1950s. The choice lay between partnership and race war. The British must therefore help to create a new kind of political association.

[23] See, for instance, Lewis H. Gann and Michael Gelfand, *Huggins of Rhodesia: The Man and His Country* (London, 1964), pp. 208–229, for the views of the leading white Rhodesian statesman.

[24] Lewis H. Gann, *A History of Northern Rhodesia: Early Days to 1953* (London, 1964), pp. 397–413, 434–437.

The imperial factor, however, would still have to play a vital role in Central Africa. The settlers could not be trusted to look after purely African matters in the north. The British, against much opposition from Rhodesian statesmen, therefore successfully insisted on a federal rather than a unitary constitution. The Colonial Office would still retain a vital say in Northern Rhodesia and Nyasaland; sensitive subjects such as police, African education, African agriculture, and African social services (except university education) would remain territorial preserves. The federal government, on the other hand, would look after noncontroversial subjects such as defense, economic planning, postal services, communications, and technical departments—a division of functions which still assumed that African affairs could be neatly sliced off from decisions of a more general kind.

In 1953, after a period of intense political agitation, the three Central African territories joined in the Federation of Rhodesia and Nyasaland, a semiautonomous state within the British Commonwealth. The country's constitution was a compromise, designed to balance the multiplicity of conflicting forces within the Federation. The constitution was complex, so full of checks and balances that few citizens, white or black, could have given an intelligible account of the exact way in which the three territories were governed. The partnership formula, designed to reconcile the various racial interests, itself became a bone of contention. European advocates of federation equated partnership with a constitution, depending on a property-weighted franchise which strongly favored the whites. The metropolitan power looked to the gradual emergence of a nonracial state where color would cease to count. African nationalist leaders interpreted partnership as a promise of ultimate African self-rule. The conflicting parties never developed a political consensus, and not only African politicians, but also many European Rhodesians, regarded the Federation as nothing but a makeshift arrangement which would ultimately break up into its constituent parts. The federal state never succeeded in building up a new national loyalty. Few Africans ever thought of themselves as Rhodesians; few Europeans considered themselves Central Africans.

From the economic standpoint the new state was a much greater success. Industrialization continued at great speed in Southern Rhodesia. According to some economists, the Federation for a time indeed achieved the fastest rate of economic advancement ever attained in any part of the world.[25] There was a remarkable rise in African real wages. The Federation's greatest achievement, in terms of brick

[25] For detailed figures see William Vernon Brelsford (ed.), *Handbook to the Federation of Rhodesia and Nyasaland* (London, 1960).

and concrete, was the construction of the Kariba Dam; this vast hydroelectric project dammed up the Zambezi River and created the greatest man-made lake on earth. However, the settlers could not win the battle for men's minds, either at home or abroad, and unlike similar Communist projects, Kariba was never accepted by world opinion as a credential of political legitimacy. Within the Federation itself there were a number of limited social reforms. But even if the Europeans had been willing to advance further on the path of integration, the very nature of the constitution prevented the federal authorities from having much direct impact on African affairs. The federal government thus found itself in the unenviable position of being blamed for errors for which it bore neither governmental nor administrative responsibility.

The federal state did not in fact create any of the evils expected by African leaders in the early 1950s. No African was driven from his ancestral acres except in a small area near the Kariba Dam; the industrial color bar was somewhat relaxed rather than tightened. The franchise, adopted on the federal level in 1958, actually gave more voting rights to Northern Rhodesian and Nyasaland Africans than had unadulterated Colonial Office rule. Africans obtained admittance to the federal civil service on terms previously unknown not merely in Southern Rhodesia, but also under the much-vaunted Colonial Office dispensation of prefederal days in Northern Rhodesia and Nyasaland. But neither liberal and humanitarian opposition in Britain nor African nationalist opinion in Central Africa was in any way appeased. Reforms that would have appeared substantial in the late 1940s seemed miniscule in the late 1950s. In the northern territories able leaders such as Kenneth Kaunda and Hastings Banda built up well-organized mass parties; these rested on wide popular support and charismatic leadership and made great promises of the social benefits that would accrue by liquidating the white man's "stupid" federation. Half-hearted attempts at repression stimulated rather than destroyed the opposition, and the political initiative passed to the northern Africans.[26] The drop in world copper prices, which had exerted such an important influence on decolonization in the Congo, also hit the Federation. Unrest steadily increased. In 1959 open violence broke out in Nyasaland, the most backward and poverty-stricken of the three territories and politically the weakest link in the federal chain. Federal troops, white and black, successfully restored order. But London now

[26] For two interesting works written from the African nationalist point of view see Kenneth D. Kaunda, *Zambia Shall Be Free: An Autobiography* (London, 1962; New York, 1963), and Guy Clutton-Brock, *Dawn in Nyasaland* (London, 1959).

began to lose faith in both the federal experiment and the traditional formula of multiracial government. There was more rioting in Northern Rhodesia, and the imperial government steadily began to shift the representation weight on the northern territorial legislatures in the Africans' favor. Racial conflict thus threatened to find constitutional expression in a deadlock between the federal authorities at Salisbury and the territorial authorities in Lusaka and Zomba. The Europeans, still numbering only a quarter of a million in the federal state as a whole, shrank back from illegality. Despite much angry grumbling, the federal authorities did not dare take the risk of seizing power in the territorial sphere and of declaring the federal state independent by a *coup d'état*.

After much further recrimination, the imperial government at last decided to break up the ill-fated federal state. In 1963 the Federation was dismantled; a year later Northern Rhodesia and Nyasaland attained full independence under black governments, becoming known respectively as Zambia and Malawi. The unified Central African economic area broke up into its component parts. Southern Rhodesia, the only Central African territory with a more diversified industrial base, now faced the danger of losing its economic hinterland beyond the Zambezi. The colony retained its local autonomy, but lacked international status. The old property-weighted franchise continued in existence, leaving the territorial state machinery in control of a mainly European electorate. In 1965 the Rhodesian government proclaimed the country's complete independence, without, however, gaining international recognition. Faced with the threat of economic and diplomatic boycott from overseas, the Europeans were forced to look for support from South Africa. British imperial devolution thereby helped to drive Britain's last African colony into the Afrikaner sphere. Zambia and Malawi, on the other hand, found themselves in the unenviable position of not controlling their own trade outlets. Zambian commerce remained dependent on Southern Rhodesian railways to the south and on Portuguese railways to the west. Malawi relied on the Portuguese-controlled port of Beira, so that a new, uneasy equilibrium came into existence along the southern frontier of African-ruled Africa.

In the Portuguese empire events took a very different course. During the scramble for Africa the Portuguese, with their extreme brand of nationalism, had confounded all prophets by successfully holding onto their overseas possessions against more powerful competitors such as the British and the Germans. The Portuguese were determined to repeat this operation during the "unscrambling" of Africa, and up to the present they have succeeded. In the interwar years lack of capital, labor, and markets had caused stagnation in the Portuguese colonies. Wartime prosperity, however, brought about drastic changes. Angola and Mozambique alike did well during the war in consequence of the worldwide shortage of colonial produce, all the more so since the Portuguese were excluded from the buying arrangements of the Allied Combined Food Board and could make their own terms. The colonies also shared in the general postwar boom. The cautious financial policy of the Portuguese government had built up sizable financial reserves, and the authorities were thus able to resume and even improve upon development schemes already announced before World War II. Even more remarkable than the economic "great leap ahead" in the two major African provinces— an upsurge that was, after all, paralleled in many other parts of Africa—was the new-found confidence of the Portuguese administration. The Portuguese felt they were safe from external attack; the Portuguese state itself was solvent; there was no serious revolutionary threat in Lisbon. These factors all combined to create a very different atmosphere from that experienced by previous Portuguese generations. Portugal had not been seriously involved in World War II; the mother country had never been overrun; Portuguese nationalism had not exhausted its impetus. Portugal also remained in some ways a kind of ideological museum, where older concepts, once current in Western Europe as a whole, retained their vigor. Patriotism and pride of empire continued to go hand in hand as nowhere else in Europe. Portugal, though short of domestic capital, thus financed a large development plan in the colonies.[27]

In addition, the Portuguese vigorously promoted white settlement in their colonies, especially in Angola. Between 1940 and 1957 the European population of Angola rose from about 44,083 to 156,703, and it is still going up. The Portuguese hope to turn Angola into a kind of African Brazil, politically linked to the motherland, infused with a common loyalty, and held together by a Portuguese national mystique that would transcend the barriers of color. The Portuguese at the same time made a number of limited social reforms which bore some resemblance to those effected by the French under the Brazzaville program. The Portuguese were successful in containing internal opposition to their rule in Mozambique. Angola, however, was struck by the backwash of decolonization in the Congo. Resistance centered on the Ba-

[27] Based on Richard J. Hammond, *Portugal's African Problem: Some Economic Facets* (Carnegie Endowment Occasional Paper No. 2; New York, 1962). According to Hammond, some 4,385 million escudos or nearly $150 million was invested in public funds in Angola and Mozambique between the years 1953 and 1955 alone. Probably about the same amount of private capital was invested during the same period.

kongo people, whose territory straddled the former Belgian Congo, and in 1961 Holden Roberto, a Bakongo, launched a liberation campaign which obtained great support from the Congolese side of the border. The rebels carried out extensive massacres, and many Europeans and their African supporters were murdered or tortured to death; numerous plantations were wiped out, and the Angolan economy sustained a temporary blow. The insurgents, however, had underestimated the strength of the Portuguese state machinery, an error all the more excusable as it was shared by most Western European and American experts. Portugal, though militarily among the weakest of the NATO powers, struck back successfully. The Portuguese strongly reinforced their troops, launched a counter terror campaign, and turned Angola into an armed camp, laced with strongholds and landing strips. They adopted an offensive based on small, mobile combat groups, supported by helicopters. Enemy partisan formations were kept on the move and were driven deeper and deeper into the forests; African refugees gradually drifted back from the Congo, and the Portuguese were able to resume work on their plantations.

The Portuguese also tried to benefit from the lessons learned by the French army in Indochina and Algeria and linked reconquest to an extensive social development program. They multiplied local schools and regrouped the scattered African villages into centralized settlements, supplied with a school, a church, local administration buildings, and a clinic. Regrouping was intended to isolate the guerrillas both physically and psychologically, but village consolidation also facilitated more active economic development. The Portuguese at the same time put up new factories and houses in the bigger urban centers, especially Luanda. Railway and port facilities were expanded, so that the economic basis of Portuguese power was substantially increased. The partisans, for their part, failed to secure adequate support from the Organization of African Unity. They were further weakened by internal divisions. The Angolan People's Union under Roberto, a nationalist, failed to see eye to eye with the Movement for the Liberation of Angola (1959), a front which had incorporated the Communist Party of Angola. Furthermore, powerful Angolan tribes such as the Ovimbundu were untouched by the Bakongo movement. In 1964, moreover, Moise Tshombe, a pro-Western former leader of the secessionist Katanga state, became Prime Minister of the Congolese Republic. The Congo for the time being could no longer effectively serve its intended role as a privileged sanctuary. Guerrilla activity, far from attaining the projected "third stage" of massive military operations postulated by Mao Tse-tung, reverted to the "first stage" of small-scale terrorism, which the Portuguese seem to have under fairly effective control. In Mozambique the Frelimo movement headed by Eduardo Mondlane has not been successful. Decolonization thus helped to bring about what has been called a white counter-revolution.[28] The Portuguese, the white Southern Rhodesians, and the South Africans consolidated their military position, and also vastly expanded their local economic potential, so that the outcome of the decolonization campaign in the southern portion of Africa now remains in doubt.

[28] The phrase comes from Jean Ziégler, *La contre-révolution en Afrique* (Paris, 1963).

22. Imperial Balance Sheet: A Summing Up

Men all through the ages have gloried in the splendor of empire. "And Solomon reigned over all kingdoms from the river unto the land of the Philistines, and unto the border of Egypt: they brought presents, and served Solomon all the days of his life," proudly wrote the Biblical chronicler. "For he had dominion over all *the region* on this side the river. . . : and he had peace on all sides round about him."[1] Zulu praise singers and *griots* from Sine-Saloum composed poems in a similar vein; they likened their respective monarchs to mighty elephants, whose victories were countless, like the stars in the sky, and against whose might none could prevail. Innumerable conquerors in history wrote in a similar fashion about their military records. The moral revulsion against all empire embodied in an active political, rather than a passive theological, creed is thus a recent phenomenon. It had its origins in the West, where it went hand in hand with a reaction against any kind of authority, moral, religious, political, or economic, which did not rest—or which elaborate and specious manipulation did not make appear to rest—on the free consent of the governed. At the same time there was a revaluation of the origins of empire. Prophets from times immemorial have cursed the strong and condemned the counselors who took gold for justice. Jesus himself drove the money changers out of the Temple. But the assumption that the religion taught in the Temple (or indeed the whole framework of political power associated with the Temple) was but the superstructure of the moneylenders' and landlords' economic power is again a modern Western concept.

The economic interpretation of history arose from Western attempts to grasp the essence of reality, to find the real behind the apparent, to psychoanalyze history, as it were, and to reveal hidden motives in the

[1] I Kings 4:21 and 24.

360

minds of the mighty, motives that might not be apparent even to the actors themselves. Applied to modern imperialism, the economic interpretation of history, as elaborated by Hobson and Lenin, made modern Western imperialism in Africa a thing apart, a force of Satanic destructiveness. The new theory associated Western conquests with money, not glory. The scramble for Africa was explained by the overabundance of capital in the bank accounts of European capitalists. The monopolists' inability to find sufficient profitable investments at home supposedly was the true driving force of Western imperialism in Africa. Colonial exploitation, the argument continued, drained Africa of its riches, furnished the West with an enormous unearned increment of wealth, and even sapped the European proletarians' will to revolt.

In Africa, the neo-Marxist or quasi-Marxist argument also states that Western conquest wrecked traditional societies and prevented a more natural and gradual indigenous evolution. Medieval English feudalists, the assumption continues, may have served a "progressive function" in subjugating the tribal Welsh, but modern English capitalists cannot boast of a similarly progressive role in subduing African tribal or feudal polities. The West as a whole thus owes a great moral and economic debt to the underdeveloped world. The African peoples, who have at last gained their independence, should now retaliate for "a century of wrong,"[2] either by extorting aid on an unprecedented scale from their former oppressors or by initiating protracted wars or bloody revolutions against pro-Western traitors on African soil.

This philosophy, or some more pacific variant, now forms part of the accepted political orthodoxy among many educated black people from the Cape to Cairo and from Dakar to Dar es Salaam. It also appeals to many Western thinkers who feel a profound concern, a secularized sense of guilt, for the iniquities committed or supposedly committed by white people in Africa. "Consciencism," the name given by Kwame Nkrumah to his own pan-Africanist philosophy, might indeed justly be used to describe the ways of thought adopted by many of the best minds in the West itself.

Our own analysis has come to different conclusions. The history of empire reveals much greater continuity than is assumed in the cataclysmic view that postulates a dialectical rhythm, punctuated by abrupt jumps, where slow quantitative changes lead to sudden qualitative changes. The scramble for Africa at the end of the nineteenth century formed part of a much longer story of imperial conquest, a story that had been going on throughout the earlier part of the nine-

[2] The phrase was actually used by a white Afrikaner speaking of British rule in South Africa.

teenth century and before. But the particularity of the new imperial motivation did not lie in the supposed overabundance of capital seeking new investment opportunities. Bismarckian Germany, not to speak of late nineteenth-century Italy and Portugal or of Russia and Japan, was not bursting at the seams with funds for which no employment could be found nearer home. Britain was sending money abroad in large quantities, but British capital exports had already attained noteworthy dimensions before the onset of the scramble. Most British capitalists preferred to place their funds in white-settlement areas such as the United States, Canada, Australia, and Argentina, rather than tropical Africa. Nor is there any justification for the romantic theory that the true imperial decisions were made by the Rothschilds and the Bleichröders from the obscurity of a countinghouse. Salisbury and Bismarck were not men to be manipulated by their bankers. Nor was it always true that "real" power invariably lay with the lending states. European capitalists could sometimes wield immense influence in a weak and backward state like Egypt or Ecuador, but their ability to do so did not necessarily arise from the strings which supposedly tied the debtor to the lender. The United States, as we have seen, used British capital in large quantities throughout the nineteenth century, but the United States never became a British dependency any more than did Prussia, which in the earlier part of the last century also borrowed British money on an extensive scale.

The African scramble becomes intelligible only through a pluralistic rather than a unitary explanation. There was not one kind of imperialism; there were many—and there were great differences in their respective motives. Insofar as the imperialists had financial incentives, they were concerned more with the protection of trade than with the investment of capital, or they looked upon colonization as a speculation in real estate which might or might not appreciate in the future and which ought to be preempted as an insurance policy against some unspecified future need. However, there were many other considerations. For Germany and Portugal especially, imperialism was a kind of "conspicuous consumption" on a national scale.[3] The desire for prestige or for strategic advantages, the demands made to pacify a "turbulent frontier" (and thereby extend empire), religious or idealistic motives, all played a vital part in different stages of Western empire building. Imperialism went hand in hand with na-

[3] The phrase has been adapted from Veblen by Richard J. Hammond, "Economic Imperialism: Sidelights on a Stereotype," *Journal of Economic History,* XXI, No. 4 (December, 1961), 596.

tional pride and was thus in many ways the highest stage of nationalism.

In a more fundamental sense, imperialism was also the result of African weakness. Many literary men in modern Africa wish to stress the black man's achievements in the past, but observing Africa's present-day backwardness, they come to the unwarranted conclusion that imperialism or the slave trade caused African backwardness. The reverse, however, is much nearer to the truth. The so-called Christian slave trade had rested on an Afro-European partnership in which powerful African potentates sold their prisoners to the white men from beyond the seas. Why then did Africans sell their captives? Because they wanted European trade goods—cloth, guns, knives, hatchets, liquor, and beads. Backward African economies could not produce some of these items at all or in sufficient quantities, or they could not buy them in the desired quantities by means of "legitimate" trade. African rulers were therefore unable on their own to cope with the problems of the slave trade, Christian or Muslim. Abolition came from without, and only European suzerainty could, for the time being, repair the ravages of the gun frontier that was converging on the African interior during the last century.[4] White conquest was often resisted, but with the exception of the Amhara and the Afrikaners, no indigenous people managed to resist European invaders in nineteenth-century Africa. The military reasons for the white man's victory were obvious. As Hilaire Belloc has put it:

> Whatever happens, we have got
> The Maxim gun, and they have not!

But why, then, did they not have the Maxim gun? The answer goes beyond a question of military technology. Maxims and Mausers were themselves the products of a highly complex industrial, technical, and scientific culture, which African tribesmen might envy but could not at the time imitate. The white man was also more advanced in the field of ideas. The production even of machine guns required ideological foundations much broader than those possessed by any contemporary African society. The white man's most important contribution to Africa did not consist of arms or even of quinine tablets. His most important imports were perhaps the very words Africa and African. The peoples of precolonial Africa had no sense of unity. They thought of themselves as Yoruba, Mashona, or Masai. Their minds remained bound by the realities of small territorial communities.

[4] See, for instance, Henri Brunschwig, *L'avènement de l'Afrique noire du XIXe siècle à nos jours* (Paris, 1963), pp. 98ff.

The larger African kingdoms all imposed tight constraints of a social and economic order. European colonial rule subsequently imposed its own barriers, but in the first place it acted as a liberating force. The whites generally desired a free labor market; in the imperial scheme of things there was accordingly no place for the slave trade or domestic servitude. Thus in 1906 British pressure forced the Barotse to emancipate the domestic slaves in their kingdom. Imperial rule and the exigencies of a wider market economy similarly did away with the restraints of trade and production imposed by indigenous authorities. Under the new dispensation there was no room for potentates like King Gezo in West Africa, who would not allow his subjects "to cultivate around Whydah coffee and sugarcane, rice and tobacco, which at times have been found to succeed," or who prohibited the growth of peanuts except for purely domestic purposes. White governance implied a rigid distinction between the new rulers and the ruled, but it did away with indigenous caste differentiation whereby "a caboceer may not alter his house, wear European shoes, employ a spittoon-holder, carry an umbrella without leave, spread over his bed a counterpane, which comfort is confined to princes, mount a hammock, or use a chair in his own home; and if he sits at meat with a white . . . must not touch knife or fork." Traditionally "only 'a man of puncto' may whitewash the interior of his house at Agbome, and the vulgar must refrain from this, as well as from the sister-luxury of plank board doors."[5] The Europeans' new order had, of course, an economic as well as an idealistic rationale. Sumptuary legislation restricted the sale of European goods; "distributor kings" interfered with the freedom of white merchants as well as black customers and suppliers; slave labor was incompatible with wage labor. Advantages for the white man did not, however, necessarily imply disadvantages for the black. For all the *ex post facto* idealizations of precolonial society and of more "organic" types of social orders, there are few records of former slaves who wished to return to servitude or of commoners who wanted to restore sumptuary laws.

In fact, the surprising thing about most imperial conquests was not the amount of bloodshed involved, but the profound contradictions imperialism produced within tribal societies. It was these contradictions which allowed such vast areas to be taken over by relatively small forces and which in so many cases turned European conquest into a multiracial affair, a matter of complex Afro-European alignments, where one black community would try to play off the imperial factor against another. The emergent intelligentsias of the

[5] Sir Richard F. Burton, *A Mission to Gelele, King of Dahome,* ed. by his wife, Isabel Burton, I (London, 1893), 119–120.

nineteenth-century African West Coast, the bulk of African teachers and evangelists in contemporary southern Africa, were usually convinced advocates of imperial domination. Africans like Bishop Samuel Crowther might criticize Western rule in some of its aspects, but they preferred the new order to the old. The people who had actual experience of precolonial Africa, of local despotism, of the social and economic limitations which beset contemporary African kingdoms, of their intellectual narrowness, their rigid social stratification, their poverty, witchcraft executions, political mass liquidations, the superstitious destruction of twins as harbingers of evil, or intertribal warfare—these people did not regard preconquest Africa in the same light as so many modern scholars, whose work is all too often infused both by a nagging sense of guilt and by a generous but deceptive romanticism concerning the glories of a departed society.

Precolonial Africa had many outstanding achievements to its credit. The best of Benin sculptures bear comparison with the best, say, of medieval German art. African dance rhythms have inspired modern music all over the world. Anticolonialists, however, must ask themselves how far and how quickly these indigenous societies could have caught up with the West if the European powers had at the time of the scramble accepted a "self-denying ordinance" and Africans had been spared the experience of foreign rule. Some scholars and politicians give a confident answer to this question. Indigenous African societies, they argue, had appreciable powers of adjustment. Tribal communities were bound to coalesce into feudal states; feudal states would in turn have developed capitalist methods of production; these in turn would have broken the capitalist matrix and would in due course have been replaced by socialism. Others believe that Africans might have avoided the Western capitalist stage altogether and found some entirely new form of social organization. Such a development, the argument continues, would have been more natural; it would also have been more productive. Africans would have been spared the evils of alien exploitation. Africa would have become more than a raw-material producer for the West, more than a hewer of wood and drawer of water for richer nations. The economic state of the continent would therefore have been much healthier. Such conjectures are difficult to evaluate. We do not really know how, say, the "small brave city-state" of Nembe-Brass in the Niger delta would have fared on its own or how social changes would have affected its indigenous house system. Speculations of this kind belong to the realm of "ifs" and "buts" or to an academic cloud-cuckoo-land.

It is, however, legitimate to look at the one and only great African state which (except for a brief period of Italian occupation from

1935 to 1941) remained independent and even managed to participate in the scramble on its own account. Ethiopia had evolved a relatively advanced form of indigenous feudalism. The Ethiopians at the
time of the partition possessed a written language as well as an ancient
cultural tradition dating back to Byzantium. Ethiopia, moreover, managed to build up a substantial armed power. In terms of military and
cultural resources, Ethiopia was far superior to most black African
states in existence in the second half of the nineteenth century, not to
mention the so-called stateless societies. Ethiopia's record indeed
impressed a number of Africans to such an extent that many separatist
churches in other parts of the continent adopted the word Ethiopian
in their names. Geographically, the country is one of the biggest in
Africa; large areas are situated in healthy mountain country. Ethiopia
has notable natural resources, many of which remain unexploited.
After World War II the previously landlocked country obtained a
direct outlet to the sea through Eritrea; in addition, foreign aid flowed
to Ethiopia in considerable quantity.

It is instructive to compare the record of Ethiopian achievement, or
more specifically that of its Amhara rulers, with that of Southern
Rhodesia. Comparisons, of course, can never be exact, for in this
case the odds favor Ethiopia. Southern Rhodesia's size and population are much smaller than Ethiopia's. Precolonial Rhodesia, moreover, was a much more backward country than the northern mountain
state. At the time of white conquest the indigenous tribes had no
written language; their material culture was less highly developed than
that of the Ethiopian ruling group; their military strength was much
smaller, and even Lobengula's warrior kingdom in Matabeleland, the
most powerful community in preconquest Rhodesia, could in no way
bear comparison with the Amharic empire. Furthermore, Southern
Rhodesia was colonized by European settlers. In the language of contemporary anticolonialism, its people became the victims of the worst,
the most oppressive, and the most reactionary form of colonial rule
in existence. Let us therefore place some of the economic achievements of Ethiopia side by side with those of Southern Rhodesia, a
country which in 1960 had been subject to European rule for just
seventy years and which in the early 1960s had only one-sixth of
Ethiopia's population.

	Ethiopia	*Southern Rhodesia*
Area	395,000 sq. mi.	150,333 sq. mi.
Population	24,600,000 (1960 estimate)	4,010,000 (1963 estimate)
Total number of African children at school	224, 934 (1959–1960)	552,000 (Africans only)

	Ethiopia	Southern Rhodesia
Enrollment in secondary schools	8,949 (1959–1960)	4,726 (1959) (Africans in academic and technical secondary schools) 11,947 (1958) (Europeans)
Hospital beds available for Africans	5,823 (1959, excludes Eritrea; includes hospitals and clinics of all kinds)	8,759 (1959, includes hospitals and clinics)
Railways	683 miles (1963)	1,345 miles
Roads	2,900 miles (1963)	36,270 miles (1963)
Electricity consumption (in million kwh)	124.4 (1961)	1,562.0 (1961)
Manufacturing plants	200 (1959)	1,059 (1961)
Workmen employed in industry	26,000 (1960)	97,000 (1961)
Total wages and salaries paid in industry	$6 million (1960)	$69 million (1959)

Such figures testify for themselves; they do not leave much ground for optimism concerning the assumed capacity for more effective African development on an indigenous basis during the imperial era.[6]

Imperial rule obtained equally impressive results in many of the tropical areas of Africa. Africa's economic development centers on a group of expanding "islands." There is no solid frontier, such as that which characterized the economic opening of North America or Australia. There are great variations in the size, distribution, and economic structure of these islands, which are often either completely separated from one another or joined only by tenuous links. Much of the economic advance has taken place on the coast where there are accessible rain-forest zones suitable for the production of cocoa, bananas, palm oil, timber, and other products. A second category, the highland islands, derives its prosperity from a rich volcanic soil or a cooler climate, greater freedom from disease, the presence of European settlement, and ecological suitability for crops like coffee, tea, tobacco, and pyrethrum. A few areas may be classified as irrigation islands; others center on great mining complexes, such as the Katangan and Zambian groups of mines. Some important regions do not fit into these four classifications. Much, for instance, depends on the presence of transport facilities; the unusual dispersion of productive enterprise in the Congo basin is explained by the presence of a great system of inland waterways.

[6] Statistics are based on Violaine L. Junod (ed.), assisted by Idrian N. Resnick, *The Handbook of Africa* (New York, 1963); William A. Hance, *The Geography of Modern Africa* (New York, 1964); and Central African Statistical Department, Salisbury, Southern Rhodesia.

Within these limits the imperial powers achieved a great deal. A widely current doctrine, obligatory among the adherents of Marxism-Leninism, popular as well among many non-Marxist economists, asserts that the underdeveloped world is not only poor, but also stagnant or actually regressing. Progress can be achieved only by breaking the shackles of colonial rule, by a new social revolution which will nationalize the means of production. The economic history of a country such as the former Belgian Congo lends no support to this theory. When the Belgians took command, they found themselves face to face with a people who had attained the technology of the Early Iron Age, whose foreign trade was largely confined to the export of such wealth as slaves, ivory, and some copper. The Belgians introduced new methods of mining; they succeeded in working vast mineral resources which had been inaccessible by traditional methods. By the end of the 1950s the Congo was one of the world's greatest copper producers and was the world's leading exporter of cobalt. Mining in turn stimulated all sorts of other enterprises. Much foreign capital had to be spent on railway construction or port facilities; additional money was invested in workshops, power plants, waterworks, and cement factories. Mining compounds required feeder roads and housing projects, public utilities and services. These in turn attracted people eager to meet the demand of the mining townships for building material, clothes, services, and so forth; the towns gave new outlets for farming enterprise; there was an increase in trade and banking, so that mining acted as a "multiplier-accelerator" of economic growth. The Congo became a great power producer and by the end of the 1950s had attained second rank among all producers of hydroelectricity on the African continent.[7]

Belgian rule provided the country with a huge network of roads and railways; there was river transport on a large scale, and the modern port of Matadi, with its three deepwater quays, a total berthing length of more than a mile, and its freight storage shed covering several hundred acres, could handle a vast volume of maritime traffic. The 1940s and 1950s also saw a rapid expansion of the country's secondary industries. The colony began to manufacture foods, beverages, textiles, chemicals, and other goods; few underdeveloped countries ever attained a swifter rate of industrial growth.[8] The mines and

[7] In 1958 copper exports amounted to 237,562 tons. Diamonds amounted to 16,673,474 carats (all types). The installed capacity of hydroelectric plants amounted to 489,200 kilowatts. *Whitaker's Almanac* (London, 1962), p. 845; United Nations, Statistical Office, Department of Economic and Social Affairs, *Statistical Yearbook, 1959* (New York, 1960), p. 274.

[8] The United Nations *Statistical Yearbook, 1959*, p. 74, gives the index numbers of industrial production as follows: 1938, 11; 1948, 40; 1953, 100; 1958, 140.

factories, the railways and ports, put up under Belgian management represented a truly creative achievement, the result of the colonizers' own enterprise capital and skills. Most of the other colonial powers could point to achievements almost as impressive.

Critics of the Belgian record in particular retort that even though the Congo may have made some social and economic advance, the progress attained was achieved at an exaggeratedly high price, that a small group of interlocking companies reaped an exorbitantly high rate of profit.[9] Defenders of the Belgian record reply that foreign investment accounted for the "capital value of practically every man-made thing in the Congo that stands more than six feet above the ground, not to mention such surface-level assets as railways, roads, harbours, wharves, electric cables, water conduits, drains, etc."[10] They calculated that the return of the total Belgian investment in the Congo of about £1,000 million had been estimated to yield at an average no more than 4 to 5 percent per annum over the years and that probably higher rates of interest could have been secured in Europe. These findings are similar to those of Frankel, who showed that the return from industries even as profitable as those of South African gold-mining concerns had not been unduly high compared with gains made in other parts of the world, after the risks and the costs of prospecting, developing, and redeveloping had been subtracted.[11] Many colonial enterprises made fortunes for their promoters, but many also yielded limited profits or involved their backers in serious losses or bankruptcy. Taking colonial development as a whole, it is nonsense to say that the imperialists joined in plundering Africa. The dramatic increases from production in most colonies benefited all concerned, the peasant producers and the workers as well as expatriate interests. None would have been possible under the rule, say, of Msidi and his Unyamwezi associates, East Coast freebooters who ruled in Katanga at the time of the partition and were toppled from power by the new colonial administration.

The imperialist record was equally impressive in the field of schooling. The Belgian Congo may serve as a convenient example. The Belgians spent about 15 percent of the Congolese budget on schooling; this expenditure got some remarkable results. As of 1960 the Congo

[9] Compare Lord Hailey, *An African Survey: A Study of Problems Arising in Africa South of the Sahara* (revised; London, 1957), p. 1298: in 1953 about 56 percent of the national income was received by Africans; over 14 percent entered the coffers of companies.

[10] George Martelli, *Leopold to Lumumba: A History of the Belgian Congo, 1877–1960* (London, 1962), pp. 215–216.

[11] See S. Herbert Frankel, *Capital Investment in Africa: Its Course and Effects* (London, 1938).

could boast of a literacy rate higher than that of most underdeveloped countries in the world. About 18,000 African schoolchildren went to secondary schools; over 19,000 Africans were technical students, so that the country was relatively well provided with future "noncoms" and junior officers of industry. The Belgian record admittedly was much less impressive in the field of higher education, and the Belgians encountered bitter criticism for their failure to provide the country with sufficient university-trained leaders. This point, nevertheless, can be overstressed. In the words of an American scholar:

> As the Congo emerged from colonialism straight into chaos, well-meaning individuals, including some who should have known better, took up the cry that there were only "sixteen college graduates" in the country when the Belgian tricolor was hauled down in Leopoldville. A good part of the confusion simply arises from the fact that few non-specialists are qualified to judge the educational equivalence of diplomas from varied educational systems. . . . Thus, an evaluation of the exact number of Congolese who now hold the equivalent of an *American* college education . . . is far larger than is usually expected—though still far too small for the Congo's present and future needs.

The number of persons in possession of Belgian diplomas equivalent to American university degrees at the time of independence has actually been estimated at 4,000. This is a figure very different from the magical number of "sixteen college graduates" that will no doubt be remembered forever as the sum total of Belgium's educational effort in the heart of Africa.[12]

The effects of Belgium's educational effort are obviously difficult to assess. If peace cannot be maintained in the Congo, there is every likelihood that education will deteriorate to such an extent that these achievements of the past will become but a memory.[13] Should the Congo manage to keep peace, however, its Belgian-founded system of education has a bright future. Based on a solid foundation of primary schools, backed up by a network of vocational schools capable of providing the country with the technical knowledge essential to a developing economy, and topped by several universities and extension centers, the Congolese educational pyramid rests upon a far more solid base than that of most underdeveloped countries.

Belgian achievement in the educational sphere has been dealt with

[12] Bernard B. Fall, "Education in the Republic of the Congo," *Journal of Negro Education*, XXX, No. 3 (Summer, 1961), 266–276; quotation, 271. See also Crawford Young, *Politics in the Congo: Decolonization and Independence* (Princeton, N.J., 1965), pp. 198–199.

[13] The killing of many educated men by the Simba or rebels has, of course, robbed the Congo of future leaders and administrative and technological cadres.

at some length because the Belgians, more than any other imperial rulers, subsequently had to face the onerous accusation of not having trained their subjects for independence. Ironically enough, these charges were often made by the very people who in the days preceding Congolese independence were most outspoken in their demand for the speedy termination of Belgian imperial rule, either on the grounds of self-government or on the notion that African backwardness was an imperialist propaganda device. The critics who use such arguments forget that only Western imperial rule has been judged by its capacity for self-liquidation. No one has ever censured the Iraqis for not preparing the Kurds for national independence, or the Soviet Union for not having done enough to equip the peoples of Kamchatka or Kazakhstan for the responsibilities of international sovereignty.

In fact, colonial empire in Africa was one of the most efficacious engines of cultural diffusion in world history. Imperial rule involved a vast transfer of human and physical capital to Africa. Much of Africa benefited not merely from enormous private and public investments in brick and mortar, but also from a great transfer of human abilities to Africa. The efforts made by privately subsidized mission societies and similar organizations alone form an outstanding chapter in the history of civilization.

The Western powers brought a host of new economic, medical, social, and administrative techniques to Africa; these in turn have played a decisive role in the history of the continent. The European influence for progress in Africa often receives insufficient emphasis as the result of a new African-centered historical approach. This approach artificially divides the story of the white man in Africa from the doings of the African peoples proper, an attitude which no serious historian would adopt in dealing, say, with the impact of English medieval conquests on tribal Wales. There is, of course, no justification for such a bias. There is no reason that the railways constructed by Belgian projectors in the Congo, or the Kariba Dam created by British, Rhodesian, French, and Italian planners on the Zambezi, should be considered a smaller part of Africa's heritage than the architectural achievements by early stone builders at Zimbabwe or Dhlo-Dhlo.

The Europeans' contribution is equally impressive in the cultural field, including the recovery of Africa's ancient past. Many scholars accuse white imperialists of having given insufficient attention to the doings of black people and of having written the history of Africa in terms of Europe's own past. This critique, however, often ignores two important points. Our knowledge of early Africa is limited, not merely because of the failings of colonial historians, but because documentation on the colonial period is infinitely more comprehensive than that of preceding eras. The colonial powers created extensive written records; they also developed registries, archives, and statistical and demographic services of a kind unknown to more primitive systems of government. Hence far more can be said with accuracy concerning, say, British policies of indirect rule on the Gold Coast than the policies of the old Ghanaian empire and its subject chiefs. Much more is known about Belgian economic policies (and their failings) in the Congo than about the commercial aims pursued by the bygone kingdom of the Bakongo. Second, the fact is often overlooked that the scientific recovery of the more ancient African past was initiated not by the indigenous peoples, but by the white rulers of Africa.

The colonial credit account is all the more impressive when measured against the time span of Western empire in Africa. The vast majority of African people experienced imperial tutelage for no more than the lifetime of a single grandmother. Even this brief period was in practice further curtailed by two world wars and a world slump, which by their impact additionally shortened the era of what might be called effective colonization. The great social and economic changes brought about by imperial rule during the last century or so were, moreover, not paralleled by the mass liquidations and mass expulsions involving millions of people which during the last two generations became part and parcel of so many totalitarian governments in Central and Eastern Europe. Imperial rule, in the long run, put an end to armed internecine conflicts; most parts of Africa remained sheltered from major foreign wars; there was administrative stability; colonial governance was generally efficient. Under the Union Jack and the Tricolor there was freedom from corruption in the white-manned layers of the colonial service. Imperial rule also had the advantage of possessing a recognized machinery for making adjustments within the rulers' own power structure. The imperial system had a built-in capacity for self-criticism. Future African historians will not quickly forget the cruelty, say, of German punitive expeditions against the Herero or the disgraceful story of "red rubber" in the Congo. The only reason that they will be able to write of these horrors with real authority lies in the ability of the imperial powers as a whole to document their failings. Future historians will necessarily draw on the material accumulated by European commissions of inquiry, parliamentary debates, metropolitan blue books, and similar records which formed part of a self-corrective mechanism of a type unknown to earlier Matabele, Somali, or Arab conquerors; they played an important part in putting a stop to imperial abuses. Imperial governance, moreover, had no parallel for the internal power struggles familiar, say, to Communist governments from Moscow to Tirana, which lack a legitimate and universally recognized procedure for changing the personnel of power holders and which so often had taken recourse to mass liquidations within the rulers' own ranks whenever shifts occur in the internal balance of power.

Imperial rule was of the limited kind. Imperial governance was never total; hence the participants played for more limited stakes, and there was evolution toward effective rule of law. Modern historiography in the underdeveloped countries usually takes such achievements for granted. So do militant African nationalists in a territory like Rhodesia, who see nothing incongruous in appealing political sentences in white Rhodesian courts. But defenders of the imperial record can really take this widespread use of a double standard as a backhanded compliment. As Margery Perham has put the matter with regard to censors of her native Britain:

> The deepest contrast of all is surely that Britain's subjects and ex-subjects have confronted her with political and, what is more, moral demands, which are new, at least in their intensity and wide acceptance. From where, we must ask, were these new standards derived? I think we shall find that, like other weapons turned against the West, they have been purloined from the West. And the ideal of democratic freedom, and an almost indefinable sense of moral obligation towards the weak, have been learned very largely from Britain herself.[14]

A modern Ghanaian critic of empire, in other words, operates from a political thesis made in Britain. His country, in its modern configuration, was unknown to traditional Africa, its boundaries, administration, and governmental structure were created by colonial rule. The literate Ghanaian's language of political process is English. He adopts modern standards of British justice. He uses terms such as "freedom," "self-determination," and "historical progress," which, in their modern formulation, would have been as incomprehensible to traditional African rulers as the terminology of space travel.

Yet there is also a very different aspect to empire. Its complexity can be obscured all too easily by what might be called the "scenic-railway" approach to writing history, in which the visitor is taken along a preordained route which never varies. The tourist on the pro-colonial track goes past hospitals and housing schemes, schools, cattle dips and wells, and massive government buildings. Sitting in his compartment, he talks to former colonial administrators; he reads statistics about rising population figures and percentile production increases;

14 Margery Perham, *The Colonial Reckoning: The End of Imperial Rule in Africa in the Light of British Experience* (New York, 1962), pp. 20–21.

he returns from his journey as an enthusiastic advocate of empire in retrospect. The rival train takes him on a very different trip. He travels past city slums, slag heaps, and refuse dumps; the train continues through eroded reserves. On the way, the traveler talks to pessimistic economists and angry "prison graduates"; he reads statistics about social evils, property, and crimes; he may return a convinced opponent of white colonialism in all its forms. He would have a good case, for, in addition to its positive aspects, empire had its grim and seamy side. In discussing this, we should differentiate between those features which arose from ignorance and neglect, those that came about through deliberate policy decisions counter to the conquerors' own professed values, and those that have beset all backward societies in the throes of industrialization under any form of government—colonial, liberal-capitalist, nationalist, or Communist.

A good many errors arose from lack of knowledge. Early missionaries, for instance, had very little idea of African religious concepts. A better acquaintance with African philosophy came only through long experience. Many early missionary pioneers thus unjustly berated all African forms of religious expression, with disastrous results for their own work. Early district officers usually failed to understand the economic rationale of slash-and-burn agriculture and gave correspondingly bad advice to their African charges. Convinced advocates of direct rule ignored the more valuable aspects of indigenous government. In the early days of Rhodesian history many British officials, for example, held as part of their faith that Barotse judges were incurably corrupt and oppressive; this prejudice bore little relationship to reality, but often affected local administration in a most deleterious fashion.

Worse even than ignorance was neglect. The preceding pages have usually emphasized the foreign rulers' more positive achievements. A modern Nigerian historian has summed them up by saying that "the colonial powers created the framework of the larger [territorial] units. They built the first railways and highways. They established cosmopolitan administrative and commercial capitals, civil services and trade unions, where new [social] unities were being forged."[15] In many instances, however, the colonial powers did far too little. Development was naturally sporadic; the richer or more accessible areas were developed first. More remote regions, like those included within the territories of modern Niger and Chad or the British High Commission Territories in South Africa, were neglected, so that their economic

15 J. F. Ade Ajayi, "The Place of African History and Culture in the Process of Nation-Building in Africa South of the Sahara," *Journal of Negro Education*, XXX, No. 3 (Summer, 1961), 209.

infrastructure continues weak to this day. Metropolitan businessmen have been the subject of much censure for their real or alleged rapacity, for their conscienceless greed which supposedly undermined or smashed indigenous social structures. The real trouble with many colonies was not the extent of enterprise, but its relative absence; there were usually too few capitalists, rather than too many. The colonial administrations themselves were generally deficient in research, resources, and recruits—the "three R's" of development; hence in many parts of the continent the old Africa remained almost unchanged. Even where knowledge was available, governments were often either unwilling to make use of other peoples' experiences or followed the line of least resistance. The Northern Rhodesian government as well as indigenous chiefs long opposed the stabilization of African labor on the Copper Belt even though they had the example of Katanga, where during the 1920s and 1930s these problems were tackled in a much more realistic fashion. Neglect often sprang from the doctrine of "indefinite time ahead." Sir Andrew Cohen, a modern British administrator, rightly points out how the lack of a sense of urgency played a major part in preventing economic expenditure in many colonies. The principle of financial self-sufficiency for each territory went together with this slow-moving approach.[16]

The British method of indirect rule likewise presupposed an extremely leisurely pace of political and administrative evolution. It was designed to cope with the requirements of people under rural conditions, who, of course, formed the vast majority of Africans in every colony. It was not conceived as part of a nation- or state-building program; still less did it take into consideration the demands of educated Africans or wider pressures in the world at large. Had the British been able to foresee how quickly they would devolve power to the indigenous people after World War II, and had they not, as it were, decolonized so absentmindedly, they might have equipped their charges in a more adequate fashion for future independence. Such arguments benefit greatly from hindsight. Even the most progressive American schools of opinion, and the bulk of educated Africans themselves, were more concerned in the interwar period with the protection of black people from abuses than with the task of building nations. The fact is that in both the economic and the political sphere a good deal of imperial practice can be summed up as "too little and too late."

Critics of the imperial record nevertheless can easily push their case too far. They do so when they assume that all Africa's social evils

[16] Sir Andrew Cohen, *British Policy in Changing Africa* (London, 1959), pp. 26–28.

—its backwardness, its rural and urban misery—must necessarily be the product of colonialism or of capitalist exploitation associated with imperial rule. This approach interprets African realities in terms of the financial manipulations carried out by "guilty men" operating from sumptuous offices in Paris, London, or Washington. In this, as in so many other instances, "the conspiratorial view of history finds considerable favour with extremists of the Right or Left, with the blindly prejudiced and with the feeble-minded. It has always been so and history is littered with examples, from the Protocols of the Elders of Zion to the curious ravings of the John Birch Society in the United States. It is evidently a comfort to certain minds to blame misfortunes or conditions arising from a variety of causes on a conspiracy by a group of sinister-minded men."[17] It is not, however, a view of history which works.

Africa's social and economic backwardness was not caused by the impact of foreign rule. On the contrary, Western domination in Africa only became possible, as we have tried to indicate, because most of the African continent had failed to keep pace with industrial, political, and military developments in Western Europe. There is little evidence to show that continued home rule would by itself have made any difference. The countries in Asia, Africa, and the New World which have been independent longest are among the most poverty-stricken; Liberia, Ethiopia, Haiti, and Afghanistan stand out as grim examples. Nor is it obvious that the political alternatives now being offered by totalitarian dictatorships would have secured better results. This has been obscured by the optimistic fashion in which the Soviet experience has been applied by Communist, and even by some liberal, writers in the West to the realities of the twentieth century. Such interpretations, however, emphasize the growth of Russia's industrial and military capacity without reference to consumer demands, to economic costs, to welfare in terms of human lives (including the mass famines of the 1930s), to standards of living, or to political terror. They take no account of mass liquidations, forced labor on a national scale, and similar impositions, which no modern colonial ruler ever dared to apply within his dominions. Such interpretations usually also fail to make reference to the comparatively advanced nature of pre-revolutionary Russia (as reflected, for example, in its agricultural surplus, its relatively high literacy rate, and the rapid rise of Russia's industrial expansion before 1914). They also fail to take account of the way in which countries such as Japan, Malaya, Hong Kong, or the colonial-ruled Gold Coast managed to make rapid strides without

[17] Brian Crozier, *Neo-colonialism: A Background Book* (London, 1964), p. 35.

large-scale socialization. They ignore the experience of postwar Germany, where the Federal German Republic has increased its production and well-being to a vastly greater extent than Communist-run East Germany, which started off on the same social and economic level as its Western competitor. Nor do these interpretations usually examine the meanings or limitations of Communist statistics, which eschew as a matter of professed political conviction the ideological crime of "objectivism."

The argument, however, leads on to the wider question of colonial exploitation. The concept of exploitation most often employed in present-day discussion of the colonial record is based, consciously or unconsciously, on Marx's theory of surplus value. Objections to this concept have been discussed earlier (see Chapter 6) and need not be recapitulated at this point. Charges of exploitation assume also more generalized formulations. Sometimes exploitation is equated with wages low in relation to the workers' needs, or in relation to salaries paid in other countries or in other occupations. Such notions of exploitation often presuppose the concept of an ideally just price for labor, but we are rarely told exactly what this price ought to be. Many modern anticolonial theorists implicitly regard differences in remuneration between, say, a highly trained white technician or a backward black recruit as unjust in themselves, even though the supply of highly skilled labor may be very scarce in a particular colony and the supply of unskilled labor plentiful. High differentials between the respective incomes of foreign entrepreneurs and indigenous workmen similarly invite condemnation, even though it may have been the foreigner's enterprise and initiative which started economic development in the first place. The charge of exploitation gains added force from nationalist fervor, but the accusation usually becomes even more imprecise. Belgian mining companies, which provide their black workmen with living conditions superior to those offered to laborers in most other parts of the continent, supposedly practiced exploitation just as much as the poorest white backveld farmer, who could afford only the scantiest wages and welfare provisions for his field hands. By a strange quirk of nationalist illogicality, few challenge the rate of remuneration paid by African employers, say Ghanaian cocoa farmers, to their workmen. Foreign financiers allegedly exploit Africans because they lend money to colonial concerns; shipping lines take their share because they transport colonial goods; overseas consumers join in the guilt because they purchase colonial produce.

There is virtually no end to the number of variations on the theme. Much of this propaganda shares in the schizophrenic quality which used to characterize the anti-Semitic propaganda of Nazi Germany. If

the colonialists invest money in African enterprises, they are max-
imizing their profit rates by illegitimate means. If they do not invest,
they are guilty of neglecting their dependencies. If Western capitalists
lend money to a non-Western government, they incur the charge of
indirect exploitation. If they refuse to put money into an African
country, they are boycotting the development of the new nations. The
Western powers are blamed if they stop giving aid, as the French did
in Guinea, and they are blamed again if they are too generous. If they
drop everything and quit, as so many white farmers have done in
Algeria and Kenya, they are showing an unseemly distrust in African
intentions. If they stay on and keep investments flowing in, as do the
white companies in Zambia and Katanga, they are confirming charges
of an unholy conspiracy to keep black Africans "in their place."[18]

Charges of exploitation, however, are meaningless without sub-
stantiation of one or more of the following points. Was there physical
appropriation of wealth which was already previously in existence and
which owed nothing to the colonizers' efforts? Did the colonizers employ forms of compulsion which forced colonial workmen or producers to accept remuneration at a rate lower than they could have
obtained in a free-market economy? Could the function of the foreign
entrepreneur have been assumed more effectively, or in a more humane and public-spirited fashion, by indigenous enterprise—whether
state-owned or run by private individuals?

The last charge can be answered with the greatest degree of confidence. The bulk of foreign enterprise in Africa—mines, farms, factories, railways—was not, and could not have been, started by the
indigenous people in precolonial Africa. In present-day Africa, indigenous capitalists or state organizations do not pay better wages or
offer better working conditions than their Western counterparts; on
the contrary, comparisons nearly always work out in favor of the
foreign firm. Nor has there been any evidence that take-over bids
have been or would be accompanied by greater economic efficiency
than obtained under the old regime. Sékou Touré, the Guinean President who had been so outspoken in support of Marxist policies, had
handed back some nationalized enterprises, including state trading
organizations, to private hands, letting it be known that he had simply
taken them over to get aid from foreign countries.[19]

There has indeed been some exploitation, though critics can easily
overestimate its extent and its value to the exploiter and overlook the
fact that the measures complained about have also occurred in the
absence of a colonial relationship. In the earliest stages of imperial

[18] Crozier, *Neo-colonialism*, p. 109.
[19] Crozier, *Neo-colonialism*, p. 81.

rule there were occasional instances of plain robbery. The British South Africa Company, for instance, confiscated cattle belonging to the vanquished Matabele and Angoni tribes, communities which had themselves practiced cattle rustling on an extensive scale. White farmers in Matabeleland were able to purchase native "scrub cattle" at low prices. But in the country's economic history as a whole this direct transfer of wealth had little importance.

Exploitation might also arise from the seizure of land, precolonial Africa's major form of wealth. But again, taking colonial Africa as a whole, the areas settled by European farmers were small. No exploitation, moreover, was involved in instances where the indigenous population was scanty and received compensation, as occurred on the Northern Rhodesian railway belt, though not in the white-settled areas of Fort Jameson in northeastern Rhodesia. In assessing the Europeans' role, account must in addition be taken of the way in which such land appreciated in value under European management, through the creation of dips, dams, fences, and tobacco barns, through new means of communication, through new farming methods such as the application of green manure, which improved the quality of the soil. Hence the balance sheet of exploitation can be compiled only with the greatest difficulty, if at all.

Exploitation occurred through the use of obligatory labor. Forced labor could be used in both an indirect and a direct fashion. The imposition of head taxes was, in the early days of empire, a means of getting tribesmen to work for wages as well as a means of obtaining revenue. Economic history, however, suggests that the importance of tax pressure as a means of mobilizing labor progressively diminishes with the expansion of a country's economy, giving way to more positive economic incentives. The social effects of taxation, moreover, are not limited to colonial situations. In a backward subsistence economy any imposts levied in cash rather than kind will drive peasants to earn money by going out to work, no matter whether a white or a black government runs the country's finances. Forced labor of a direct kind was practiced in the early days of Kenyan and Rhodesian history and, to a much wider extent, in the French and Portuguese colonies. The system persisted longest in the Portuguese empire—up to the abolition of the *indigenato* in 1961. Portuguese Africans were under obligation to work in a manner approved of by the administration for at least six months of the year, or else be contracted by the government. The threat of such contracts in turn impelled Africans who might otherwise have stayed at home to hire themselves out for pay as "voluntary" workers. No economist has as yet tried to estimate the total amount of wealth extorted from Africans in this fashion. However, forced labor was by no means always a paying proposition for employers. Forced labor went hand in hand with primitive conditions. Its effectiveness was also limited by the weakness of the early colonial state machinery. The scanty numbers of administrators and policemen at the disposal of the ruling powers prevented the imposition of human tribute in a totalitarian fashion. Furthermore, forced labor did not fit in with a more advanced economy. A backveld farmer keeping some scrub cattle and planting a little corn might profitably employ native conscripts. A modern agriculturist has no intention of letting an unwilling and ill-qualified draftee drive an expensive tractor or run a milking machine.

A more subtle form of exploitation may be practiced through tariff arrangements that tie colonial producers to a metropolitan market and prevent them from obtaining the same price for their exports which they might have secured in other countries. Portuguese policies of trade discrimination in favor of the mother country through tariffs and shipping regulations have thus benefited Portuguese textile manufacturers. Portuguese millowners have been able to sell goods inferior in quality and higher in price than those available in neighboring territories. Portuguese policy has also benefited other special interests, such as the Lisbon entrepôt trade, which has gained by the policy of discouraging direct shipments to colonial territories from foreign ports. These and related financial expedients have inevitably contained an element of economic duress—more so in some ways for the European entrepreneurs resident in the colonies than for the Africans; they have helped to account for the separatist demands that used to be made not only by educated Africans, but also by white settlers in Angola.[20]

Discriminatory practices of this kind are not, however, confined to colonial situations, nor are they the necessary result of a colonial nexus. Tariff discrimination, whether in colonial or in noncolonial trade, always benefits some special-interest group at the consumers' expense. Resentment on the part of raw-material-producing countries toward industrial states is not, moreover, confined to the capitalist world. Rumanian Communists have protested against Russian attempts to keep Rumania as a producer of primary products within COMECON; they have insisted that under existing barter arrangements they have had to pay higher prices for their imports and have received less money for their exports than they could have obtained on the world market.

[20] Richard J. Hammond, *Portugal's African Problem: Some Economic Facets* (Carnegie Endowment Occasional Paper No. 2; New York, 1962), pp. 21–22, 34–35.

There is, too, the question of whether such practices serve the long-term interests of the dominant power. Many economists have doubted that Portuguese tariff policies, for example, have benefited the interests of even the Portuguese bourgeoisie as a whole. Imperial preference favors some domestic producers. It also gives a premium to colonial as against foreign producers. Hence metropolitan industrialists as well as consumers have to buy colonial primary products at prices higher than those obtaining in a free market. Imperial preference, in other words, may also be interpreted as a means of exploiting major metropolitan interests. The French and Italians pay more for Senegalese peanuts and Somali bananas than world prices call for. Other experts have doubted that even the most favored groups really derive as much advantage from such arrangements as is thought. Even today Portugal has a much less important share in the commerce of its colonies than any other metropolitan country, so that *dirigisme* may well have backfired.[21]

Similar considerations apply to the manner in which European trade unions have in the past secured economic privileges that are designed to increase wage rates for their members. Their policy may, in some sense, be regarded as a means of exploiting both the consumers and semiskilled and unskilled black workers. Trade-union practices of this kind are not, however, confined to Africa. There is no economy in the world, capitalist or Communist, which does not contain elements of "exploitation" in the sense that well-placed labor lobbies are able to secure special terms for their services. Critics of white labor practices must, on the other hand, also remember the positive aspects involved in a large-scale transfer of laboring skills. Kenneth Kaunda's United National Independence Party bitterly attacked the white miners' and the white railway workers' superior position. Zambia has, however, realized the value of the white worker; the Zambians as yet have made no attempt to get rid of their white labor force or to reduce their pay.

Independent Algeria, on the other hand, embarked upon a different policy. Many critics of the French colonial record used to put the full blame for Algeria's social problems on the *petits blancs,* the small employees, the skilled workers and craftsmen who supposedly exacted

---

[21] The Portuguese, moreover, can plead with some justification that the economic significance of Portuguese control cannot be measured solely in terms of trade figures. The Portuguese have established not merely a governing and managerial class, but a whole urban civilization; they have introduced numerous skilled white workmen and artisans; the towns and the lingua franca are a major cohesive force in their territories. In fact, the whole "exchange sector" of the territories—and hence their whole prospect of further economic development—depends on Portuguese participation.

unmerited privileges from their colonial status and whose presence restricted opportunities for Muslim Algerians. Today some 900,000 white Algerians have fled the country as refugees, leaving most of their property behind. The departure of whites has not brought prosperity to Algeria; on the contrary, the loss of skill and purchasing power from this mass transfer of population has immeasurably worsened Algeria's economic problems and, interestingly enough, has created large-scale unemployment for Muslim Algerians.

To summarize, historical balance sheets are always hard to draw up. They involve their accountants in problems of extreme complexity, of differing standards of comparison, and of making value judgments. But the imperialists can plead that, even within their critics' own unspoken terms of reference, the colonial record involved tremendous achievements for good as well as ill. In our view, the imperial system stands out as one of the most powerful engines for cultural diffusion in the history of Africa; its credit balance by far outweighs its debit account.

23. The New Rulers in Charge: An Epilogue

Perhaps Africa's most difficult problem is that of legitimacy. Empire on its decline was already suffering from a lack of inner confidence. Both the bulk of the Western intelligentsia and the vast majority of educated Africans were convinced that the imperial mandate of heaven had expired, the more so since the old rulers made such feeble attempts to broaden the basis of their governance and to associate the emergent African intelligentsia in the task of top-level administration. Decolonization set up a new ruling class composed of educated black people. But as Sir Eric Ashby, a Cambridge don, has put it:

> The spread of higher education in tropical Africa has driven apart the Westernised élite and the masses. The African graduate occupies the place previously occupied by the expatriate colonial administrator; he lives in the expatriate's house; he drives a similar car; he is paid on the high salary scale previously reserved for expatriates. Within five or ten years of leaving college he may find himself propelled into the permanent secretaryship of a ministry, into a position where rivalries are fierce, where idealism struggles with self-interest, where success is very uncomfortable and very precarious. From this altitude it is virtually impossible for him to remain in close sympathy with the great mass of his fellow countrymen. Part of the price which the African graduate pays for his higher education is his loneliness. . . .
>
> In England the side-effects of social mobility are negligible compared with their effects in Africa. For an African the impact of a university education is something inconceivable to a European. It separates him from his family and his village (though he will, with intense feeling and loyalty, return regularly to his home and accept what are often crushing family responsibilities). It obliges him to live in a Western way, whether he likes it or not. . . . Some of his primeval responsibilities to a traditional society remain; at the same time new "Western" responsibilities pile up on his desk, of the kind which an equivalent graduate in Europe might not get until after twenty years' experience. He has no adequate

supporting staff. . . . In the United Nations, in the markets of the world, at conference tables, it is the African graduate who carries on his shoulders the destiny of his continent.[1]

At its best, the speedy rise of the new ruling class produced a great sense of exhilaration. As in France during the Revolution, young men quickly went to the top and sometimes brought to their jobs new energy and a new idealism. At its worst, the rapid Africanization that followed, and often preceded, independence produced jobbery, corruption, and an outlook which associated administrative position with political status rather than executive functions. White-collar workers and intellectuals, who had commonly led the independence struggle, often used the state machine to provide their own group with a multitude of jobs at the taxpayer's expense. Some states thus developed vast, parasitic party bureaucracies whose very existence now forms a crushing burden on the state.[2] The postindependence concepts of African socialism, *étatism,* or "monism" thus often developed into nothing more than the ideological superstructure to justify the existence of an expensive white-collar elite. In most parts of Africa "the black élite . . . possess little of the substantive skills and resources . . . necessary for them to play a progressive or decisive role in directing the modernization of African societies. . . . In this situation the use of power by what is, so to speak, a pseudo-élite, is inevitably distorted and abused." All too often the new elites resort to "indulgence in a ritualistic game of acting out élite roles that they in fact cannot fulfill."[3]

The unequal fruits of independence, moreover, were likely to cause intense resentment on the part of the "outs" toward the "ins." The old imperialists may have had plenty of faults; they had lacked contact with the masses and had often felt themselves strangers. But the white district commissioner in some sense had stood outside local struggles; he had belonged to a foreign caste whose technical qualifications, at any rate, were rarely challenged and who had been known to stand above the competing interests of tribes and clans. Independ-

---

[1] From Sir Eric Ashby, *African Universities and Western Tradition* (London, 1964). The first paragraph is on p. 101, the second on pp. 41–42.

[2] Guinea, for instance, a country with an estimated population of some 3 million and a backward economy, now supports a corps of 226,000 party officials, or something like 7 percent of the population. In the "imperialistic" Federation of Rhodesia and Nyasaland, with about three times the population of Guinea and a much more highly developed economy, there were in 1956 no more than about 10,000 white and about 40,000 black people in state administrative services of all kinds, that is to say, less than .5 percent of the population.

[3] Martin Kilson, "African Autocracy," *Africa Today,* April, 1966, p. 5.

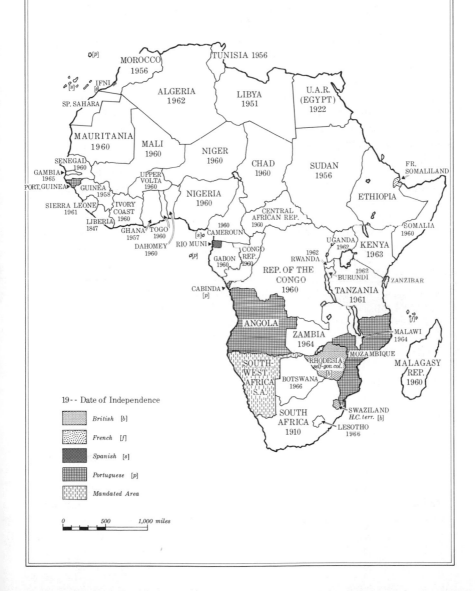

AFRICA in 1966

O [p]

MOROCCO
1956

TUNISIA 1956

IFNI
[s]
SP. SAHARA

ALGERIA
1962

LIBYA
1951

U.A.R.
(EGYPT)
1922

[s]

MAURITANIA
1960

MALI
1960

NIGER
1960

CHAD
1960

SUDAN
1956

FR.
SOMALILAND

SENEGAL
1960
GAMBIA
1965
PORT.GUINEA

UPPER
VOLTA
1960

NIGERIA
1960

ETHIOPIA

GUINEA
1958
SIERRA LEONE
1961
LIBERIA
1847

IVORY
COAST
1960

CENTRAL
AFRICAN REP.
1960

SOMALIA
1960

GHANA
1957
DAHOMEY
1960

TOGO
1960

1960
[s] CAMEROUN

UGANDA
1962

KENYA
1963

RIO MUNI
[p]

GABON
1960

CONGO
REP.
1960

RWANDA
1962

1962
BURUNDI

ZANZIBAR

CABINDA
[p]

REP. OF THE
CONGO
1960

TANZANIA
1961

ANGOLA

ZAMBIA
1964

MALAWI
1964

MOZAMBIQUE

MALAGASY
REP.
1960

SOUTH-
WEST
AFRICA
S.A.

RHODESIA
self-gov. col.
[b]

BOTSWANA
1966

SWAZILAND
H.C. terr. [b]

SOUTH
AFRICA
1910

LESOTHO
1966

19-- Date of Independence

British [b]

French [f]

Spanish [s]

Portuguese [p]

Mandated Area

0   500   1,000 miles

ence swept this privileged order away. All things suddenly seemed possible to all men; hence the losers in the race for property, power, position, and privilege became even more resentful than in the past. Bitterness was apt to be intensified by the age level of the new ruling party. Many of the original militants had moved into high office at a youthful age. Their rapid advancement often created a promotion blockage for the next generation of university graduates, who would now have to wait many years for the original incumbents to retire. The new rulers, at the same time, were asked to honor political checks which they had endorsed during the independence struggle as against the postcolonial future. Many African nationalists had been able to mobilize mass support against the old rulers by promises of great social benefits which would accrue to the common people from the impending transfer of power. After the completion of the nationalist victory, many of these checks began to bounce. The new governors still had to face all the perennial problems of Africa, its lack of social and physical capital, impediments in the way of communications, the presence of tropical disease, the problems arising from irregular rainfall, and a host of other difficulties. The resources of Africa remained as unevenly distributed and as unevenly developed as in the days of colonial rule; indeed, independence sometimes led to loss of economic confidence.

The new rulers stepped into their predecessors' governmental inheritance; they had to run territories which owed their very existence to the imperial impact; they had, in some sense, to become their own colonizers. A historian might indeed trace some interesting tentative parallels between the problems of government at the beginning of the imperial epoch and those facing the colonial successors at the start of the postimperial era. The first generation of imperialists commonly consisted of capable all-around men, often with strong charismatic personalities, such as Rhodes and Wissmann. Such men frequently lacked an established bureaucracy and recruited generalists—explorers, hunters, and soldiers—into their service. The early white administrators perforce had to live in close contact with the villagers and normally acted like local chiefs. Some tried to follow rigidly Victorian precepts of morality; others were cruel and lecherous. But they all "knew their Africans." These frontier officials were succeeded in turn by trained civil servants, men such as Sir William Milton in Southern Rhodesia; administration became routinized; the bureaucracies expanded; native commissioners assumed many new tasks; they often became tax gatherers, census takers, and public-works supervisors rather than "father and mother" to their districts, so that contact between the rulers and the ruled began to disintegrate.

The problems now encountered by the new rulers were similar. The new men were also generalists, often of strong personality, men who had gained their influence by organizing the masses. As long as the party leaders carried on the struggle against the colonial regimes, they necessarily remained in touch with the people, but having once assumed the reins of power, they too tended to become more remote from the villagers. The ablest party officials became ministers, chief secretaries, or district heads and often lost touch with their old constituents. Party organizations began to decay; the enthusiasm of the remaining militants evaporated, and for all their rhetoric, even radical parties such as Nkrumah's Convention People's Party and Sékou Touré's Parti Démocratique de Guinée could not fill the widening gap between the new regimes and the masses.

There were also parallels of policy between the new imperialism and the new pan-Africanism of the postcolonial variety. In the 1890s many of the white empire builders had seen colonization primarily in terms of global foreign policy, of the international balance of power and national glory. Imperialism was "future-directed" in its outlook and often neglected local problems of a more mundane kind. The bureaucratization of empire to some extent changed the nature of the colonial administrations and led to a more sober approach and increasing preoccupation with the local and technical problems of the various colonial territories. The new rulers will probably have to face a similar development. During the early years of independence the postcolonial rulers generally placed special emphasis on political questions concerned with pan-Africanism, foreign policy, and the United Nations; local problems in many cases came second. This trend is likely to be reversed as technical, economic, and administrative problems loom larger, as the new rulers become increasingly absorbed in local issues, and as they realize that even in foreign affairs their position depends primarily on a strong domestic base.

The new rulers face many other difficulties. In many cases they have to carry out their tasks with an administrative machine much weaker than that controlled by their predecessors. Independent Africa had insufficient experts to man its technical services and execute its ambitious development programs. To some extent the deficiency continued to be made up by foreign experts. By 1964 something like 40,000 French and 15,000 British civil servants were still at work in independent countries. But the governments were under strong internal pressure to replace these expatriates with trained people of their own nationality. No African government was able to emulate Southern Rhodesia which, on obtaining responsible government in 1923, had taken over the British South Africa Company's very efficient civil service *in toto* and had refused to "Rhodesianize" the civil service with job-hungry white party stalwarts. In many cases the very prospect of being "Africanized" induced European civil servants to emigrate before the expiration of their expected terms of office. The substitution of experienced people with those inexperienced frequently led to loss of administrative efficiency at the very time when calls on the state machinery were steadily increasing. African nationalists and their liberal supporters overseas had, by their own political campaigning, helped to accelerate the "revolution of rising expectations" with which the old rulers had been unable to cope. The new rulers now often had to pay the price of their own propaganda.

The position was worst in the Congo, where postindependence troubles struck a serious blow to the country's cash economy. There was runaway inflation, the old budgetary surpluses disappeared, and agricultural exports dropped, though mining maintained its position. Congolese politicians faced acute urban problems even more serious than those which had beset their predecessors. Many cities expanded in an uncontrolled fashion. Between 1960 and 1965, for instance, the population of Léopoldville is supposed to have grown from 300,000 to 1 million. But this was only one of many urban centers where the population had outgrown the means of production, where too many people were chasing too few jobs, and where miserable shanty towns kept sprawling beyond the city's outskirts. Power now rested with the "new men," but the new men in turn found themselves under attack as "the profiteers of the regime." The new men were probably not sufficiently cohesive or conscious of their common interests to be called a class. They were, however, sufficiently well-off to be readily identifiable. They wore collar and tie; they made their living in politics and administration both on the central and on the provincial level; they served in the army and the police; they worked as bus owners, contractors, and commercial agents; some had benefited from currency depreciation through money transfers and other financial manipulations. The new ruling group numbered perhaps about 400,000 people, a small minority, who in turn had to face new forms of social radicalism from people who looked for a "second independence." The Congo and other unstable governments like those of Rwanda and Burundi were in the worst position, but all the new governments faced the problem of an uncontrolled drift of impoverished peasants into the cities where there might not be enough jobs for newcomers. None of them could impose rigid movement controls of the kind whereby South Africa prevented the emergence of an unemployed and potentially revolutionary city mob. In the countryside the new rulers encountered similar difficulties. The new party functionary, unlike the

old-style district commissioner, had to compete directly with traditional chiefs for the allegiance of the rural people. Hence the new
elites, bent on modernization, generally wished to do away with tribal
dignitaries and tribal bonds. (There was, in fact, a strange parallel
between the new course and the policy of deliberate detribalization
originally advocated by British South Africa Company theoreticians
in the Rhodesia of the early 1900s.) Such a course, however, had
many dangers. The tribesmen, unless economically and socially integrated into wider communities, might simply be deprived of their
accustomed institutions and sink to the level of a dispirited peasantry,
subject alternatively to apathy or to wild outbursts in the pursuit of
millennium movements or Jacqueries.

Hence even purposeful and comparatively well-run governments
like those of Zambia found themselves face to face with a host of
economic, political, and administrative difficulties of a kind that had
already faced their predecessors, now made worse by outside circumstances beyond the new rulers' control. Above all, there was the question of capital investment. By the beginning of World War II funds
to the value of some $6 billion had been placed in Africa; most of the
money came from Europe. Of this total, colonial governments had
accounted for around 45 percent and had used these loans to build
railways, ports, and other public works. The rest came from the pockets of private investors, and a large percentage was used for the development of mines. Colonial rule had therefore created a pattern in
which much reliance was placed on local governments to start economic development.[4] While theories of African socialism are of fairly
recent origin, much of its practice, including development planning
and the resulting network of marketing boards and other statutory
economic controls, had been inherited from the old imperial rulers.
World War II and its aftermath gave strong impetus to the various
African economies. Changes in economic thought at the same time
added emphasis to the assumption that the government should promote economic development and social welfare and that the more
developed countries should give assistance to backward regions. Until
1960, that is to say, until about the end of the colonial period, Africa
did extremely well. Many experts believe that economic development
in Africa between 1945 and 1960 went on at a faster pace than in any
other major underdeveloped region of the world. The continent's gross

[4] See Andrew M. Kamarck, "Recent Economic Growth in Africa," *Annals of
the American Academy of Political and Social Science,* CCCLIV (July, 1964),
46–53. Some $2.5 billion was placed in the Union of South Africa, about $2
billion in other British territories, about $700 million in the Congo, $350
million in the French territories, and $300 million in the Portuguese territories.

national product grew 4 to 6 percent a year in real terms; areas like the Rhodesias, the Belgian Congo, Morocco, Gabon, and Kenya grew at rates of 6 to 11 percent a year, among the highest rates in the history of the world. During the same period funds to the value of around $15 billion flowed into Africa, of which something like $5 to $6 billion derived from private lenders, with the balance from governments.[5] This large influx of capital provided a minimum of administrative and welfare and transport services essential for economic growth, but it also helped to accelerate new demands.

In 1960, however, Africa's relative position in the world market began to deteriorate. Many successor governments found themselves faced with extraordinarily difficult situations at the very time when the imperial bonds had broken or were about to be broken. The capacity for the production of primary products had finally caught up with the needs of the industrialized world. In many countries the prevailing sense of insecurity occasioned not merely a stoppage in the inflow of capital, but also a sizable outflow of private funds and emigration of key personnel. During the postcolonial period world prices were generally more favorable to the African countries than they had been in the 1930s, but many African governments overspent their incomes and thus were more dependent on external assistance. These questions gave serious concern to most independent African countries, except South Africa, which still attracted many white newcomers and which had become largely independent of further foreign capital investment. The new African governments had, of course, the advantage of being able to rely on a much greater volume of foreign help than their predecessors; by 1964 external aid to Africa was running around $1 billion to $1.5 billion a year. But most of the successor governments still found themselves in difficult straits.

The independent African states differ to some degree in their reaction to these and related predicaments. They vary in background and outlook. Hence generalizations with regard to the Africans are just as dangerous as those concerning the old imperial powers. By 1966 Ghana was well on the road toward what might be called Afro-fascism. This was characterized by a pronounced leadership cult, the *Gleichschaltung* of voluntary associations and of the judicature, a corporate parliament, forged election results, the privileged position allotted to the new party bureaucracy, the use of political indoctrination and sporadic terror, as well as a militant nationalist ideology which emphasized the alleged conflict of interests between the "have" and the "have-not" nations and which aimed to lift the class struggle from the social to the national plane.

[5] Kamarck, "Recent Economic Growth," p. 51.

In 1966, however, both Ghana and Nigeria succumbed to military coups, as did several other states in French-speaking Africa. Control of the military establishment presents the new rulers with a problem from which the colonial powers had escaped. The military strength of the former imperial states had rested primarily on their metropolitan establishment. Control of the military was a domestic, not a colonial, problem, and the colonies were largely shielded both from aggression abroad and from military coups at home. The new rulers, on the other hand, find themselves in a dilemma. If their national forces remain small, their emergent state cannot play a strong role in foreign policy and might face internal subversion. But if politicians expand their country's army to cope with foreign problems (as Zambia is now doing), the strengthened army might become a contender for power on its own. In underdeveloped countries the armed forces are likely to occupy a peculiarly strong position. Armies are disciplined bodies, trained to employ violence. But they do not rely on machine guns alone. An efficient army needs support services capable of coping with staff organization, personnel questions, engineering matters, transport, intelligence, and so forth. These support services can act as schools for administration in general and provide the country with scarce skills. The command structure of an army is easier to understand than a constitution, and simple people may look to the "man on horseback" rather than to the politician. Armies moreover often act as "pressure cookers," where ethnic loyalties (still overwhelmingly strong in most parts of Africa) take on a kind of corporate and national identity. Armies may thus step in where the politicians fail, and as African armies expand, civilian rule may well contract.

However, all African states, whether based on armies, on single parties, or on parties using paramilitary formations of a political kind, share certain common features. There is generally little loyalty to the state as such. Political legitimacy lies rather with the ruling party or with an individual, a powerful president or prime minister who controls both party organization and the state executive.[6] There is a mood of vague social radicalism; there is a widespread proclivity toward dictatorial rule; there is a frequent, though by no means universal, penchant for *étatiste* solutions. This outlook oddly combines leftovers from the old rulers' intellectual armory with a more recent revolutionary legacy. The new radicalism does not require much explanation. The African leaders wish to jump into the twentieth century and free

---

[6] For a recent legal view of a "presidential" state see J. S. R. Cole and W. N. Denison, *Tanganyika: The Development of Its Laws and Constitution* (London, 1964), especially pp. vi–vii, 26–33. This account is, however, already somewhat out of date.

their people from the bondage of backwardness. Many also suffer from a burning sense of racial or national grievance; they wish to cast away the badge of shame which they believe black people have carried in the past; they wish to become the white man's equals; they battle for parity of esteem, for a sense of dignity. Many have accepted the curious ideology that rules in both China and the Soviet Union, a mode of thought that thrives on the comparative, that measures the achievements of one country by the standards of another, and that envisages the international scene as a race in which the participants are under a constant obligation to overtake their neighbors in arbitrarily selected arenas of power. The new race for esteem has become all the more difficult, since the most advanced powers no longer measure their achievements purely in terms of territorial power, but in terms of technology—a field in which the new countries are least able to compete. The new men who now sit in the main offices of the government house and in the secretariat share their predecessors' bias toward *étatiste* solutions as well as the old colonial civil servant's impatience with parliamentary interference.

This outlook is easy to understand. In newly independent Africa, the formation of states always preceded the development of new nations. Gambia and Zambia, Mali and Malawi, Niger and Nigeria, are now recognized political entities, but Gambians and Zambians, Malians and Malawians, are still to be formed. The new states lack any kind of ethnic or linguistic cohesion. Their very existence, for the most part, has little reality to the mass of the people, who remain bound up with village and family affairs. Nationalism requires a national mystique, a spirit of sacrifice. But few Africans are willing to die for the banners of Upper Volta or the Republic of the Congo (Brazzaville). In Mali the Tuareg of the desert do not willingly recognize the authority of southern Negroes. The Somali of Kenya wish to secede and to join their neighbors in the Greater Somali Republic. Academic theoreticians may speak of the politicization of the African, but this is a difficult task in countries where the mass of the people farm the land and are infinitely more interested in the prospects of the coming rain than the next elections, because a good crop makes all the difference between hunger and happiness. In a state such as the Republic of Niger most people are too poor to buy a newspaper; the sparsity of the population and the vast distances involved further impede the circulation of the printed word. The radio helps to some extent to fill the gap, but again, not every peasant can buy one. Much depends on the quality of local party cadres; yet party organizations are not easily maintained in out-of-the-way villages, and even convinced modernizing militants may find the going as hard as did the old-fashioned religious evangelists. Most African countries remain divided in their religious allegiance, so that a religious creed cannot normally serve as a national cement. There are exceptions. The Somali practice Islam and the Amhara practice a Coptic form of Christianity; these opposing creeds do serve to underline national distinctions. But in most parts of Africa the new rulers have to make national bricks without ideological straw. They must persuade regional and ethnic units to acknowledge a central state authority; they have to forge new bonds of a territorial variety. All this has to be done through the medium of English or French, the former colonizers' tongues which for the purpose of government, administration, and technology are unlikely to be replaced on any large scale by indigenous languages. The new rulers in some ways have to be their own colonizers, but they often have to work with resources less extensive than those of their predecessors in office. They have not only to maintain, but also to strengthen, the inherited apparatus of government. They have to rely on military forces which, although weak in numbers and equipment and often poorly trained and unreliable, must control vast territories with small armies. They cannot automatically rely on reinforcements from overseas in case of trouble,[7] yet, like the old rulers, they still have to govern unstable countries where, in some cases, even a few hundred well-led, determined fighters can easily seize power, as was done in Zanzibar. Although the new men have taken over much of the old-time civil servants' authoritarian outlook, they often lack the old colonial functionary's sense of administrative permanence.

The vast majority of African leaders have sought to escape from their troubles by one-party rule. By 1965, only five out of thirty-six independent African countries still managed to cling precariously to parliamentary government in something like the Western sense. One-party rule seems to offer numerous advantages. Parliamentary government requires a stable administrative structure and a complex system of polling booths and of counting votes; secret ballots require administrative integrity and efficiency, qualities which the new states commonly lack. The fairest elections have usually taken place under the old imperial system; the new rulers are often too deeply involved in the game to stick to the rules. One-party rule, on the other hand, has acquired intellectual respectability through the Soviet precedent and seems to facilitate the mobilization of resources. (Most Africans have forgotten that during World War II the British were much more successful than the Nazi dictatorship in the task of harnessing the nation's economic strength to warlike tasks.) One-party rule corresponds to

[7] The French do have agreements with most of the former French colonies to give help if asked.

the self-interest of the "ins" as against the "outs." It also tends to increase ethnic tensions. The old colonial governments, for all their authoritarian character, had been limited. The new rulers generally aimed at a much greater degree of state power. Hence the question of who was to control the state machinery became more important than ever before, and competing ethnic groups were often likely to take recourse to violence. But one-party rule also owed something to the old colonial functionary's outlook, his predilection for undivided authority, his impatience with the ruminations of elected bodies. Throughout much of the earlier colonial period administrative struggles within the ranks of the governmental hierarchy had, to some extent, taken the place of "open" politics. Such habits were easily passed on to the new rulers.

One-party government is often accompanied by detailed attempts at economic planning and sometimes by an intense suspicion of private enterprise, especially of foreign undertakings. These attitudes again parallel ideas found in the ranks of old-style colonial rulers, the Portuguese in particular, but all others as well. The new rulers' widespread faith in state controls thus owes much to two opposing and yet sometimes oddly complementary traditions—socialist doctrine and the belief in development planning evinced by the colonial authorities, in the last stage of colonial rule especially. Many colonial governments had been impressed by the claims of economic experts drawn in from outside. Some of these advisers went beyond the relatively straightforward task of collecting and evaluating specialized information; they tried to endow their science with predictive powers and ignored both the multiplicity of variables involved in the making of economic forecasts and the unsatisfactory nature of the statistical evidence on which their calculations were so often based. In the imperial period development plans had already sometimes become a kind of international status symbol, valuable more as a means of producing psychological satisfaction and political prestige for its makers than as economic tools. The new rulers often took over these attitudes and sometimes placed an unjustified trust in the counsel proffered by itinerant academic advisers. In their generous enthusiasm for modernization, many African statesmen assume, like so many intellectuals on both sides of the Iron Curtain, that there must be some magical formula, some philosopher's stone or elixir of life, by which Africa might attain within ten or twenty years the standards of economic development and of social welfare which Western Europe has built up over many centuries. Needless to say, such hopes have little foundation in fact and are to be compared with the faith which many seventeenth-century German princelings put in the claims made by wandering alchemists and astrologists. They do, however, form an important element in that "revolution of rising expectations" which endangers the stability of all African regimes.

Single-party government and tight economic controls are not, however, always capable of dealing with such problems; they do not necessarily lead to political stability. Perhaps fortunately for Africa, the multiplicity of ethnic claims, the bonds of the extended family system, lackadaisical attitudes toward time (as measured in terms of Western punctuality), and financial carelessness or corruption all militate against the creation of tightly disciplined, centralized, and dependable party cadres. Reliable, unquestioning party functionaries of the East German variety are just as hard to train in Africa as reliable civil servants of the British kind. Single-party rule, moreover, does not by itself ensure political or financial integrity. The inordinate luxury often displayed by the president-leader cannot be legitimately challenged in public; subordinates follow the example set from above; checks on illegitimate public expenditure for private ends disappear. Monopolies of power are, in fact, likely to make political struggles increasingly all-embracing in character. In a situation where power, prestige, position, and property are tightly linked, the "ins" have too much at stake. The political kingdom, once attained, must be defended at all costs, lest all other things are also lost. The "ins" are therefore under constant temptation to rely on increasingly tougher methods. The "outs" in turn try to escalate the political struggle and sometimes seek external support. The process has been graphically described by Colin Legum, a modern British writer who strongly sympathizes with the pan-African cause.[8] The process of transferring power within the single-party state frequently originates in the palace. It usually has two stages. First, the claims of acknowledged pressure groups within the ruling party produce continuous internal rivalry for power. Second, there is growth of an active opposition, acting subversively within the state, in exile, or both. The exile group often finds a safe haven in a neighboring state—Congolese rebel radicals in Brazzaville and Burundi, the Sawabah Party of Niger in Ghana. Internal party splits thereby achieve an external dimension; these may involve other African states as well as major foreign powers and may as a result become part of the new scramble for Africa, in which the United States, the old colonial powers, China, and Soviet Russia all stake out new claims for indirect influence. As Legum puts it, the process of driving the opposition underground forces the leaders to look under their beds as well as out their windows. The rulers, fearing persecution, may there-

[8] See Colin Legum, "What Kind of Radicalism for Africa?" *Foreign Affairs* (New York), XLIII, No. 2 (January, 1965), 237–250.

fore persecute whomever they fear. Their dread of losing office becomes all the more obsessive if politics is their only means of livelihood. Nkrumah, the Ghanaian President, may well have been justified in believing that one plot against his life was planned by his most trusted lieutenant and a second by the most senior members of his security forces. In the Ivory Coast, President Houphouet-Boigny had to deal with no fewer than three conspiracies in a single year, all of them involving ministerial colleagues. Political suspicion may lead to the creation of a restrictive society; trade unions are controlled; organs of information are supervised; the civil service is rendered liable to purges; the promotion system tends to work in favor of party acolytes; the security forces are multiplied.

But the degree of oppression should not be exaggerated. Political terror as yet has not even remotely attained the bloody standards set up by Nazi or Communist dictatorships in Europe. Africans have not acquired the art of mass liquidations as formerly practiced by Germans and Russians. Active opposition is in the main usually confined to limited groups among intellectuals, to pressure groups such as the trade unions, or to ethnic minority groups with particularist grievances, such as the Negroid peoples of the southern Sudan, the Watutsi of Rwanda, and the Somali of Kenya and Ethiopia. Nevertheless, ethnocentric centers of disaffection are likely to make common cause with other discontented groups in neighboring countries; alternatively, they may look to the established governments of adjacent states for help. The Somali of Kenya and Ethiopia thus place their trust in the Greater Somali Republic; the Watutsi of Rwanda put their hopes into the Watutsi-ruled government of Burundi. Links between opposition elements and neighboring countries naturally lead to the familiar checkerboard pattern of foreign policy, whereby countries seek allies among states with whom they do not have a common boundary for use against their neighbors.

Internecine tensions of this kind strongly militate against pan-African aspirations. The new nationalist establishments all favor a great African bloc which will smash white rule in South Africa, Rhodesia, and the Portuguese colonies and form a great power in its own right. But pan-Africanism, like comparable movements in other parts of the world, comes into conflict with established vested interests in existing states. Prime ministers do not usually want to vacate a ministerial suite for a provincial governor's office; heads of department do not want to step down in favor of some other civil servant in some other capital. Pan-Africanist aspirations cannot easily overcome the ancient barriers of geographical distance and of ethnic variety which separate the various states, not to mention the differences brought about by conflicting imperial legacies of the French, Belgian, and British variety. The new leaders are sometimes torn between ambitious programs of a continental scale and extreme parochial concern for national interest in the narrowest sense. The intermediate field of practical cooperation in limited fields is often neglected. The new rulers frequently confuse rhetoric with the realities of administrative execution, a failing by no means unknown to their predecessors in office. Ghana's union with Guinea has never left the declaratory stage. Ghana's pact with Guinea, Mali, Morocco, Algeria, and the United Arab Republic as a radical caucus in neutralist affairs soon foundered on the conflicting goals of its members. Existing weaknesses are aggravated by lack of cadres with a tradition of public service, lack of experience in committee work, the absence of a common language—an acute problem to negotiators without a polyglot staff—and a widespread lack of economic understanding. In many cases there is no common economic impulse to negotiate for cooperation, since traditional trade links connect the emergent countries with the imperial power rather than with other African states. In many ways the new rulers find cooperation just as difficult as did their predecessors, who similarly possessed little knowledge of the problems besetting other African territories and who also tended to work in territorial isolation.

Despite all their weaknesses, the new rulers nevertheless have substantial achievements to their credit. Most independent African countries have successfully preserved their existing state machinery, and some, like Ghana and Zambia, have even expanded it. Independence has rarely led to a breakdown of the economy. Even in the Congo, civil war had little effect on the mining industry.[9] Independent Africa is just beginning to be troubled by the perils of militarism (seven coups in 1965–1966). But black Africa as a whole has had a better record of political stability than, say, the Spanish-speaking countries of Latin America after their wars of independence in the first decades of the nineteenth century. The new Africa has produced a whole crop of able statesmen, figures such as Kenneth Kaunda and Léopold Senghor who, for all their disagreements, compare very favorably with many nineteenth- and twentieth-century Latin American leaders. African politicians, notwithstanding their frequently militant radical phraseology and their penchant for using colonialism and neocolonialism as an ever-ready alibi, display a great deal of shrewdness in playing not merely Americans and Western Europeans, but also Chinese and Russians against each other. Independent Africa not

[9] J. Anthony Lukas, "Rebellion Dims Hope for Congo," *The New York Times,* January 25, 1965, pp. 47, 63.

only has become an object of world politics, but also has succeeded in exercising some influence in its own right. Even though the African states have not been able to coalesce into a solid voting bloc at the United Nations, they have managed to exert diplomatic pressure quite out of proportion to their real power, as measured in terms of population, military force, and economic strength. The mere existence of the new African nations has played a role in the American Negro struggle. The Soviet Union for its part has had to face unaccustomed problems in dealing with countries that do not easily fit into the rigid framework of Marxist-Leninist sociology, countries whose complex politics may even have played some part in modifying certain Marxist theories in action.[10]

The future is impossible to chart. Men of good will can only hope that the new rulers will achieve a Pax Africana to replace the former imperial peace.

[10] For a detailed discussion of these and related problems see Zbigniew K. Brzezinski (ed.), *Africa and the Communist World* (Stanford, Calif., 1963).

Bibliography

ADSHEAD, STANLEY DAVENPORT. Diary, 1930. Copy in AD 1, Historical Manuscripts Collection, National Archives of Rhodesia, Salisbury.

African Advancement in Rhodesia. Salisbury, Southern Rhodesia, Service Press, 1965. 31 pp.

AJAYI, J. F. ADE. "The Place of African History and Culture in the Process of Nation-Building in Africa South of the Sahara," *Journal of Negro Education,* XXX, No. 3 (Summer, 1961), 206–213.

ALAGOA, EBIEGBERI JOE. *The Small Brave City State: A History of Nembe-Brass in the Niger Delta.* Madison, University of Wisconsin Press, 1964. 173 pp.

ANSTEY, ROGER. *Britain and the Congo in the Nineteenth Century.* Oxford, Clarendon Press, 1962. 260 pp.

ASHBY, SIR ERIC. *African Universities and Western Tradition.* (Godkin Lectures at Harvard University, 1964.) London, Oxford University Press, 1964. 113 pp.

ASHTON, THOMAS SOUTHCLIFFE. "The Treatment of Capitalism by Historians," in Friedrich August von Hayek (ed.), *Capitalism and the Historians.* Chicago, University of Chicago Press, 1954. Pp. 33–63.

AUSTIN, DENNIS. *Politics in Ghana, 1946–1960.* London, Oxford University Press, 1964. 459 pp.

BARBOUR, NEVILL (ed.). *A Survey of North West Africa (The Maghrib).* 2d ed. London, Oxford University Press, 1962. 411 pp.

BARNES, LEONARD. *Soviet Light on the Colonies.* Harmondsworth, Middlesex, Eng., Penguin Books, 1945. 288 pp.

BARTH, HENRY. *Travels and Discoveries in North and Central Africa: Being a Journal of an Expedition Undertaken under the Auspices of H.B. Majesty's Government by Henry Barth, Ph.D., D.C.L.* New York, Drallop Publishing Co., 1896. 3 vols.

BAUER, PETER T. *Economic Analysis and Policy in Underdeveloped Countries.* Durham, N.C., Duke University Press, for the Duke University Commonwealth-Studies Center, 1957. 145 pp.

————. "Regulated Wages in Under-developed Countries," in Philip D. Bradley (ed.), *The Public Stake in Union Power*. Charlottesville, University of Virginia Press, 1959. Pp. 324–349.

————. *West African Trade: A Study of Competition, Oligopoly and Monopoly in a Changing Economy*. Cambridge, Eng., Cambridge University Press, 1954. 450 pp. Reissued with a new preface; London, Routledge & Kegan Paul, 1963.

BENNETT, GEORGE. *Kenya: A Political History; The Colonial Period*. London, Oxford University Press, 1963. 190 pp.

————, and CARL G. ROSBERG. *The Kenyatta Election: Kenya, 1960–1961*. New York, Oxford University Press, 1961. 230 pp.

BLANCHARD, MARCEL. "Administrateurs d'Afrique noire," *Revue d'Histoire des Colonies*, XL (1953), 377–430.

BODELSEN, CARL ADOLF GOTTLIEB. *Studies in Mid-Victorian Imperialism*. Reprint of 1924 ed. London, William Heinemann, 1960. 226 pp.

BOVILL, E. W. *Caravans of the Old Sahara: An Introduction to the History of the Western Sudan*. London, Oxford University Press, 1933. 300 pp.

————. *The Golden Trade of the Moors*. London, Oxford University Press, 1958. 281 pp. (Rewrite of *Caravans of the Old Sahara*.)

BRAILSFORD, HENRY NOEL. *The War of Steel and Gold: A Study of the Armed Peace*. London, G. Bell & Sons, 1914. 320 pp.

BRAUSCH, GEORGES. *Belgian Administration in the Congo*. London, Oxford University Press, 1961. 92 pp.

BRELSFORD, WILLIAM VERNON (ed.). *Handbook to the Federation of Rhodesia and Nyasaland*. London, Cassell & Co., 1960. 803 pp.

BRODIE, BERNARD. *Seapower in the Machine Age*. Princeton, N.J., Princeton University Press, 1941. 466 pp.

BROGAN, DENIS WILLIAM. "The Word That Lost Its Savour," *The Observer*, May 31, 1964, p. 28. (Review of Koebner and Schmidt, *Imperialism*.)

BRUNSCHWIG, HENRI. *L'avènement de l'Afrique noire du XIXe siècle à nos jours*. Paris, Librairie Armand Colin, 1963. 247 pp.

————. *L'expansion allemande outre-mer du XVe siècle à nos jours*. Paris, Presses Universitaires de France, 1957. 208 pp.

————. *Mythes et réalités de l'impérialisme colonial français, 1871–1914*. Paris, Librairie Armand Colin, 1960. 204 pp.

BRZEZINSKI, ZBIGNIEW K. (ed.). *Africa and the Communist World*. Stanford, Calif., Stanford University Press, 1963. 272 pp.

BUELL, RAYMOND LESLIE. *Liberia: A Century of Survival, 1847–1947*.

Philadelphia, University of Pennsylvania Press, University Museum, 1947. 140 pp.

———. *The Native Problem in Africa.* New York, Macmillan Co., 1928. 2 vols.

BURNS, SIR ALAN. *History of Nigeria.* 6th ed. New York, Barnes & Noble, 1963. 363 pp.

BURTON, SIR RICHARD F. *A Mission to Gelele, King of Dahome; with Notices of the So-called "Amazons," the Grand Customs, the Yearly Customs, the Human Sacrifices, the Present State of the Slave Trade, and the Negro's Place in Nature.* Ed. by his wife, Isabel Burton. London, Tylston & Edwards, 1893. 2 vols. Abridged edition ed. and with an introd. by C. W. Newbury. New York, Frederick A. Praeger, 1966. 378 pp.

"Cape Colony," in *Encyclopaedia Britannica,* 14th ed., IV (1929), 777–787.

CAROTHERS, JOHN COLIN. *The Psychology of Mau Mau.* Nairobi, Kenya, Government Printer, 1955. 35 pp.

CHARPY, JACQUES (ed.). *La fondation de Dakar (1845–1857–1869): Documents recueillis et publiés par Jacques Charpy.* Paris, Larose, 1958. 596 pp.

CHILDS, GLADWYN MURRAY. *Umbundu Kinship and Character.* New York, Oxford University Press, 1949. 245 pp.

CLARK, GROVER. *The Balance Sheets of Imperialism: Facts and Figures on Colonies.* New York, Columbia University Press, 1936. 136 pp.

CLUTTON-BROCK, GUY. *Dawn in Nyasaland.* London, Hodder & Stoughton, 1959. 192 pp.

CODRINGTON, ROBERT. "Report of the Administrator of North-eastern Rhodesia for Two Years Ending March 31st 1900," in *British South Africa Company: Reports on the Administration of Rhodesia, 1898–1900.* n.p., n.d.

COHEN, SIR ANDREW. *British Policy in Changing Africa.* London, Routledge & Kegan Paul, 1959. 118 pp.

COILLARD, FRANÇOIS. *On the Threshold of Central Africa: A Record of Twenty Years' Pioneering among the Barotsi of the Upper Zambezi.* 2d ed. Trans. from the French and ed. by his niece Catherine Winkworth Mackintosh. London, Hodder & Stoughton, 1902. 663 pp.

COLE, J. S. R., and W. N. DENISON. *Tanganyika: The Development of Its Laws and Constitution.* (Vol. XII of *The British Commonwealth: The Development of Its Laws and Constitutions.*) London, Stevens & Sons, 1964. 339 pp.

COLEMAN, JAMES S. *Nigeria: Background to Nationalism.* Berkeley, University of California Press, 1958. 510 pp.

COLSON, ELIZABETH. "Baselines of Change in Africa." Training Brief No. 2, prepared at Boston University for the Agency for International Development, December, 1962.

CORFIELD, F. D. *Historical Survey of the Origins and Growth of Mau Mau.* London, H.M. Stationery Office, 1960. 321 pp.

COUPLAND, SIR REGINALD. *East Africa and Its Invaders, from the Earliest Times to the Death of Seyyid Said in 1856.* Oxford, Clarendon Press, 1938. 584 pp.

―――. *The Exploitation of East Africa, 1856–1890: The Slave Trade and the Scramble.* London, Faber & Faber, 1939. 507 pp.

COURT, W. H. B. "The Communist Doctrines of Empire," in William Keith Hancock (ed.), *Survey of British Commonwealth Affairs:* Vol. II, *Problems of Economic Policy, 1918–1939,* Part I. London, Oxford University Press, 1940. Pp. 293–305.

CRAWLEY, C. W. "The Mediterranean," in *The New Cambridge Modern History:* Vol. X, *The Zenith of European Power, 1830–70.* Cambridge, Eng., Cambridge University Press, 1960. Pp. 416–441.

CRIPPS, ARTHUR SHIRLEY. *An Africa for Africans: A Plea on Behalf of Territorial Segregation Areas and of Their Freedom in a South African Colony.* Preface by Philip Kerr. London, Longmans, Green & Co., 1927. 203 pp.

CRONJÉ, J. M. *En daar was Lig: Die Sending van die Ned. Geref. Kerk in die O.V.S. in Noord en Suid Rhodesië gedurende die Jare 1899–1947.* Bloemfontein, South Africa, Algemene Sendingskommissie van die Ned. Geref. Kerk in die O.V.S., 1948.

CROWDER, MICHAEL. "Indirect Rule—French and British Style," *Africa* (London), XXXIV, No. 3 (July, 1964), 197–205.

CROZIER, BRIAN. *Neo-colonialism: A Background Book.* London, The Bodley Head, 1964. 112 pp.

―――. "The Struggle for the Third World," *International Affairs,* XL (July, 1964), 440–452.

CURTIN, PHILIP D. *African History.* (American Historical Association, Service Center for Teachers of History, Pub. No. 56.) New York, Macmillan Co., 1964. 55 pp.

―――. *The Image of Africa: British Ideas and Actions, 1780–1850.* Madison, University of Wisconsin Press, 1964. 526 pp.

DALLIN, ALEXANDER. "The Soviet Union: Political Activity," in Zbigniew Brzezinski (ed.), *Africa and the Communist World.* Stanford, Calif., Stanford University Press, 1963. Pp. 7–48.

DAVIDSON, BASIL. *The Lost Cities of Africa.* Boston, Little, Brown & Co., 1959. 366 pp.

DAVIES, KENNETH GORDON. *The Royal African Company*. London, Longmans, Green & Co., 1957. 390 pp.

DAWSON, JOHN. "Race and Inter-group Relations in Sierra Leone," Part I, *Race*, VI, No. 2 (October, 1964), 83–99.

DEANE, PHYLLIS. *Colonial Social Accounting*. Cambridge, Eng., Cambridge University Press, 1953. 360 pp.

DE KIEWIET, CORNELIS W. *A History of South Africa, Social and Economic*. 2d ed. London, Oxford University Press, 1950. 292 pp.

DELAVIGNETTE, ROBERT LOUIS. "Faidherbe," in Charles-André Julien (ed.), *Les techniciens de la colonisation (XIXe–XXe siècles)*. Paris, Presses Universitaires de France, 1946. Pp. 75–92.

―――. *Freedom and Authority in French West Africa*. London, Oxford University Press, 1950. 152 pp.

DESCHAMPS, HUBERT JULES. "Et maintenant, Lord Lugard?" *Africa* (London), XXXIII, No. 4 (October, 1963), 293–306.

―――. *Les méthodes et les doctrines coloniales de la France du XVIe siècle à nos jours*. Paris, Librairie Armand Colin, 1953. 222 pp.

DIA, MAMADOU. *The African Nations and World Solidarity*. Trans. from the French by Mercer Cook. London, Thames & Hudson, 1962. 145 pp.

DIKE, KENNETH ONWUKA. *Trade and Politics in the Niger Delta, 1830–1855: An Introduction to the Economic and Political History of Nigeria*. Oxford, Clarendon Press, 1956. 250 pp.

DUFFY, JAMES. *Portugal in Africa*. Cambridge, Mass., Harvard University Press, 1962. 239 pp.

DUIGNAN, PETER JAMES. "Native Policy in Southern Rhodesia, 1890–1923." Doctoral dissertation, Stanford University, 1961. 372 pp.

―――, and CLARENCE CLENDENEN. *The United States and the African Slave Trade, 1619–1862*. Stanford, Calif., Hoover Institution, Stanford University, 1963. 72 pp.

EASTON, STEWART COPINGER. *The Rise and Fall of Western Colonialism: A Historical Survey from the Early Nineteenth Century to the Present*. New York, Frederick A. Praeger, 1964. 402 pp.

EDWARDS, JAMES A. "Southern Rhodesia and the London Daily Press, 1890–1893," *Occasional Papers of the National Archives of Rhodesia and Nyasaland*, No. 1 (June, 1963), pp. 58–70.

EGERTON, F. CLEMENT C. *Angola in Perspective: Endeavour and Achievement in Portuguese West Africa*. London, Routledge & Kegan Paul, 1957. 272 pp.

EMERSON, RUPERT. "Colonialism Yesterday and Today," in Kurt London (ed.), *New Nations in a Divided World: The International Relations of the Afro-Asian States*. New York, Frederick A. Praeger, 1963. Pp. 3–18.

ENGELS, FRIEDRICH. *Über die Gewaltstheorie: Gewalt und Ökonomie bei der Herstellung des neuen deutschen Reiches.* Berlin, Verlag Neuer Weg, 1946. 88 pp.

ERASMUS, S. (pseud. of D. Blackburn). *Prinsloo of Prinsloosdorp.* London, Macleary, 1899.

FABRI, D. FRIEDRICH. *Bedarf Deutschland der Colonien? Eine politisch-ökonomische Betrachtung.* 3d ed. Gotha, Friedrich Andreas Perthes, 1884. 112 pp.

FAGE, JOHN D. *Ghana: A Historical Interpretation.* Madison, University of Wisconsin Press, 1959. 122 pp.

———. *An Introduction to the History of West Africa.* 3d ed. Cambridge, Eng., Cambridge University Press, 1962. 232 pp.

FALL, BERNARD B. "Education in the Republic of the Congo," *Journal of Negro Education,* XXX, No. 3 (Summer, 1961), 266–276.

FANON, FRANTZ. *Les damnés de la terre.* Preface by Jean-Paul Sartre. (Cahiers libres, Nos. 27–28.) Paris, François Maspero, 1961. 242 pp.

FAURE, CLAUDE. *Histoire de la presqu'île du Cap Vert et des origines de Dakar.* Paris, Emile Larose, 1914. 164 pp.

FAY, SIDNEY BRADSHAW. *The Origins of the World War.* New York, Macmillan Co., 1928. 2 vols.

FEIS, HERBERT. *Europe, the World's Banker, 1870–1914: An Account of European Foreign Investment and the Connection of World Finance with Diplomacy before the War.* Introd. by Charles P. Howland. New Haven, Conn., Yale University Press, for the Council on Foreign Affairs, 1930. 469 pp.

FIELDHOUSE, D. K. " 'Imperialism': An Historiographical Revision," *Economic History Review,* 2d Ser., XIV, No. 2 (1961), 187–209.

FISCHER, FRITZ. *Griff nach der Weltmacht: Die Kriegszielpolitik des kaiserlichen Deutschlands, 1914/18.* Düsseldorf, Droste Verlag, 1961. 896 pp.

FLINT, JOHN E. *Nigeria and Ghana.* Englewood Cliffs, N.J., Prentice-Hall, 1966. 176 pp.

FORDE, DARYLL. "Social Anthropology in African Studies," *African Affairs,* special issue (Spring, 1965), pp. 15–28.

FRANKEL, SALLY HERBERT. *Capital Investment in Africa: Its Course and Effects.* London, Oxford University Press, 1938. 487 pp.

———. *The Economic Impact on Under-developed Societies: Essays on International Investments and Social Change.* Oxford, Basil Blackwell, 1953. 179 pp.

FYFE, CHRISTOPHER. *A History of Sierra Leone.* London, Oxford University Press, 1962. 773 pp.

GAILEY, HARRY A., JR. *A History of the Gambia.* London, Routledge & Kegan Paul, 1964. 244 pp.

GALBRAITH, JOHN S. "Myths of the 'Little England' Era," *American Historical Review,* LXVII (October, 1961), 34–48.

————. *Reluctant Empire: British Policy on the South African Frontier, 1834–1854.* Berkeley, University of California Press, 1963. 293 pp.

GANN, LEWIS HENRY. "Archives and the Study of Society," *Rhodes-Livingstone Journal,* No. 20 (1956), pp. 49–67.

————. *The Birth of a Plural Society: The Development of Northern Rhodesia under the British South Africa Company, 1894–1914.* Manchester, Eng., Manchester University Press, 1958. 230 pp.

————. "The End of the Slave Trade in British Central Africa, 1889–1912," *Rhodes-Livingstone Journal,* No. 16 (1954), pp. 27–51.

————. *A History of Northern Rhodesia: Early Days to 1953.* London, Chatto & Windus, 1964. 478 pp.

————. *A History of Southern Rhodesia: Early Days to 1934.* London, Chatto & Windus, 1965. 354 pp.

————. "The Northern Rhodesian Copper Industry and the World of Copper, 1923–1952," *Rhodes-Livingstone Journal,* No. 18 (July, 1955), pp. 1–18.

————. "The White Settler: A Changing Image," *Race,* II, No. 2 (May, 1961), 28–40.

————, and PETER DUIGNAN. *White Settlers in Tropical Africa.* Harmondsworth, Middlesex, Eng., Penguin Books, 1962. 169 pp.

————, and MICHAEL GELFAND. *Huggins of Rhodesia: The Man and His Country.* London, George Allen & Unwin, 1964. 285 pp.

GELFAND, MICHAEL. *Lakeside Pioneers: Socio-medical Study of Nyasaland (1875–1920).* Oxford, Basil Blackwell, 1964. 330 pp.

————. *Livingstone the Doctor, His Life and Travels: A Study in Medical History.* Oxford, Basil Blackwell, 1957. 333 pp.

————. *Northern Rhodesia in the Days of the Charter: A Medical and Social Study, 1878–1924.* Foreword by Col. the Lord Robbins. Oxford, Basil Blackwell, 1961. 291 pp.

————. *Proud Record: An Account of the Health Services Provided for Africans in the Federation of Rhodesia and Nyasaland.* Foreword by Brendan P. Berney. Salisbury, Southern Rhodesia, Government Printer, 1960. 67 pp.

————. *Shona Ritual, with Special Reference to the Chaminuka Cult.* Foreword by M. Hannan. Cape Town, Juta & Co., 1959. 217 pp.

————. *Tropical Victory: An Account of the Influence of Medicine on the History of Southern Rhodesia, 1890–1923.* Foreword by His Excellency, the Governor of Southern Rhodesia, Major-General Sir John Kennedy. Cape Town, Juta & Co., 1953. 256 pp.

GERSDORFF, RALPH VON. *Wirtschaftsprobleme Portugiesisch-Afrikas.* Bielefeld, Verlag Ernst und Wolfer Gieseking, 1962. 360 pp.

GIBBS, JAMES LOWELL, JR. (ed.). *Peoples of Africa.* New York, Holt, Rinehart & Winston, 1965. 594 pp.

GILLESSEN, GÜNTHER. *Lord Palmerston und die Einigung Deutschlands: Die englische Politik von der Paulskirche bis zu den Dresdener Konferenzen (1848–1851).* Lübeck, Matthiessen Verlag, 1961. 160 pp.

GLUCKMAN, MAX. "Civil War and Theories of Power in Barotseland: African and Medieval Analogies," *Yale Law Journal,* LXXII, No. 8 (July, 1963), 1545–1546.

———. *The Economy of the Central Barotse Plain.* (Rhodes-Livingstone Institute Papers, No. 7.) Livingstone, Northern Rhodesia, Rhodes-Livingstone Institute, 1941. 130 pp.

———. *The Judicial Process among the Barotse of Northern Rhodesia.* Manchester, Eng., Manchester University Press, 1955. 386 pp.

GONCHAROV, L. "New Forms of Colonialism in Africa," *Journal of Modern African Studies,* I (December, 1963), 467–474.

Great Britain. Parliament. House of Commons. *Higher Education: Report of the Committee Appointed by the Prime Minister under the Chairmanship of Lord Robbins, 1961–63.* Cmnd. 2154. London, H.M. Stationery Office, 1963. 335 pp. plus appendixes.

GREENBERG, JOSEPH H. *Studies in African Linguistic Classification.* New Haven, Conn., Compass Publishing Co., 1955. 116 pp.

GREENE, MURRAY. "Schumpeter's Imperialism—A Critical Note," in Harrison M. Wright (ed.), *The "New Imperialism": Analysis of the Late Nineteenth-Century Expansion.* Boston, D. C. Heath & Co., 1961. Pp. 62–67.

GUTKIND, PETER C. W. *The Royal Capital of Buganda: A Study of Internal Conflict and External Ambiguity.* Foreword by A. I. Richards. The Hague, Mouton & Co., 1963. 330 pp.

HAILEY, WILLIAM MALCOLM HAILEY, 1ST BARON. *An African Survey: A Study of Problems Arising in Africa South of the Sahara.* London, Oxford University Press, 1938. 1837 pp. Revised 1956, London, 1957, 1676 pp.

———. *Native Administration in the British African Territories.* London, H.M. Stationery Office, 1950–1953. 5 vols.

HALLGARTEN, GEORGE WOLFGANG FELIX. *Imperialismus vor 1914: Theoretisches, soziologische Skizzen der aussenpolitischen Entwicklung in England und Frankreich; Soziologische Darstellung der deutschen Aus-*

senpolitik bis zum Ersten Weltkrieg. Munich, C. H. Beck'sche Verlagsbuchhandlung, 1951. 2 vols.

HAMMOND, RICHARD JAMES. "Economic Imperialism: Sidelights on a Stereotype," *Journal of Economic History*, XXI, No. 4 (December, 1961), 582–598.

————. *Portugal's African Problem: Some Economic Facets* (Occasional Paper No. 2.) New York, Carnegie Endowment for International Peace, 1962. 42 pp.

HANCE, WILLIAM A. *The Geography of Modern Africa.* New York, Columbia University Press, 1964. 653 pp.

HARGREAVES, JOHN D. *Prelude to the Partition of West Africa.* London, Macmillan & Co., 1963. 383 pp.

HARING, CLARENCE HENRY. *The Spanish Empire in America.* New York, Harcourt, Brace & World, 1963. 371 pp.

HARLOW, VINCENT, and E. M. CHILVER (eds.), assisted by Alison Smith. *History of East Africa*, Vol. II. Introd. by Margery Perham. Oxford, Clarendon Press, 1965. 766 pp.

HARRIS, JOHN H. *The Chartered Millions: Rhodesia and the Challenge to the British Commonwealth.* London, Swarthmore Press, 1920. 320 pp.

HEINE, HEINRICH. "Geständnisse," *Deutschland. II.* (Vol. XIII of *Sämtliche Werke.*) Leipzig, Max Hesse Verlag, 1898.

HENDERSON, IAN, and PHILIP GOODHART. *Man Hunt in Kenya.* Garden City, N.Y., Doubleday & Co., 1958. 240 pp.

HENDERSON, WILLIAM OTTO. *Studies in German Colonial History.* London, Frank Cass & Co., 1962. 150 pp.

HEUSSLER, ROBERT. *Yesterday's Rulers: The Making of the British Colonial Service.* Foreword by John Macpherson, introd. by Margery Perham. Syracuse, N.Y., Syracuse University Press, 1963. 260 pp.

HILFERDING, RUDOLF. *Das Finanzkapital: Eine Studie über die jüngste Entwicklung des Kapitalismus.* (Marx-Studien, Blätter zur Theorie und Politik des wissenschaftlichen Sozialismus, Vol. III.) Vienna, Ignaz Brand & Co., 1910. 575 pp.

HILL, POLLY. *The Migrant Cocoa-Farmers of Southern Ghana: A Study in Rural Capitalism.* New York, Cambridge University Press, 1963. 265 pp.

HOBSON, JOHN ATKINSON. *Imperialism: A Study.* London, George Allen & Unwin, 1902. 386 pp.

HODGKIN, THOMAS LIONEL. *African Political Parties: An Introductory Guide.* Harmondsworth, Middlesex, Eng., Penguin Books, 1961. 217 pp.

————. *Nationalism in Colonial Africa.* London, Frederick Muller, 1956. 216 pp.

————, and RUTH SCHACHTER. *French-speaking West Africa in Transition.* (International Conciliation, No. 528.) New York, Carnegie Endowment for International Peace, 1960. Pp. 375–436.

HOLDSWORTH, MARY. "The Application of Soviet Nationality Theory to Africa in Soviet Writing," in Kenneth Robinson and Frederick Madden (eds.), *Essays in Imperial Government; Presented to Margery Perham.* Oxford, Basil Blackwell, 1963. Pp. 209–226.

HONE, PERCY F. *Southern Rhodesia.* London, G. Bell & Sons, 1909. 406 pp.

HUNTER, GUY. *The New Societies of Tropical Africa: A Selective Study.* London, Oxford University Press, 1962. 376 pp.

HUXLEY, ELSPETH. *White Man's Country: Lord Delamere and the Making of Kenya:* Vol. I, *1870–1914;* Vol. II, *1914–1931.* 2d ed. London, Chatto & Windus, 1953. 315, 333 pp.

HYMANS, JACQUES LOUIS. "L'élaboration de la pensée de Léopold Sédar Senghor: Esquisse d'un itinéraire intellectuel." Doctoral dissertation, University of Paris, 1964. 478 pp.

INGHAM, KENNETH. *A History of East Africa.* London, Longmans, Green & Co., 1962. 456 pp.

JAURÈS, JEAN. *Contre la guerre au Maroc.* (Classiques français du socialisme.) Paris, Bureau d'Editions, 1936. 63 pp.

JOHNSON, R. W. M. *African Agricultural Development in Southern Rhodesia, 1945–1960.* Stanford, Calif., Food Research Institute, Stanford University, 1964. 59 pp. Reprint from *Food Research Institute Studies,* IV, No. 2 (1964), 165–223.

JOHNSTON, SIR HARRY HAMILTON. *A History of the Colonization of Africa by Alien Races.* New ed., rev. and enl. Cambridge, Eng., Cambridge University Press, 1930. 505 pp.

————. *Liberia.* London, Hutchinson & Co., 1906. 2 vols.

JONES, ARNOLD HUGH MARTIN, and ELIZABETH MONROE. *A History of Ethiopia.* Reprint of *A History of Abyssinia* with the addition of chronology. Oxford, Clarendon Press, 1955. 196 pp.

JULIEN, CHARLES-ANDRÉ. *Histoire de l'Algérie contemporaine: La conquête et les débuts de la colonisation (1827–1871).* Paris, Presses Universitaires de France, 1964. 632 pp.

JULY, ROBERT W. "Nineteenth-Century Negritude: Edward W. Blyden," *Journal of African History,* V, No. 1 (1964), 73–86.

JUNOD, VIOLAINE L. (ed.), assisted by Idrian N. Resnick. *The Handbook of Africa.* New York, New York University Press, 1963. 472 pp.

KAMARCK, ANDREW M. "Recent Economic Growth in Africa," *Annals of the American Academy of Political and Social Science,* CCCLIV (July, 1964), 46–53.

KANTOROWICZ, HERMANN. *The Spirit of British Policy and the Myth of the Encirclement of Germany.* English ed. rev. by the author and trans. by W. H. Johnston. Preface by Gilbert Murray. London, George Allen & Unwin, 1931. 541 pp.

KARIUKI, JOSIAH MWANGI. *"Mau Mau" Detainee: The Account by a Kenya African of His Experiences in Detention Camps, 1953–1960.* Foreword by Margery Perham. London, Oxford University Press, 1963. 188 pp.

KAUNDA, KENNETH D. *Zambia Shall Be Free: An Autobiography.* London, William Heinemann, 1962. 202 pp. New York, Frederick A. Praeger, 1963. 208 pp.

KAUTSKY, KARL. *Nationalstaat, imperialistischer Staat und Staatenbund.* Nürnberg, Fränkische Verlagsanstalt und Buchdruckerei, 1915. 80 pp.

KIMBLE, DAVID. *A Political History of Ghana: The Rise of Gold Coast Nationalism, 1850–1928.* Oxford, Clarendon Press, 1963. 587 pp.

KIMBLE, GEORGE HERBERT TINLEY. *Tropical Africa:* Vol. I, *Land and Livelihood;* Vol. II, *Society and Polity.* New York, Twentieth Century Fund, 1960. 603, 506 pp.

KLEIN, MARTIN A. "Sine-Saloum, 1847–1914: The Traditional States and the French Conquest." Doctoral dissertation, University of Chicago, 1964. 300 pp.

KNOWLES, LILLIAN CHARLOTTE ANNE. *The Economic Development of the British Overseas Empire.* (London School of Economics and Political Science, Studies in Economics and Political Science, No. 76.) London, G. Routledge & Sons, 1924. 555 pp.

KOEBNER, RICHARD. "The Concept of Economic Imperialism," *Economic History Review,* 2d Ser., II, No. 1 (1949), 1–29.

————, and HELMUT DAN SCHMIDT. *Imperialism: The Story and Significance of a Political Word, 1840–1960.* Cambridge, Eng., Cambridge University Press, 1964. 432 pp.

LACERDA E ALMEIDA, F. J. M. DE. *The Lands of Cazembe: Lacerda's Journey to Cazembe in 1798.* Trans. and annotated by Captain R. F. Burton. . . . Published by the Royal Geographical Society. London, John Murray, 1873. 271 pp.

LA GORCE, PAUL-MARIE DE. *The French Army: A Military-Political History.* Trans. by Kenneth Douglas. New York, George Braziller, 1963. 568 pp.

LANDES, DAVID S. "Some Thoughts on the Nature of Economic Imperialism," *Journal of Economic History,* XXI, No. 4 (December, 1961), 496–512.

LANGER, WILLIAM LEONARD. *The Diplomacy of Imperialism, 1890–1902*. 2d ed., with supplementary bibliographies. New York, Alfred A. Knopf, 1951. Reprinted, 1956, 1960. 797 pp.

LEFEVER, ERNEST W. *Crisis in the Congo: A United Nations Force in Action*. Washington, D.C., Brookings Institution, 1965. 215 pp.

LEGUM, COLIN. *Congo Disaster*. Baltimore, Penguin Books, 1961. 174 pp.

————. "Pan-Africanism and Communism," in Sven Hamrell and Carl G. Widstrand (eds.), *The Soviet Bloc, China and Africa*. Uppsala, Scandinavian Institute of African Studies, 1964. Pp. 9–29.

————. "What Kind of Radicalism for Africa?" *Foreign Affairs* (New York), XLIII, No. 2 (January, 1965), 237–250.

LEMAIGNEN, ROBERT, LÉOPOLD SÉDAR SENGHOR, and PRINCE SISOWATH YOUTÉVONG. *La communauté impériale française*. Paris, Editions Alsatia, 1945. 133 pp.

LEMARCHAND, RENÉ. "Congo (Leopoldville)," in James S. Coleman and Carl G. Rosberg, Jr. (eds.), *Political Parties and National Integration in Tropical Africa*. Berkeley, University of California Press, 1964. Pp. 560–596.

LENIN, V. I. "Imperialism: The Highest Stage of Capitalism; A Popular Outline," *Imperialism and Imperialist War (1914–1917)*. (Vol. V of *Selected Works*.) New York, International Publishers, 1935. Pp. 3–119.

LEROY-BEAULIEU, PAUL. *De la colonisation chez les peuples modernes*. 2d ed., rev., corr., and enl. Paris, Guillaumin et Cie., 1882. 659 pp.

LEVALLOIS, MAURICE. "Les tendances anti-colonialistes des Etats-Unis, de l'U.R.S.S. et de la Chine," *Renaissances*, No. 15 (October, 1945), pp. 22–38.

LE VINE, VICTOR T. *The Cameroons, from Mandate to Independence*. Berkeley, University of California Press, 1964. 329 pp.

LEWIS, BERNARD. *The Middle East and the West*. Bloomington, Indiana University Press, 1964. 160 pp.

LIEBENOW, J. GUS. "Liberia," in Gwendolen M. Carter (ed.), *African One-Party States*. Ithaca, N.Y., Cornell University Press, 1962. Pp. 325–386.

LIVINGSTONE, DAVID, and CHARLES LIVINGSTONE. *Narrative of an Expedition to the Zambesi and Its Tributaries and of the Discovery of the Lakes Shirwa and Nyassa, 1858–1864*. New York, Harper & Bros., 1866. 638 pp.

LLOYD, ALAN. *The Drums of Kumasi: The Story of the Ashanti Wars*. London, Longmans, Green & Co., 1964. 208 pp.

LORD, ALBERT B. "Nationalism and the Muses in Balkan Slavic Literature in the Modern Period," in Charles Jelavich and Barbara Jelavich (eds.), *The Balkans in Transition: Essays on the Development of Balkan Life and Politics since the Eighteenth Century.* (Russian and East European Studies.) Berkeley, University of California Press, 1963. Pp. 258–296.

LUGARD, FREDERICK JOHN DEALTRY LUGARD, 1ST BARON. *The Dual Mandate in British Tropical Africa.* Edinburgh, William Blackwood & Sons, 1922. 643 pp.

LUKAS, J. ANTHONY. "Rebellion Dims Hope for Congo," *The New York Times,* January 25, 1965, pp. 47, 63.

LUXEMBURG, ROSA. *Die Akkumulation des Kapitals: Ein Beitrag zur ökonomischen Erklärung des Imperialismus.* Leipzig, Frankes Verlag, 1921. 2 vols. in 1. (446, 120 pp.)

MACAULAY, THOMAS BABINGTON MACAULAY, 1ST BARON. *The History of England from the Accession of James II,* Vol. I. Chicago, Belford, Clarke & Co., 1888. 601 pp.

MACMILLAN, WILLIAM MILLER. *Bantu, Boer, and Briton: The Making of the South African Native Problem.* Rev. and enl. ed. New York, Oxford University Press, 1963. 382 pp.

McWILLIAM, MICHAEL. "Economic Policy and the Kenya Settlers, 1945–1948," in Kenneth Robinson and Frederick Madden (eds.), *Essays in Imperial Government; Presented to Margery Perham.* Oxford, Basil Blackwell, 1963. Pp. 171–192.

MAIR, LUCY PHILIP. *New Nations.* London, Weidenfeld & Nicolson, 1963. 235 pp.

———. *Primitive Government.* Baltimore, Penguin Books, 1962. 288 pp.

———. *Studies in Applied Anthropology.* London, Athlone Press, University of London, 1957. 81 pp.

MANOÏLESCO, MIHAÏL. *Teoría del proteccionismo y del comercio internacional.* Prologue by Ilmo. Sr. D. Manuel Fuentes Irurozqui. Madrid, Biblioteca de Economía Comercial Teórica, 1943. 350 pp.

MARTELLI, GEORGE. *Leopold to Lumumba: A History of the Belgian Congo, 1877–1960.* London, Chapman & Hall, 1962. 259 pp.

MARX, KARL. *Capital: A Critique of Political Economy:* Vol. I, *The Process of Capitalist Production.* Trans. by Samuel Moore and Edward Aveling, ed. by Friedrich Engels, rev. and amplified according to the 4th German ed. by Ernest Untermann. Chicago, Charles H. Kerr & Co., 1906. 869 pp.

———. *Revolution und Kontre-Revolution in Deutschland.* Trans. into German by Karl Kautsky. 6th ed. Stuttgart, J. H. W. Dietz Nachf., 1920. 141 pp.

MBOYA, TOM. *Freedom and After.* London, Andre Deutsch, 1963. 271 pp.

MEISSNER, BORIS. "Soviet Russia's Foreign Policy: Ideology and Power Politics," *Modern Age,* VIII (Winter, 1963–1964), 7–24.

MERRIAM, ALAN P. *Congo: Background of Conflict.* Evanston, Ill., Northwestern University Press, 1961. 368 pp.

METCALFE, GEORGE E. *Maclean of the Gold Coast: The Life and Times of George Maclean, 1801–1847.* London, Oxford University Press, 1962. 344 pp.

MICHAEL, FRANZ H. "China in Africa," in Friedrich-Ebert-Stiftung, *Studien zur Aktivität des Ostblocks in den Entwicklungsländern.* (Schriftenreihe der Forschungsstelle.) Hanover, Verlag für Literatur und Zeitgeschehen, 1963. Pp. 65–78.

MICHON, GEORGES. *The Franco-Russian Alliance, 1891–1917.* Trans. by Norman Thomas. London, George Allen & Unwin, 1929. 340 pp.

MOON, PARKER THOMAS. *Imperialism and World Politics.* New York, Macmillan Co., 1927. 583 pp.

MOREL, EDMUND DENE. *The British Case in French Congo: The Story of a Great Injustice, Its Causes and Its Lessons.* London, William Heinemann, 1903. 215 pp.

―――. *Great Britain and the Congo: The Pillage of the Congo Basin.* Introd. by Sir A. Conan Doyle. London, Smith, Elder & Co., 1909. 291 pp.

―――. *King Leopold's Rule in Africa.* London, William Heinemann, 1904. 466 pp.

―――. *Morocco in Diplomacy.* London, Smith, Elder & Co., 1912. 359 pp.

MORISON, DAVID. *The U.S.S.R. and Africa.* London, Oxford University Press, 1964. 124 pp.

MOSSE, GEORGE L. *The Culture of Western Europe: The Nineteenth and Twentieth Centuries; An Introduction.* London, John Murray, 1963. 437 pp.

MULLER, C. F. J. *Die Britse Owerheid en die Groot Trek.* 2d ed., rev. and illus. Johannesburg, Simondium, 1963. 341 pp.

MURROW, EDWARD R. Speech made November 5, 1961. Salisbury, Southern Rhodesia, American Consulate General. Cyclostyled.

NAMIER, SIR LEWIS. *England in the Age of the American Revolution.* 2d ed. London, Macmillan & Co., 1961. 450 pp.

NEUMARK, S. DANIEL. *Economic Influences on the South African Frontier, 1652–1836.* Stanford, Calif., Stanford University Press, 1957. 196 pp.

―――. *Foreign Trade and Economic Development in Africa: A Histori-*

cal Perspective. Stanford, Calif., Food Research Institute, Stanford University, 1964. 222 pp.

NEVINSON, HENRY WOODD. *A Modern Slavery.* London, Harper & Bros., 1906. 215 pp.

NKRUMAH, KWAME. *I Speak of Freedom: A Statement of African Ideology.* New York, Frederick A. Praeger, 1961. 291 pp.

NUSSBAUM, MANFRED. *Vom "Kolonialenthusiasmus" zur Kolonialpolitik der Monopole: Zur deutschen Kolonialpolitik unter Bismarck, Caprivi, Hohenlohe.* (Studien zur Kolonialgeschichte und Geschichte der nationalen und kolonialen Befreiungsbewegung, No. 8.) Berlin, Akademie-Verlag, 1962. 167 pp.

NXOBBE, MICKA. Micka Nxobbe to Lobengula, March 3, 1893. Copy in WI 6/1/1, Historical Manuscripts Collection, National Archives of Rhodesia, Salisbury.

OLIVER, ROLAND A., and JOHN D. FAGE. *A Short History of Africa.* Harmondsworth, Middlesex, Eng., Penguin Books, 1962. 279 pp.

————, and GERVASE MATHEW (eds.). *History of East Africa,* Vol. I. Oxford, Clarendon Press, 1963. 480 pp.

ORDE BROWNE, GRANVILLE ST. JOHN. *The African Labourer.* London, Oxford University Press, 1933. 240 pp.

PADMORE, GEORGE. *How Britain Rules Africa.* London, Wishart Books, 1936. 402 pp.

————. *Pan-Africanism or Communism? The Coming Struggle for Africa.* London, Dennis Dobson, 1956. 463 pp.

———— (ed.). *Colonial and Coloured Unity: A Programme of Action; History of the Pan-African Congress.* Manchester, Eng., Pan African Federation [1947?]. 79 pp.

PAISH, GEORGE. "Great Britain's Capital Investment in Individual Colonial and Foreign Countries," *Journal of the Royal Statistical Society,* LXXIV, Part 2 (January, 1911), 167–187.

PARVUS (pseud. of Alexander Helphand). *Die Kolonialpolitik und der Zusammenbruch.* Leipzig, Leipziger Buchdruckerei Aktiengesellschaft, 1907. 155 pp.

————. *Marineforderungen, Kolonialpolitik und Arbeiterinteressen.* Dresden, Verlag de "Sachsischen Arbeiter-Zeitung" (Herman Wallfisch), 1898. 35 pp.

PATTERSON, SHEILA. *The Last Trek: A Study of the Boer People and the Afrikaner Nation.* London, Routledge & Kegan Paul, 1957. 336 pp.

PEPPARD, NADINE. "Migration: Some British and European Comparisons," *Race,* VI, No. 2 (October, 1964), 100–107.

PERHAM, MARGERY. *The Colonial Reckoning: The End of Imperial Rule in Africa in the Light of British Experience.* New York, Alfred A. Knopf, 1962. 203 pp.

"Resolution on the Negro Question," *Resolutions & Theses of the Fourth Congress of the Communist International Held in Moscow Nov. 7 to Dec. 3, 1922.* London, Communist Party of Great Britain, for the Communist International [1922]. Pp. 84–87.

REYNOLDS, REGINALD. "The Emigrant Ship," *Africa South,* III, No. 4 (July–September, 1959), 4.

ROBINSON, RONALD E., and JOHN GALLAGHER. *Africa and the Victorians: The Climax of Imperialism in the Dark Continent.* With Alice Denny. New York, St. Martin's Press, 1961. 491 pp.

————. "The Partition of Africa," in *The New Cambridge Modern History:* Vol. XI, *Material Progress and World-wide Problems, 1870–1898.* Cambridge, Eng., Cambridge University Press, 1962. Pp. 593–640.

ROGERS, CYRIL A. "The Organization of Political Attitudes in Southern Rhodesia," *Rhodes-Livingstone Journal,* No. 25 (March, 1959), pp. 1–19.

ROLIN, HENRI. *Les lois et l'administration de la Rhodésie.* Brussels, Etablissement Emile Bruyland, 1913. 531 pp.

ROWSE, ALFRED LESLIE. *The Expansion of Elizabethan England.* London, Macmillan & Co., 1955. 449 pp.

RYCKMANS, PIERRE. *Dominer pour servir.* Rev. and enl. ed. Brussels, Edition Universelle, 1948. 189 pp.

SALZ, ARTHUR. *Das Wesen des Imperialismus: Umrisse einer Theorie.* Leipzig, B. G. Teubner, 1931. 201 pp.

SCALAPINO, ROBERT A. "Sino-Soviet Competition in Africa," *Foreign Affairs* (New York), XLII, No. 4 (July, 1964), 640–654.

SCHELER, MAX FERDINAND. *Der Genius des Krieges und der deutsche Krieg.* Leipzig, Verlag der Weissen Bücher, 1915. 443 pp.

————. *Die Ursachen des Deutschenhasses: Eine national-pädagogische Erörterung.* Leipzig, Neuer Geist Verlag, 1917. 157 pp.

SCHULZE-GAEVERNITZ, GERHART VON. *Britischer Imperialismus und englischer Freihandel zu Beginn des zwanzigsten Jahrhunderts.* Leipzig, Duncker und Humblot, 1906. 477 pp.

SCHUMPETER, JOSEPH ALOIS. *Imperialism and Social Classes.* Trans. by Heinz Norden, ed. and with an introd. by Paul M. Sweezy. New York, Augustus M. Kelley, 1951. 221 pp.

SEELEY, SIR JOHN ROBERT. *The Expansion of England: Two Courses of Lectures.* London, Macmillan & Co., 1891. 309 pp.

BIBLIOGRAPHY 415

SEGAL, HARVEY H., and MATTHEW SIMON. "British Foreign Capital Issues, 1865–1894," *Journal of Economic History,* XXI, No. 4 (December, 1961), 566–581.

SELIGMAN, CHARLES GABRIEL. *Races of Africa.* 3d ed. London, Oxford University Press, 1957. 236 pp.

SEMMEL, BERNARD. "The Philosophic Radicals and Colonialism," *Journal of Economic History,* XXI, No. 4 (December, 1961), 513–525.

SENGHOR, LÉOPOLD SÉDAR. "What Is 'Négritude'?" *West Africa,* November 4, 1961, p. 1211.

SHELTON, AUSTIN J. "Historiography and 'New' African 'History': A Short Exposition," *Genève-Afrique,* III, No. 1 (1964), 81–89.

SHEPPERSON, GEORGE. "An Early African Graduate," *University of Edinburgh Gazette,* No. 32 (January, 1962), pp. 23–26.

————, and THOMAS PRICE. *Independent African: John Chilembwe and the Origins, Setting, and Significance of the Nyasaland Native Rising of 1915.* Edinburgh, Edinburgh University Press, 1958. 564 pp.

SHONFIELD, ANDREW. *British Economic Policy since the War.* Harmondsworth, Middlesex, Eng., Penguin Books, 1958. 288 pp.

SÍK, ENDRE. *Histoire de l'Afrique noire,* Vol. I. Trans. by Frida Lédcrer. Budapest, Akadémiai Kiadó, 1961. 406 pp.

SITHOLE, NDABANINGI. *African Nationalism.* Foreword by the Hon. R. S. Garfield Todd. Cape Town, Oxford University Press, 1959. 174 pp.

SKLAR, RICHARD LAWRENCE. *Nigerian Political Parties: Power in an Emergent African Nation.* Princeton, N.J., Princeton University Press, 1963. 578 pp.

SLADE, RUTH M. *The Belgian Congo: Some Recent Changes.* London, Oxford University Press, 1960. 55 pp.

SNYDER, LOUIS L. (ed.). *The Imperialism Reader: Documents and Readings on Modern Expansionism.* (University Series in History.) Princeton, N.J., D. Van Nostrand Co., 1962. 619 pp.

SOMBART, WERNER. *Händler und Helden: Patriotische Besinnungen.* Munich, Duncker und Humblot, 1915. 145 pp.

SOMERVELL, DAVID CHURCHILL. "The Victorian Age," in William N. Medlicott (ed.), *From Metternich to Hitler: Aspects of British and Foreign History, 1814–1939.* London, Routledge & Kegan Paul, 1963. Pp. 73–99.

South Africa. *State of the Union: Economic, Financial, and Statistical Year-Book for the Union of South Africa, 1960–61.* Johannesburg, Da Gama Publications, 1961. 527 pp.

————. General Staff Defence Headquarters, Pretoria. "Military Report re Industrial Upheaval on the Witwatersrand . . . January to March

1922." Copy in Southern Rhodesian Defence Records, B. 2)2)10, National Archives of Rhodesia, Salisbury.

SOUTHALL, AIDAN W., and PETER C. W. GUTKIND. *Townsmen in the Making: Kampala and Its Suburbs.* (East African Studies, No. 9.) Kampala, Uganda, East African Institute of Social Research, 1956. 272 pp.

SOUTHORN, BELLA SIDNEY (WOOLF), LADY. *The Gambia: The Story of the Groundnut Colony.* Foreword by Sir John Gray. London, George Allen & Unwin, 1952. 283 pp.

STENGERS, JEAN. "L'impérialisme colonial de la fin du XIXe siècle: Mythe ou réalité," *Journal of African History,* III, No. 3 (1962), 469–491.

STERNBERG, FRITZ. *Der Imperialismus.* Berlin, Malik-Verlag, 1926. 614 pp.

STOKES, ERIC. "Milnerism," *Historical Journal,* V, No. 1 (1962), 47–60.

STRACHEY, JOHN. *The End of Empire.* London, Victor Gollancz, 1961. New York, Frederick A. Praeger, 1964. 351 pp.

SUMMERS, ROGER. *Inyanga: Prehistoric Settlements in Southern Rhodesia.* With contributions by H. B. S. Cooke [and others]. Cambridge, Eng., Cambridge University Press, 1958. 335 pp.

TAYLOR, ALAN JOHN PERCIVALE. *The Struggle for Mastery in Europe, 1848–1918.* Oxford, Clarendon Press, 1954. 638 pp.

This Is Southern Rhodesia. (ISP No. 7.) Salisbury, Southern Rhodesia, Government Printer, 1964.

THOMAS, THOMAS MORGAN. *Eleven Years in Central South Africa.* London, John Snow & Co., 1873. 418 pp.

THOMPSON, VIRGINIA, and RICHARD ADLOFF. *The Emerging States of French Equatorial Africa.* Stanford, Calif., Stanford University Press, 1960. 595 pp.

———. *French West Africa.* Stanford, Calif., Stanford University Press, 1957. 626 pp.

"Town and City Planning," in *Encyclopaedia Britannica,* XXII (1956), 334–337.

United Nations. *Compendium of Social Statistics, 1963 (Data Available as of 1 November 1962).* (Statistical Papers, Ser. K, No. 2.) New York, 1963. 586 pp. (Compendium issued as a joint undertaking of the UN, International Labour Office, FAO, UNESCO, and WHO.)

———. Statistical Office. Department of Economic and Social Affairs. *Statistical Yearbook, 1959.* New York, 1960. 618 pp.

VAN DER HORST, SHEILA T. *Native Labour in South Africa.* London, Oxford University Press, 1942. 340 pp.

VAN DER MERWE, PIETER J. *Trek: Studies oor die Mobiliteit van die*

Pioniersbevolking aan die Kaap. Cape Town, Nasionale Pers Beperk, 1945. 312 pp.

VANSINA, J. "Long-Distance Trade-Routes in Central Africa," *Journal of African History*, III, No. 3 (1962), 374–390.

———, R. MAUNY, and L. V. THOMAS (eds.). *The Historian in Africa: Studies Presented and Discussed*. (4th International African Seminar, Dakar, Senegal, 1961.) London, Oxford University Press, 1964. 428 pp.

WAKEFIELD, EDWARD GIBBON. *England and America: A Comparison of the Social and Political State of Both Nations*. New York, Harper & Bros., 1834. 376 pp.

——— (ed.). *A View of the Art of Colonization, with Present Reference to the British Empire: In Letters between a Statesman and a Colonist*. London, John W. Parker, 1849. 513 pp. (Wakefield is also one of the writers—the Colonist.)

WALKER, ERIC ANDERSON. *A History of Southern Africa*. 3d ed. London, Longmans, Green & Co., 1957. 973 pp.

WALLERSTEIN, IMMANUEL. "Pan-Africanism as Protest," in Morton A. Kaplan (ed.), *The Revolution in World Politics*. New York, John Wiley & Sons, 1962. Pp. 137–151.

WERTHEIMER, MILDRED S. *The Pan-German League, 1890–1914*. New York, Columbia University Press, 1924. 256 pp.

Whitaker's Almanack. London, J. Whitaker & Sons, 1962. 1189 pp.

WIGHT, MARTIN. *The Development of the Legislative Council, 1606–1945*. London, Faber & Faber, 1946. 187 pp.

WILLEQUET, JACQUES. *Le Congo belge et la Weltpolitik, 1894–1914*. Brussels, Presses Universitaires de Bruxelles, 1962. 499 pp.

WINSLOW, EARLE MICAJAH. *The Pattern of Imperialism: A Study in the Theories of Power*. New York, Columbia University Press, 1948. 278 pp.

WODDIS, JACK. *Africa: The Way Ahead*. London, Lawrence & Wishart, 1963. 174 pp.

WOOD, ALAN. *The Groundnut Affair*. London, The Bodley Head, 1950. 264 pp.

WOOLF, LEONARD SIDNEY. *Economic Imperialism*. London, Swarthmore Press, 1920. 111 pp.

———. *Empire and Commerce in Africa: A Study in Economic Imperialism*. London, George Allen & Unwin, 1919. 374 pp.

YOUNG, CRAWFORD. *Politics in the Congo: Decolonization and Independence*. Princeton, N.J., Princeton University Press, 1965. 659 pp.

ZIÉGLER, JEAN. *La contre-révolution en Afrique*. Paris, Payot, 1963. 242 pp.

Index